# Two decades
# in British politics

This book has been produced in collaboration with the Politics Association and is dedicated to those people who have been members and officers of the Association since its formation in 1969.

# Two decades in British politics

*Essays to mark twenty-one years of the Politics Association, 1969–90*

*edited by* Bill Jones *and* Lynton Robins

Manchester University Press
Manchester and New York

*Distributed exclusively in the USA and Canada by St. Martin's Press*

Copyright © Manchester University Press 1992

Whilst copyright in the volume as a whole is vested in Manchester University Press, copyright in individual chapters belongs to their respective authors, and no chapter may be reproduced wholly or in part without the express permission in writing of both author and publisher.

*Published by* Manchester University Press
Oxford Road, Manchester M13 9PL, UK
*and* Room 400, 175 Fifth Avenue,
New York, NY 10010, USA

*Distributed exclusively in the USA and Canada*
*by* St. Martin's Press, Inc.,
175 Fifth Avenue, New York, NY 10010, USA

*British Library Cataloguing in publication data*
A catalogue record for this book is available from the British Library

*Library of Congress Cataloging in publication data applied for*

ISBN 0–7190–3531–7 *hardback*
    0–7190–3532–5 *paperback*

Phototypeset in Great Britain
by Northern Phototypesetting Company Limited, Bolton
Printed in Great Britain
by Bell and Bain Ltd, Glasgow

# Contents

*Foreword:* Twenty-one years of the Politics
Association   *Bill Jones and Lynton Robins*                    vii

**Part I   The representative process**

1   The social context of British politics: class, gender
and race in the two major parties, 1970–1990
*Bill Coxall*                                                   3

2   All you never wanted to know about British political
parties   *Stephen Ingle*                                      22

3   Pressure groups and the British political system:
change and decline?   *Rob Baggott*                            37

4   Broadcasters, politicians and the political
interview   *Bill Jones*                                       53

5   Changes in the political class   *Dennis Kavanagh*         79

6   The political socialisation of young people
*David Denver and Gordon Hands*                                94

**Part II   The legislative process**

7   What happened to the constitution under
Mrs Thatcher?   *F. F. Ridley*                                 111

8   Voting behaviour and the party system
*David Butler*                                                 129

9   The House of Commons: from overlooked to
overworked   *Philip Norton*                                   139

10  The House of Lords: the best second chamber we
have got?   *Donald R. Shell*                                  155

**Part III**   **The executive process**

   11   The civil service: twenty years of reform
        *John R. Greenaway*                                          173

   12   The judiciary: justice with accountability?
        *Stephen P. Savage*                                          191

   13   Local government   *R. A. W. Rhodes*                         205

**Part IV**   **Policy areas**

   14   Government and the economy   *Colin Thain*                   221

   15   Britain and the European Community: twenty years
        of not knowing   *Lynton Robins*                            243

   16   Northern Ireland: a putting together of
        parts   *Arthur Aughey*                                     256

**Part V**   **Political education**

   17   Citizenship and education   *Bernard Crick*                  273

   18   Britain, Europe and citizenship   *Derek Heater*            287

   19   New curricula, new directions   *John Slater*               305

   20   Political education: a government view
        *Alan Howarth*                                              318

        *Epilogue:* Reasons to be cheerful   *Peter Hennessy*       327

        *Notes on contributors*                                     332

        *Officers of the Politics Association, 1969–1990*           337

        *Index*                                                     340

Bill Jones and Lynton Robins

# Foreword: Twenty-one years of the Politics Association

In 1967 an article appeared in the *Guardian* written by the Liberal leader Jo Grimond entitled 'A syllabus for AD 2000'. In response, Derek Heater, a young lecturer from Brighton College of Education, wrote a letter to the correspondence columns of the same newspaper, proposing the formation of a professional association for teachers of politics together with a supporting journal. As he recalls, 'this proved the moment of conception for the Politics Association'. Letters flooded in from interested teachers but Heater had difficulty in raising sufficient finance or interest until he met Bernard Crick, then professor of politics at Sheffield University. Once convinced the idea was right, Crick persuaded the Hansard Society to part with £250 and convene a conference at University College London on 5–7 September 1967.

Over 200 turned up to listen to lectures – including one from the Speaker, Dr Horace King – and to launch the new association. Several proposals for a name were considered and rejected and it eventually took Crick's casting Chairman's vote to decide on the 'Politics Association'. In retrospect Heater thinks a title embodying the idea of 'citizenship' would have been better but the name chosen expressed the straightforward wish of many 'to promote in our schools and colleges of Further Education the teaching of politics, controversy and all'.[1] Over two decades later the title has survived the controversy and the Association has flourished.

In September 1990 a conference was held at Holly Royde College, Manchester University, to celebrate twenty-one years of the Politics Association. The theme of the conference was a retrospective analysis of various developments in British politics and political education since that founding year. The two founding fathers of the

Association, Derek Heater and Bernard Crick, addressed the conference together with three of its distinguished former Presidents, Fred Ridley, David Butler and Dennis Kavanagh; a current Vice-President, Peter Hennessy; and the current President, John Slater. This book has grown out of the papers delivered at that conference, supplemented by those of other academics who have been associated with the Politics Association in various ways. Also included is the text of a speech delivered by Alan Howarth MP, in his capacity as Education Minister at a House of Commons reception held in honour of the Politics Association on 4 July 1990.

By happy chance the lifetime of the Politics Association coincides with two extremely eventful decades in British history. It includes the last decade of the, by then, fragmenting post-war consensus and the following Thatcher decade of so-called 'conviction-led' politics. *Two decades in British politics*, therefore, offers a timely opportunity to reassess the continuities and changes in the governments led by Harold Wilson, Edward Heath, James Callaghan and Margaret Thatcher. Was 1979 the political watershed it has been widely upheld to be by numerous academics and commentators? Or was it simply another undistinguished step in the politics of Britain's economic decline?

Appropriately enough the book contains twenty-one chapters in honour of the Association's achievements over twenty-one years. They are reflective and thematic; some pursue broad themes whilst others apply a narrow focus. The political demise of Margaret Thatcher in November 1990 provides a neat cut-off point for the period studied, but readers might wonder at the absence of a chapter specifically upon the dominating figure of the last decade. The answer is that the editors felt her presence would so permeate every chapter that one on her alone would be unnecessary. The book is divided loosely into sections according to their relevance to the political process: the representative process, the legislative process, the executive process and policy issues. A separate section addresses issues in political education.

What, then, have been the achievements of the Politics Association which are worthy of celebration? Under the guidance of Bernard Crick the Association participated in the Programme for Political Education which was funded by the Nuffield Trust. The final report, *Political Education and Political Literacy*, received considerable attention when it was published in 1978 and still provides the benchmark for current discussions. The inclusion of citizenship as a cross-curricular theme in the national curriculum provided a new context for developing political education. In 1991 the Association published an edited text, *Political Understanding Across the Curriculum*, which was firmly rooted within the philosophy of the original Programme for Political Education. The campaign to promote political education has also been pursued through a variety of other activities – the findings of periodic surveys into levels of pupils' political understanding conducted in association with member schools; the numerous conference papers delivered by Politics Association members together with books published on various aspects of political education; occasional publications and position papers produced by the Association have all helped to keep the flame of political education burning, even during the darkest days when the prospects for survival, let alone success, seemed minimal. (For a tribute to this side of the Association's work see Chapter 20 by Alan Howarth, MP.)

In the area of politics teaching the Association has wielded considerable influence on the way in which the discipline at 'A' level has developed from the dusty legalistic study of the British constitution into a wide approach to politics which frequently includes a comparative or international element. The Association is represented on most 'A' level GCE Boards as well as on other bodies concerned with curriculum development. The Association has also provided a growing range of resources for both teachers and students. The Politics Association Resources Bank, known by all members as PARB, has grown like Topsy in terms of the written resources, study packs and audio and video cassettes of lectures available for purchase. PARB was set up originally to serve the Manchester Branch but its success led to its rapid 'nationalisation' and by 1990 it employed the equivalent of two full-time staff who serve over 5,000 customers a year. (In 1991 it changed its name to the PA Resources Centre.)

The organisation of conferences has also been an area of increasing activity. In addition to the Annual Conference for members, there are now regular regional and London-based day conferences for students and, since 1983, an annual Politics Week held at Manchester University. These conferences have employed some of the best speakers in the country from the worlds of academe, journalism and politics. Indeed most of the leading politicians of the day have graced such events, including the likes of Tebbit, Owen, Kinnock,

Heseltine, Scargill, Powell and Joseph. Over the years the conferences have stimulated thousands of young people to regard politics in its proper light as a subject which is both exciting and essential
for citizens in a democratic society. Indeed, if imitation is the highest
form of flattery, the Association has also been much complimented
by the assortment of profit-making organisations which have subsequently sprung up to exploit the sixth-form politics market.
Despite the accusation by Lord Arran in 1970 that the Association
was a 'socialist conspiracy', political speakers chosen reflect a
scrupulous balance between the parties. The only survey of members' political affiliations, incidentally, was a straw poll taken by
Professor Anthony King at the 1981 Annual Conference revealing an
equal balance between Labour and Conservative supporters.

The Association has also been active in the world of publishing.
Numerous textbooks on a wide range of subjects have been produced by or with the co-operation of the Politics Association. Longman has published two series – *Political Realities* and *Contemporary
Politics* – whilst both Manchester University Press and Macmillan
have published books in conjunction with the Association. The
Politics Association moreover has its own journal, *Talking Politics*.
Published originally by Longman, then by Sage, as *Teaching Politics*,
its future was frequently at risk. Indeed, other journals in the field,
such as *Teaching Political Science*, the *International Journal of
Political Education* and *Education and Social Science*, did collapse
and cease publication. But reborn on a more secure commercial
footing as *Talking Politics*, the journal has gone from strength to
strength, having experienced a sixfold increase in circulation over its
predecessor.

This touches on a topic much debated at the 1990 Conference and
which is raised by a number of contributors to the political education
section. Some members feel that what they see as the original thrust
of the Association – the development of political education in
schools and colleges – has been vitiated in recent years and that the
Association has become too much a service organisation for teachers
of 'A' level politics. The demise of *Teaching Politics*, which used to
include articles on the theory and method of political education, is
particularly cited together with its replacement, *Talking Politics*,
which does not. Against this it is argued that the Association
operates in an open market. To generate essential income it has to
organise events which recruit viable numbers; to retain members it

has to give them what they want. All the evidence is that members want conferences and resources on British politics more than conferences and articles on political education. The correct balance between these and other functions of the Association's will doubtless be debated well into the third decade of the Association's existence.

It was an article in 1967 looking forward to the curriculum in the year 2000 which first provided the stimulus for the creation of the Politics Association. We feel sure that when this year arrives the teaching curriculum will reflect the very substantial contributions made by the Association during the intervening period. And we would look even further ahead. This book celebrates the Politics Association's twenty-first birthday. We cannot do better than repeat the sentiment expressed in John Slater's final sentences and look forward to reading the celebratory publication marking the Association's golden jubilee.

A final note of thanks is due to the Greater Manchester branch of the Politics Association for financial assistance connected with this volume and to Hazel Gordon and Judith Martin for additional typing.

Bill Jones<br>Lynton Robins

**Note**

1   D. Heater, 'The origins of the Politics Association: a personal view', in *The Politics Association 1969–70: the First 21 Years* (Manchester, Parsonage Press, 1990) 3–4.

# Part I
# The representative process

# 1  Bill Coxall

# The social context of British politics: class, gender and race in the two major parties, 1970–1990

The reasons for studying the social context of British politics strengthened during the two decades after 1970. With the emergence of a wider ideological division between the two major parties than at any time since the war, together with the impact of 'second wave' feminism and the increasing vociferousness of the ethnic minorities, the social representativeness of political institutions attained greater salience in national debate than it had had since the demand for increased working-class representation in Parliament in the early years of the century. Without maintaining that Parliament should be an exact microcosm of the social make-up of the nation, women and blacks followed the working class in legitimately arguing for greater representation in Parliament and other leading institutions, first on the grounds of fairness and second, in the belief that it would make a significant difference to policy-making. This chapter considers trends in the class, gender and ethnic composition of the major parties at constituency, parliamentary and Cabinet levels since 1970. It begins with an examination of changes in the class background of the two major parties. It then considers the changing positions in national politics of women and ethnic minorities before concluding with a discussion of the overall importance of the social background of politicians to an understanding of their political behaviour.

## Social class and party elites

Certain trends are discernible in both of the major parties between 1970 and 1987. In both the Conservative and Labour Parties the proportion of MPs educated at public schools declined slightly (from 74 to 68 per cent and from 17 to 14 per cent respectively) as did the proportion of Oxbridge-educated MPs (from 52 to 44 per cent and from 24 to 15 per cent respectively). At the same time, each party registered an increasing proportion of graduates: university-educated MPs rose from 64 to 70 per cent of the Conservative Party and from 53 to 56 per cent of the Labour Party. The broad contrast in the educational backgrounds of the parties remained. The Conservatives are still mainly public-school educated, although there has been a continuing decline in the proportion of old Etonians (from 18 to 11 per cent); Labour remains predominantly state-school educated, but with a much-reduced proportion of MPs with elementary education only – 19 per cent in 1970; under 2 per cent in 1987.[1] A significant shift in the Conservatives towards becoming a more meritocratic and less patrician party was observable in 1979. Non-Oxbridge graduates constituted a mere 12 per cent of the party in 1970, but in 1979 the non-Oxbridge element increased to 19 per cent; it rose again – to 26 per cent – in 1983, and stayed at that level in 1987. It has been aptly remarked by Byron Criddle that these figures reflect both 'a drift of the party away from the upper middle class; and a drift of the upper middle class away from political careers now seen as less rewarding both in pay and status'.

In occupational background also, the two major parties remained strongly contrasted. MPs from the professions continued to be the largest single element in both: they constituted 45 per cent of the Conservative Party in 1970, 42 per cent in 1987; 40 per cent of the Labour Party in 1970, 40 per cent still in 1987. But the professions from which each party predominantly drew were very different. In 1970, half of Conservative professionals and 22 per cent of the party as a whole were lawyers and this profession, although a declining proportion, still represented just over two-fifths of all professionals and 17 per cent of the party in 1987. By contrast, the Labour Party drew most strongly upon the teaching profession; former teachers constituted 39 per cent of the professional element and 19 per cent of the entire party in 1970 and their presence was even more marked in 1987, when they made up 59 per cent of the professional segment and just under one-quarter (24 per cent) of the party as a whole. The next best represented professions in the Conservative Party in 1970 were the armed services and consultants but, after the 1987 general election, a marked change appeared, with the most numerous professions (after law) being chartered secretaries/accountants and, more surprisingly, school teachers (each 11 per cent of all professionals), with the armed services reduced from 16 per cent of the professions to 10 per cent. The major change in the professions as a group in the Labour Party in this period – after the large increase in former teachers – was the sharp decline in lawyers: 34 per cent of all Parliamentary Labour Party (PLP) professionals in 1970, this category was reduced to 19 per cent in 1987. In both parties, the proportion of MPs with local government experience increased (to nearly two-fifths of Conservatives and just under half of the PLP in 1983), reflecting a trend towards the growing perception of politics as a career in both parties.[2]

The Conservatives continued to contain a far higher proportion of MPs with business backgrounds than Labour – just under 31 per cent in 1970 rising to 37 per cent in 1987, compared with Labour's 10 per cent in both years. But the Conservatives remained unsuccessful in raising their proportion of working-class MPs – a mere 1 per cent in 1970, and still no higher in 1987. The attempts of Central Office to encourage the adoption of more working-class and trade-union candidates continued to be frustrated by the desire of autonomous constituency associations to be represented by middle-class MPs.[3] By contrast, Labour's manual worker element was much larger, and even appears to have grown slightly – from 26 per cent in 1970 to 29 per cent in 1987. The desire of Constituency Labour Parties to pick well-educated individuals led to the selection of increasing numbers of middle-class candidates, but many selectors would certainly like to choose more working-class candidates.[4]

The basis of the increasing proportion of graduates in the House of Commons has been in the expansion of educational opportunities since 1945. Broader developments in society – as well as party competition – underlie shifts in the social composition of both parties: away from the upper middle class and the very rich by the Conservatives, away from its working-class base by Labour – two-thirds of the trade-union sponsored MPs in 1987 had no experience of manual work. Despite the slight increase in its manual worker element since 1970, the PLP has experienced a *long-term* decline in this group as well as a large-scale growth in its proportion of university graduates.

But this apparent convergence of the parties should not be exaggerated. The increasingly well-educated Labour Party which has emerged remains very different from the Conservative Party in its social composition, despite greater recruitment by the latter of MPs with more modest origins. Approximately 50 per cent of Labour MPs in the new 1979 Parliament had working-class parents. As Michael Moran has pointed out, whereas pre-war the typical Labour MP achieved mobility out of the working class in one step by entering Parliament, in the post-war period, the typical Labour MP first rose out of the working class by education, and then capped this social process by election to the House of Commons.

The House of Commons as a whole remains a socially very unrepresentative body. In 1987, university graduates formed 6 per cent of the population but 64 per cent of MPs. Whereas only about 6 per cent of the population had attended public school, 46 per cent of MPs in that year had done so. Managerial, administrative and professional jobs expanded rapidly in the 1970s and 1980s – from 23.5 per cent of the occupied population in 1971 to 29 per cent in 1983 and then further to 31 per cent in 1985. But a much larger proportion of MPs – over two-thirds – was drawn from these occupations. Manual workers continued to decline as a proportion of the workforce (from 62.6 per cent in 1971 to 57 per cent in 1983 and 56 per cent in 1985) but they constituted a much smaller proportion of the House of Commons – a mere one-eighth in 1983.[5]

A comparison of the leadership (Cabinets and Shadow Cabinets) of the two major parties in 1970 and 1990 reveals certain continuing trends but more change at the top of the Labour Party than of the Conservative Party. It also reveals that the two elites remain quite dissimilar. In Conservative Cabinets, the long-term trend for ever larger proportions of ministers to have received university educations continued: fifteen of the eighteen ministers in Heath's 1970 Cabinet had received a university education but twenty out of the twenty-two ministers in Thatcher's final Cabinet had been educated at university (83.3 per cent compared with 90.9 per cent). These figures may be set in the context of an average of 71.4 per cent university-educated ministers in Conservative Cabinets between 1916 and 1955 and an average of 81.6 per cent between 1955 and 1984.[6] Conservative Cabinets remained predominantly Oxbridge-educated (fifteen out of eighteen in 1970, a slightly fewer sixteen out of twenty-two in 1990) but the long-term domination of the two foremost public schools was in decline. Five Cabinet ministers in 1970 but only three in 1990 had attended Eton or Harrow; old Etonians and old Harrovians formed nearly half of Conservative Cabinets in the period 1916–55 and just over one-third of Conservative Cabinets between 1955 and 1984. The overwhelming majority of both the Heath and Thatcher Cabinets was educated at public school but each contained a significant minority of grammar-school-educated Ministers. There was a continuation of the long-term trend for the number of ministers with aristocratic origins to fall. There were four such members of the Heath Cabinet but only two in the final Thatcher Cabinet, compared with five out of eighteen in Eden's (1955) and eight out of twenty-one in Chamberlain's (1937) Cabinets. The tendency for Conservative Cabinets to become more uniformly middle class in the post-war period continued.

Significant differences in social and educational background existed between the Labour Shadow Cabinet led by Neil Kinnock in November 1990 and the contemporary Conservative Cabinet. Members of the Labour elite were also largely university-educated (nineteen out of twenty-two) but all except four of these attended provincial universities rather than Oxbridge. Fifteen had attended state schools; seven had been educated at independent schools. Of the state-school-educated, most were products of grammar schools; three went to secondary and technical schools. Whereas the Thatcher Cabinet was largely drawn from the worlds of law, commerce and finance, and career politics (it included six barristers, one solicitor, four company directors, two bankers, two consultants, and four political researchers), the Labour Shadow Cabinet contained an even larger proportion from the 'talking professions' than did the PLP. No fewer than nine had been lecturers, tutors and teachers, and in addition there were three journalists, two local government officers, a former trade-union official and a political researcher. There were fewer lawyers (three barristers, one solicitor) than in the Conservative Cabinet; collectively, there was minimal experience of finance, commerce and industry. About two-thirds hailed from Wales, Scotland and the North of England – an enduring Labour tradition.

Overall, the Labour leadership in 1990 differed in certain important ways from Labour Cabinets of the 1960s and 1970s. It was normal for approximately half the members of those Cabinets to have been Oxbridge-educated (in 1970, twelve out of twenty-one had been) and for about one-third to have attended public school. By 1990, the proportion of university-educated people at the top of the party had increased, as had the grammar-school element, and the proportion of members educated at Oxbridge and public schools was much reduced – to just under one-fifth and just over one-quarter respectively.

Analysing the social background of Labour Cabinets between 1964 and 1979, Dennis Kavanagh concluded that one-half were 'meritocrats', one-quarter were 'proletarians' and one-fifth were 'patricians'. Meritocrats were from working- or lower-middle-class backgrounds, with university and usually grammar-school educations; proletarians were from working-class families who left school at an early age and then became manual workers, trade-union organisers or clerical workers; and patricians came from middle-class professional families and, after public school and Oxbridge, usually entered one of the professions.[7] Clearly, by 1990 the meritocratic element had become even more pronounced, and the proletarian and patrician elements much smaller. A Labour Cabinet of the future would seem likely to contain a higher proportion of individuals of achieved middle-class status than ever before.

At constituency level, whereas the middle class is dominant in the Conservative Party, the Labour Party is socially more diverse. Writing in 1980, on the basis of information about Conservative Associations collected between 1964 and 1969, Butler and Pinto-Duschinsky found that the higher the level of the party, the smaller the degree of participation by working- and lower-middle-class Conservative supporters. Thus, one out of 105 working-class Conservative identifiers carried out some activity within the party, one out of thirty lower-middle-class (C1) identifiers did so and one out of twenty-seven upper-middle-class Conservatives assisted the party in some way. There was a pronounced tendency for each step of the hierarchy in local Associations to be composed of a higher social group than the one below it. Although both lower-and upper-middle-class members of Conservative Associations carried out a similar amount of political activity, constituency chairmen were predominantly upper middle class. Constituency chairmen were normally a notch lower on the social scale than Tory MPs.

Unlike Conservative MPs who were more likely to possess professional than business backgrounds (45 per cent professional, 30 per cent business in 1970), constituency leaders were generally businessmen (66 per cent) rather than professionals (24 per cent). Of these, 84 per cent had been educated at public schools or grammar schools. By the 1960s, such groups had largely replaced the landowners and very wealthy businessmen who had taken leading roles before the war. At the highest level locally, the working class and lower middle class were virtually shut out of office-holding. In 1969, 1 per cent of the Conservative constituency chairmen were drawn from the manual working class – exactly the same as the percentage of Conservative MPs with working-class origins. Conservative chairmen in Labour-held seats were less likely to have been educated at public schools than chairmen in Conservative-held seats (under 25 per cent, compared with about 50 per cent) and more likely to have attended elementary school only (25 per cent, compared with 5 per cent).[8] Conservative Associations have always contained a high proportion of women who by tradition have seldom been prominent in leadership roles. However, Ingle has suggested that in the 1980s this situation began to change substantially.[9] In the absence of detailed evidence, it is hard to estimate how much of this picture of Conservative Associations remains true of the late 1980s. Party membership was probably about 1½–1¾ million in 1969–70; about 1½ million in the mid-1970s (based on the Houghton estimate of 2,400 members per constituency) and declined to about one million in 1990.[10]

The social make-up of the leadership of Constituency Labour Parties (CLPs) is very different. Janosik's 1968 study distinguished between the social composition of CLPs in Labour 'strongholds' and in Labour 'marginals'. In Labour strongholds, 31 per cent of local leaders came from professional (21 per cent) or business (10 per cent) backgrounds, 32 per cent from the skilled and semi-skilled working class (each 16 per cent) and 19 per cent were trade-union officials. Over two-thirds (69 per cent) of leaders had received elementary education only, whilst 17 per cent had received post-secondary education. Over 80 per cent of members in such constituencies were affiliated trade unionists.

In Labour marginals, the same proportion of leaders had business or professional backgrounds (although an even higher proportion were professionals (26 per cent) rather than businessmen (6 per cent), slightly more were trade-union officials (21 per cent), but significantly fewer (16 per cent) were from the skilled (9 per cent) and semi-skilled (7 per cent) working class. A lower proportion of leaders (49 per cent) had elementary education only and a higher proportion (23 per cent) had received post-secondary education. Of party members, 64 per cent were trade unionists. The full social profile of all the CLP leaders in the study (including those in constituencies Janosik categorised as 'weak' Labour divisions) was as follows: professional 20 per cent, business 12 per cent, white collar 17 per cent, skilled worker 12 per cent, semi-skilled worker 14 per cent, trade-union (and party) officials 16 per cent, housewives 9 per cent.

Janosik also analysed the age-structure of local party leaderships. Just under half (46 per cent) of leaders in strong constituencies were over 56 and a mere 6 per cent were under 35; 40 per cent of activists had become involved before the General Strike. In marginals, the age profiles of leaders and activists were younger, the proportions in these categories being respectively 11 per cent, 17 per cent and 9 per cent.[11]

The social composition of CLP leaderships in the 1960s contrasts sharply with that of contemporary Conservative constituency elites. CLP leaderships were much less middle class (only about one-third were businessmen and professionals, compared with 90 per cent of Conservative chairmen from these groups); they were often very limited educationally compared with their predominantly public-school or grammar-school-educated Conservative counterparts; and they contained a very substantial working-class/trade-union element, which groups were virtually absent from Conservative Associations.

Individual Labour Party membership appears to have dropped substantially in the late 1960s, probably to little over 300,000 in 1970.[12] Active constituency organisations 'shrivelled to a mere skeleton' between 1966 and 1970, the consequence, as Patrick Seyd has written, of social change, neglect and mass disillusionment.[13] Membership trends in the 1970s are a matter of dispute: Seyd argues that membership increased but there is no agreement that it did.[14] What appears to be incontestable was a shift in the social base of CLPs as a result of an influx from three sources – young, more highly educated, public-sector professionals, often with working-class parents, militant trade unionists and radical feminists. The overall result seems to have been a tilting of the social balance within CLPs away from the older generation of working-class activists towards middle-class professionals, often in public-sector employment.

However, this generalisation needs to be made with caution. Seyd's 1986 study of two contrasting Sheffield constituencies, Conservative Hallan, where non-manual occupations and owner-occupation were predominant, and Labour Attercliffe, in which manual workers were in a large majority and nearly half the house-

holders were council tenants, shows that in certain types of constituency working-class activists could still be by far the largest social
group. Hallam CLP was mainly composed of highly qualified,
middle-class, public-sector professionals, most of whom worked for
the local council, whereas the Attercliffe CLP largely consisted of
working-class trade unionists, one-third of whom were employed by
private firms. A strong similarity between the two local parties,
however, was that over half of their respective activists had joined
after 1975, recruitment being especially vigorous between 1980 and
1984.

## Women in national political life

Underlying the intensification of pressure in the 1970s and 1980s to
increase the representation of women in elite roles in all spheres of
national life was the emergence of 'second wave' feminism in the late
1960s, with its angry reaction against the failure of post-war
feminists sufficiently to improve the status of women. By no means
all of the new feminists of the 1970s engaged directly in political
activity but the consequences of radical feminism may ultimately
prove more transformative than the effects of the suffragette campaigns. By 1990, women's actual representation within political
elites had improved only to a limited extent, but the issue had
attained a far greater significance on the national political agenda
than it had had twenty years before.

In 1970, only ninety-nine women candidates stood for Parliament,
of whom twenty-six were elected, a mere 4.1 per cent of the House.
Fifteen of the women MPs were Conservative (out of twenty-six
candidates), ten were Labour (out of twenty-nine candidates). After
that, each election saw a rise in the number of women candidates –
143, 161, 210, 280 in the general elections of 1974 (February and
October) 1979 and 1983 respectively, but the result was a small
decrease rather than an increase in the number of women MPs: 23,
27, 19, 23. In 1983, women constituted 10.7 per cent of candidates,
but only 3.5 per cent of the House of Commons. A large proportion
of the increasing numbers of women candidates represented the
minor parties: in 1983, the two major parties put forward only 118
women candidates (Conservatives 40, Labour 78) – 42 per cent of
the total number of women candidates, compared with their combined 55 per cent in 1970. In all parties – and especially in the minor

parties – the vast majority of women candidates was standing in hopeless seats.[15]

The 1987 general election marked a modest but significant advance. Three hundred and twenty-five women candidates stood – 14 per cent of all candidates – and forty-one were successful, the largest number ever to be elected to the House. Labour, as is normally but not invariably the case, had the largest number of women MPs: twenty-one of its ninety-two candidates were elected, as compared with seventeen out of the forty-six Conservative candidates. Labour selected more women in safe seats than ever before. However, it remained far more difficult for a female candidate to get elected than for a male: one in three of male candidates was successful compared with one in eight women candidates. Moreover, the proportion of women MPs – at 6.3 per cent – was still one of the lowest in Europe. In Germany (15 per cent), Denmark (30 per cent) and Sweden (38 per cent), elected women representatives are far more numerous in their national legislatures. In addition, women's representation in 1989 among British Euro-MPs (15 per cent), although higher than their representation in the Commons, was not only 'near the bottom of the European league' but also slightly lower than in 1979 (16 per cent) and 1984 (17.3 per cent).[16]

At the level of government, only twice since 1945 has there been more than one woman minister in any Cabinet, and after Mrs Thatcher's departure, there were none at all in the new Cabinet. Labour appointed four women ministers in 1966, but not until 1988 did any government include more than two women ministers again. In 1990, including Mrs Thatcher, there were five women in the government.

At the end of 1989, the House of Lords contained sixty-five women peers, of whom forty-five were life peers and twenty were peers by succession. At 13 per cent of life peers, women are obviously better represented in the Lords than in the Commons. However, with women receiving only about one-eighth of life peerages, this proportion, which is still very low, is unlikely to improve dramatically in the future.

Outside Westminster, women have tended to play a larger role. Of Conservative Conference delegates in 1980, 38 per cent were women but, down to the early 1980s, women did not exceed 11 per cent of Labour Conference delegates. In 1986, women constituted 27 per cent of Labour's National Executive Committee (NEC) and, during the 1970s, they formed 20 per cent of the Executive Committee of the Conservative National Union. Traditionally, women have been both numerous and active in Conservative Associations, although many see the local Conservatives primarily as a social organisation. A new generation of women joined the CLPs in the 1970s. First came a women's trade-unionist influx concerned about discrimination against women at work; then, beginning in the late 1970s, socialist women's liberationists, who were disillusioned with extra-parliamentary Leninist groups, began to move into the party.

Explanations of women's continuing low representation in elective positions, particularly in the House of Commons, have emphasised both the factors which discourage women from coming forward for such roles and the discrimination against them when they do present themselves as candidates for selection. The main situational constraints are first, the problem of combining domestic responsibilities, which still largely fall on women, with the demands of a full-time political career and second, women's inferior position in the structure of educational and occupational opportunity. For example, although women form an increasing proportion of university students (30 per cent, 1970–1; 43 per cent, 1987–8), in the economically active population (aged 25–69) in 1987–8 only 5 per cent of women were university graduates compared with 8 per cent of men. This is a situation which clearly disadvantages women in competing for a place in the Lower House, where nearly two-thirds are university graduates. Women form only a small minority in the upper echelons of business and commerce and a scarcely higher proportion of the professions, occupations which dominate the House of Commons. Women constitute only 21 per cent, 17 per cent and just under 10 per cent of the important recruitment areas for parliamentary careers of law, university teaching and chartered accountancy. The UK Inter-Professional Group report in 1990 found that women formed only 17.5 per cent of the fourteen professions in its survey.

Women also often face discrimination – direct or indirect, deliberate or sub-conscious – when they come before selection committees. Discrimination is another reason why women constitute such a small proportion of the major parties' lists of candidates – in 1983, 15 per cent of Labour's list B, 10 per cent of the Conservative list. An even smaller proportion of women – a mere 4.5 per cent – was selected for Labour's A list of trade-union sponsored candidates in that year.

Sponsorship of women candidates by trade unions is of particular importance in increasing the representation of women in the House of Commons: in 1987, thirteen of Labour's twenty-one women MPs were union-sponsored.

Systems of proportional representation favour the adoption of larger numbers of women candidates, but failing the (unlikely) introduction of such a system in the UK, the best prospect for women's political progress is determined action by the major parties over the selection of parliamentary candidates. By the late 1980s, there were some indications that this had begun to happen. In the early 1980s, the SDP adopted the policy of positive discrimination, declaring that at least two women must be included on every shortlist; the Liberals followed suit and then, in 1988, Labour also adopted a policy of compulsory representation of women on shortlists. The Conservatives rejected this idea in favour of simply encouraging more women to come forward. At its 1990 Conference, Labour agreed a ten-year programme to ensure that half the PLP is composed of women and gave the NEC the task of devising ways to achieve this objective.

Both major parties in the 1980s gave women more prominent roles. Emma Nicholson became Vice-Chairman of the Conservative Party with special responsibility for women. Having in 1985 agreed to establish a Ministry for Women's Rights, Labour in 1990 gave Shadow Cabinet positions to Margaret Beckett (Chief Secretary, Treasury), Jo Richardson (Women), Ann Clwyd (Development and Co-operation) and Ann Taylor (Environmental Protection). Its 1990 Conference agreed to establish a quota of at least 40 per cent women on its NEC and other national policy-making bodies and also that at least 50 per cent of the official positions on CLPs should be occupied by women.

### The representation of the ethnic minorities in national politics

This period has witnessed an increasing involvement and representation of the ethnic minorities in British politics. In the 1970 general election, the race issue probably helped defeat Dr David Pitt, the Labour candidate at Clapham and the first West Indian to contest a winnable seat for either of the major parties. In the 1974 elections, race relations and immigration hardly surfaced as issues. But since then, whilst taking care as far as possible to avoid provoking a backlash by white voters, politicians of both major parties have for several reasons begun to take the votes of the ethnic minorities more seriously.

One factor was the increase in the Afro-Caribbean and Asian population, which went up from 1.2 million (2.3 per cent of the total population) in 1971 to 2.1 million (3.9 per cent) in 1981 and thence rose to a 2.35 million average (4.3 per cent) in 1983–5. A second factor was the increasing registration and turn-out rates of these groups. In 1974, non-registration by West Indians was estimated at 37 per cent and by Asians at 27 per cent, compared with 6 per cent for whites. However, non-registration amongst ethnic minorities declined – to 23 per cent for West Indians and 18 per cent for Asians in 1979 – and turn-out rates increased, amongst Asians to a very similar level, according to one survey of the 1979 election, to that of whites.[17] Lastly, the closeness of the electoral contest in 1974 forced both parties to pay more attention to those constituencies in major cities which contained a significant proportion of black voters. In particular, the Conservatives came to realise that their failure to appeal to ethnic minority voters could have played a part in the Labour victory in the 1974 elections, since a high proportion of Labour gains were in seats where its majority was less than the black population.

The number of black candidates gradually increased. There were five in 1979 (two Conservative; one Labour; two Liberal); eighteen in 1983 (four Conservative; six Labour; eight Alliance), when one candidate – Paul Boateng (Labour) – stood for a winnable seat; and twenty-eight in 1987 (six Conservative; fourteen Labour; eight Alliance). In 1987, six of Labour's ethnic-minority candidates stood for winnable seats and four were successful: Keith Vaz (Leicester East), Paul Boateng (Brent South), Diane Abbott (Hackney North and Stoke Newington) and Bernie Grant (Tottenham). All four won in seats which contained a high proportion of West Indian and Asian voters.

The results confirmed the 1983 election evidence that black Labour candidates do not necessarily suffer discrimination by white voters. However, many black Labour candidates did experience swings against them, as did all of the black Conservative candidates (unlike in 1983) and all of the Alliance candidates.[18] Black voters mainly support Labour: a poll of Afro-Caribbean and Asian voting intentions in 1987 showed 72 per cent in favour of Labour, 18 per cent Conservative and 10 per cent Alliance. However, Afro-Caribbeans vote more strongly for Labour (86 per cent) than do Asians (67 per cent), and Labour may be losing ground among the latter group. Labour's black MPs soon established a black parliamentary caucus and a black section councillors' group.

The Labour Party has encouraged the involvement of Asians and West Indians in the party since the 1970s, with growing success in the last decade. The NEC's 1980 advice note, *Labour and the Black Electorate*, was a key document which recognised that the party had to increase its efforts if it was to retain its support among black voters. The early 1980s saw Afro-Caribbean and Asian political involvement in the party most marked in the London area. By 1984, Labour had eighty Afro-Caribbean and Asian councillors there and a further seventy in the rest of the country, and by 1986, there were over 200 black Labour councillors in London. Its six parliamentary candidates in 1987 all had backgrounds in London local government.

These candidates were also indentified with the demand for black sections which first appeared in the party in 1983. A working party report in 1985 recommended black sections with delegates at local, regional and national level and some representation on the NEC. But the leadership and probably most Labour grass-roots activists were opposed and the NEC rejected the recommendation. Instead, Labour established a Black and Asian Advisory Committee and appointed a full-time Black and Asian adviser to assist the committee.[19] But the campaign for black sections continued and in 1990, although still rejecting black sections, Conference agreed to set up a single affiliated organisation for people of African, Caribbean and Asian descent. Its probable name would be the Black and Asian Socialist Society. It would be entitled to vote in elections for the Socialist Society's seat on the NEC and, if it gained sufficient members, it could be entitled to its own seat on the NEC. This decision in principle, for which the rules had still to be worked out, meant that groups open only to black and Asian members would be established at constituency level.

The Conservatives have had less success in recruiting blacks and Asians. In 1976, a new Central Office Department of Community Affairs was established to promote the party among target groups including black voters. One of its first initiatives was to create an Anglo-Asian Conservative Society and an Anglo-West Indian Conservative Society to stimulate recruitment but these societies had only limited success. In 1985, the Anglo-Asian Society had thirty-two branches with 2,000 members and the Anglo-West Indian Society had a mere seven branches with 200 members. The Anglo-Asian Society was disbanded in 1986 following claims that it had been taken over by Sikh extremists and a year later the Conservatives decided to form a 'One Nation Group' to replace both societies. The Conservatives have also been less successful than Labour in promoting black and Asian candidates at local level. Of the seventy-nine Asian and Afro-Caribbean councillors elected for London boroughs in May 1982, only seven were Conservative — five Asian and two Afro-Caribbean. In 1985, the party had only twenty ethnic minority councillors nationwide.

## The social context of British politics

What difference does the social background of politicians and political activists make to their political behaviour? The relationship between the social context of politics and the ideas and actions of its practitioners is neither straightforward nor well-understood. Few political scientists doubt that a relationship exists but rightly they give more cautious expression to it than do elite theorists.

At parliamentary level, the considerable social homogeneity of the Conservative Party has long been and, despite some evidence of recent weakening, remains a source of political cohesion. Political attitudes among Conservative MPs rarely reflect the rather small differences in social background.[20] Moreover, the very pronounced social unrepresentativeness of an almost exclusively middle-class party has not prevented it from attracting significant levels of working-class support. In 1979, working-class support for the party increased and remained high in the two following elections. In 1987, the Conservatives gained 43 per cent of the votes of skilled workers and 31 per cent of the votes of semi-skilled and unskilled workers. The social differences between party activists and parliamentarians are not pronounced and, in any case, tend to cement political loyalty rather than undermine it. It remains a valid point that the privileged backgrounds and limited social experience of most Conservatives can be an impediment to effective policy-making when the party is in government, especially, it might be added, with regard to reform of the state educational and health services, and of local taxation.

In research relating to the period 1955–76, some correlation was found between the social background and political attitudes of Labour MPs. The research by Finer, Berrington and others showed that Labour MPs from the newer professions (including journalists, publicists and party organisers) tended to be more strongly associated than other groups in the party with support for the principles of socialism; and that the group classified as 'workers' (largely the trade-union-sponsored MPs) were strong on 'material' issues (cost of living and welfare) and the least concerned of any group with ideological positions. Despite its continuing 'embourgeoisement', the PLP remains more socially diverse than the Conservative Party, a factor which has a bearing on its lesser political cohesiveness. This is especially the case when issues closely involving working-class interests, such as trade-union reform, become prominent when the party is in government. The increasingly middle-class composition of the PLP, it has been suggested, has led to a growing social distance between the party in Parliament and its 'natural' working-class constituency. The party's weakening support from working-class voters in the 1970s and 1980s led to intense debate on the left about whether the 'forward march of Labour' had been halted.[21]

The party's traditionally strong attachment to the importance of symbolic representation has also led to strains at constituency level. Labour selectors in the CLPs largely choose middle-class candidates, but a 1976–79 study of constituencies in Scotland and the north-east suggested that the majority disapproves of this practice. The two most frequently expressed reasons for this disapproval were that middle-class MPs lose touch with the working class and that middle-class MPs cannot represent the working class. The most disapproving were left-wingers which suggested that some Labour selectors saw the social class of a candidate as indicative of his or her ideological position.[22]

Insufficient evidence exists to confirm the view that the new university-educated, public-sector-employed Labour constituency activists who became prominent in the 1970s and early 1980s are uniformly more left-wing than working-class activists. According to Seyd's 1986 study, left-wing attitudes were 'firmly-based' amongst activists both in working-class Attercliffe and middle-class Hallam. But the study, which was written at a time when left-wing views were extremely influential in the constituencies, showed that, on all issues except public ownership, the Attercliffe CLP was less left-wing than the Hallam CLP, often significantly so. In Liverpool, rank-and-file Militant supporters who became prominent in the local party in the early 1980s have been described as 'aggressively proletarian' but in Manchester the battle for the local party was between 'moderates' who were generally Manchester-born skilled workers or local businessmen and left-wing former student activists from middle-class south of England backgrounds.

The increased representation of women in the House of Commons has been advocated both on symbolic and substantive grounds. Whilst the symbolic argument posits the unfairness of massive under-representation, the substantive case suggests that a larger contingent of women in Parliament would make a difference to its functioning because women possess a distinctive point of view. But the evidence on how far women do behave differently and how far their political behaviour resembles that of male politicians is inconclusive. One study based on the 1987 British Candidate Survey found that, although party was the strongest predictor of attitudes to social change, there was 'a significant gender gap' on many of the issues studied. The authors are cautious on the question of whether the gender difference in political attitudes they find is sufficient to matter. They raise the point, however, that women are unlikely to be in a position to transform public policy until they form a much higher proportion of the legislature than they do at present.[23]

The greater parliamentary representation of blacks (who form only 0.6 per cent of the House of Commons) has also been advocated on both symbolic and substantive grounds. The involvement of blacks in the major parties as members and supporters in similar ways to whites can help incorporate blacks into the British political mainstream. Black participation in class-based institutions can be endorsed by advocates of the multi-cultural society as preferable to such alternatives as black parties based on black consciousness, participation of blacks in the system through 'buffer' institutions like the Community Relations Commission, large-scale withdrawal from the system by alienated blacks or outbreaks of rioting and urban violence.[24] But the liberal integrationist outcome depends on the major parties' selection of increasing numbers of black candidates for winnable seats and the success of those candidates in winning them.

## Notes

1 D. Butler and M. Pinto-Duschinsky, *The British General Election of 1970* (London: Macmillan, 1971) 301, 303; and D. Butler and D. Kavanagh, *The British General Election of 1987* (London: Macmillan, 1988) 202.

2 M. Moran, *Politics and Society in Britain* (London: Macmillan, 1989) 157.

3 J. Greenwood, 'Promoting working class candidature in the Conservative Party: the limits of Central Office power', *Parliamentary Affairs*, vol. 41 (1988) 467–8.

4 J. Bochel and D. Denver, 'Candidate selection in the Labour Party: what selectors seek', *British Journal of Political Science*, vol. 13 (1983) 56–8.

5 M. Ball, F. Gray and L. McDowell, *The Transformation of Britain* (London: Fontana, 1989) 427, 432; M. Rush, *Parliament and the Public* (London: Longman, 1986) 63–4.

6 M. Burch and M. Moran, 'The changing British political elite, 1945–1983: MPs and Cabinet Ministers', *Parliamentary Affairs*, vol. 38 (1985) 15.

7 D. Kavanagh (ed.), *The Politics of the Labour Party* (London: Allen & Unwin, 1982) 101.

8 D. Butler and M. Pinto-Duschinsky, 'The Conservative elite, 1918–1978: does unrepresentativeness matter?', in Z. Layton-Henry (ed.), *Conservative Party Politics* (London: Macmillan, 1980) 194–8.

9 S. Ingle, *The British Party System* (Oxford: Blackwell, 1987) 83. See further M. Pugh, 'Popular Conservatism in Great Britain: continuity and change, 1880–1987', *Journal of British Studies*, vol. 27 (1988) 266–7.

10 D. Butler and G. Butler (eds.), *British Political Facts 1900–1985* (London: Macmillan, 1986) 139.

11 E. Janosik, *Constituency Labour Parties in Britain* (London: Pall Mall Press, 1968) 9–25.

12 P. Seyd, *The Rise and Fall of the Labour Left* (London: Macmillan, 1987) 40.

13 L. Minkin, *The Labour Party Conference* (London: Allen Lane 1978) 87; Seyd, *Rise and Fall of the Labour Left*, 43.

14 Seyd, *Rise and Fall of the Labour Left*, 44; and P. Whitely, 'The decline of Labour's local party membership and electoral base', in Kavanagh, *Politics of the Labour Party*, 115–16.

15 E. Vallance, 'Women candidates in the 1983 General Election', *Parliamentary Affairs*, vol. 37 (1984) 304–6.

16 S. McRae, 'Women at the top: the case of British national politics', *Parliamentary Affairs*, vol. 43 (1990) 341–7; for a European comparison, see E. Kolinsky, 'Political participation and parliamentary careers: women's quotas in West Germany', *West European Politics*, vol. 14 (1991) 56–72.

17 Z. Layton-Henry and D. Studlar, 'The electoral participation of Black and Asian Britons: integration or alienation?', *Parliamentary Affairs*, vol. 38 (1985) 308–9.

18  Butler and Kavanagh, *General Election 1987*, 341; and M. Fitzgerald, 'Race in the 1987 Election Campaign', in I. Crewe and M. Harrop (eds.), *Political Communications: the General Election Campaign of 1987* (Cambridge University Press, 1987) 283–4.

19  C. T. Husbands, 'Race and Gender', in H. Drucker *et al.* (eds.), *Developments in British Politics 2* (London: Macmillan, 1986) 298.

20  C. Mellors, *The British MP* (Farnborough: Saxon House, 1978) 120.

21  E. Hobsbawm, 'Labour: rump or rebirth?', *Marxism Today* (March 1984).

22  Bochel and Denver, *'Candidate Selection in the Labour Party'*, 56–7.

23  P. Norris and J. Lovenduski, 'Women candidates for Parliament: transforming the agenda', *British Journal of Political Science*, vol. 19 (1989) 114—15.

24  Z. Layton-Henry, *The Politics of Race in Britain* (London: Allen & Unwin, 1984) 166–70.

# All you never wanted to know about British political parties

Rather surprisingly, political parties have not been the object of rigorous analysis over the past two decades. Instead, they have been regarded as part of the furniture. I should like to remedy this omission by examining the nature of parties and the party system as they have emerged over the last twenty years or so. But I must start with an admission: it is wrongly assumed that to throw the spotlight on a subject necessarily makes it more easily comprehended, that illumination equals simplification. Unfortunately this is not always the case and to throw light on a very complex subject simply focuses the mind's eye on a pattern of paradox and confusion which was hitherto unsuspected. So it is with political parties. There is no student of politics who does not have an idea of what parties are or how they operate in the British context; indeed John and Jane Citizen, if put to it, could give a reasonable working definition of a British political party. Perhaps in making sense of the political land-scape this 'idea' is as much as is needed. Certainly it could be argued that many who have written about or commented upon the British political system over the past twenty years or so have tended not to question the conventional wisdom. If we seek a clearer insight into the nature of British parties and the system of which they are a part, however, we must start again from the beginning: we must question basic assumptions and examine available evidence, and we must expect some cherished beliefs to be called into question, some reassuring 'truths' to appear less certain. I propose to proceed along these lines, then: stating the most important of the assumptions and then examining each, with the intention of concluding with a restatement of the nature of British party politics.

## The nature of the British party system

To begin, we can agree that most commentators during the past two decades would accept the following as the guiding assumptions concerning the operations of the British party system:

1. Britain has a predominantly two-party system in which the major parties represent competing ideologies which distinguish each from the other and unite the adherents of each against the other.

2. This two-party system makes voters' choice possible by canalising policies into two broad alternatives, thus allowing for the popular endorsement of one alternative which takes the form of a mandate to the victorious party.

3. The defeated party makes the government accountable by scrutinising policy and performance through a range of parliamentary procedures which were designed with this objective in mind.

4. In a two-party system the need to win support from the uncommitted voters in the centre of the spectrum presses both parties towards consensus politics, thus restricting partisanship (or adversarianism) to rhetoric and encouraging continuity of policy.

5. Over a period of time both major parties will share power more or less equally.

6. The victorious party in a general election will *usually* represent the majority of voters (not always: that would be too much to expect).

7. As a consequence of the operation of these principles Britain has, during the last twenty years or so, possessed a party system which, despite its acknowledged deficiencies (such as the under-representation of minorities), allows for strong, efficient and legitimate government.

Perhaps. In any event we shall be in a better position to judge after we have examined each of the assumptions. First, then, we will examine assumptions concerning the two-party system and competing ideologies.

## Two competing parties

Even a cursory study of party history will indicate that British politics have not traditionally been dominated by two parties. Only for comparatively brief periods in British history have two national parties, organised and disciplined especially for that end, dominated the Houses of Parliament. This is not a matter of judgement but of easily verified fact and it is thus all the stranger that most recent writers on the party system have operated on the assumption of a two-party norm. Robert McKenzie's *British Political Parties*, published in 1955, perhaps the major contribution to the literature, devoted only two of its 597 pages to the Liberal Party (and those in the appendix), and none at all to any other minor party. No doubt this made sense in the 1950s when the Liberal Party in the House of Commons had been reduced to a rump of six and over 90 per cent of voters were supporting the two major parties. McKenzie, rather like Bagehot before him, seemed to assume that he lived in typical times and that the system had little dynamic for change. McKenzie though, unlike Bagehot, occupied a pivotal position, being not only a senior political scientist but also a media person. The advent in the late 1950s of mass-media coverage of politics provided a natural plat-form for his views and the nature of the medium of television did much to underwrite those views. The 'for' and 'against' model of presentation had much to commend it. The format benefited from the presentation of 'both sides of the argument' in an overtly balanced and democratic manner, and it scarcely seemed to occur to producers that there might be more than two sides. This allowed the coverage of party politics, especially electoral politics, to follow the successful model of sports presentation, with greater excitement added by virtue of the fact that the observer doubled up as par-ticipant (voter). The match commentator was none other than McKenzie himself, complete with his swingometer, which, origi-nally, was one-dimensional, measuring only the swing from one major party to the other.

The limitations of the two-party model were exposed, though, as early as 1958 by a Liberal by-electoral victory at Torrington and although one chance victory could be written off, the subsequent victory in suburban Orpington in 1962, with a swing to the Liberals from the Conservatives of over 20 per cent, and a total Liberal vote of over 3 million in the 1964 general election could not be. Neverthe-less, the two-party model managed to incorporate this apparently irreconcilable development without much difficulty. Research indi-cated that much of the Liberal vote was a protest – against the malfunctioning of the two-party system. If it were to function properly, then, the protest would go away. Moreover, it was dis-covered that for others the Liberal Party was a half-way house, a brief refuge on a once-in-a-lifetime journey from left to right, or vice versa. So rather than challenging the two-party model the Liberals actually confirmed it, operating as a necessary safety valve. The intermittent success of the Scottish National Party (SNP) and Plaid Cymru in the late 1960s and 1970s clearly represented a different phenomenon and yet they were treated in much the same manner, as being vehicles of protest concerning very specific failures of the two-party system.

Politicians and political commentators who subscribed to the two-party model had always assumed that protest votes were primarily by-electoral indulgences and that, come the general election, the model would reassert itself. It failed to do so in February of 1974 when there were major successes for the nationalists and over 5 million voted Liberal. The result was a slender Labour victory, so slender that eight months later Prime Minister Wilson gave the electorate another opportunity to come to its senses. The result, however, was much the same, and it became obvious that, in the medium term at least, the two-party model, for all its convenience, would have to be shelved. Quite suddenly British political commentators began to write about multi-party politics and to ask questions about the party system which some continental commentators had been asking a decade before.

By the 1980s the Liberals had established a regular support of between 15 and 25 per cent and when, in 1981, they formed an alliance with the newly emerged social-democratic defectors from the increasingly left-wing Labour Party, the Social Democratic Party (SDP), they enjoyed public support in the opinion polls of over 40 per cent for more than six months. Clearly no commentator could dismiss this as simply a safety valve.

In the general election of 1983 the Alliance came desperately close to gaining more votes nationally than the Labour Party, though it failed to make any impact in terms of representation, gaining only twenty-three MPs from its 7 million votes. A less successful result in the 1987 general election led to the merging of the Liberals and the majority of the SDP to form (eventually) the Liberal Democrats. A substantial minority of the SDP strove to retain its independence under the leadership of Dr David Owen, but Owen disbanded the party in 1990. The merged Liberal Democrats went through two trying years of internal disputes, a leadership contest, intense financial difficulties, and a fierce struggle for the centre vote with the rump SDP in a background dominated by a Labour Party successfully attempting to re-establish itself as a force for moderate left-of-centre politics. In the European elections of 1989 the Liberal Democrats' lacklustre campaign led to their securing a substantially smaller proportion of votes than the Green Party and most commentators were speaking of a return to two-party politics. By 1990 however, Liberal Democrat finances were in better order, the new leader Paddy Ashdown had begun to establish himself as a national figure, and the SDP had vanished; an unexpected by-electoral victory at Eastbourne set the seal on the party's (re?)emergence as a national force.

With increasing support for the SNP (including a by-electoral victory in Govan in 1988) and with the Liberal Democrats revived, the future of the British party system began to seem less predictable. The unexpected departure of Margaret Thatcher as Conservative leader in late 1990 magnified this growing unpredictability substantially.

What this review of recent party history indicates is that the two-party model is not only inappropriate for analysing British politics historically but, apart from a brief period in the 1960s and 1970s, it is by no means wholly appropriate even to the modern era.

## Two competing ideologies

If the picture of two parties completely dominating British politics is seen to be somewhat inappropriate, the picture of two associated dominant ideologies must fall *ipso facto*. It is possible to take the argument further though and to examine the extent to which, irrespective of their lack of dominance, the two major parties have, in the past two decades, possessed ideologies which actually do distinguish them from their opponents and unite their supporters. Investigation of the policy commitments of both the Conservative and Labour Parties reveals what might euphemistically be called some interesting anomalies.

Anthony Quinton speaks of three chief principles of Conservatism: traditionalism, which he describes as a strong emotional attachment to existing procedures, faith in a fixed constitution and a strong belief in the rule of law; organicism, which compares society to a natural living body comprising an ecology of mutually beneficial relationships, implying, in political terms a hierarchy built on duties and privileges (Disraeli's 'one nation'); finally scepticism, frequently associated with the Christian concept of original sin, which emphasises the limitations of human endeavour, and finds political form in a strong belief in limited government.[1] For O'Sullivan this last is the lynchpin of Conservatism, its major distinguishing feature.[2] We might add pragmatism to this list, since Conservatives have traditionally claimed to be prepared, unlike socialists, to put 'reality' before ideology. In the nineteenth century, however, the Conservative Party was opposed by *laissez-faire* Liberalism and became the party of intervention, in its attempt presumably to act 'organically' and secure the interests of all citizens. In the twentieth century too, under leaders like Neville Chamberlain and Harold Macmillan, the party supported substantial government intervention in the economy, afterwards earning the opprobrium of neo-liberals in the party like Lord Joseph. Later, Edward Heath's neo-corporatist policies showed scant regard for limited government.

More recently, under the leadership of Margaret Thatcher, a Conservative government embarked on an enterprise nothing less grand than to reshape society – precisely the kind of task Conservatives would traditionally have considered to be both inappropriate and indeed obnoxious. The 1988 Education Reform Act, for example, conferred no fewer than 240 new powers upon the Secretary of State, over sixty of which were the direct result of government-backed amendments. It would be no exaggeration to say that the sweeping reforms of the Thatcher era exhibited a distaste for tradition, a complete rejection of the ethos of organicism – indeed Thatcher argued that there was no such thing as society – and a willingness to strengthen the powers of the central government in so profound a way as to change the shape of the constitution (*vis-à-vis* local government for example). As for pragmatism, whilst it is clear that nearly all governments will trim their policies in the light of 'reality', Thatcher made a fetish of conviction politics and in pursuing single-mindedly the establishment of the community charge against all good advice, she actually came to epitomise the very antithesis of pragmatism. Thus the Conservative government under Margaret Thatcher represented the polar opposite of the chief Conservative virtues. To put it simply, the policies of the Thatcher government strongly reinforced the message of history, that in office Conservative governments show little more than a random or at most a symbolic relationship with Conservative ideology.

Marxists would argue that Conservatism can only be understood as an ideology in the Marxist sense, as a veiled statement of the interests of the property-owning class. To the counter-argument, that the Conservative government's policy of high interest rates has been injurious to the interests of their supporters, Marxists would argue: yes, but only to a minority and only in the short term. However, they would have to explain the government's attempted long-term reform of the legal, medical and educational professions, against the wishes of the groups themselves, all of them part of the Conservatives' 'natural' constituency. In fact, the whole ethos of Thatcherism has been profoundly un-Conservative, in nothing more than its attempt radically to change values. In short, whilst Conservatism can be shown to be at least in part a reflection of class interest, Conservative governments can be found pursuing mutually conflicting policies with regularity.

As for the Labour Party, it has been demonstrably riven by ideological disputes since its inception.[3] Has its role been to establsih socialism or to pursue the interests of the working class? If it were to be argued that these are two sides of the same coin, then how should the party react to the fact that the working class does not seem to perceive this unity? For the Fabians, socialism required the establishment of an elite which would run society in the interests of all, but for others socialism implied a diffusion of power, giving people some control over their own lives. In office Labour governments tended to increase state control via nationalisation, but such a policy became increasingly unpopular with the working class who, faced with great bureaucratic administrative structures, felt no sense of ownership of the state's industries and services, but rather a sense of alienation towards them. By the late 1950s, following the party's third successive electoral defeat, strenuous efforts were made to 'liberate' the party from its commitment to nationalisation, but Labour Conferences saw this as treachery and resisted.

The Wilson government of 1966 was the only post-1950 Labour government with a strong majority. Its trumpeted commitment, though, was not so much to socialism as to the 'white heat of the technological revolution'; that is, to spreading greater wealth and to improving services through transforming industrial performance rather than transforming the structure of power within society. This policy, which anyway was not successful, earned the displeasure of many backbenchers, one of whom declared that he had not struggled so hard to replace a middle-class Conservative government with a working-class Conservative government. When Wilson's government attempted, through its Bill *In Place Of Strife* to reform the trade-union movement, this sense of betrayal became greater. When Wilson returned to office in 1974 and when, after his retirement, James Callaghan became Prime Minister, a knife-edged majority and a pact with the Liberal Party made a full-blooded redistributive socialist policy impossible. Yet it was quite plain that no such policy had been envisaged by the party and one is forced to conclude that, with the exception of the 1945–50 government, when a centralised command economy already existed as a legacy of the war, Labour governments have not conspicuously advanced the cause of socialism. When, from 1979 onwards, the left-wing of the party sought to wrench power from the right, this was partly a response to a double failure: the deeper failure of not having advanced socialism but also the more present failure of having lost electoral support through general ineptitude. By 1983 the left had secured some notable victories: the programme of compulsory re-selection for MPs, the electoral college for choosing the party leader, greater party involvement (through the National Executive Committee) in drawing up the manifesto and the election to leader of that doughty champion of the left, Michael Foot. If Labour had been elected in 1983 the country could have expected its most radical government since 1945; in the event Labour was humiliated. Ex-Labour Cabinet minister Peter Shore referred to the party's manifesto as 'the longest suicide note in history'.

By 1987 Labour's radicalism was already being undermined. Neil Kinnock urged the electorate to vote not for socialism, nor even for Labour, but for Kinnock. After a good but unsuccessful campaign Kinnock and his allies set about a review of all aspects of Labour's policies and structure. The consequences of this review could hardly have been greater. David Marquand, writing in 1987 of the future of British politics, advanced the view that for Labour to become electorally victorious it would need to win the votes of those seduced into supporting the Alliance, and to do that it would need to review its pro-nuclear disarmament policy, its anti-European policy, its general faith in nationalisation and its strong alignment to the trade-union movement: 'in other words', he concluded, 'to cease to be the Labour party'. His words might have been prophetic for Labour has done (or is doing) each of these things and more.

The voter might legitimately express some bewilderment about what the Labour Party has stood for over the years. Bound by its 1918 constitution to bring the means of production and exchange into social ownership – to a socialist economy – it has signally failed to do so despite internal pressure. Currently the party has made it plain that it has no such commitment and yet the most recent and most detailed study of the party membership[4] indicates that the party rank-and-file remain strongly in favour of extending nationalisation, pro-nuclear disarmament, strongly pro-trade union (wishing to see the restoration of the right to secondary picketing, for example) and strongly in favour of increasing taxation to improve services. If the 1987 position is any guide, a parliamentary party with a majority of more than fifty would be substantially to the left of the current leadership and perhaps substantially less amenable to the blandishments of Kinnock's reformism.

In short Labour Party history presents a pendulum swing back and forth from socialism to social democracy, with the swing to the latter normally synchronising with (admittedly rare) periods of government. This division is substantially the one which confronted the party at its inception and the subsequent failure to resolve it means that the party presents no ideological consistency to the voter. Kinnock's Labour Party in the 1990s is as different from the party of Callaghan and Foot as Thatcher's Conservative party was from the party of Macmillan and Heath. The idea of two competing ideologies which are consistent and which distinguish each from the other and unite the adherents of each against each other is not simply borne out in reality.

## Two competing policy programmes?

Having established this lack of consistency concerning party ideology – and not just over the past twenty years – it becomes difficult to take too seriously the idea of the major parties canalising policy into two broadly understood alternatives for popular choice and endorsement. Irrespective of ideological inconsistency, however, it is clear that during the modern period party identification has become much less pronounced amongst the electorate than was once the case. A study by Rose and McAllister, for example, using a factor analysis of voter preference amongst Conservative, Labour and Alliance supporters, indicated a substantial measure of agreement in the three key policy areas of welfare, morality and racialism.[5] Indeed, only fifteen of forty-five policy issues elicited any measure of disagreement among supporters of the three major parties. The authors concluded that only socialism excited real disagreement but the split was not along party lines: attitudes to socialism divided both Labour and the Alliance and united (in hostility) only the Conservative voters.[6] Moreover, Labour voters were in disagreement over twenty-six out of forty-five issues, Alliance voters on twenty-five and Conservatives on nineteen. There is no evidence that Margaret Thatcher's electoral victories owed anything to public support for her policies; indeed the Conservative vote actually fell in 1983. On the basis of their analysis the authors were able to suggest two conclusions: that disagreement is commonly within and not between parties and that how a person thinks about issues is a poor guide to how he/she votes. If these conclusions were out of line with other findings we might have cause to question them but they are not; they make it clear that a claim made on behalf of any party which secured an electoral victory that it has a mandate from the people to enact its policies is always likely to be dubious. If, as is almost invariably the case, the victorious party represents only a minority of the electorate, the claim must be meaningless. Each Nuffield electoral study teaches us that only a minority of voters read election manifestos. Of that minority only a further minority agrees with the policies outlined. So the mandate claimed by the present government, for example, is based upon the support of a minority of a minority of a majority. And, as Pimlott pointed out, that original minority (constituting the Conservative vote in 1987) represented the 'smallest proportion of the popular vote of any Tory administration since 1922'.[7]

## Two-party accountability

The third generalisation to be considered concerns government accountability through vigilant opposition, made the more important because, in a two-party system, the opposition is also the alternative government. Parliamentary procedures ensure that government policy is scrutinised by the opposition, which is able to focus public attention upon policies it considers harmful. It is quite obvious that any government during the past twenty years with a working majority, if it had the support of its own backbenchers, need have no fear that its policies would be defeated. Norton has shown that, since the Heath ministry, government backbenchers have acted with a measure of independence and have been able to influence their own party leaders.[8] What he cannot show is any measure important to a government with a working majority being defeated in the House, nor can he show the opposition having any noticeable direct influence. It would be a nonsense to suggest that debate in the House of Commons is a charade simply because, when a government has a working majority, the result is always predictable. Nevertheless, it is fair to question the extent to which accountability may be said to exist in a parliamentary system which allows a government to put on the statute book a law as widely reviled by politicians and people of all political persuasions as the community charge. It is also fair to question the effectiveness of Question Time, especially Prime Minister's Questions, if government ministers set their minds to self-advertisement rather than answering questions. During Margaret Thatcher's prime ministership the average number of questions 'answered' fell from around nine per session to around five.[9]

Indeed, it can be argued that far from ensuring government accountability the British two-party system actually hinders the process. Since information is seldom neutral it tends to be a commodity which governments hoard; consequently British government is arguably the most secretive of the Western democracies. The present government has sought to prevent the select committee system, for example, from attaining anything like the influence of its American counterpart by placing strictures on the kind of information that civil servants may make available. State security is a goal for which it is worth making sacrifices of openness; government embarrassment is not.

Even when it is readily available, however, the nature of information has changed. As policy has come to cover areas of increasing complexity so it has become more technical and indeed technological. It has, as a direct consequence, become less amenable to adversarian scrutiny. Yet the procedures which Parliament uses for purposes of scrutiny remain largely unchanged. Even where they have changed, as in the system of select committees established after 1979, the partisan–ideological confrontation of the two major parties places strict limits on their capacity to effect change as well, as mentioned, as on their freedom of enquiry. What this means is that the opposition will tend to engage the government on aspects of its policy which are amenable to adversarian presentation rather than its more important aspects. A detailed study of health politics between 1970 and 1975 exemplified the consequences of this quite clearly.[10] The hugely expensive structural changes envisaged by the National Health Reorganization Act were less effectively discussed than the decision not to provide birth control free on prescription. Although only £3 million of public funds were involved, this issue proved very suitable for adversarian debate, with the traditional rallying cries of equality, responsibility, welfare and bureaucracy punctuating debate regularly. One- or two-tier administrative structures, co-terminosity with local government and the role of family practitioner committees did not fire the blood. Nor is it simply the manner in which such matters are debated; as policy becomes more complex and technical so the inputs come 'increasingly not from parties but from experts within the executive. The procedures for assessing these policies, however, continue to operate as if they *were* partisan–ideological and so remain basically adversarian.'[11] Ian MacLeod, as Parliamentary Private Secretary to Winston Churchill when the latter was leader of the opposition in the late 1940s, was asked to provide the great man with 'statistics' for a debate that afternoon on infant mortality. The information services of the House were even worse then and MacLeod worked hard to provide the information. Churchill made no reference whatever to the details painstakingly provided and when MacLeod later remonstrated with him, his leader retorted that when he asked for statistical information on infant mortality he expected that information to prove conclusively that fewer children had died when he was Prime Minister than during under the Labour government of the day! So much for adversarian scrutiny.

### Two-party consensus

The next generalisation concerns the alleged centripetal tendency of British politics: the need to win votes in 'the middle ground' draws both parties towards consensual politics. This is an argument especially associated with Richard Rose's *Do Parties Make A Difference*.[12] In crucial areas of the economy, says Rose, major developments are not much influenced by change of government; whether we examine inputs (matters within the government's control, such as setting the minimum lending rate, the level of public-sector borrowing and of public expenditure) or economic outcomes only partly under government control (such as inflation, unemployment and economic growth), it is 'long-term secular trends undependent of party which influence the direction of the economy, not party policy'.[13] Moreover, his studies led him to conclude that party politics were consensual and not adversarian in character for three reasons: the electorate tends to agree on major issues; parties in government moderate their ideological preferences for fear of what their opponents might do when they come to power; finally, new governments face old problems with old advice and the same kinds of restraint. Adversarianism, then, he concludes, is largely rhetorical and not real.

On the other hand, it can be argued that rhetoric is very much a part of reality. In S. H. Beer's words, rhetoric establishes 'the framework of public thinking about policy'[14] and Labour's comments about what it intends to do when in government will only be ignored if it is quite certain either that Labour will not be able even to try to do what it promises or that it is not at all likely to gain power. As to the argument that parties are prisoners of economic trends, this is at most only partly true; there is no justification, for example, for assuming that Labour would have responded to the economic problems of the 1980s by a policy of privatisation. Outside economic policy there are probably even greater differences of party, none more so than in education, for example: Labour's ideology in the 1960s and Conservative ideology in the 1980s have had profound and profoundly different effects upon Britain's education system. Their combined impact can only have been harmful.

## Two party power sharing

The fifth generalisation suggests that the two major parties would, over a period of time, share power more or less equally. In fact this is far from the truth. Parties of the left have been in government with a good working majority on only three occasions in this century: 1906, 1945 and 1966. Their total number of years in office with good majorities this century amounts to thirteen. The Conservatives have done as well since 1979! By contrast, if we include coalitions which they dominated, the Conservatives have been in power with good majorities for some fifty-six years. On average then, the Conservatives are more than four times as likely to be in power than Labour. The last twenty years have been typical, with the Conservatives in office with a good working majority for sixteen years, Labour enjoying five years with a tiny and disappearing majority.

The sixth generalisation suggested that, by and large, victorious parties represent the majority of the electorate. In fact on only three occasions in the last century has an incoming government represented a majority of the electorate: in the first, 1900, the victorious Conservatives were in alliance with Liberal Unionists; in the second and third, 1931 and 1935, they were the dominant partner in coalitions. Only in 1931 when the coalition secured the support of 67 per cent of those who voted could a British government genuinely be said to represent a clear majority of the voters: only once in a hundred years. No surprise, then, that no government in the past two decades has represented a majority of the voters because not once in the last *century* has a major party fighting on its own won a majority, which casts an intriguing reflection on the notion of legitimacy.

## Two-party efficiency

The final generalisation declares that the operation of the British two-party system provided for a government which, if not fair to minorities, was at least efficient, legitimate and strong. Perhaps having turned the spotlight on the system, its efficiency and legitimacy appear substantially more flawed and ambiguous than we thought. As for its strength, two final thoughts. If a government is single-minded enough, against all opposition, to pass a particular measure only for it to be reversed later by another government when it proves unworkable, is that an indication of strength on the part of both governments although the net consequence is nothing? Second, if the British two-party system produces strong government, why is it that, in times of national emergency, when it is almost universally agreed that strong government is needed, it is to coalitions that Britain tends to turn?

In addition to these deep-seated anomalies and ambiguities, the spotlight also reveals, finally, that since 1979 the Conservative Party has, to all intents and purposes, provided not only the country's government but, through its backbenches, the chief opposition. With the departure of Thatcher it unseated the government and provided a change in government. In all this the official opposition parties, and indeed the electorate, were merely observers.

In brief conclusion, the spotlight seems to show that party politics over the past two decades has been far more complex than most commentators have allowed. Perhaps we should turn off the spotlight; it brings only confusion. Or alternatively, if we are to make better sense of the next twenty years, perhaps we need to think again about the British party system.

## Notes

1   Anthony Quinton, *The Politics of Imperfection* (Oxford: Blackwell, 1978) 24.

2   N. K. O'Sullivan, *Conservatism* (London: Dent, 1976) 24.

3   For a full account of the origin and nature of these disputes see R. N. Berki, *Socialism* (London: Dent, 1975).

4   Patrick Seyd, Paul Whiteley and David Broughton, 'Labour reorganization down at the grassroots', paper presented to PSA Specialist Group on Parties and Elections, 1990.

5   R. Rose and I. McAllister, *Voters Begin to Choose* (London: Sage, 1986).

6   *Ibid.*, 143.

7   *Sunday Times*, 20 November 1988.

8   Philip Norton, 'Independence, scrutiny and rationalization: a decade of change in the House of Commons', *Teaching Politics*, vol. 15, no. 1 (1986) 69–97.

9   Ian Aitken, *Guardian*, 12 December 1990.

10   Stephen Ingle and Philip Tether, *Parliament and Health Policy: The Role of MPs 1970–75* (Farnborough: Gower, 1981).

11   *Ibid.*, 155.

12   Richard Rose, *Do Parties Make A Difference?* (London: Macmillan, 1984, 2nd ed).

13   *Ibid.*, xxix.

14   S. H. Beer, *Modern British Politics* (London: Faber & Faber, 1965) 347.

# Pressure groups and the British political system: change and decline?

The belief that there has been a general decline in the influence of pressure groups in Britain is not without foundation. For some this belief springs directly from the style and method of government over the last decade. The confrontational style of the Thatcher regime, its radical programme, its distrust of special interests and, of course the large parliamentary majorities it enjoyed, have, it is argued, made it more difficult for pressure groups to influence policy. This feeling of decline has also been reinforced by the complaints of well-established pressure groups that government no longer listens to them. But are pressure groups really less powerful today than, say, in the 1970s? The task of this chapter is to explore the changes in the pressure-group universe over the last two decades, to assess whether or not these changes constitute a decline, and to predict the future conduct and role of pressure groups.

Such a task is far from simple. It is notoriously difficult to generalise about pressure groups, given their number and diversity. Also, as pressure groups are concerned with a range of issues, it is possible that their influence may have declined in some policy areas whilst increasing in others. Furthermore, pressure groups are an integral part of the political system and it is often difficult to distinguish their influence from that of other political institutions, such as parties, Parliament, the media and government departments, with which they interact. Finally, the task is complicated by the fact that many pressure groups operate quietly, invisibly and effectively on issues attracting little public attention. As a result, their contribution to policy-making may be more difficult to gauge than that of groups operating on front-line issues. Put another way, an assessment of the influence of pressure groups may be distorted by focusing purely on those policy issues at the forefront of public concern.

Before going any further it is of course important to clarify the term 'pressure group'. For the purpose of this chapter a pressure group is defined as an organisation which seeks to influence the details of a comparatively small range of public policies. Factions of political parties and government departments or agencies are not in this context regarded as pressure groups. The following analysis is broken down into four stages. First, an examination of the role and influence of pressure groups in the 1970s. Second, an evaluation of the impact of the Thatcher governments' style on the conduct of pressure-group politics. Thirdly, a consideration of other developments in this field over the last two decades. Finally, some concluding remarks along with an assessment of the future course of pressure-group politics.

## The 1970s: the heyday of pressure-group politics?

The late 1960s and early 1970s are often depicted as the heyday of modern pressure-group politics. During this period observers became increasingly aware of sharply conflicting styles of interaction existing between pressure groups and the principal governing institutions. On the one hand, there was an unstable, sporadic, unpredictable style, of which more will be said later. On the other, there was the stable, predictable and continuous form of interaction, largely embodied in the relationships between government departments and the major producer interest groups.

The latter had been the dominant form during the post-war period. This was largely because in most policy areas economic intervention and the welfare state, against a background of political consensus, had brought government into a strong relationship with a wide range of producer groups (a term which in the sense used here includes trade unions and labour organisations). These groups had access to Whitehall and their leaders were usually consulted on policy matters prior to the introduction of parliamentary legislation and official statements. In some cases, notably agriculture, government departments had a statutory obligation to consult certain organised interests when making policy.

In the absence of statutory provisions, there were a number of reasons why government still felt it desirable to bring groups into the policy-making process. First of all, this process made it more difficult for the group to oppose the policies which they had helped create. Prior consultation also helped to pre-empt criticism of government policy at a later stage, where it would represent an open attack on the government's authority. Governments preferred to retreat on policy issues in private discussions rather than be defeated openly in public. The consultation process also provided government with specialist information and advice on policy matters. As government did not have a monopoly of information and expertise, it became dependent on the provision of these resources by the groups. Finally, governments realised that in many cases pressure groups and their members could influence the implementation of policy. Without their co-operation on a practical level, policies would remain largely statements of intent.

The interface between government and the major producer groups was well oiled and for the most part worked smoothly. Consultation took a variety of forms, ranging from the formal Whitehall committee to the informal chat with senior group officials over lunch. The most prominent groups boasted of daily (and at times, hourly) contact with government. But for the most part the consultation process was rather routine, much time being spent on highly detailed matters of little public interest. Even so, the access which the large producer groups enjoyed was extremely useful when more controversial issues were raised. Moreover, the channels of influence were largely hidden. The consultation process was insulated from public and parliamentary scrutiny, the leaders of the producer groups were not public figures, and media interest in their activities was low.

When issues did attract wider public interest, governments sometimes found it politically difficult to exclude other groups and their views would be sought. A variety of means were employed when a broader range of views needed to be consulted. Departmental committees of enquiry, such as the Erroll Committee on the liquor licensing laws set up in the early 1970s, were usually established when the issue in question was focused on one government department (in this case the Home Office). For issues that cut across the responsibilities of many government institutions, or which were of special public importance, the government would establish a Royal Commission. One example, the Royal Commission on the National Health Service, which reported in 1979, received evidence from over 1,200 groups and organisations. These methods of garnering wider opinion were criticised, largely because of both the expense involved and their potential for removing issues from the political agenda. Governments could postpone decisions during the period of the enquiry (which often took two years or more) and then reject the recommendations. But commissions and committees were useful in that they did consult widely and could provide a clearing house for ideas and evidence, promoting debate on important issues of public policy.

The principal focus of policy-making, however, remained in the continuous, stable relationships between producer groups and government departments, exemplified by the National Farmers Union–Ministry of Agriculture and the British Medical Association–Health Ministry cases, which have been well documented. Of course, from time to time, the stable relationship was threatened. For example, doctors in their pay dispute of 1965 at one point threatened mass resignation from the National Health Service. But even when, as in this case, relationships became strained, stability was usually restored. It was not until the late 1960s and early 1970s that such crises became far more frequent. By this time in many policy areas the dominant style of interaction appeared to be giving ground to a more open and unstable form, particularly amongst labour groups.

The late 1960s and early 1970s were a time of rapid growth in the pressure-group universe. Many new groups emerged in this period. Some were offshoots of established producer groups, dissatisfied with the achievements of the parent group and its stable relationship with Whitehall. But many were consumer and client groups, representing interests which had previously been excluded from the policy process. New cause groups also sprang up, particularly in the area of environment and welfare.

The style of these consumer and cause groups was very different from the mainstream producer interests described above. The form of interaction between government and such groups was less stable, more sporadic and less predictable. Indeed, some groups achieved remarkable successes, against the odds. The decision to alter plans for the siting of the third London airport, for example, was a direct result of cause-group pressure. The tactics of these groups were also different from those employed by the producer interests. The media, Parliament and the general public were the main targets of their campaigns, rather than Whitehall. The newer consumer and cause groups were also very innovative in the lobbying techniques they employed. Many were highly skilful in mobilising the media and public and parliamentary opinion through well-organised campaigns. Some groups also went in for 'direct-action' tactics leading to open confrontation with the authorities.

As the 1970s unfolded, direct-action tactics were increasingly taken up by a number of producer groups, particularly the trade unions. The incomes and industrial-relations policies of successive governments bred conflict and confrontation. This reached its climax in 1974, when the Heath government called an election following its confrontation with the unions. The defeat of Heath added to the climate of concern about the power of pressure groups. The incoming Labour government adopted a more conciliatory approach, attempting to accommodate trade unions through formal and informal consultation on a range of policy issues. It was in the end unable to contain union power, culminating in the 'winter of discontent' and electoral defeat. But it was not just the unions who were confronting government during the 1970s. The Labour government's nationalisation plans provoked hostile campaigns from the banks, amongst others. Meanwhile the doctors were incensed over the policy of phasing out pay beds in NHS hospitals. Although the stable, negotiated order persisted on many less controversial issues, the adoption of confrontational strategies by established producer interest groups was definitely on the increase. Some academics saw Britain as becoming increasingly ungovernable. According to them, many pressure groups – and not just the unions – exercised what amounted to a veto power over policies with which they were closely connected. The result was that difficult decisions were not made, particularly with regard to economic policy. Others saw the threat posed by pressure groups in even more serious terms. For them pressure groups undermined the authority of elected governments and thereby posed a threat to democracy itself.

### The Thatcher decade

The defeat of Heath in 1974 led the Conservative Party to develop plans aimed at avoiding a similar situation in the future. Two internal reports prepared whilst in opposition, the Ridley and the Carrington Reports, provided the basis for future Conservative strategy. The Conservatives realised that the unions would have to be confronted at some point, but thought in the short term some appeasement would be inevitable. A Conservative government would only fight from a position of strength. Hence it decided to back down in the face of the miners' dispute of 1981, but fought in 1984–85 once contingency plans were in place. In an attempt to improve its position the government also passed a number of laws restricting and regulating trade-union activities in the early 1980s. Yet it was the dramatic growth of unemployment that was most effective in cutting the ground from under the unions, leading to a decline in their power.

The refusal of the Thatcher government to consult the unions on policy matters (with the exception, until recently, of training policy) was in part the result of its ideological stance. The New Right philosophy, which provided the rationale for much of the government's programme, was highly critical of special interests. The power of such interests is, according to this philosophy, closely related to the size and growth of government. In theory the government's withdrawal from certain policy commitments and programmes would undermine the power of pressure groups involved in these policy areas. Yet the style of the Thatcher government was as important as its underlying philosophy. Mrs Thatcher's brand of conviction politics set the tone for the government as a whole. This gave rise to a policy style that placed less emphasis on prior consultation with pressure groups, and more on how to achieve the priorities that had already been determined.

The signals were clear. No new Royal Commissions were created. A number of advisory bodies on which groups were represented were abolished, and others (such as the National Economic Development Councils) were downgraded. As the Thatcher decade progressed, and as the more radical and controversial measures were outlined, the relationship between some groups and government deteriorated rapidly. Groups representing public-sector institutions (such as the local authority associations, for example), workers and professionals experienced this most sharply. Even some business groups felt excluded, the director-general of the Confederation of British Industry (CBI) calling in 1981 for a bare-knuckle fight with the government.

The main complaint amongst many established producer groups during the tenure of the Thatcher governments was that prior consultation had become a thing of the past. This is certainly true of the radical policies which lay at the heart of the governments' programme. But producer groups still maintain contact with government departments and discuss policy issues with ministers and civil servants. The British Medical Association, for example, despite its hostile attacks on the government's NHS reforms, remains connected to the Department of Health through a range of formal and informal contacts. Government continues to consult pressure groups, often in advance of policy decisions, on matters of technical complexity and low political significance. Moreover, some producer groups have been consulted more frequently than they were before the Thatcher government came to power. The privatisation programme, for example, led the government to consult a range of financial and public relations advisers. The firms involved have, as a result, enjoyed increased access to government. This access was no doubt useful when other issues affecting their interests, notably changes in financial and advertising regulations, were being considered by government.

But it is nevertheless true that producer interests in many policy areas have exerted less influence over the early stages of policy-making than was previously the case. This has been partly because government has been able to turn to alternative sources of advice. Right-wing think tanks, like the Adam Smith Institute and the Centre for Policy Studies, have provided many ideas for policy change. The Prime Minister's Policy Unit has also been a major engine of policy development. Co-opted special advisers, invariably businessmen like Lord Rayner, Sir Roy Griffiths and Sir Robin Ibbs, have also played a central role in policy development. Government departments are also obtaining more policy advice from management consultants than previously. The Department of Health, for example, spent £47 million 'buying in' advice from management consultants in 1989 compared with only £400,000 in 1979. It should be noted that the recommendations of management consultants can have a major impact on policy. One example was the Department of Energy's decision in 1989 to withdraw nuclear power from the electricity privatisation programme, a move prompted by the department's financial consultants.

Pressure groups which have been unable to influence policy through the consultation process have to resort to other means. Many producer groups, feeling increasing frustration with the consultative process, have therefore followed cause groups in diverting resources into publicity campaigns and parliamentary lobbying.

This perhaps explains in part the perceived increase in parliamentary lobbying over the last decade. Yet most agree that such lobbying requires much more effort than in the 1970s. It is more highly competitive, given the larger number of groups involved, whilst at the same time the succession of large government majorities has made the task of opposing government legislation much more difficult.

Party discipline has of course been broken on many occasions over the last decade. But substantial backbench rebellions, fuelled by pressure-group lobbying in Parliament, have hardly dented the government's majority in the vast majority of cases. Defeats in the Upper House have been more likely, though the most challenging of the Lords' amendments have usually been overturned at a later stage in the parliamentary process. For example, in 1989 the House of Lords passed an amendment to the Electricity Bill permitting tighter regulation of energy efficiency. The government was strongly opposed to this measure since it would saddle the soon-to-be-privatised electricity industry with possible financial burdens, making it less attractive to potential investors. This direct challenge to government policy was later defeated when the Bill returned to the Commons for final consideration.

Even so, pressure groups have in certain circumstances been able to succeed in the face of government hostility. The 1986 Shops Bill, for example, stimulated overwhelming pressure from shopworkers, small businesses and church interests, leading to a spectacular Commons Second Reading defeat for the government. A further example was the massive pressure exerted by the brewers in 1989, which led to a remarkable backdown by Lord Young, the then Trade and Industry Minister, on his plans to introduce competition into the industry. On a less visible level, though, government has often conceded points during the passage of legislation through Parliament. It has on a number of occasions tabled its own amendments to Bills, often following parallel discussions with pressure groups. For example, a government amendment to the NHS Bill in 1990 introduced a new system of monitoring service quality in the health service. This amendment was tabled by the government following discussions with groups representing health professions, in which the latter had expressed their concern about the possible impact of the reforms on standards of care.

If pressure groups fail to influence the emergence and course of legislation, there may still be a card left to play. Some commentators have noted that groups are increasingly reasserting their influence at the policy implementation stage.[1] For although prior consultation appears to be less common and less effective for many producer groups, government still consults widely when it is implementing policies. To give an example, around 130 organisations were consulted by the Ministry of Agriculture on the implementation of the 1985 Food and Environment Protection Act. Pressure groups may still have a great deal of power at the implementation stage. At the very least, by withdrawing co-operation they may be able to slow the pace of reform. They may be able to persuade ministers to incorporate changes which attract less publicity, but which significantly alter the impact of the policy. Education policy seems to be a good example of this process at work. Since the passage of the Education Reform Act in 1988, ministers have diluted a number of the reforms, particularly with regard to testing pupils at key stages of the national curriculum, following pressure from groups in the education sector.

The changing nature of pressure-group politics over the last decade has to be recognised. Established producer groups no longer automatically expect prior consultation, whilst new groups – particularly those associated with the implementation of the privatisation programme – have increased their access to the consultative process. Most groups – whether producer, consumer or cause group – tend to rely on three main strategies: patiently building support amongst peers and Conservative backbenchers in the hope of winning concessions at the parliamentary stage; public and media relations in an attempt to create a climate which will force government to change its mind at a later stage in the policy process; and finally, limited co-operation at the implementation stage in an attempt to dilute the reforms. Using these tactics groups have in many cases been able to dilute proposals and soften the impact of change. But they have been unable to influence the direction of policy, and have found it near impossible to persuade government to adopt policies which are not compatible with its radical programme.

## Other changes and developments

Over the last two decades pressure groups have become an important focus for public participation. This is part of a general trend within the political culture. Most evidence seems to suggest that the public is more assertive than before, especially in respect to collective action.[2] Public participation in pressure groups over the last two decades, at least in terms of membership, appears to have grown. In contrast, figures for the political parties reveal declining membership over this period. Some pressure groups have enjoyed a spectacular growth, notably the environmental groups. Following a period of growth in the early 1970s, the combined membership of the main national environmental groups in Britain more than doubled during the last decade to a total of over 5 million. Such growth appears to reflect the increasing importance of post-materialist values and quality of life issues, and the fact that hitherto the major parties have failed to give priority to these issues. This development may also herald a long-term shift in the distribution of power from producer to consumer and cause groups. Indeed, it is important to note that membership of some producer groups, notably the trade unions, fell during the 1980s. However, it could be argued that the degree of member participation in union matters has actually improved during this period, as a result of the new laws aimed at making unions more responsive to their rank and file.

A further aspect of pressure-group politics over the last two decades has been the growing importance of the European dimension. During the 1980s some pressure groups became increasingly aware of the implications of the Single European Act and the new European Community initiatives in areas such as the environment, social policy and the internal market. Constitutionally, European Community law overrides national laws and by lobbying at the European level, pressure groups can pre-empt battles which otherwise would be lost at national level. An example of this was the recent backdown by the British government with regard to the European water-quality directives on nitrate levels. Lobbying at the European level by Friends of the Earth and other environmental groups is believed to have been a major factor in the application of these standards to Britain. Another current example is the European-wide rules on advertising. At the time of writing the British tobacco and alcohol companies fear that their products will be subjected to an advertising ban as a result of the proposed rules and have been vigorously lobbying the European institutions to prevent this from happening.

Other developments in the pressure-group universe over the last two decades involve the rules which govern the relationship between decision-makers and pressure groups. There has been much concern in recent years about the dramatic growth of political consultancy firms. Grantham, in a recent review, estimates that the industry is worth £10 million a year, three times larger than only six years earlier.[3] Political consultancy firms, in return for a fee, supply the client with a wide range of political services. They operate a current-awareness service for the client, informing the organisation about developments on the political front. Incidentally, the mass of direct-ives and regulations emanating from European Community has stimulated a growing market for this kind of service. Political con-sultants also supply a lobbying service for clients, putting them in touch with politicians and civil servants who may be able to influence the course of policy in favour of the client.

There is much disagreement about the impact of political con-sultants. The consultants themselves are not afraid to talk about their potential for influence: after all, they are unlikely to undersell their abilities. Others see the consultants as threat to democracy, a hidden yet powerful force in the policy process, unaccountable to anyone but the client. Another school of thought doubts their effectiveness, believing many consultants themselves fail to appre-ciate the subtleties of the political system, and dismisses them as an expensive waste of time and money. Despite the range of views about political consultants, there is broad support for a procedure which explicitly recognises their existence. One answer would be a system of registration, where political consultancies would be allowed to practise lobbying in return for disclosing certain details about their work. The question of who should perform this role is much more controversial; practitioners generally prefer self-regulation, whilst those harbouring darker suspicions about the practices of political consultants have called for an explicit system of licensing to be introduced.

The disquiet about political consultancy has also revitalised the debate about the propriety of the relationship between pressure groups and decision-makers. This debate has come to the surface on a number of occasions over the last two decades, focusing attention on groups' relationships with sitting MPs, ex-ministers and former civil servants. This in turn has produced proposals for reforming the rules which govern aspects of these relationships.

The Select Committee on Members' Interests has in recent years censured a number of MPs for failing to disclose payments from special interests. A great deal of attention was focused on the case of John Browne, the MP for Winchester, who was criticised in 1990 by the select committee for not disclosing a payment of $88,000 from a Saudi Arabian bank. Cases such as this have produced calls to tighten up the registration of members' interests. The present register of interests established in 1975 only applies to the House of Commons; some believe it should be extended to the House of Lords. Furthermore, as only pecuniary interests currently have to be registered (though some MPs do list non-pecuniary interests), the requirement could be widened to cover other relationships with outside interests. Enforcement might also be improved by the imposition of stronger penalties on those MPs who fail to register interests or who do not obey the rules of disclosure when speaking in debates.

Another cause for concern in recent years has been the taking of jobs by ex-ministers in privatised corporations – Lord Young (Cable and Wireless), Peter Walker (British Gas) and Norman Tebbit (British Telecom). Whilst there is nothing new in ministers accepting boardroom positions once leaving office, many now feel that the involvement of ministers with companies they helped to create raises serious questions about their conduct. Though ministers may have acted fairly and honestly in office, the taking of such jobs leaves them open to accusations of impropriety and bias in favour of special interests. Some believe that the rules governing ex-ministers' conduct should be brought into line with those already in force relating to civil servants. Civil servants at under-secretary level and above require permission to join any company within two years of leaving. Those in lower grades also need permission to join a firm with which they have had direct dealings, or if they have had access to classified information about the firm's competitors which constitutes trade secrets.

But there may also be a need to redraw the civil service rules. Over the last decade the number of civil servants taking private-sector jobs has increased. Around 200 a year now apply for permission to do so. There has also been an increase in inward secondment (the taking of short-term appointments in the civil service by individuals currently working for outside organisations) particularly from business. This increased mobility creates the suspicion that special interests could benefit from the inside knowledge of former civil servants to a far greater extent than in the past. It could also lead to accusations of impropriety. This was noted in 1984 by the Select Committee on the Treasury and Civil Service, which called for a tightening of the rules covering the appointment of ex-civil servants. Amongst other things the committee recommended that civil servants be delayed for a maximum of five years from taking outside appointments. But the report was not implemented by the government. In 1988 the Select Committee on Defence returned to the issue. The committee was critical of the movement of staff from the civil service to the defence industry, and did not believe that the current rules regarding these appointments adequately protected the public interest. Their calls for more information and openness on the appointment of former civil servants also fell on stony ground.

In the short term at least, radical reform of the formal rules of the game – that is, the codes and provisions regarding the relationship between pressure groups and decision-makers – looks unlikely. However, the Select Committee on Members' Interests is currently considering tightening up the rules on the disclosure and registration of interests, and this may bring some changes in detail.

## Concluding remarks . . . and the future

The resurgence of concern about the nature of the relationship between pressure groups and decision-makers would seem to confirm that pressure groups remain as important features of the political process. Undoubtedly the decline of pressure-group power has been exaggerated by some observers. But there have been important changes in the conduct of pressure-group politics, as noted above. Groups have had to adjust to a changing political scene. Some groups have found the process of adjustment easier than others, and some have even relished the new environment in which they have found themselves. The result has been a redistribution of influence within the pressure-group world.

It is true that the conduct of pressure groups is largely shaped by the wider political system within which they operate. A number of emerging trends are therefore likely to have a considerable impact on pressure-group politics in the future: the growing importance of the European Community; centralisation of political authority in Britain; changes in the electoral and party context; and changes in political culture.

Clearly the European dimension will continue to grow in importance. This may disadvantage small and less powerful groups who, for example, may not be able to afford the expense of running a European-based office. However, if further institutional reform in the Community leads to an increase in the powers of the European Parliament, as part of a move to reduce the 'democratic deficit', smaller groups may find lobbying on the European level more accessible. Decision-making at community level also raises the possibility of cross-national alliances between smaller groups, making possible the formation of larger and more powerful pressure groups at the European level.

Although Europe is likely to grow in importance as a focal point for pressure-group politics, this does not necessarily mean that pressure groups will desert Whitehall and Westminster. The concentration of political authority over the past ten years has, if anything, made national political institutions an even more attractive target for lobbying efforts. This concentration of power is unlikely to be decentralised in the short term. One can therefore expect to see national political institutions – government departments, Parliament and the national media – continue as the main targets for pressure-group lobbying in the foreseeable future.

Changes in the electoral and party context will have wide implications for pressure groups. If the Conservatives continue their run of general election successes into the 1990s, pressure groups may adapt to this 'one-party system' by building more permanent links with the party. To an extent this adjustment has already taken place, with Conservative backbench MPs increasingly becoming a major target for pressure-group campaigns. But this does not mean that Labour will necessarily be neglected. Most pressure groups are by nature cross-partisan. They believe that the electoral pendulum will swing back at some time, and will no doubt continue to canvass the Labour leadership even if it should suffer further election defeats. Moreover the opposition party has been a useful focus for pressure-group campaigns in recent years – the counter-attack on the government's NHS reforms being one recent example – and this is likely to continue. Other important factors in this context will be the size of future parliamentary majorities and the effectiveness of party discipline, which affect the ability of government to force through legislation in the face of opposition from pressure groups.

Finally, the changing political culture of Britain will have wide implications for pressure-group politics. The continued fragmentation of British society will probably produce a continued growth in pressure groups to cater for these new interests. Much will depend on the willingness of individuals to participate in groups. The sharp growth in the membership of environmental groups, mentioned earlier, is at least illustrative of the willingness to join. The growth of the environmental movement also raises a further point related to political culture. For, as suggested earlier, it may indicate a shift in the balance of power between consumer and cause groups on the one hand and producer groups on the other. Traditionally the latter have been far more powerful, but this may change if people's political preferences become shaped more by the environment in which they consume and live than that in which they produce and work.

Communication is an important element in the development of political culture. The information revolution may continue to improve communication between individuals making it easier to organise groups. We may see in future an increasing use of facilities like electronic mailing and desktop publishing by pressure groups. This, coupled with the developments in the field of broadcasting, could widen and diversify the channels through which groups present their views, and could herald a new pluralism. On the other hand, however, concentration of ownership in the media and the costs of communication technology may simply reinforce the influence of those who are already powerful.

Looking to the future is always more hazardous than describing the past, but it is unlikely that pressure groups will decline significantly as a political force. Indeed, the future trends outlined above suggest that pressure groups will continue to be an important feature of British politics. After all, as has been shown, pressure groups have had to adjust to a changing political context over the last two decades. There seems no reason why a similar process of adjustment will not take place in response to future changes in the political environment of pressure groups.

## Notes

1  J. J. Richardson, *Government and Groups in Britain: Changing Styles* (Glasgow: Strathclyde Papers on Government and Politics No. 69, University of Strathclyde, 1990).

2  A. Heath and R. Topf, 'Political Culture', in R. Jowell, S. Witherspoon and L. Brook (eds.), *British Social Attitudes: The 1987 Report* (Aldershot:

Gower/Social and Community Planning Research, 1987).

3  C. Grantham, 'Parliament and Political Consultants', *Parliamentary Affairs*. vol. 42, no. 4 (1989) 503–18.

# Broadcasters, politicians and the political interview[1]

When he started as a young man on *The Times* Louis Heren was given a piece of advice by an old hack. He was told you should always ask yourself when talking to a politician: 'Why is this lying bastard lying to me?' I think that is quite a sound principle from which to operate. Jeremy Paxman, *The Media Programme*, Channel Four, 29 October 1989.

During the February 1974 general election campaign a BBC television news team was covering one of Harold Wilson's rallies in the north of England. Anxious not to waste time or film they asked Wilson where in his speech he would be saying something quotable. He replied that they were not to worry; as soon as he said 'turn over' they should start their cameras. After Wilson triumphantly mounted the stage – to the forgettable strains of 'Hello Harold' – he begun his speech and sure enough paused at a particular point before quietly saying 'turn over'. The phrase was missed by the audience but immediately set the cameras rolling. By this time Wilson had become so much the television professional that he had learnt the technical command used to start filming and was thereby able to project his prepared sound bite from the podium into the news bulletins.

This event struck one young member of the news team as worryingly significant; now at Granada Television it was he who suggested it might provide a starting point for an essay on the changing relationship between broadcasters and politicians over the last two decades. This relationship has always been uneasy and infinitely complex; I propose to narrow my focus to a single important item: 'the political interview'. By this I mean broadcast discussions between politicians and interviewers from the three to five minute interrogations on Radio 4's *Today* Programme, to the 'set piece' affairs on *Walden*, *Panorama* or similar programmes.

I begin by discussing the provenance and nature of the interview, go on to consider how politicians strengthened their hands against interviewers in the 1970s and 1980s; and conclude with a consideration of whether the set-piece political interview is in decline.

## Origins and nature of the political interview

Searching for the origins of the political interview entails some (I hope forgivable) cheating with the twenty-year parameters of this volume. Opinions differ upon the first definitive example but almost inevitably it involves Robin Day. Some say it was his interview with President Nasser one year after Suez in 1957 when Day was given *carte blanche* to ask whatever questions he chose and did so to great effect.[2] Day himself chooses his interview with Harold Macmillan in February 1958: 'by far the most important interview' he had done with a British politician up to that point and the first one in which Macmillan himself believed he had 'really mastered television'.[3] Until that time senior British politicians had treated television with great caution: both Attlee and Churchill detested it and those few politicians who had embraced it, like Robert Boothby, did not obviously enhance their political careers. The Fourteen Day Rule, invented during the war but preserved in peace, in any case prevented coverage (or discussions involving MPs) of any issue likely to be debated in Parliament within the following two weeks. Party political broadcasts (PPBs) were allowed on television for the first time in 1951 but Lord Samuel's leaden scripted address on behalf of the Liberals and Anthony Eden's obviously staged interview with television announcer Leslie Mitchell failed to impress public and politicians alike.[4] However, the fact that 20 million television viewers watched the Coronation in 1953, together with Richard Nixon's decisive use of television to defend his vice-presidential nomination (the famous 1952 'Checkers' broadcast) alerted the more prescient politicians to the fact that here was a medium of immense potential power.

Television was used more widely in the 1955 election with Eden as Prime Minister making a highly effective PPB: an unscripted direct address to the nation. After the election, however, politicians closed ranks on any attempt to use television to discuss current affairs. After the BBC challenged the Fourteen Day Rule in July 1955 it was strongly reasserted by the Postmaster-General Charles Hill and given the force of law. In the event the challenge was eventually taken up by one of the new thrusting commercial television companies. Granada Television defied the law by covering the Rochdale by-election in 1958: there were no repercussions. Television had flexed its muscles and won. This was the new atmosphere in which Robin Day confronted Macmillan on 23 February 1958 in an ITN studio. Previously, television interviews with ministers had been uncontroversial deferential affairs 'where the interviewer was regarded as a useful one-man audience for the carefully prepared views which famous men and women deigned to impart to their viewers and listeners'.[5] Day's interview marked a sharp break with such practices. He addressed Macmillan as 'Prime Minister' not 'Sir' and posed some challenging questions, including one on the competence of the much criticised Foreign Secretary, Selwyn Lloyd. 'The most vigorous cross-examination a Prime Minister had been subjected to in public', commented the *Daily Express* the next day.

Elsewhere the press was critical. *The Daily Telegraph*'s editorial asked whether the Prime Minister should be asked such questions 'before a camera that shows every flicker of the eyelid'; *The Observer* worried lest 'the television screen begins to by pass the House of Commons'; and the *Daily Mirror*'s Cassandra opined that 'the Idiots Lantern is getting too big for its ugly gleam'.[6] But between them Day and Macmillan had forged a new relationship between broadcasters and politicians and a new distinctive kind of media event which would play an important part in British politics from thereon. Day was the foremost of a new brand of interviewers, like Ludovic Kennedy, Robert McKenzie, John Freeman and James Mossman, who successfully established this important innovation. The BBC's *Annual Report* for 1960 recognised the controversial nature of this new development and stressed the need for interviewers to be 'scrupulously fair and objective ... The crux of the matter is to satisfy the enquiring mind of the public – and this may be critical – while at the same time encouraging the person interviewed to display his case, or his thoughts as he would wish.'[7]

Why did the political interview develop at this particular time? The answer is more to do with the evolution of the medium than with the politicians. By the late 1950s television was establishing itself as Britain's major leisure activity. A consequent shift had taken place in the balance of power: instead of broadcasters seeking access to politicians for news stories and comment, it was now the politicians who sought access to the air waves to influence a mass audience. As John Whale points out, television's need for a 'constantly changing picture' made the interview more interesting than the talking head of a ministerial broadcast.[8] Tough questions, moreover, made better television than soft ones, and the new competition between the BBC and independent television now made such considerations more than a mere professional concern. Broadcasters were able to set the rules for access. Politicians concurred because they had no choice. Macmillan reluctantly bowed to the inevitable and at the age of 62 resolved to endure the camera's 'hot, pitiless, probing eye' and the uncertainty of answering unknown questions in front of millions.[9] He recognised that the interview was now a more effective means of winning support than the straight talk to camera which in any case, as Whale observed, seemed by that time to belong to a 'stratfied order of society which had passed away'.[10] He was prepared in the process to sacrifice some of the distance and mystique which had traditionally protected British political leaders and buttressed their authority. The political interview, therefore, was both a reflection of declining political deference and a catalyst for it throughout the next decade. Harold Wilson responded immediately to the new form. According to Peter Hennessy, 'He changed the nature of the discourse, making it relaxed and conversational but recognising that it is the well-fashioned phrase or sentence which will glow and be remembered.'[11]

To some extent the interview represented the extension of journalistic values to television. There was no formal constitutional basis for it but print journalists saw themselves as the Fourth Estate: the guardians of truth in a pluralist democracy and the public's guarantee that politicians would be called to account. Television interviewers now assumed the journalist's role and title. Writing in 1961, Robin Day devised ten guidelines for the new profession, one of which enjoined its members to remember the interviewer is 'not employed as a debater, prosecutor, inquisitor, psychiatrist or third-degree expert but as a journalist seeking information on behalf of the viewer'. In his 1989 memoirs Day describes himself merely as a seeker of 'truth or clarity from a public figure on behalf of the viewer'. He reprints his guidelines adding that he would 'not alter a word'.[12]

It is true that close to the heart of the political interview lies a

Socratic search for truth through informed and persistent questioning, but the kind of interview which Day did so much to pioneer
and develop was surely something more. In his hands it *was* something of an inquisition (why else did Day choose the title of 'Grand
Inquisitor' for his memoirs?) and to some extent a prosecution.
Whilst his prepared questions were usually 'fair, proper and in the
interrogative'[13] Day's tone of voice could appear at times aggressive
and accusing. Indeed, his style was more reminiscent of his former
profession as a barrister than an MP at Question Time. With his
distinctive bow tie and heavy spectacles, Day was clearly more than a
questioner on the public's behalf. His personality and presence
added an essential new ingredient; he looked and was formidable,
something which invested his interviews with tension and made
compelling television. *The Times* commented in the wake of one of
his interviews in February 1964 [The] supreme test for a party leader
these days has become the ordeal by television.'[14] A Robin Day
interview was essentially adversarial, a duel. Day himself recalls how
Harold Wilson enjoyed the 'sword-play of a good television interview' and would chide him afterwards over the really tough questions he had neglected to ask.[15] This anecdote reveals yet another
layer in the composition of this new media form. Day and his fellow
interviewers were not just interested in extracting the truth but in a
particular species of it. They wished to catch the politicians out, to
force an admission or revelation, maybe an error, or otherwise make
their interviews newsworthy – and thereby enhance their own reputations. Interviewers may indeed feel a commitment to pluralist
democracy – and it is to the citizen's advantage that they should – but
it is debatable whether their first loyalty lies here or to their medium
and their careers in it.

At the heart of the relationship between politicians and broadcasters is in Peter Hennessy's phrase an 'unspoken contract':
publicity in exchange for good television.[16] Speaking to a television
interviewer in 1986 Bryan Gould, MP, summed it up neatly: 'I'm a
politician and I'm trying to get across a message . . . your main
function is to keep the viewer watching.'[17] According to Hennessy
broadcasters need:

people who can make the language get up and walk from the first sentence.
Content has to be fairly good but, above all it's the way it's said rather than
what is said which is important. Those who are sufficiently plausible and
voluble, who know how to fashion little bullets of the right length and

content and deliver them live will be invited time and time again. That's why you see the same people on *Newsnight* night after night. Remember that out of 650 MPs a fair number will be ruled out on ground of age, dreariness, alcholism and so forth, so it's quite a small pool of those who can perform, who can shine.[18]

But is the public interest being served by this process? It all depends upon the nature of the contract. To compress a complex argument, an efficient pluralist democracy requires correct information and clear explanations from politicians conveyed via an independent and unbiased media. The contract should not therefore be too cosy or collaborative nor, for obvious reasons, should it be too one sided. A tension born of mutual respect is the best guarantee of the public interest. It is understandable and inevitable that both sides will strive for the advantage but essential that neither should achieve dominance. Politicians seek unrestricted access on their terms: television journalists try to hold them to certain conditions. In the late 1950s ITN established two basic ground rules which have been subsequently jealously guarded by the BBC as well: no questions should be submitted to politicians in advance, though areas of likely interest should be indicated; and no rehearsals should be allowed. In his own guidelines Robin Day added some additional advice to interviewers: do not be overawed or omit 'awkward topics'; withdraw rather than participate in an interview rigged to secure a 'prestige appearance'; and do not press questions merely to 'sound tough'.[19]

By the mid-1960s the political interview had been born. David Cox of London Weekend Television believes Day 'could justly claim to have invented the political interview', and it must be allowed that if the distinguishing feature of this new media form is an inquisitorial fearlessness then it is also the hallmark of Day's interviewing style.[20] But it must be remembered that politicians also play an essential reciprocal role: unless they are prepared for the most part to reply freely to such direct questions then the interview could never have evolved. Are we describing a uniquely British phenomenon? Brian Walden (whose own contributions are later discussed) does not believe that the particular British form of the interview can be found in the USA, France or Germany and attributes it to our tradition of 'robust public argument and peculiar intimacy of our political culture'.[21] It is certainly the case that few governments face such sustained and uninhibited public criticism as the British: the American

President for example does not have to survive the twice-weekly bear-pit of Prime Minister's Questions. Day is quick to claim his questions are in 'the vigorous . . . parliamentary style' and that the training and experience of British politicians enables them to cope with them, easily – in some cases with relish.[22] Nevertheless, as the political interview developed as an important part of the political process, politicians worked hard to change the balance of power with broadcasters. During the 1960s, as Day writes, 'television got tough with the politicians. Not surprisingly the politicians got tough with television.'[23] They did so in a number of ways during the next two decades, some of them concerned with the external context within which the interview occurs and others within the internal context of the interview itself.

## The politicians get tough

### The external context

As long as broadcasters are truly independent they can insist politicians gain access to mass audiences only on their terms. However, politicians have the power to threaten this independence and make broadcasters fearful, causing them to withhold certain programmes, leave others unmade and interview questions unput. Legally, broadcasting organisations are obliged to present controversial political questions in a fair and unbiased way. The problem according to Lord Hill, former BBC Chairman, is that 'they regard something that is impartial as biased against them and something that is biased in their favour as beautifully impartial'.[24] Given this tendency, it is hardly surprising that politicians of both major parties should regularly have perceived hostility towards them in the broadcasting organisations and sought to neutralise it. The means available to politicians have been widely chronicled and need only be summarised here. But the record shows that during the period studied, political pressure on broadcasters increased, especially during the 1980s. They fall under five major headings.

1. *Power of appointment*    Governments appoint the chairman of the BBC and the IBA and also members of their governing boards. Harold Wilson believed it essential that Labour should show well on television as the press was effectively a Conservative preserve. He was notoriously paranoid about a supposed anti-Labour bias in the

BBC and in 1967 'punished' the Corporation by making the aforementioned Charles Hill its Chairman. Hill, it will be recalled was the Conservative politician who had given the hated Fourteen Day Rule the force of law in 1955. In the event he proved to be more the protector than the persecutor of the BBC. Mrs Thatcher was no less convinced that during the 1960s left-wing sympathisers had flooded into the BBC and, now in positions of power during the 1980s, were undermining her efforts to swing Britain to the right. Her response in 1986 was to appoint as Chairman Marmaduke Hussey, former Managing Director of *Times* newspapers to, according to Norman Tebbit's office, 'get in there and sort it out – in days not months'.[25] Shortly afterwards the BBC's Director-General Alasdair Milne was summarily sacked. (Hussey, however, like Hill before him, proved to be no Tory placeman and has subsequently fought the Corporation's corner on a number of issues.)

2. *Finance*   Governments set the BBC's licence fee and the legal framework within which independent television companies raise money through advertising. Politicians in power are therefore provided with a perfect weapon with which to intimidate recalcitrant broadcasters. In 1966 Wilson countered a BBC request for a higher licence fee by backing a plan to introduce commercials prepared by no less a person than Tony Benn – in his pre-left-wing Anthony Wedgewood incarnation.[26] Thereafter the BBC wrestled regularly with governments over licence fees until the spectre of advertising again emerged in 1985 when Mrs Thatcher set up the Peacock Committee hoping it would recommend such an option. Instead it came down against advertising and (to the Corporation's joy) urged that the licence fee be tied to inflation until 1991. Undaunted, Mrs Thatcher set about deregulating the IBA, but this attempt was more to do with her free-market passions than a desire to counter perceived left-wing bias.

3. *Opposition to particular programmes*   Governments of both parties have generated intense political rows over particular programmes. Often these have related to security issues – like the BBC's *Real Lives* series on Northern Ireland in 1985 or Thames Television's *Death on the Rock* in 1987 – but they also target programmes which direct unwelcome attention or comment upon their parties. One programme in particular severely weakened the broad-

casters' position. *Yesterday's Men* was a 1971 BBC programme about the Labour opposition front bench. Its title, irreverent tone and intrusive questions so outraged Harold Wilson and mobilised so much political pressure upon broadcasters that even its producer, Angela Pope, declared 'I would not try it and no one else would for a very long time. Nobody must do *Yesterday's Men* again.' In the wake of the programme its presenter David Dimbleby perceived a 'rather hideous softening' in television's approach to politicians.[27]

4. *Political campaigns*   These can be of a generalised nature – like the Bennite right-wing conspiracy theories or the routine attacks upon the BBC launched by Thatcherite backbenchers – but they can also be centrally co-ordinated. The best example was Norman Tebbit's assault on the BBC, when he fired off regular salvos in the run up to the 1987 election. The campaign against alleged left-wing bias on Radio 4's *Today* programme in 1990 led by Lord Wyatt also bore the hallmark of a Central Office campaign.[28]

5. *Cutting up rough*   Senior politicians regularly put pressure upon broadcasters either just before or just after programmes with which they find fault. Tony Benn is notoriously wary of broadcasters, personally tape-recording every interview he gives and loudly objecting to perceived misrepresentation. In June 1988, for example, Granada Television invited him to be interviewed on their *Under Fire* programme. Whilst waiting in the studio he heard the presenter rehearsing the introduction in which Benn was described as coming from an 'establishment' background. He took exception to this and asked that the offending passage be reworded. With transmission time looming the producer, somewhat meekly, agreed: thereby conceding the first round (and subsequently earning his editor's wrath).

Examples also abound of politicians exploding with fury after an interview or programme – Harold Wilson's rage after *Yesterday's Men* is possibly the most famous. On other, rare, occasions interviewees have unilaterally ended the interview. In 1982 John Nott, then Defence Minister, ended a robust Robin Day interview with the words 'I'm sorry – I am fed up with this interview. It is ridiculous.' He thereupon walked out of the studio. The next day Nott's walkout was the news, not the interview, but according to Day this was a 'unique event' for him and it had no long-term implications for the

political interview. How much of this behaviour goes on behind the
scenes is impossible to know but according to Jeremy Paxman:

There are politicians who say 'If you ask me that question you will regret it. If
you ask me that question I will take it up with the DG. If you ask me that
question I will walk out.' Now clearly it does concentrate the mind when you
are on the air in 20 seconds and a politicians is saying that to you.

In such circumstances Paxman believes that unless the question is
ruled out for legitimate legal or personal privacy reasons

you absolutely have to ask it or you betray those people on whose behalf you
are putting the questions. You can't possibly agree to these attempts at
blackmail and bullying.[29]

The 1970s and 1980s then were decades when the politicians turned
up the pressure. They increased the external pressures upon broadcasters, especially Mrs Thatcher who, in the parlance of the decade
'handbagged' the BBC and severely alarmed independent television
companies. It is impossible gauge the impact of such pressure but it
showed in small ways. On the day before the 1987 election Mrs
Thatcher recorded a morning interview with David Dimbleby.
During it she excoriated those who 'drool and drivel' about caring
for those in need. When challenged to explain her choice of words
the Prime Minister was forced into a rare public apology. Quite a
coup for the interviewer. Michael Cockerell, however, recounts how
this telling exchange was deliberately held back by the BBC until the
late evening when it could have little effect on voting behaviour: 'It
seemed that the browbeating of the past year had worked.'[30]

*The internal context: how politicians improved their game*
If politicians got tough, they also got clever. In 1970 a freelance
television journalist caught sight of some rejected film footage for a
PPB featuring an up and coming politician. He perceived potential
where others did not and offered his unpaid advice: their subsequent
twenty-year partnership earned Gordon Reece his knighthood and
helped Mrs Thatcher to achieve political hegemony over the 1980s.
It also established unelected media advisers as important political
actors in British politics. True, media advisers were not new –
Macmillan, Heath and Wilson had used them – but Thatcher's
approach, drawing upon American experience, was qualitatively
different. By comparison, according to Joe Haines, Wilson's
arrangements amounted to 'a one man and a dog operation'. The key

difference was that under Mrs Thatcher media advice evolved into *media management*.

In the 1979 campaign Reece was supplemented by a public-relations firm, Saatchi and Saatchi, and other figures including Tim Bell, Harvey Thomas – who used to organise rallies for Billy Graham – and subsequently the incomparable Bernard Ingham, an erstwhile Labour-supporting journalist who joined the civil service as an information officer and rose to be Mrs Thatcher's media manager in chief. Both advisers and managers knew how much truth there lay in Harold Wilson's apparently cynical dictum that 'most of politics is presentation and what isn't is timing'.[31] Policies and personalities were carefully packaged: presentation requirements became an important input into the decision-making process. At the beginning of the 1980s Labour was relatively backward both in comparison with the Conservatives and their own previous practice – for example, the slickly run 1959 and 1964 election campaigns. When appointed in 1985 as Director of Communications, Peter Mandelson centralised co-ordination and control and personally introduced a tough new professional ethos of media management. He also contributed importantly to the policy-making process itself to help make policies more attractive and presentable.[32] By 1987 Labour was a match for the Conservatives in terms of presentation and fought the better election campaign. Within this more professionalised context the evolution of the political interview was influenced in a number of ways.

1. *Exploitation of other media opportunities*   Leading politicians were advised to look beyond the tough confrontations with heavyweight interviewers to exploit easier opportunities for exposure. This included choosing 'friendly' interviews and rejecting media invitations – something which Mrs Thatcher did for extended periods throughout her years in office. In 1979 Thatcher's advisers also dramatically upgraded the importance of photo-calls in election campaigns. Instead of giving interviews or press conferences in which she might be caught out, Mrs Thatcher was presented in a series of eloquent visual settings, the most enduring perhaps, being the calf which she obligingly cuddled in an East Anglian field whilst the equally obliging media worked their cameras. (One school of thought urges a boycott of such manipulative events.) Thatcher also broke new ground by appearing on light-entertainment programmes

like *Jim'll Fix It* in 1977 and in 1984 was the first Prime Minister to appear on a chat show. On the latter occasion, at the height of the miners' strike she succeeded in softening what she confessed was a 'tough and hard' image on television.[33] There were obvious gains to be made by avoiding the fast bowling of Sir Robin Day and hitting easy sixes off the likes of Michael Aspel and Jimmy Young in front of much bigger audiences. Neil Kinnock did his best to play the same game, even appearing on a Tracy Ullman pop video (one area at least into which Mrs Thatcher would certainly never have dared venture).

2. *Rules of engagement*   Media advisers encouraged politicians to toughen up the 'rules of engagement' with broadcasters. Phillip Harding, a former *Panorama* producer and now editor of Radio 4's *Today* programme provides the following analysis:

Certainly politicians got cannier over time. They have become more eager for coverage but on their own terms. Now one enters into discussion about the format of a programme in a much more calculated way than one might have done say ten years ago. And that has been accentuated by the government information machinery which has taken views about whether or not ministers should do certain types of interview. Bernard Ingham obviously played a part in that. He also wanted ministers to have the last word and believed they should not take part in debates with other politicians: the job of government ministers was to explain policy uninterrupted and unmediated.[34]

Harding did not feel, however, that any 'quantum change' occurred in 1979; it was merely part of a gradual sophistication over time by politicians of both parties: the opposition could be just as 'sensitive over who appeared when and on what programme'. The battle lines had become clearer and were more hotly contested but negotiations were usually

a mixture of principle and practice. It depends on how badly you want the interview as to how much you are prepared to deviate from the ideal. And it's the same with the other side. It also depends on the personality of the particular politician. This is much more true now; some ministers (for example Kenneth Clarke) are quite happy to debate – others will not.[35]

Stuart Prebble, editor of Granada's *World in Action* during the Thatcher years reports a different experience:

Ingham's way of handling the media marked a complete break with previously accepted practice. On *World in Action* we were constantly asking for ministers to appear to answer on some issue raised by one of our programmes. We found that information officers wouldn't return our calls, and when they did they would frequently suggest a range of conditions which they knew would be unacceptable. For example, they wanted a complete written list of questions, or they wanted to view all the other interviews in the film, or a guarantee of uninterrupted airtime, or a promise that there would be no editing. Sometimes they said they would only appear live, knowing that *World in Action* is not a live programme. In the end it became clear that the minister concerned simply had no intention of giving the interview, but they did not want us to be able to say that 'the minister declined . . .' The effect of this was simply to deny the principle of accountability; if it didn't suit them to appear and answer for their policies, they would not do so.[36]

Ingham's memoirs tend to reinforce Prebble's view. In a revealing section Ingham confirms his hostility to the *Today* programme, adding that Brian Redhead 'once called me a conspiracy. From then on I was. His failure to apologise meant that he never got another interview with Mrs Thatcher as Prime Minister.'

3. *Impression management* Advisers worked hard to improve the appearance of their political masters. Such considerations were not new: astute politicians had long ago realised television was a medium of impressions. Radio listeners thought Nixon 'won' his 1960 presidential debates, but television viewers gave the contest to the handsome and comprehensively packaged Kennedy. Politicians realised early on that 'the momentary impression they give will have an effect on the view a massive audience takes of them', and in Goffman's phrase they applied themselves to 'impression management'.[38] Macmillan consequently changed from a tweedy old Tory into an elegrant, perfectly groomed Edwardian gent. Wilson travelled on election campaigns with several freshly pressed blue suits to appear at his best on the screen. His tendency to emphasise points by aggressive shakings of his fist was countered by Marcia Williams: she advised him to smoke a pipe thus occupying his hands whilst conveying a homely trustworthy image.[39] Mrs Thatcher's impression management was of a different order, however. From early on Reece advised her sternly on her wardrobe: fewer fussy clothes and never a hat. By the mid-1980s as Peter Mandelson comments

Every part of her had been transformed: her hair, her teeth, her nose I suspect, her eyebrows. Not a part of Mrs Thatcher was left unaltered.[40]

By contrast, Michael Foot appeared wholly unreconstructed. It was his crumpled appearance, unruly hair and thick bi-focals which reminded Labour that personal appearance on television was of

prime importance. Kinnock responded well: according to one producer he would turn up to interviews carrying a freshly laundered
suit which he would don minutes before going on air. Mandelson
denies that Walworth Road staff paid close attention to Kinnock's
appearance, but after the trauma of 1983 leading Labour figures
probably needed no encouragement to appear in regulation dark-
blue suits and sober ties.[41] The same applied to other party leaders:
in 1989 Granada's *World in Action* wickedly captured David Owen
personally adding the final touch to his coiffure from a hair spray can
just before going on air.

4.   *The set*   At that historic 1958 interview Robin Day sat on a
comfortable swivel seat behind a table whilst Macmillan was per-
ched on a hard-backed chair. The Prime Minister joked that he
appeared to be 'on the mat' but when Day offered to swap places
demurred: 'No No, I know my place.'[42] Today no politican would be
so naively accommodating. If the PM suspected he might appear to
be in the subordinate role then it was likely a damagingly large
proportion of viewers would think the same. Media managers now
engage in frequently tough negotiations with television producers
over the interview set. Roger Bolton, another *Panorama* producer,
was shocked at his first contact with Gordon Reece who

would ask what would be the colour of the set, would there be flowers – he
thought that was necessary – what sort of chairs did we plan? [He] was the
first such person in British politics to do his job properly; he took what I
would regard as the depressing view that the image was more important than
the message and he concentrated on leaving an impression with the viewer of
what Mrs Thatcher was like rather than drawing attention to what she said
in detail.[43]

Once similarly convinced, Mrs Thatcher became equally demanding: on one occasion a chair had to be flown in specially from Sweden
for Mrs Thatcher's appearance on *TV Eye*: 'she had approved the
design but not the colour of the one Thames had planned for her'.[44]
A Channel 4 *Media Programme* in October 1990 revealed Mandelson shared a similar attention to detail and a 'disciplined professionalism' which won praise from such seasoned political columnists
as Michael White of the *Guardian*. Whilst Mandelson probably was
not so demanding over interview sets, it is noticeable that in recent
years Kinnock has been filmed increasingly in his own oak-panelled

Westminster office, a setting which enhances his prime ministerial claims.

5. *Performance skills* Perhaps most importantly, advisers helped politicians to improve their performance on their side of the microphone. Major political interviews are undeniably daunting occasions, even for skilled and experienced parliamentarians. Macmillan by his own admission suffered agonies before speeches and likened appearing on television to 'going over the top' in the First World War. Oddly, Robin Day saw not a trace of this and perceived Macmillan as perfectly relaxed before and during interviews. Whatever Macmillan did to cope with his nerves he did it virtually unaided. Margaret Thatcher was also a highly keyed-up personality – an 'adrenalin factory' as she once described herself. Reece helped to soothe her down, relax her so that her nervous energy could be translated into what became excellent performances. Reece also coached Thatcher's voice when private polls revealed it to be offputtingly shrill and upper class. He encouraged her to lower the tone and sound more like her Grantham self. A tutor from the National Theatre was employed and according to Max Atkinson she achieved a reduction in pitch of 46 Hz, a figure which is almost half the average difference in pitch between male and female voices. The lower tone also tended to slow down her rate of speech and enhance its statesmanlike quality.[45] Mandelson claims that neither Neil Kinnock nor any of his front-bench colleagues receive more than a few hours' coaching by Walworth Road staff. Kinnock certainly has a natural affinity for television. His biographer Robert Harris writes

he took to the medium from the moment he first encountered it and the medium took to him in return. Kinnock looks good on television – open and straightforward. Other politicians are told the tricks and try to learn them; Kinnock does it all naturally.[46]

It might be worth reflecting however, that this natural talent has possibly nourished a degree of over-confidence. 'You don't have to tell me what to do' Kinnock told his advisers before appearing for the first time on *Weekend World*, 'I got to be leader of the Labour Party by being good on television'.[47] Whilst undeniably a skilful communicator, Kinnock has often been criticised for being too vague and verbose and often too defensive and straightfaced in major interviews.

Body language is also important. Television interviewees are advised not to fidget or move hands to the face, make extravagant gestures and to look at the interviewer all the time.[48] Harold Wilson lost points for allowing his eyes to slide away sideways, giving an untrustworthy, dissembling impression. They are also advised to look relaxed yet alert, composed yet interested, with lively eyes and expressive, frequently smiling faces. Mrs Thatcher was even advised to move slightly from buttock to buttock when answering questions as this was believed to indicate interest in the question.[49] The scope for props in interviews is slight and is limited in practice to notes or, in the case of male interviewees, pipes. Notes can give an impressive image but too frequent reference to them can easily detract from it. Wilson used his pipe to good effect; relighting it allowed him more time to think and slowed down the pace of the interview.

Personal manner inevitably reflects personality and media advisers encourage interviewees to be themselves. Many politicians, like Wilson and Healey, use the interviewer's first name to suggest a friendly relaxed nature and to create a matey atmosphere. Callaghan chose to be more formal and employed what Robin Day called a 'don't try any of your nonsense with me' approach.[50] On occasions he would choose to become 'very angry if a particularly sensitive subject were raised' and then in the studio, according to Tom McNally his former aide, 'he would bang on the table and be indignant'.[51] According to Robin Day this style, 'if not designed to intimidate . . . often did so'.[52] Perhaps to match or legitimise his own aggression Callaghan 'rather liked a rude television interviewer because the public sympathy would be on the side of the man being heckled rather than the man doing the heckling'.[53] Unsurprisingly, Callaghan tended to ask for Robin Day.

Mrs Thatcher's personal style as Prime Minister was controlled, courteous and formal. Combined with her immaculate appearance it could accurately be described as both regal and imperious. From such heights she could deploy majestic indignation or condescension to great effect. She invariably took control of the interview and very few interviewers were able to seize back the initiative from her.

Finally, media advisers encouraged the strategic use of evasion: the avoidance of direct answers to questions put. The device can take several forms. The most obvious is the short answer which is economical with the truth. Clement Attlee used to nonpluss inter-viewers with a series of one-word answers; Callaghan used airily to dismiss difficult questions with the word 'speculation'. Less obvious but much studied by psycholinguists are the deliberate evasions designed to deflect attention from sensitive areas or to enable a prearranged agenda to be pursued. Peter Bull and Kate Mayer of York University studied a number of television interviews given by Kinnock and Thatcher and concluded that both evaded more than half the questions posed – Thatcher 56 per cent, Kinnock 59 per cent – utilising eleven main devices including: ignoring the question, acknowledging the question without answering, questioning the question, attacking the interviewer, declining to answer, giving an incomplete answer, making a political point instead of answering the question, and claiming to have already answered the question.[54] Another researcher, Sandra Harris of Nottingham Polytechnic applied a different analysis to speeches by the same politicians but came up with similar results: Mrs Thatcher gave direct answers to 50 per cent of questions compared with Kinnock's 40 per cent; gave indirect answers to 40 per cent compared with Kinnock's 29 per cent; and challenged 10 per cent of the questions compared with 39 per cent by Kinnock. Both politicians unsurprisingly evaded significantly more questions than subjects analysed in other institutional settings, like magistrates, policemen and nurses.[55]

Another study by Bull and Mayer on 'Interruptions in political interviews' reveal how these politicians resist attempts to deflect them from their evasions. Mrs Thatcher, however, was much more tenacious in this respect than Kinnock. The devices she used – all of which have a familiar ring – include:

no please let me go on . . . may I just finish? . . . one moment . . . just let me say this . . . I must beg of you . . . I would love to go on . . . will you give me time? . . . Yes, but one moment . . . no, don't stop me.

The researchers conclude that Mrs Thatcher's interruptive style is unusual

in that she voices frequent objections to being interrupted, although the objective evidence in fact shows a striking degree of similarity in the way the interviewers treat both political leaders. The impression that she is badly treated is compounded by her tendency to personalise issues, to take questions and criticisms as accusations and frequently to address the interviewers formally by title and surname, as if they need to be called to account for their misdemeanours whereas in fact they are simply doing their job. [She] shows a striking mastery of the arts of political oneupmanship, continually wrong-footing interviewers and putting them on the defensive such that they feel obliged to justify or even apologise for their role as interviewers.[56]

Roger Bolton noticed a Thatcher device which helped her to deal with interruptions: she did not 'take a breath or halt at the end of sentences. This means the interviewer can't get his question in or seems to be rudely interrupting if he is.'[57]

### Is the political interview in decline?

By the late 1980s it appeared to some commentators that politicians, counselled by their media advisers, had so mastered the interviewee's art, especially evasion techniques, that they were able to 'hijack' the situation and use it to convey carefully rehearsed arguments, often employing key emotive words and phrases. Robin Day himself believed this to be the case, not to mention Paul Johnson writing in the *Spectator*. In his memoirs Day complains

the significance, news value and appeal of the 'setpiece' television encounter greatly declined . . . It is now rarely a dialogue which could be helpful to the viewer'.

Day names Thatcher as the principal culprit and cites several examples of her hijacking style as well as the findings of Bull and Mayer already mentioned. He concludes these developments are 'bad for the people, bad for democracy, bad for television and bad, in the end for politicians'.[58] At a conference on political communication following the 1987 elections various experts agreed. One of them, Ivor Gabor, suggested that a stalemate had been reached between politicians and their interrogators. He wondered if 'We've moved beyond the time of . . . the set piece interview as the most effective way of putting politicians through the mill.'[59] Citing the success of Mrs Diana Gould's rattling of Mrs Thatcher on *Nationwide* over the sinking of the *Belgrano* issue in 1983 he suggested we should broaden the use of interviewers and let 'everybody have a go at the politicians'. (There may be something in this. When being questioned by a studio audience in the 1987 election campaign Mrs Thatcher's 'If I could just make one more point' was answered with a resounding collective 'No!')[60]

Can it be that twenty years after Day perceived the politicians 'getting tough' with the broadcasters that the set-piece political interview has indeed been neutralised? And has it no longer any useful role to play in the democratic process? Against this end-of-the-interview-as-we-know-it argument a number of points can be made.

Firstly, politicians have always been skilful evaders. A student of political interviews in the 1960s devised an 'index of evasiveness' and calculated that in one interview with Robert McKenzie, Harold Wilson scored 48 per cent whilst in another with Robert McNeill, Edward Heath was close behind with 45 per cent.[61] Neither needed special coaching to achieve their high scores. It is, moreover, fairly certain that had the political interview existed during the times of Robert Walpole and Lloyd George similar analyses would have been made.

Secondly, it is true that an interviewer cannot repeat evaded questions endlessly for fear of appearing boring, or interrupt incessantly for fear of appearing aggressive. But the viewer does not have to be too attentive or discerning to perceive these evasions and draw appropriate conclusions about the character of the politician concerned. This process is assisted if, as the 1990 BBC guidelines recommend, interviewers draw particular attention to evasion attempts ('evasion should be exposed').[62]

Third, there are limits to the role of media advisers. They can touch up the good points, tone down the bad and improve performance up to a point. But they cannot invent a new person. As Joe Haines observes, 'You can't act an image over a period of many years, so when you see the Prime Minister it *is* more or less the Prime Minister.'[63] Austin Mitchell moreover argues that despite all the articles written about them relatively few politicians have attended the so called 'charm schools'.[64] Nor can advisers help once a live interview is under way: the politician is alone, in full public view, usually with a well-informed and quick-witted adversary. This is still a formidable test and how politicians cope has became an important index of their quality and an occasion when the public can learn a great deal about them. Peter Riddell for example believes that

the most revealing insights into Mrs Thatcher over the last decade have come in the big interview. Whereas her speeches are so carefully worked over . . . it is when she spurts out during the course of an interview – normally after the first half hour – that she is so revealing.[65]

Fourth, leading on from Riddell's point, other forms of the political interview seem to be in good shape – the short news interview, for example. Such judgements are subjective but Jeremy Paxman on *Newsnight* and the trio of Brian Redhead, Sue McGregor and John

Humphrys on Radio 4's *Today* programme are well informed, objective, politely insistent and commendably tenacious in the face of the inevitable evasions. Nor are they deferential. Consider Jeremy Paxman's devastating opening question to Lord Young during an early-morning interview in the 1987 election campaign and Young's somewhat feeble response:

*Paxman:* Lord Young, since your party came to power more people are without a job, more people without a home, more people are afraid to go out of their homes, more people are being raped, being mugged and more people are being murdered. Not much of a record is it?
*Lord Young:* Well if you put it like that, but you know anyone can make facile comments like that.[66]

Day's complaint, moreover, focused only on the party leaders: it does not follow that interviews with other leading politicians in the Cabinet or Shadow Cabinet have been similarily undermined.

Finally, a powerful refutation of Day's analysis has been made by David Cox, executive producer of the *Walden Interview*. He insists that the political interview is 'alive and well': it all depends upon how it is conducted.[67] His strategy is to eschew the multi-topic approach for a single focus: for example, can Sir Geoffrey Howe stand up to Mrs Thatcher? (3 September 1989). The approach is to assume the politician is not lying but telling the truth: questions are formulated to test the underlying assumptions and internal consistency of arguments deployed. To do this intensive preparations are undertaken with a team of producers and researchers. Each possible response by the politician is anticipated and countered with more probing interrogation. A bulky programme document is then produced and handed to the eponymous interviewer who, added to his thirteen years in the House of Commons enjoys the advantages of a razor-sharp mind and total recall. The document absorbed, Walden proceeds into battle usually without notes but with every conceivable line of evasion covered. The transcripts of six Brian Walden interviews published in 1990 reveal how subtly and insistently he probes the defences of his subject, frequently drawing together half answers, hints and allusions into potentially embarrassing and testing summations of what has (allegedly) been disclosed.

Cox points out that in his interview with Thatcher after Nigel Lawson's resignation as Chancellor on 29 October 1989 she employed ten out of Bull and Mayer's eleven forms of evasion but still believes the interview was a striking success. 'This interview alone', he declares, 'could be taken as proof that politicians have not destroyed the political interview'. He prefers to lay the blame for any possible decline not with the politicians but the broadcasters. Politicians may have improved their performance to the extent that they can 'walk all over interviewers', but only those who are 'insufficiently informed, astute or prepared or who lack real confidence in what they are doing'. Politicians will often answer questions clearly but when they do try to evade 'it is the interviewer's job to frustrate them not to cry "Foul"'. 'All too often today' Cox concludes, 'the interviewer is not as adept at his own craft as the politician he is interviewing.'

It is not surprising that Cox should champion the *raison d'être* of the series he edits nor that he should extol the excellence of its principal asset, but his criticism of other interviewers, by implication, must include Day himself. Day's memoirs, however, not to mention his performance, attest to the thoroughness of his preparations and no one could have had more confidence in his own chosen trade.[67] Certainly the most able politicians over the last twenty years have succeeded in redressing the balance of power with interviewers. Helped by their advisers they have analysed the chess game of the political interview more thoroughly than hitherto and have refined an impressive repertoire of ploys and defences. Certainly, too, some interviewers have failed to appreciate the new level at which the game is now played and have surrendered some advantage to the politician. (Walden, incidentally, is an excellent chess player and once had ambitions to play professionally.) But Day's fear that the political interview is dead has possibly more to do with the feature that dominated virtually every other aspect of politics in the 1980s: Mrs Thatcher's personality. As Peter Hennessy puts it:

She mesmerised because of her voice, her appearance, her caveat-free sentences and a determination to terrorise the interviewer and say what she intended whatever the question.[69]

Once again, judgments must be subjective but Day, though never terrorised often seemed uneasy with Mrs Thatcher; by his own admission he mishandled his big 1983 *Panorama* election interview with her, allowing himself to become embroiled in a sterile statistical debate. Perhaps Day's 'insider' clubland background made it difficult for him to relate to this powerful 'outsider' female? Walden fared better, possibly because he is something of an outsider too, and possibly because he 'was never in awe of her'.[70] He also struck that relaxed tone to which Mrs Thatcher responded best and was rewarded by more interviews with her than anyone else. But he did not allow personal friendship to compromise his professionalism and in that celebrated October 1989 interview gave no quarter. Walden could handle Mrs Thatcher, some of the time at least, but many other interviewers (David Dimbleby and perhaps David Frost excepted) had less success.

It is tempting to conclude from this discussion that all that was needed for the big political interview to be restored to its former effectiveness was the departure from the political stage of its most dominant and exasperating performer. Tempting but untrue. Sir Robin was right to a degree but for the wrong reasons. The set-piece interview is indeed under threat – from both parties to that unspoken contract.

Politicians have realised that the media has many more congenial and welcoming rooms in its mansion than those presided over by professional interrogators. Things can go wrong in interviews: John Biffen was sacked after Brian Walden tempted him into suggesting Mrs Thatcher could be less dominant; Kinnock was pressed into a grievous error when he suggested a non-nuclear Britain would respond to a Soviet invasion with guerilla warfare – attracting Owen's 'Dad's Army' jibe four days before the 1987 general election. How much easier to disseminate messages via photo opportunities, talk shows or (if in government) the semi-political government advertising campaigns. These strategies reach millions whilst political interviews attract real interest only retrospectively when gaffes are reported. For leading politicians in the 1980s the set piece interview became a high-risk, low-return option; they could afford to play hard to get.

For their part, broadcasters are perhaps less interested now in the big interview than they were a decade ago. They have found it increasingly difficult to provide interviewers who can put politicians under any real pressure and even when they do the result is usually some distance away from that key broadcasting concept, 'good television'. The Sunday interviews for example are watched by relatively tiny audiences. Even Walden's interview with Thatcher at the height of the Lawson resignation crisis, attracted only 3 million viewers and on those occasions when something substantive has been divulged, more people are likely to read about it in the press the next day. Furthermore, given the financial pressures all television companies are facing, pressures which will intensify under the government plans to deregulate independent television, senior executives are casting unfriendly eyes upon what has similarily become for them high-cost, low-return enterprises.

Is John Major's accession to power likely to have a remedial effect? Possibly. As in so many areas, John Major's relationship to the media represents a sharp break with his predecessor. When invited to condemn the BBC's coverage of the Gulf War in January 1991, for example, he took the opportunity to offer the Corporation fulsome praise. But as an interviewee he palpably lacks the ability, in Hennessy's phrase, to make the 'language get up and walk' and often uses predictable prefactory clichés before getting his answers under way. Significantly, the media never chose him to comment before his elevation made whatever he said important. Peter Hennessy reflects that it would be

nice if we had a Prime Minister who had no gift for the language but instead used unvarnished plan words – like Attlee. The whole fashion might change.[71]

But it is doubtful if Attlee's bathetic style would score so many points in the television age.

Major's interview with Walden on 14 April 1991, moreover, suggested he is less well armoured than his predecessor and within the current rules of the game risks losing by default. In the face of Walden's aggressive questioning on his leadership qualities, Major often seemed defensive, lacklustre and even prolix. Consider this response to Walden's suggestion that the Prime Minister's 'consultation' over the poll tax expressed his own indecisiveness:

What I think is important is that whenever you're considering a matter of importance that you do consider it, you listen to the points that are being made, you consider these points, you examine them, you consider how they will affect the people whose lives will be affected about it, and then you decide. Now that is always the way I have conducted affairs before I became Prime Minister and it's how I will continue to conduct affairs. At the end of the day you have to decide. But it is folly to decide until you have the right evidence, the right consideration and are able to reach the proper judgment.

Mrs Thatcher threatened the interview's viability by being over-whelming. Mr Major's personality has removed this threat but replaced it with another. Even at her most overweening Mrs Thatcher could not fail to fascinate and, in a peculair kind of way, entertain. The danger with the mellow Mr Major is that we will not bother to turn on our televisions in the first place.

## Notes

A surprisingly large number of people have helped me in writing this relatively short piece. Of them, I would like to thank Stuart Prebble, Peter Mandelson, Gerry Northam, Phillip Harding and Peter Hennessy for granting interviews and Bob Franklin, Philip Norton, David Murphy, Martin Harrison, Paul Habbeshon and Andrew McLaughlin for being helpful in a variety of other ways. My inevitable debts to Michael Cockerell's excellent *Live from Number Ten* and Sir Robin Day's memoirs will be obvious from the notes below.

1  I am grateful to Stuart Prebble, Head of Regional Programmes at Granada Television for the suggestion of this title.

2  Ivor Yorke, *The Techniques of Television News* (London: Focal, 1978) 109.

3  Sir Robin Day, *Grand Inquisitor* (London: Pan, 1989) 1–2.

4  Michael Cockerell, *Live from Number Ten: The Inside Story of Prime Ministers and Television* (London: Faber & Faber, 1988) 12.

5  E. G. Wedell, *Broadcasting and Public Policy* (London: Michael Joseph, 1968) 205.

6  *Daily Telegraph*, 7 March 1958; *Observer*, 2 March 1958; and *Daily Mirror*, 25 February 1958.

7  *BBC Annual Report and Accounts*, 1959–60, 10–11.

8  John Whale, *The Politics of the Media* (London: Fontana, 1977) 116.

9  Cockerell, *Live from Number Ten*, 56.

10  Whale, *Politics of the Media*, 116.

11  Interview with Peter Hennessy.

12  Day, *Grand Inquisitor*, 122 and 121. See also Robin Day, *Television: A Personal Report* (London: Hutchinson, 1961).

13  *Ibid.*, 7.

14  *The Times*, 18 February 1964.

15  Day, *Grand Inquisitor*, 260.

16  Interview with Peter Hennessy.

17  *Is Democracy Working?*, Tyne Tees Television, April 1986.

18  Interview with Peter Hennessy.

19  Day, *Grand Inquisitor*, 122.

20  David Cox (ed.), *The Walden Interviews* (London: Boxtree, 1990) vii.

21  *Ibid.*

22  Day, *Grand Inquisitor*, 272.

23  *Ibid*, 206.

24  Cockerell, *Live from Number Ten*, 141.

25  *Ibid.*, 312.

26  *Ibid.*, 134.

27  *Ibid.*, 180.

28  See 'The new hounding of the BBC', *Observer*, 25 February 1990.

29  *The Media Programme*, Channel Four, 29 October 1989.

30  Cockerell, *Live from Number Ten*, 331.

31  Austin Mitchell provides a slightly different version of the quotation in his *Westminster Man* (London: Thames Methuen, 1982) 207.

32  Interview with Peter Mandelson.

33  Cockerell, *Live from Number Ten*, 285.

34  Interview with Phillip Harding.

35  *Ibid.*

36  Interview with Stuart Prebble.

37  Quoted in the *Sunday Times*, 18 May 1991. See B. Ingham, *Kill the Messenger* (London: Harper Collins 1991); and also Robert Harris's *Good and Faithful Servant* (London: Faber & Faber, 1991), especially Chapter 7.

38  Erving Goffman, *The Presentation of Self in Everyday Life* (London: Penguin, 1984) 219 and see Chapter 6.

39  Cockerell, *Live from Number Ten*, 88.

40  Interview with Peter Mandelson.

41  *Ibid.*

42  Day, *Grand Inquisitor*, 1.

43  Cockerell, *Live from Number Ten*, 268.

44  *Ibid.*, 268.

45  Max Atkinson, *Our Masters' Voices* (London: Routledge, 1986) 113.

46  Robert Harris, *The Making of Neil Kinnock* (London: Faber & Faber, 1984) 111.

47  Harris, *Good and Faithful Servant*, 11.

48  See for example Denis MacShane, *Using the Media* (London: Pluto Press 1978) 126–55.

49  Cockerell, *Live from Number Ten*, 340.

50  Day, *Grand Inquisitor*, 273.

51  Cockerell, *Live from Number Ten*, 232.

52  Day, *Grand Inquisitor*, 273.

53  Cockerell, *Live from Number Ten*, 228.

54  Day, *Grand Inquisitor*, 290.

55  Text of inaugural lecture delivered in January 1991, kindly sent to author by Professor Harris. See also article in *THES* 25, January 1991.

56  Peter Bull and Kate Mayer, 'Interruptions in political interviews: a study of Margaret Thatcher and Neil Kinnock', *Journal of Language and Social Psychology*, vol. 7, no. 1 (1988) 44–5.

57  Cockerell, *Live from Number Ten*, 261.

58  Day, *Grand Inquisitor*, 283 and 292.

59  Ivor Crewe and Martin Harrop (eds.), *Political Communications: The General Election Campaign of 1987* (Cambridge University Press, 1989) 132.

60  Martin Harrison in David Butler and Dennis Kavanagh, *The British General Election of 1987* (London: Macmillan, 1988) 161.

61  Kenneth Pease, 'The great evaders', *New Society*, 2 October 1969.

62  Interviewing on the BBC: a new guideline (internal document), June

1990, 6.

63   Joe Haines, *Is Democracy Working?*, Tyne Tees Television, April 1986; 'Harold and I were a couple of television amateurs', Cockerell, *Live from Number Ten*, 226.

64   Austin Mitchell, 'Televising the House', *Talking Politics* (Winter 1990–91) 64.

65   Crew and Harrop, *Political Communications*, 134.

66   Shown on the *Media Programme*, Channel Four, 29 October 1989.

67   Cox, *The Walden Interviews*, vii–xiv.

68   See also Day, *Grand Inquisitor*, 7 and 120.

69   Interview with Peter Hennessy.

70   Cox, *The Walden Interviews*, ii.

71   Interview with Peter Hennessy.

# Changes in the political class

This chapter describes and analyses some of the main social and stylistic changes within the British political class in the past two decades. It looks at three groups: politicians, civil servants and, for want of a better term, political entrepreneurs. The latter refers to political advisers, members of think tanks, researchers and others who, holding no formal party position, contribute to the formulation of party policy.

## Politicians

In the election of party leaders there has been a modest broadening of the opportunity for participation. Both the Liberal and Social Democratic Parties, partly out of a commitment to participation but also because of a shortage of MPs as candidates, extended the election of the party leaders to the membership at large. In the Conservative Party the election of the party leader by a secret ballot of MPs was broadened in 1975 to allow for the incumbent leader to be challenged. Until then the party had a procedure for election of the leader but not for a challenge to or dismissal of the incumbent. Under the new system Mrs Thatcher deposed Mr Heath and went on to win the leadership. Sir Anthony Meyer in 1989 was the first to use the machinery when he stood against Mrs Thatcher. But his action overturned assumptions about the 'unthinkability' of challenging a Prime Minister. In 1990, Michael Heseltine challenged Mrs Thatcher and did well enough to force her resignation.

The Labour Party has made the most radical changes in its leadership selection. The election of the party leader and deputy leader, once the preserve of MPs, has, since 1981, been opened to the party membership, organised in an electoral college of affiliated trade unions, constituency parties and MPs. In addition, sitting MPs, hitherto virtually guaranteed re-nomination, have to undergo a reselection in the lifetime of the Parliament. The introduction of these changes had less to do with party democracy than a battle about power. For all the competing claims about the political sovereignty of Parliament or Conference, independence of MPs and accountability of the Parliamentary Labour Party (PLP) to the membership, the reforms were pushed by the political left as a means of extending its power and resisted by the political right as a means of protecting its power.[1]

What is so remarkable is that in spite of the constitutional changes, designed to close the gap between the myth of sovereignty of Conference and the autonomy in practice of the parliamentary leaders, the parliamentary domination of the Labour Party under Neil Kinnock is as strong as ever. Mr Kinnock regularly gets his way on the National Executive Committee (NEC), ran a highly personalised general election campaign in 1987, and Conference has acquiesced in a policy review which has buried many left-wing policies. In spite of the mandatory reselection, some 70 per cent of MPs in the last Parliament were re-nominated without a contest. In so far as the constitutional reforms, the high-tide of Bennery in the early 1980s, were designed to make the party safe for socialism and the leaders beholden to the allegedly left-wing grass roots, they have failed.

If one turns to the educational background of MPs, it is no surprise to find that the Conservatives are still overwhelmingly from public school and Oxbridge backgrounds. But the slight trend to greater social representativeness in the post-war Parliaments has speeded up since 1970. New Conservative MPs in recent Parliaments increasingly have been educated at state secondary schools and non-Oxbridge universities. In 1970 only 17 per cent of Conservative graduates had been to a non-Oxbridge university: in 1987 the figure was 38 per cent. In 1983 and 1987 there were record lows of 12 and 11 per cent of old Etonians among Conservative MPs. In the 1970 Parliament 25 per cent of Tory MPs had attended Eton, Harrow or Winchester. In the 1987 Parliament the figure was down to 15 per cent. This feature is part of a drift in the Conservative Party from the upper middle class and of that class from a political career.[2] There has also been a steady increase in Conservative MPs with experience in local government. But although 40 per cent of Conservative MPs

Table 5.1 *The changing educational background of Conservative MPs*

| | 1970 Con. MPs (330) | | 1987 Con MPs (376) | | 1987 intake (53) | |
|---|---|---|---|---|---|---|
| Oxford | 90 | } (49%) | 90 | } (44%) | 14 | } (41%) |
| Cambridge | 71 | | 76 | | 8 | |
| Other university | 38 | (17%) | 97 | (38%) | 14 | (28%) |
| | 208 | (63%) | 263 | (70%) | 36 | (68%) |
| Eton | 59 | } (25%) | 43 | } (15%) | 3 | } (7%) |
| Harrow | 14 | | 8 | | 1 | |
| Winchester | 9 | | 4 | | – | |
| Other public school | 161 | | 201 | | 28 | |
| | 243 | (75%) | 256 | (68%) | 32 | (60%) |
| Public school and university | 147 | (51%) | 194 | (51%) | 23 | (43%) |

*Source:* First two columns from Nuffield election studies. The third column is updated by B. Criddle from his table in D. Butler and D. Kavanagh, *The British General Election of 1987* (London: Macmillan, 1988) 202.

in 1987 had served on local authorities, only two of the twenty-two members of Mrs Thatcher's final Cabinet had done so.

Labour MPs are increasingly middle class, white collar and university-educated. Between 1945 and 1987 the proportion of graduates on Labour benches increased from 33 per cent to 56 per cent (on the Conservative side the increase was from 59 per cent to 69 per cent). Some part of the embourgeoisement is a consequence of social mobility; more Labour MPs are 'meritocrats', first-generation graduates of universities, from working-class or lower-middle-class homes. This has been a consequence of the gradual shift from manual to 'service' jobs in the occupational structure of society, the expansion of higher education and the increase in relatively 'open' careers like teaching and welfare.

Of recent Labour MPs, 30–40 per cent are drawn from the 'communicating' occupations (largely school teachers, lecturers in further and higher education and researchers). In 1987 one-quarter of the party's MPs and one-third of its candidates were lecturers or teachers and one in ten had worked in local government. In terms of trade-union sponsorship the white-collar Association of Technical and Managerial Staffs (ASTMS) and National Union of Teachers (NUT) are replacing the Transport and General Workers Union (TGWU) and the National Union of Mineworkers (NUM). If Labour's middle class is drawn in the main from the public sector and the non-commercial part of it, particularly the social services and teaching, the Conservative middle class is drawn largely from the private sector – particularly law.

There has been a modest shift in the direction of greater social representativeness in terms of gender and race. In the 1987 general election a record number of 243 women candidates was selected by the three main parties and a record 41 were elected. Both Labour and the Liberal Democrats provide for the inclusion of at least one woman on every shortlist. In the 1987 Parliament there was a record number of four black and Asian MPs (all Labour). Labour's new rule of electing at least three women to the Shadow Cabinet ensures that any future Labour government will have a record number of women Cabinet ministers. Like the Democratic Party in the United States, the Labour Party is moving in the direction of giving representation as of right in the party to hitherto neglected social groups.

Further up the political ladder, one notes that in recent Conservative Cabinets there has been a steady reduction of old Etonians, old Harrovians and products of the more prestigious public schools. Although Mrs Thatcher's 1990 Cabinet had sixteen Oxbridge graduates, only seven (Howe, Belstead, Hurd, King, Wakeham, Gummer and Brooke) went to prestigious public schools. Labour's frontbench represents the triumph of the 1944 Education Act and now virtually extinct 11+ examination. Most shadow ministers went in the 1950s and 1960s to grammar schools, many of which have since turned independent or comprehensive. The Shadow Cabinet has as many graduates from Hull University (with Hattersley, Prescott and McNamara) or Edinburgh (Smith, Brown, Cook) as from Oxford (Blair, Kaufman and Gould). There are none from Cambridge.

But one feature has not changed. Mrs Thatcher was as likely as her predecessors to move around her Cabinet ministers. The turnover rate of two years as head of a department is still one of the highest in the West. Of the last Thatcher Cabinet the average minister, prior to his then post, had served in 2.7 departments (excluding service in the Whips' Office). One gain from this accumulated experience of different departments could be that ministers' 'generalist' skills and knowledge may increase and the quality of Cabinet deliberations improve. There was some clustering of the departmental experiences of the last Thatcher Cabinet. Of the nineteen Cabinet ministers who sat in the Commons, seven had previous experience in the Whips' Office, and seven had served in the Treasury before assuming their 1990 posts. Four (Major, Wakeham, Brooke and MacGregor) served in both. Experience in two of the most centrally oriented departments – those concerned with the economy and with party discipline – was important for Mrs Thatcher's ministers.

For all the available data on social background it is not immediately obvious what its implications are for the behaviour and values of politicians. Will a better-educated (in terms of graduates largely in the arts and social sciences) House be more ideological, more interested in abstract ideas? In the case of Labour does the decline in the numbers of former manual workers and the embourgeoisement (when elected) of former workers lead to a deradicalisation of views? Has the reduction of MPs from upper-class backgrounds led to a decline of the 'One Nation' outlook on the Conservative benches? Mrs Thatcher once spoke disparagingly of the 'bourgeois guilt' of her predecessors, claiming that their privileged backgrounds made them shrink from taking tough but necessary measures. Will Conservative MPs of a more modest social background, who owe so much to their own efforts (the recent memoirs of Norman Tebbit, *Upwardly Mobile*, and Lord Young, *The Enterprise Years*, are revealing in this respect), be less sympathetic to state provision of services and emphasise more the virtues of self-help and self-reliance? We do not know.

We have numerous typologies of the styles and character of Prime Ministers and theories about whether the styles fluctuate cyclically ('strong' Premiers followed by 'consolidators', and so on) or are moving in a particular direction ('the rise of prime ministerial government'). Mrs Thatcher, partly because of her performance and partly because of her lengthy period of office, will continue to provide much material for the 'power of the PM' debate. Though a Conservative, she was deeply dissatisfied with the condition of British society and economy she inherited. She was a political mobiliser, wanting to change attitudes, institutions and policies. She paraded her beliefs and convictions and celebrated the tutelary role of political leadership[3] Ivor Crewe comments, 'Not since Gladstone has Britain been led by such an opinionated and evangelical prime minister.'[4] It is all very different from another Conservative Premier

(Macmillan) who once said that if people wanted a sense of purpose they should get it from bishops not from politicians.

Mrs Thatcher had a strong sense the sovereignty of the British state, the authority of (her) government, and the power of her office. Many of her ministers, domestic pressure groups and outside bodies like the European Commission felt the force of this assertiveness. Because she made few changes to the office of Prime Minister any expansion of prime ministerial power was largely a consequence of her forceful personality. She ran economic and foreign policies independently of her Chancellor of Exchequer and Foreign Secretary, fired or transferred two Foreign Secretaries in humiliating circumstances, and kept strict control of the Cabinet agenda (ostensibly the cause of Mr Heseltine's resignation at the time of Westland). Over the past decade commentators increasingly saw No. 10 as a powerhouse separate from the Cabinet. Here was a peacetime model of the premiership which has been undeniably successful in terms of achieving policy objectives and winning general elections. It was also a self-conscious repudiation of the style of her immediate predecessors. All the same, the circumstances of her downfall provide a warning.

It will be interesting to see whether she has set a new trend or bred a reaction: will the mobiliser be followed by the consolidator, the presidential style by collective Cabinet rule? In view of the limited changes in the office, much will depend on the assessment of her *personal* style. Although she built up the Downing Street Policy Unit, in part to develop her own agenda, she did not develop a Prime Minister's Department. Her record demonstrates how circumstances, political skill and personality can radically shape the power rating of a British Prime Minister.[5]

The reflections of Lord Hunt of Tamworth (Secretary of the Cabinet 1973–79) on the difficulties of running a collective (i.e. Cabinet) executive are relevant here.[6] His view is that Cabinet government suffers today because of the excessive departmental load on ministers, the lack of a collective briefing body for the Cabinet as a whole and, regardless of the character of Mrs Thatcher or any other incumbent, the pressures on the Prime Minister to intervene across the board. In large part these include the increase in summitry and the speed of modern communications under which Prime Ministers are expected to react quickly to the latest developments. As Secretary to the Cabinet Lord Hunt found that more and more of his time was taken with advising the Prime Minister than with running the business of the Cabinet Office. Advocates of the creation of a Prime Minister's Department take the view that presidentialism is a fact of modern political life, and that British government should adapt to it.[7]

In the face of these increased demands on Prime Ministers what has given way in the post-war period has been the parliamentary role. The twice-weekly Question Time in the House of Commons still takes a good deal of time in preparation. But a recent study has dramatically shown how the number of statements and interventions in debate in the Commons by post-war Premiers has declined. And compared to other British premiers Mrs Thatcher's parliamentary role was minimal.[8]

## Civil servants

It was often said that Mrs Thatcher attached more importance to individuals than to institutions. Her lack of interest in reforming government institutions may have been a reaction against the activism of Heath and Wilson in this respect. But for all her institutional conservatism she accepted the *Next Steps* programme, which may produce a radical transformation in the civil service by the end of the 1990s. She had a say in the appointment in the 1980s of virtually all permanent secretaries and most deputy secretaries. There have been claims that she has politicised the service, but few impartial observers are convinced that this has happened. Her support for particular people was probably determined more by personal than political chemistry; she preferred to promote 'doers' even where this disturbed established lines of seniority.[8]

Civil servants have had to compete with ministers receiving outside advice on policy, notably from the think tanks (see below), and from Mrs Thatcher, supported by her Policy Unit. For much of the post-war era many observers have been struck with the strength of departmentalism in Whitehall. Under Mrs Thatcher one was impressed by the presence of a stronger centre. The tendency for permanent secretaries to have spent earlier years in the Treasury and/or the Cabinet Office, departments concerned with central co-ordination and planning, may actually serve to increase what Theakston and Fry have called a 'centre perspective'.[10]

Many of the government's policies, with a few exceptions for favoured parts of the public sector, seem to have been based on the dictum; public bad, private good. Mrs Thatcher did not need the public-choice school to reinforce her beliefs that much of the public sector was unproductive, self-serving and a parasitic drag on the wealth-creating private sector. As a new Secretary of State for the Environment in 1979, Mr Heseltine informed his senior officials that he had made a million pounds before he was thirty: what had they achieved? Mrs Thatcher is also alleged to have told Sir Ian Bancroft, then head of the service, 'Clever people should not be here.' Certainly the civil service has felt the lash of her actions as well as her tongue. Although an attempt to curb some of their 'privileges', notably index-linked pensions, came to nought, she has reduced the size of the service by one-seventh since 1979.

The emphasis on changing the ethos of the service, to promote good management, cost-cutting and value for money are the alleged virtues of what Professor Hood calls a new public management, imported largely from the private sector.[11] Some of the qualities traditionally prized among policy-oriented senior administrators, such as balance, judgement, and a critcally detached rather than enthusiastic appreciation of proposals to change the status quo, were not appreciated by Mrs Thatcher. The new emphasis is on setting objectives and allocating resources to realise the objectives, performance appraisal, use of quasi-markets and contracting-out of services to create or encourage greater competition, and greater freedom to manage. As Peter Jackson observes, the language of public-sector management has replaced that of public administration.[12] The new culture has been reflected in the Raynor efficiency scrutinies, the Financial Management Initiative (FMI) and the *Next Steps* programme, under which many departments will be transformed into agencies. The agencies will have their own chief executives, with control over staffing, salaries and goals and will therefore, in theory, be more accountable.

We lack good evidence on the effects of the Thatcher years on the senior civil service. Has there been a decline in the sense of public service as a motivation for entering the civil service? Will the changes attract people with a strong interest in management, as opposed to people who are interested in policy formulation? Is there a greater perception of the civil service as deliverers of services to customers? Has there been a decline in the intellectual input to policy making? One does not have to be opposed to the reforms to point to the imperfections of some of the features of the Educational Reform Act, the health service reforms, and the poll tax. Brought in hurriedly, with a short period of time for consultation, they have had to be amended rapidly. The complaint of Sir Kenneth Clucas, Permanent Secretary at the Department of Trade and Industry until 1982, is that ministers have been too keen to achieve quick results and followed the line of 'Give me the answer on one sheet of paper.'

The service has also experienced difficulty in filling posts and retaining high-quality people. Some part of the problem may be a matter of paying relatively low London salaries and increased competition from other sectors for the best and the brightest. Some may also be a matter of a perceived lack of appreciation of public service by the government. The problems are likely to increase in the next decade with the downturn in the number of young people entering the labour-market and competition from other sectors.

On the other hand, some features of Whitehall life have hardly changed at all. One is the relative lack of public interest. While 150 journalists are in the political lobby, only two or three are attached to Whitehall. David Walker, till recently of *The Times*, and Peter Hennessy of the *Independent* have been lonely pioneers. Training is still modest and departments are reluctant to release their best people for courses. Hennessy has recently quoted the head of the Civil Service College: 'The fundamental philosophy is that you learn to do your job in government at your desk, not in a school.'[13] In spite of demands for more outsiders to be brought in to top posts, *à la* Sir John Hoskyns, little has been done. Hoskyns indeed also called for the dismissal of everybody over fifty and the virtual politicisation of the service. It is still an Oxbridge arts-dominated higher civil service. Sir Peter Levene, at Defence Procurement, stands out because his appointment is exceptional. It is not surprising that there is so little change in the social background of top civil servants, as long as they are chosen from the ranks of the higher civil service.

## Political entrepreneurs

The entrepreneurs are a more shadowy group, simply because for many of them political activity is part-time or a by-product of other roles. We are familiar with the role of the early Fabians in permeating elites with their general ideas and specific policy proposals, and acting as brokers between the worlds of ideas and political practice.

In the United States think tanks like Brookings, American Enterprise Institute and Hoover Institution have long provided bases for advisers moving between government and academe. Britain has lacked such institutes, culture and, apart from in wartime, a system of 'in and outers' in Whitehall – although outstanding individuals like Keynes and Beveridge (both in wartime) moved between different careers and influenced the political agenda.

Yet since the mid-1970s the Institute of Economic Affairs, the publishing house for promoting free-market ideas, has gone from strength to strength, and been joined by many other think tanks. One can point to the Adam Smith Institute, Centre for Policy Studies (CPS), Social Affairs Unit and various small specialist groups, sympathetic to the Conservative Party, promoting health and education reforms. By means of pamphlets and seminars these groups have floated such ideas as privatisation, contracting-out local government services, school vouchers, student loans and the winding up of the Inner London Education Authority. They helped to change the climate of opinion and in turn profited from that change. Reforming ministers could use these ideas to challenge 'yes minister' officials in their departments. Members of Mrs Thatcher's Policy Unit kept in touch with the think tanks and helped her in her battles against status-quo inclined departments.

One is struck by the interpenetration between members of these think groups, Conservative MPs, special advisers to ministers and desk officers in the Conservative Research Department. Members of think tanks get appointed to Conservative policy groups and consult with special advisers to ministers. Thus Lord Young of Graffham and Sir John Hoskyns started off in the Centre for Policy Studies in the late 1970s before joining government as adviser then minister in the former case and head of the No. 10 Policy Unit in the latter. John Redwood headed the Policy Unit before becoming a Conservative MP. David Willetts is presently Director of Studies of the Centre for Policy Studies and prospective candidate for a safe Conservative seat. But between 1978 and 1984 he worked in the Treasury as an official, including spells as Private Secretary to Nigel Lawson and Nicholas Ridley, and then worked in the Policy Unit. Robin Harris was at once time a special adviser in the Treasury for Nicholas Ridley, was for four years (1985–89) the Director of the Conservative Research Department and has recently joined the Policy Unit. Graham Mather, at present Director of the Institute of

Economic Affairs, was previously head of the Policy Unit at the Institute of Directors and has stood as a Conservative parliamentary candidate. Of the last Thatcher Cabinet, Hurd, Patten, Newton, MacGregor, Lilley and Lamont all took their first steps on the political ladder by working in the Conservative Research Department. Indeed, in the present House twenty-seven Conservative MPs have been employed in the Conservative Research Department and eight are former Central Office employees.

Two points are of interest here for understanding the character of the Conservative Party in Parliament today. One is that these positions provide a useful launching pad for a political career for young men and women. According to Byron Criddle, 68 of the 376 Conservative MPs returned in the 1987 Parliament have backgrounds as employees in the Research Department, or Central Office or as political advisers, and sometimes in more than one. Another is that this network helps to keep issue specialists in touch with each other and, on balance, heightens interest in policy questions in the Conservative Party.

Labour has been much slower to develop such an infrastructure of institutions which provide bases for the entrepreneurs to move between employment in the party, government and think tanks. But the recently established Institute of Public Policy Research, under James Cornford, a one-time academic and former Director of the Nuffield Foundation, and Patricia Hewitt, senior research fellow and formerly press and broadcasting secretary to Neil Kinnock, is a modest attempt to emulate Conservative practice. It seems, however, that, as in 1964 and 1966, a future Labour government will be heavily dependent on special advisers drawn from social science departments, notably economics and social administration/social policy, in the universities. At local government level, however, Labour councillors have combined office with employment in neighbouring local authorities, or as trade-union officials.

## Conclusion

In many respects the main theme, apart from the emergence of the political entrepreneurs, appears to be lack of change in the political class. That should not surprise: radical changes are more likely to accompany the collapse of or a fundamental shift in the regime and the replacement of one elite by another. Changes in the social backgrounds of politicians and top civil servants, though noticeable, are modest and broadly confirm the direction of earlier years.

There is also no discernible change in the narrow range of occupations from which politicians are recruited. The rule about starting early in politics (entering Parliament in one's mid-thirties) – and therefore probably not achieving a high level of competence in other fields – still holds. This means that politicians are overwhelmingly drawn from other para-political jobs (for example, in local government or as political advisers or researchers), or professions which are flexible (for example, law and communications). The top levels of Whitehall and Westminster are as much a closed shop as ever. Virtually all Cabinet ministers continue to be drawn from elected MPs and all permanent secretaries from 'lifers' in the Whitehall establishment. In Downing Street Mrs Thatcher may have chosen members of her Policy Unit and advisers for their technical and managerial skills (for example, Hoskyns, Strauss, Griffiths, Walters) but in government only Lord Cockfield and Lord Young have come from outside – in both cases from a business background. A possible force for change in the civil service is the *Next Steps* programme which may promote more interchange between managers from the executive agencies and the policy-makers in Whitehall.

It is worth noting how national leaders in other countries can recruit Cabinet ministers from outside the legislature, from law, business or academe. Countries with vigorous federal systems (for example, West Germany, the United States and Australia) provide opportunities outside of central government for gaining executive experience (as state governors or local mayors), not least for the opposition. In the United States and West Germany, reputations are first made at the state or regional levels. Moreover, both in France and Sweden more than half of the parliamentarians simultaneously hold local political office as well. Here is a neglected cost of the centralised system of government in Britain. A party in opposition for a lengthy period of time, as Labour was after 1951 and has been since 1979, is likely to lack potential ministers with experience of government. Opposition spokesmen will be catapulted into the Cabinet without the opportunity to ascend the ladder as a permanent private secretary and junior minister. In federal systems or countries which have vigorous local government, opposition party leaders at least have the opportunity of formulating and implementing programmes. Reduction of the power of local government in recent years have further reduced this avenue in Britain.

The role requirements of political leadership, particularly in party management, remain much the same. Although Mrs Thatcher had strong views and appointed and sacked many ministers, she rarely if ever in the past eleven years had a Cabinet of Thatcherites. For the most part she took account of the talent available and the political balance of the party. It is interesting that the stars on Labour's frontbench – John Smith, Gordon Brown, Jack Cunningham, Bryan Gould, Roy Hattersley and Robin Cook – score in parliamentary debates. Such a skill remains the key to winning the plaudits of parliamentary colleagues and political commentators. It is a mark of the importance which political leadership in Britain attaches to such qualities, and a reflection of the narrow socialisation of ministers: on average present Cabinet ministers have spent twelve years in the Commons before gaining office. Such a background cultivates and rewards communicating and debating skills.

It is likely that the presentational aspects of politics have increased, particularly in the past decade. Mr Heath, Mr Foot and Mr Callaghan made few concessions to their media and public-relations advisers. It would be difficult to imagine either man nestling a calf in a field in Norfolk for thirteen minutes for the benefit of press and television photographers, as Mrs Thatcher did in the 1979 general election. This is not a matter of different party values, for Mr Kinnock has been as willing as Mrs Thatcher to adapt himself to the requirements of the media – making time for photo-opportunities and sound bites.[14] Voters' impressions about politics are increasingly gained from television: being 'good on the box' is a great asset.[15]

There has been some emphasis on a macho or can-do style of management in much of the public sector, in industry and in political life. Mrs Thatcher prided herself on providing strong leadership, being effective in a crisis, and the electorate credited her with these qualities. There has been pressure on Mr Kinnock to emulate her and his standing with colleagues and the public has soared when he has hammered the left of his party. Some of this may be a reaction to the 1960s and 1970s when it was widely thought that British leaders were too respectful of established (usually restrictive) practices in industry and the professions, and too accommodating to group demands. Leaders, it was said were 'overloaded' by group demands and the political system suffered a 'pluralistic stagnation'. Both

Wilson and Heath started as mobilisers, promising major changes, and ended as conciliators; indeed as Prime Minister in 1974 Wilson promised the electorate 'a bit of peace and quiet'. What seemed to count in the 1970s was the government's ability to strike agreements with the social partners.

Mrs Thatcher rejected this outlook. Under her there was a greater sense of the autonomy of the centre, which was reflected in the government's unwillingness to court groups and its withdrawal from established responsibilities, for example, full employment. Mrs Thatcher also displayed a greater confidence in her sense of what needed to be done and was more interested in seeking advice about implementation. She did not appoint any Royal Commissions. A Cabinet colleague commented: 'She likes to start a discussion with the conclusion.'

It has often been noted that Mrs Thatcher was dismissive of the largely centrist establishment – senior civil service, universities, lawyers, bankers, church leaders and the BBC. These institutions provided many members – the 'good and the great' – of the Royal Commissions and are 'The Lost Tribe of British Public Life'.[16] John Lloyd, of the *Financial Times* has talked about the emergence of a new and different anti-establishment. Whereas the old one was assured, middle-class, paternalist and not very materialistic – in a word, satisfied – the new one consists predominantly of rule- or code-breakers, materialists, and people who are demotic and efficient. It includes people like Alan Sugar, Lord Hansen, James Goldsmith, Lord Raynor, Rupert Murdoch and Andrew Neil. Mrs Thatcher, like many of these, was sceptical of consensus-seeking Royal Commissions and the time-honoured rules of the professions, and saw herself as outside the old establishment. In a notable speech in 1985 she attacked her clerical and academic critics, and praised the risk-takers and wealth-creators, people who are frequently from a modest background:

And nowhere is this attitude [opposition to wealth-creation] more marked than in the cloister and common room. What these critics apparently can't stomach is that wealth-creators have a tendency to acquire wealth in the process of creating it for others.

She continued:

They didn't speak with Oxford accents. They hadn't got what people call the right 'connections', they had just one thing in common, they were men of action.

Here perhaps is the most noticeable change: the great casualty of the past two decades has been the 'fixer' style of politics, and with it the consensus-seeking fixers.

## Notes

1 See D. Kogan and M. Kogan, *The Battle for the Labour Party* (London: Fontana, 1982).

2 See B. Criddle, 'Candidates', in D. Butler and D. Kavanagh (eds.), *The British General Election of 1987* (London: Macmillan, 1988).

3 D. Kavanagh, *Thatcherism and British Politics*, 2nd ed (Oxford University Press, 1990) Chapter 9.

4 I. Crewe, 'Values: the crusade that failed', in D. Kavanagh and A. Seldon (eds.), *The Thatcher Effect* (Oxford University Press, 1989) 240.

5 A. King (ed.), *The British Prime Minister* (London: Macmillan, 1985).

6 See W. Plowden (ed.), *Advising the Rulers* (Oxford: Blackwell, 1987).

7 See P. Hennessy, *Cabinet* (Oxford, Blackwell, 1986); and A. Berrill, 'Strength at the centre: the case for a Prime Minister's Department', in A. King (ed.), *The British Prime Minister* (London: Macmillan, 1985).

8 See P. Dunleavy, G. Jones and B. O'Leary, 'Prime Ministers and the Commons', *Public Administration*, vol. 68 (1990).

9 RIPA, *Top Jobs in Whitehall* (London: RIPA, 1987).

10 K. Theakston and G. Fry, 'Britain's administrative elite: permanent secretaries 1900–86', *Public Administration*, vol. 66 (1988).

11 C. Hood, *Beyond the Public Bureaucracy State?* (London School of Economics, 1990).

12 P. Jackson, *Measuring the Efficiency of the Public Sector* (Manchester Statistical Society, 1988).

13 P. Hennessy, *Whitehall* (London, Secker & Warburg, 1989) 529.

14 See D. Butler and D. Kavanagh, *The British General Election of 1987* (London: Macmillan, 1988).

15 M. Cockerell, *Live From Number 10* (London: Faber & Faber, 1988).

16 P. Hennessy, *The Great and the Good* (London, Policy Studies Institute Research Report No. 654, 1986).

# The political socialisation of young people

Just over twenty years ago, in 1969, the age at which people in Britain became eligible to vote was lowered from twenty-one to eighteen. As a result, in 1970 just under 2½ million young people between the ages of eighteen and twenty were able to vote in a general election for the first time. This sudden influx of a large number of young people into the electorate raised a number of questions at the time. How well qualified were young voters to use their new political power? How would they use it? Did their political attitudes differ markedly from those of older voters? Might these new voters tip the balance of power in general elections?

Looking back over the past twenty years we are now in a better position to answer questions like these and to see that some of the fears expressed at the time were ungrounded. It is true that the political parties have sometimes tried to 'target' young people in their campaigns – by making use of rock music and 'pop' artists, for example – but, on the whole, eighteen to twenty-one-year olds have simply been absorbed into the larger electorate. Nonetheless, there remain important questions about the political attitudes and behaviour of the young, including those who have not yet reached voting age. How are their political opinions shaped and have there been any significant changes in their attitudes over the past twenty years? Does the political behaviour of young people today show any major differences from that of young people in the 1960s? How well prepared are they to undertake the duties of citizenship?

Perhaps the most obvious starting point for any discussion of questions such as these is the theory of political socialisation. Put simply, socialisation theory suggests that individuals' political knowledge, attitudes, values and beliefs (or, more generally, their 'orientations' to politics) are the product of a learning process begun in early childhood and carried out by 'agencies' such as the family, the school, peer groups and the mass media.

In the 1960s and early 1970s, in research heavily influenced by similar work in the United States, there were a number of empirical studies concerned with political socialisation in Britain. Much of this work concentrated on the very young, often focusing on children under ten years of age, and it had two main themes. First, it was concerned with 'cultural transmission' – the processes by which young people acquired knowledge about and loyalty towards the political system as a whole and developed attitudes consonant with the political culture.[1] In this context, it was argued that the stability of the British system required the effective socialisation of young people. Second, there were studies of the process by which political interest and specific partisan attitudes and identifications were developed among children. It was demonstrated, for example, that 63 per cent of boys had developed a party preference by the age of twelve.[2]

Although political socialisation quickly became a standard topic in textbooks on comparative politics and political sociology, some of these studies, and the theory itself, were severely and effectively attacked. Critics were sceptical of the claims that early childhood experiences had such great importance and also queried the supposed links between attitudes and behaviour. Further, they argued that the concept of political socialisation had simply been stretched to include all possible influences upon political attitudes; they mocked attempts to explain the stability of democratic regimes by reference to the attitudes of ten-year-old children.[3] One critic entitled an extended critique 'An obituary to political socialisation'.[4]

In addition to these theoretical problems, many of the events of the 1970s and early 1980s also cast doubt on the validity of a theory which was originally intended to account for regime stability. During these years there were signs that political extremism was on the increase, racial tension erupted into violence on a number of occasions, political nationalism in Scotland and Wales threatened to fragment the state, the established party system came under serious threat and the 'ungovernability' of Britain was a recurrent theme of political debate

In the 1980s, however, there has been a more mature reconsideration of socialisation theory and the beginnings of a renewed, if more modest, research interest. Scholars have acknowledged the weaknesses of some aspects of earlier research but have argued nonetheless that there is a valuable core to socialisation theory which needs to be preserved. It may be helpful to summarise this core.

The central claim of socialisation theory is that people's attitudes and patterns of behaviour are learned. As they grow up young people belong to or come into contact with a variety of social groups and institutions – most obviously the family, peer groups and the education system. For a variety of reasons there is a tendency for individuals to come to share the attitudes and behaviour patterns that are typical of the groups with which they come into contact. This may be the result of a conscious desire to imitate friends and colleagues or an unconscious desire to conform to group norms, but it may also be a product of group sanctions and pressures brought to bear by groups on their members. These groups act also as agencies of socialisation into the wider national culture, since many of the attitudes and behaviour patterns typical of the groups reflect that wider culture. The mass media too, and in particular television, play an important part in this process of socialisation into the national culture, being a major source of information and of role models.

It would not be claimed, of course, that socialisation *determines* attitudes and behaviour or that it is their sole source. Individuals are individuals and have their own personal predilections and preferences. Perhaps even more important, they have their own very different patterns of experience of the world in which they live, and these are bound to have a major impact on the way in which their attitudes develop. Modern socialisation theory, then, does not claim that all beliefs and behaviour are consequences of the influence of socialising agencies, only that for many individuals their socialisation experience is an important source of their current attitudes and opinions.

It is still held, however, that the influence of socialising agencies is likely to be at its strongest in the early years of life. The personalities of the young are less clearly formed, their range of experience is narrower, and for a variety of reasons they are more exposed to and more susceptible to socialising influences. We need make no claim about the lasting effects of early childhood socialisation, but if we are interested in the attitudes and behaviour of young people as they enter adult life then the effects of socialisation agencies in these and the immediately preceding years seem bound to be of considerable importance.

An account of socialisation theory in something like these terms would, we suggest, be accepted by most scholars now working in the area. It remains to add that *political* socialisation is only one aspect of the more general process of socialisation. Learning about the political system and forming attitudes towards political parties and the central issues of politics is simply one of the learning processes that most young people experience during their adolescence – although it is, no doubt, one of the more important.

This reassessment of the central claims of the theory of political socialisation in the 1980s coincided with increased concern among politicians and policy-makers about some aspects of youth behaviour – 'lager loutism', football hooliganism and so on – and there were also worries about the long-term effects of high levels of unemployment among young people. As a result, then, there has been a cautious reawakening of interest in socialisation, focusing now not on young children but on teenagers and young adults, and setting socialisation more clearly alongside a range of other factors likely to affect young people.

In particular, a number of research projects have been undertaken which have been concerned to explore the nature and sources of the belief systems of the young with respect to politics as well as other areas of life. Partly in response to the sorts of concerns of politicians noted above, the Social Science Research Council set up a major research programme, called the *Young People in Society Initiative*, in the early 1980s. The focus of this research was particularly on the psychological development of young people and it stressed the use of participant observation, as well as more conventional survey methods. The researchers were primarily interested in what they called 'normal psycho-social development', rather than 'problems', but the study also investigated topics such as delinquency, attitudes to alcohol consumption and the effects of the experience of unemployment.[5] As part of this project, Billig and Cochrane studied the political attitudes of mainly working-class young people in the West Midlands, using sample surveys and group discussions, and some of their conclusions are discussed below.

A second major study of young people in Britain, arising out of the *Young People in Society Initiative*, is currently in progress. This is the *16–19 Initiative*, which is a complex longitudinal study of a cross-section of 6,400 young people in four different areas of Britain. It involves a series of annual surveys between 1987 and 1991 as well as more specific detailed research in each of the four areas, and it is expected that it will produce much useful material on young people's attitudes to politics.[6]

A third piece of work in this area is our own study of young people aged between sixteen and nineteen studying for 'A' levels in schools and colleges throughout England and Wales. This research involved a series of surveys undertaken between 1986 and 1988 which investigated political knowledge, attitudes and behaviour. One of the major themes of the research was the impact of formal political education upon the political knowledge and attitudes of young people and we refer to some of our results below.

## Recent changes in the agencies of political socialisation

We have suggested that the theory of political socialisation, in the more careful and modest reformulation we have outlined above, provides a useful basis for explaining the political orientations of young people. But many of the main agencies of socialisation in British society have undergone substantial change in recent years, and this might lead us to expect correspondingly important changes in the political attitudes and behaviour of the young.

For example, the family, which on most accounts is the most powerful agency of socialisation, has been significantly affected by the rising divorce rate and by the increasing number of births outside marriage. Largely as a result of these trends, the proportion of all families with dependent children which were single-parent families rose from 8 per cent in 1971 to 14 per cent in 1987 (*Social Trends* (1990) 37–38). Family ties may as a result have been weakened, and this in turn may mean that the family has become a less effective mechanism for transmitting ideas about politics.

There have also been important changes in the education system. The last twenty years have witnessed a major change from the secondary-modern and grammar-school system of secondary education to comprehensives in most parts of the country. The proportion of children in Britain attending comprehensive schools rose from 38 per cent to 88 per cent between 1971 and 1988 (*Social Trends*, (1990) 53). There have been more modest, but still significant increases in the proportion of students attending universities – the figure rose by 31 per cent between 1970/71 and 1987/8 (*Social*

*Trends* (1990) 59). Also of some interest is the fact that there has been a considerable expansion in the teaching of politics in schools, partly as a response to concern about the perceived political ignorance of young people and partly in response to a sustained campaign on the part of the Politics Association. Almost all examination boards now offer GCSEs and 'A' levels in British government and politics. Of course, only a small minority of school pupils take such courses, but one might expect that those who do will end up having more knowledge and awareness of politics, and perhaps more sophisticated attitudes than those who do not.

The mass media clearly play an important role in the process of political learning and media coverage of politics has been transformed since the 1960s. On the one hand, the rise of the tabloid press has meant a new stridency in political coverage, as well as a much greater pro-Conservative bias. Whereas in 1964 60 per cent of the adult population read a pro-Conservative newspaper and 49 per cent read a pro-Labour one, by 1983 the corresponding figures were 75 per cent pro-Conservative and only 24 per cent pro-Labour.[7] On the other hand, television, with its balanced coverage of politics, has become the dominant medium of communication and this has transformed both the availability and the presentation of information about politics. We now have almost round-the-clock news and political comment and, since 1989, the televising of Parliament as well.

The agencies of political socialisation which we have described operate within a given political environment and this political environment has also seen some remarkable changes in the past twenty years. Until the 1960s, the British political system was characterised by consensus, stability and pragmatism. The two-party system seemed highly stable, and voters generally displayed a rock-like fidelity to their chosen party. Furthermore, the system was underpinned by a political culture which was generally agreed to be characterised by deference and trust in government.[8]

Young people coming of age in the late 1980s and 1990s will have experienced none of this. The period in which they have become conscious of and learned about politics has been one of 'conviction politics' with a great emphasis on ideology; it has seen the electoral dominance of one party (and of one powerful leader) as well as a serious challenge to the established two-party system; and recently it has seen signs of the possible emergence of 'Green' politics as an alternative to the traditional political agenda. Those coming of age in the 1990s have had no experience of stable two-party politics based on class, which was the norm in Britain for thirty years following the Second World War. Rather, they have grown up in an era in which the party system and party support have been fluid. Some commentators have in turn related these developments to more fundamental changes in the political culture – a breakdown in trust and a decline in deference – which together, they argue, have transformed the context of British politics.[9]

We have, of course, only sketched a few of the most obvious changes in the political socialisation process and we cannot consider all of their effects upon young people. In what follows, however, we pick out and comment on a number of themes that appear to be of particular importance and interest.

## Political knowledge

The first major study of the extent of political knowledge among young people in Britain was carried out in the mid-1970s. Surveying a sample of over 4,000 fifteen and sixteen year olds, Stradling found that there was widespread political ignorance: 'it is apparent that they lack much of the kind of basic information which the political consumer needs if he is to understand decisions and actions which affect him and if he is to make political choices between actions, policies, parties or candidates. One of the most disturbing findings . . . is ignorance of where the political parties stand on the main issues of the day.'[10] Stradling points out that there was no evidence of significantly higher levels of political knowledge among adults, and the results of his study were widely quoted as evidence of the need for improved political education in schools.

As noted above, some advances in the provision of formal political education have been made over the past twenty years and, in addition, television has increasingly provided a wealth of political information for those who want it, but in spite of this there is very little evidence to indicate any general improvement in political literacy. Billig and Cochrane gloomily conclude from their 1979–82 surveys of working-class youth referred to above that 'young people will continue to exist in a condition of ignorance in which simple solutions . . . will have appeal'.[11] In 1985, another survey, which sought to update Stradling's work, concluded that 'the present state of political knowledge and literacy is appallingly low and has not improved in some ten years'.[12]

Our own study of 'A' level pupils in the late 1980s produced some rather more positive results. We found that levels of political knowledge among English and Welsh school children in the sixteen-to-nineteen age group were moderately high and, in particular, our results showed that those who were studying politics were significantly more politically literate and more sophisticated and aware about politics than were other pupils.[13] This may appear a rather obvious conclusion, but in fact it contradicts a great deal of previous research on the effects of the school curriculum on student attitudes – research in the United States, for example, had consistently been unable to find any significant effect of formal political education upon young people in general.[14] Our results are, of course, not directly comparable with those of the surveys quoted earlier because of the narrow nature of our sample – the young people we surveyed were part of the minority which goes on to post-compulsory education – although they may give some comfort and ammunition to supporters of formal political education in schools.

While 'A' level courses may have improved the position as far as a small minority is concerned, then, there is no evidence as yet that the developments of the last twenty years have in fact led to any significant changes in knowledge about politics among young people in general. This rather pessimistic conclusion reinforces the arguments of those who continue to press for better provision of political education, especially for those who leave school at the minimum age.[15]

## Political participation

It is easy to get the impression that young people nowadays are highly active politically. They are often well to the fore in 'demos', they are seen selling political newspapers on street corners, they seem to take a leading part in many 'single-issue' groups, and so on. But in fact this impression is highly misleading. Much closer to the mark is the report of a 1986 survey which began 'Thatcher's children are politically apathetic.'[16] This apathy extends even to the relatively simple act of voting. The two major survey studies of election turn-out in Britain both agree that age is one of the very few social characteristics which is significantly related to levels of non-voting. Swaddle and Heath, for example, found that in the 1987 election turnout in the eighteen to twenty-four age group was almost 20 per cent lower than among twenty-five to sixty-four-year-olds. Crewe, Fox and Alt suggest that the main reason for this lower turnout is that young people are less exposed to social networks in which the norm of voting is well-established, and are thus isolated from community pressures to vote.[17] Furthermore, young people have frequently not developed the firm attachment to a party which simplifies the task of voting and provides a powerful motivation.

Unfortunately there is little systematic evidence about the extent or form of political participation on the part of young people who have not yet reached voting age, or of non-electoral participation by young electors. The youth movements of the various parties appear to have been declining in strength over the years, but we have little or no reliable information about participation in minor parties such as the Greens, the Socialist Workers Party, the National Front and so on. In addition, episodic participation in the campaigns of pressure groups or on particular issues remains a subject which has been largely untouched by social scientists.

## Party preference

There is a well-known aphorism which suggests that if people are not radical in their youth then they have no heart, but if they are not conservative by middle age then they have no head. In the 1950s and 1960s this piece of folk-wisdom found some empirical support. Academic surveys and opinion polls regularly found that young people – and particularly the youngest group of eligible voters – were substantially more inclined to vote Labour than the rest of the electorate.[18] By the elections of the 1980s, however, this youthful bias towards Labour had all but disappeared. In each of the elections of 1979, 1983 and 1987 a plurality of first-time voters supported the Conservatives.[19] Similarly, in our study of 'A' level students the distribution of party support in 1987 was close to that among the electorate as a whole.

It would appear, then, that as far as party choice is concerned there has been a genuine change among young people. How this change is to be explained is not at all clear, but one possibility is that it may be a result of the increasingly pro-Conservative bias of the popular press. Alternatively, it might reflect the dominant Conservative mood of the country in the 1980s or even, paradoxically, more effective family socialisation. Interestingly, however, young men have been more affected by this trend than young women. Up to the 1960s it was almost a law of political behaviour that women were more inclined to support the Conservatives than men. In elections from 1979 onwards, however, this 'gender gap' has virtually disappeared. More surprisingly, in the late 1980s a series of polls and surveys found that among younger voters the gender gap actually went into reverse, with women being more left-wing than men. Clear evidence of such a reversal was also found among young people of pre-voting age.[20] It is possible that this difference might be accounted for in terms of Mrs Thatcher's 'tough' image – her stance on defence, welfare and so on might be attractive to young men, but not to young women. But our own analysis of sixth-formers suggested that the most obvious explanation was simply that on a whole range of issues girls were more left-wing than boys.

One of the best-supported findings of voting research over the past twenty years is that there has been a decline in the strength of party identification among the electorate, i.e. a weakening of voters' psychological commitment to parties. It might be thought that this weakening could be the result of a generational effect: new generations of young voters coming into the electorate may be less strongly committed to the established parties and this might account for the weakening of party identification in the electorate as a whole. But this hypothesis has been fairly convincingly disproved. Analysing survey results from the early 1970s, Crewe, Sarlvik and Alt showed that although party identification was weaker among the young, as would be expected, the decline in the strength of party identification was similar amongst all age groups. Replicating this analysis in the early 1980s, Clarke and Stewart reached a similar conclusion.[21] Weakening partisanship among the electorate as a whole, therefore, cannot be explained by the entry into the electorate of new cohorts of especially weak partisans.

## Political extremism

It has been suggested by some writers that the young, or at least some sections of the young, may be particularly susceptible to the appeals of extremist political groups. Billig and Cochrane, for example, argue that support for the National Front and the prevalence of more generally racist views, particularly among young working-class men and women, may be a product of political ignorance and the fear of unemployment. In their study of young people in the West Midlands between 1979 and 1982, Billig and Cochrane found surprisingly high levels of support for extreme right-wing parties. In 1979, 7 per cent of their respondents gave the National Front or the British Movement as their first-choice party. By 1982, 14 per cent reported a first choice and 16 per cent a second choice for one of these parties. In addition, Billig and Cochrane interpret the surge in support in 1982 for the SDP as, paradoxically, an expression of authoritarianism.[22]

Billig and Cochrane viewed their results with some alarm but, although some evidence of political extremism among the young has also been found in Liverpool,[23] it is worth sounding a note of caution about levels of support for extremist parties. We ourselves found no evidence of significant support for extremism among 'A' level pupils in the late 1980s. When asked to order their preferences among seven different parties, fewer than 1 per cent of our respondents placed the National Front first, and less than 4 per cent placed it first or second; 1 per cent placed the Communist Party first and 4 per cent placed it first or second. More than half of our respondents were unwilling to indicate *any* preference for these parties. In addition, at the time of the 1983 election a survey of a substantial group of mainly unemployed working-class youngsters, found that there was 'almost total rejection of extremist political parties'.[24] Apathy and resignation were commoner responses to unemployment than extremism.

More generally, there has been no increase in support for the extreme right or left in either general or local elections in Britain during the 1980s. Indeed, in electoral terms extreme right support has been smaller than it was at times during the 1970s, and it remains tiny. Similarly left-wing parties such as the Socialist Workers Party, despite their extensive involvement in the popular anti-poll-tax campaign, remain very much on the fringe of British politics. It may be that a small number of young people flirt with the extreme left or extreme right in some localities, but this is not usually reflected in adult voting behaviour.

## Thatcher's children?

Although we have argued that the weakening of partisanship over the past twenty years cannot be interpreted as the result of a generational effect, the notion of political generations is, nonetheless, a very useful one. It can be argued that as each age cohort enters the electorate its opinions and behaviour are heavily influenced by the major political events of the time and by the prevailing political mood. As the cohort ages there will, of course, be some change, but the influences which were important during its formative years will continue to shape attitudes and behaviour for a long time afterwards. The generation of the 1960s, for example, who are the parents of the current generation, will still be influenced politically by the events of their youth – the Vietnam War, the successes and failures of the Wilson government, the 'permissive society' and so on.

One of the themes most frequently discussed by political commentators in recent years has been whether the political generation which has come of age in the 1980s will be 'Thatcher's children'. The suggestion is that the members of this generation have been strongly influenced by the radical shift to the right in British political debate brought about by Mrs Thatcher, and that they will carry these new ideas with them into the 1990s and beyond.

What evidence is there to substantiate such a view? Survey evidence is unfortunately limited. As our discussion so far has perhaps illustrated, it is a difficult and expensive matter to get a representative sample of young people, and the numbers of young respondents in the large-scale national BES surveys conducted after each election are too small to allow any but the most basic analysis.[25] What evidence we have is, then, fragmentary, but nonetheless most of it seems to point in the same direction.

Surveys of the electorate as a whole suggest that there is little evidence that the Thatcherite agenda has made a deep impression. While on some of the issues associated with management of the economy there may have been some movement to the right, on a whole range of issues relating to the welfare state, the National Health Service, education and so on, the electorate remains predominantly social democratic in its outlook; for example, people continue to favour higher expenditure on public services even if this means higher taxes. Survey results on these sorts of questions have been thoroughly investigated by Crewe, who concludes that the electorate's 'economic values are solidly social democratic, their moral values only half-Thatcherite, and on both fronts they have edged to the left since 1979. There has been no ideological sea change.'[26]

There seems no good reason to suppose that young people have been any more susceptible to the allure of Thatcherism than have older generations. A survey of 2,417 social studies students in the fourteen-to-nineteen age range by Williams in 1985 suggested that they were predominantly 'wet' in their outlook, though the theme of apathy once again emerged: half the sample said they were 'not political at all.' Our own survey of sixth-formers between 1986 and 1988 found majorities or substantial pluralities taking right-wing positions on unilateralism and renationalisation of privatised industries, but left-wing positions on the redistribution of wealth, the health service and the welfare state. In September 1986 *The Times*, although giving little hard information, reported a survey conducted by MORI which found in general terms that on the key issues of employment and unemployment Thatcherite positions had had little effect on young people.[27]

We must conclude, then, that in a variety of ways young people in the 1970s and 1980s seem to have displayed continuity rather than change, despite the significant changes in the agencies of socialisation to which we referred earlier. There are still low levels of knowledge about politics and lower than average levels of formal participation, and there is some evidence of more general apathy. Young voters today are less inclined to support Labour than they were twenty years ago, but there is no support for the view that among the young party loyalties have weakened more than among other age groups. There is also little support for the more general proposition that the young have been particularly influenced by Thatcherism. It is not clear whether one should find in these results depressing evidence of lack of progress, or comforting support for the forces of continuity and stability.

Notes

1   See, for example, F. Greenstein, V. Herman, R. Stradling and E. Zureik, 'The child's conception of the Queen and the Prime Minister', *British Journal of Political Science*, vol. 4 (1974) 257–88; J. Dennis, L. Lindberg and D. McCrone, 'Support for nation and government among English schoolchildren', *British Journal of Political Science*, vol. 1 (1971) 21–44.

2   R. Dowse and J. Hughes, 'Girls, boys and politics', *British Journal of Sociology*, vol. 22 (1971) 53–67; R. Dowse and J. Hughes, 'The family, the school and the political socialization process', *Sociology*, vol. 1 (1971) 21–45.

3   See D. Marsh, 'Political socialization: the implicit assumptions ques-

tioned', *British Journal of Political Science*, vol. 1 (1971) 453–65; A. H. Birch, 'Children's attitudes to British politics', *British Journal of Political Science*, vol. 2 (1972) 519–20; D. Kavanagh, 'Allegiance among English children: a dissent', *British Journal of Political Science*, vol. 2 (1972) 127–31; R. Dowse, 'Some doubts concerning the study of political socialization', *Political Studies*, vol. 16 (1978) 403–10.

4   Ted Tapper, 'An obituary to political socialization', paper presented at the annual conference of the Political Studies Association, Nottingham, 1976.

5   H. McGurk (ed.), *What Next?* (London: Economic and Social Research Council, 1987).

6   See K. Roberts, 'ESRC – young people in society', *Youth and Policy*, vol. 22 (1987) 15–24; and J. Bynner, 'Coping with transition; ESRC's new 16–19 initiative', *Youth and Policy*, vol. 22 (1987) 25–8.

7   R. Negrine, *Politics and The Mass Media in Britain* (London: Routledge, 1989).

8   G. Almond and S. Verba, *The Civic Culture* (Princeton University Press, 1963).

9   See S. Beer, *Britain Against Itself* (London: Faber & Faber, 1982).

10   R. Stradling, *The Political Awareness of The School Leaver* (London: Hansard Society, 1977) 23.

11   M. Billig and R. Cochrane, 'Adolescents in politics', in McGurk (ed.), *What Next?*, 51.

12   G. Mardle and M. Taylor, 'Political knowledge and political ignorance: a re-examination', *Political Quarterly*, vol. 58 (1987) 208–16.

13   D. Denver and G. Hands, 'Does studying politics matter? The political knowledge, attitudes and perceptions of school students', *British Journal of Political Science*. vol. 20 (1990) 263–88; D. Denver and G. Hands, 'Political education, political parties and the party system in Britain', *Youth and Policy* (1991).

14   See K. P. Langton and M. K. Jennings, 'Political socialization and the high school civics curriculum', *American Political Science Review*, vol. 62 (1968) 852–67; A. Westholm, A. Lindquist and R. G. Niemi, 'Education and the making of the informed citizen: political literacy and the outside world', paper presented to the Workshop on Political Socialisation and Citizenship in Democracy, Tel Aviv, 1987.

15   See L. Robins, 'The delegitimation of political education in Britain: a working paper', in M. van der Dussen and H. Hooghoff (eds.), *Towards a Global Political Science: a report on the 14th World Congress of IPSA, Washington 1988 with Selected Papers* (Enschede, The Netherlands: NICD, 1989) 59–76.

16   M. McCarthy, 'Thatcher's children', *The Times* (1–3 September 1986).

17   See K. Swaddle and A. Heath, 'Official and reported turnout in the British general election of 1987', *British Journal of Political Science*, vol. 19 (1989) 537–51; I. Crewe, T. Fox and J. Alt, 'Non-voting in British general elections 1966–October 1974', in C. Crouch (ed.), *British Political Sociology Yearbook*, vol. 3 (London: Croom Helm, 1977).

**18**   See, for example, R. Rose, 'Britain: simple abstractions and complex realities', in R. Rose (ed.), *Electoral Behaviour* (New York: Free Press, 1974).

**19**   See D. Denver, *Elections and Voting Behaviour in Britain* (London: Philip Allan, 1989) 66.

**20**   For accounts of gender voting see, for example, P. G. Pulzer, *Political Representation and Elections in Britain* (London: Allen & Unwin, 1967); P. Norris, 'Conservative attitudes in recent elections: an emerging gap?', *Political Studies*, vol. 34 (1986) 120–8; D. Denver and G. Hands, 'A new gender gap: sex and party choice among young people', *Talking Politics*, vol. 2 (1990) 109–12.

**21**   See I. Crewe, B. Sarlvik and J. Alt, 'Partisan dealignment in Britain 1964–74', *British Journal of Political Science*, vol. 7 (1977) 129–90; H. D. Clarke and M. C. Stewart, 'Dealignment of degree: partisan change in Britain, 1974–83', *Journal of Politics*, vol. 46 (1984) 689–718.

**22**   Billig and Cochrane, 'Adolescents in politics'.

**23**   K. Roberts and G. Parsell, 'The political orientations, interests and activities of Britain's 16 to 18 year olds in the late 1980s', unpublished working paper, University of Liverpool, 1988.

**24**   M. H. Banks and P. Ullah, 'Political attitudes and voting among unemployed and employed youth', *Journal of Adolescence*, vol. 10 (1987) 201–16.

**25**   See, however, A. Brown, 'Thatcherism and the young: the death of the Left?' (paper presented at the PSA Conference, Lancaster, 1991) which analyses the changing opinions of first-time voters and reaches conclusions which are broadly similar to ours.

**26**   I. Crewe, 'Has the electorate become Thatcherite?', in R. Skidelsky (ed.), *Thatcherism* (Oxford: Blackwell, 1988) 44.

**27**   See M. Williams, 'The Thatcher generation', *New Society*, vol. 75 (1986) 312–15; D. Denver and G. Hands, 'Political socialisation in The United Kingdom', in H. Dekker and R. Meyenberg (eds.), *Political Socialization in Eastern, Central and Western Europe* (Frankfurt: Peter Lang, 1991); M. McCarthy, 'Thatcher's Children', *The Times*, 1–3 September 1986.

# Part II
# The legislative process

# What happened to the constitution under Mrs Thatcher?

Twenty years ago we had a relatively clear idea of what the British constitution meant. Even if it wasn't necessarily the best in the world, it worked well enough on principles understood and generally respected by our political leaders. A little over a decade ago this was still broadly true. Some critics were already calling for a Bill of Rights, but the understandings that underlay our system of government were still in place. Then Mrs Thatcher came to power and everything changed. Power, how obtained and how used, is my focus here. We have an unrepresentative government exercising almost unfettered powers (a 'miselected dictatorship', if one corrects Lord Hailsham's phrase) which can be used to impose laws the public does not want and to maintain its own hold on office. Written constitutions, we were often told by smug defenders of the unwritten British system, are no defence against dictatorship if the enemies of democracy can mobilise sufficient force. True enough. But without a revolution or a *coup d'état* our constitution has been used, not to establish a real dictatorship – one must keep a sense of proportion – but to allow a manner of government that must be the least democratic among Western democracies. The point I want to make, in other words, is that the British constitution was always a poor defender of democracy. Democrats didn't abuse it. A new breed of politicians did.

It is suprising how often one hears uncontradicted references to Mrs Thatcher's electoral victories. She lost three elections in a row with a declining share of the vote at that, less in 1983 than in 1979, less in 1987 than in 1983, when she obtained a record low for the Conservative Party. Only 42 per cent of the voters (and only one-third of the electorate) supported her when she was last elected. A substantial majority opposed her. A few years ago I calculated the proportion of voters supporting the government in office in seventeen West European states: Britain came bottom of the list. That raises questions of democratic legitimacy far more serious than discussion about the 'fairness' of the electoral system.

At the same time, many of the policies the Thatcher government imposed through its control of Parliament were rejected by the public when the public was asked (not by the government, of course, but by pollsters), and the broad thrust of government policy seemed the opposite of what most people said they wanted. In fact, opinion polls, as in E. Jacobs and R. Worcester's recent *We British* (1990), show exactly this. In February/March 1989, 78 per cent of those asked approved of higher taxes to improve the National Health Service, 71 per cent to support the elderly and the poor. A number of questions contrasted 'socialist' and 'Thatcherist' values ('Which view of society comes closest to your ideal?'). A society in which caring for others is more highly regarded was favoured by 81 per cent, against 12 per cent who favoured one in which wealth creation is more highly regarded; 54 per cent favoured a society which emphasises the social and collective provision of welfare, against 40 per cent for one where the individual is encouraged to look after himself; 47 per cent favoured a mainly socialist society in which public interest and a more controlled economy are most important, against 39 per cent for a mainly capitalist society in which private interests and free enterprise are most important. In May 1990 only 25 per cent were satisfied with Mrs Thatcher as Prime Minister and only 23 per cent approved her government's record. The Iraq crisis improved her rating somewhat (one thinks back to the Falklands: it seems that military affairs alone put the majority behind her) but this did not last, as opinion polls at the time of the party leadership contest showed.

Well, one might say, never mind the electorate, disregard the opinion polls, it is the performance of government that counts. 'For forms of government let fools contest; whate'er is best administer'd is best.' But did the indicators justify strong, if unpopular, government? Inflation, unemployment, balance of payments, economic growth, interest rates – all seemed to put us low on European league tables. In September 1990 the papers announced record figures for business insolvencies and the CBI warned that a serious recession was imminent. The figures were not better in other fields: crime rate, drug abuse, illegitimate births, homeless youths. We had the highest rate of political killings in Europe. The number of people in relative poverty was increasing, as was the health gap between rich and poor. The papers told of a 75-year old widowed rape vicitim who was deprived of her social-security benefits by a ministry rule which took account of the modest Criminal Injuries Board compensation she received (a ruling civil servants would hardly have made without explicit or assumed ministerial support). We read that ambulances in parts of London would no longer take the blind or amputees to hospital for out-patient treatment. What sort of a society was created by ten years of strong government?

Nor can it be said that the government was efficient even if its policies were a painful medicine to cure our ills, encouraging the disciplines of the market. It staggered from one incompetence to another, ill-considered decisions with embarrassing side-effects, banana-skin misjudgements. The Wright affair, the Westland affair, the Rover affair, the Lawson/Walters affair. More often than not its policies were rejected by its own supporters – football identity cards by the police, students' loans by the banks, high interest rates by industrialists (beating inflation by undiscriminating high interest rates leads to bankruptcies and reduces investment, thus wealth creation). Whatever the theoretical arguments in favour of something like a poll tax, would any practical person have rushed into a scheme so impractical to administer?

How could a government representing a declining minority of the electorate push through radical policies disliked by a majority of the population? The centralisation of power our constitution allows makes it possible, and above all the principle of parliamentary sovereignty which can translate into the sovereignty of a government that controls a disciplined majority in Parliament. Until the Thatcher era such power was held in check less by restraints of public opinion (the British are a remarkably patient, law-abiding people, notwithstanding miners' strikes and anti-poll tax demonstrations) than by the understanding of democracy our ruling politicians showed. Before discussing how the powers available to government could be used and abused in governing the country, however, let us look at how that power was acquired and retained.

That Mrs Thatcher won power with 60 per cent of the voters against her was, of course, the result of the single-member-constituency electoral system. The parliamentary majority the system gave her was not her doing but the result of the failure of the opposition to unite. It does seem odd that one should expect citizens to jump into the fire (if that is how Labour and Liberal Democrats see each other) if they want to get out of the frying pan, but she neither created the system nor abused it. What I want to do here, instead of discussing this well-rehearsed topic, is to run through the ways in which our so-called constitution allows those in power to manipulate elections and influence voters in order to remain in power.

The first point is that governments can plan (or at least try to plan) so that favourable policies or their outputs come on stream at election time. This is not uncommon in other countries, but nowhere else have governments such unfettered power over taxation and spending, for example, as in Britain, where the House of Commons allows budgets to be implemented within minutes of their presentation. And it is clear that raising or lowering income tax, increasing or cutting expenditure on health, education or the police, are looked at with the electorate in mind, however much economic theory is spoken. Certainly that is how the Whitehall-watchers of the press see it, as reflected in newspaper discussion of forthcoming rounds of ministerial budget negotiation.

Linked to this is the power to choose when to hold an election. At the end-of-term address to Conservative backbenchers in July 1990 Mrs Thatcher said: 'I am entitled to ask for a fourth term on our record, but we must look at each possible date and ask are we going to win?' The timing is in the hands of the Prime Minister. I do not think there are many democracies (in fact I can think of none) where it is possible to dissolve Parliament and call an election for no other reason than that the opinion polls look good, or the economy will soon get worse, or a battle has recently been won. As Roy Jenkins put it, it is having a race in which one of the runners is also the starter – and fires the gun when he sees his competitors tying their shoelaces. True, we know that all Prime Ministers play this sort of game, but in the past it seems to have been fairly amateur guesswork with the Prime Minister and a few confidants. Now it has become a professional public-relations business, a different sort of operation altogether. It may be that the public relations/advertising world has blossomed to such an extent in recent years that it is bound to influence all politicians. Nevertheless, I believe the change reflected a change in the character of Conservative politicians. A new breed of Conservative ministers saw government as just another career and used sales techniques just as they would in commerce. Calling an election involved the same sort of decision for them as when to launch a soap-powder campaign.

Then there is the possibility of influencing the electoral roll. It is true that the extension of expatriates' right to vote was approved by Labour in the House of Commons. But it was obviously the product of Conservative strategists, with Labour MPs the innocents, who discover too late they have been tricked by sharp operators. Some 2½ million people who left Britain up to twenty years ago (instead of five, as before) are entitled to vote in British elections. They do not pay taxes in Britain: in many cases, indeed, they left to avoid paying taxes. That is worth emphasising because the government that gave them the vote was the same government that justified the poll tax by saying that voters should pay taxes, otherwise they would vote irresponsibly. But why be consistent when Conservative Central Office estimated that 80 per cent of expatriates would be Conservative supporters? Spread through the USA, Canada, Australia and South Africa, there are also half a million in Spain – and these are relatively easy to organise since they live in expatriate communities. The Conservative Party is busy mobilising them, dinner dances included. And they have been asked to sign a form which authorises Central Office to register them (will it really be possible to ensure that it is in the constituencies in which they lived twenty years ago, or will some appear on the registers of marginal constituencies?) and (at least as an option) appoint a proxy to vote Conservative on their behalf.

If there are double standards as regards 'no representation without taxation', there are also double standards as regards the spending of public money. In addition to Conservative Party spending on the mobilisation of expatriates, the Home Office has allocated £750,000 for the purpose, compared to the £500,000 it made available for electoral registration advertising in this country (where lost electors are more likely to support Labour). That seems to be an example of how the understandings of the unwritten British constitution altered as ministers used public money for what is inescapably party political gain.

The registration of electors brings one to the fact that a record number of adults failed to register in the UK. According to the Office of Population, Census and Statistics, summer 1990 saw 50 per cent fewer of those eligible to register as new voters doing so compared to three years before. Was this an unforeseen, unhoped-for side effect of the poll tax? The likelihood that it would happen had been pointed out, after all. So we got Conservative voters abroad added to the register, Labour voters lost at home.

Conservative spending on national election campaigns seems also to have increased considerably after Mrs Thatcher took over. Whether it achieved anything or not, Lord MacAlpine, the Conservative Treasurer, must have thought he was buying something when he spent £5 million on press advertising over a few days in 1987. The Conservatives can raise money from big business. The chairman of the companies concerned do not have to delve into their own pockets, of course – they use company funds. Ostensibly, they do so because Conservative rule is in their companies' interest (even when government policies seem far from beneficial) – but one suspects that personal advantage is the real motive. The correlation between company donations and chairmen's appearance in the honours list cannot be entirely accidental.

It may be said that this is not new, even if the extent to which Mrs Thatcher favoured businessmen donors is remarkable. It may be said that the law which allows vast company-financed national campaigns is not of her making: it dates from a time when corruption, the buying of votes, was at constituency level. It is significant, however, that Mrs Thatcher put through legislation designed to make it harder for Labour by changing the rules about trade-union political funds, without any thought of applying similar rules to business. A rich sauce for the Conservative goose, but restrict Labour gander's gravy if you can.

Mrs Thatcher also used the honours system to reward and punish MPs: more than a hundred knighthoods for faithful backbenchers, but Julian Critchley, longer serving than most (and long service is the most important criterion), was deliberately excluded (presumably for disloyalty). Her nominations of politician life peers reflected even more clearly political bias and served to benefit her government by starving Labour and Liberals of new blood in the House of Lords, thus affecting the working membership of the legislature.

Then we have the whole range of ways in which the government tried to shape public opinion. The selling of Mrs Thatcher was a case in point. How effective would her speeches have been without the script-writers? An example taken from the press about her last party conference: Mrs Thatcher coached at No. 10 by her script-writing team, the playwright Sir Ronald Miller, a member of her policy unit and a political adviser, for the John Cleese 'dead parrot' section of her party conference speech (the Liberal Democrat parrot bit her at the Eastbourne by-election shortly after, of course). How many would have noticed Mrs Thatcher without her image-builders? Gordon Reece and his successors played a leading role in the Prime Minister's conduct. The moment she left her office, everything became a carefully planned and carefully packaged photo-opportunity: we saw her picking up litter, hard-hatted on a crane, white-coated in a factory, pearled like the Queen at the bedside of disaster victims. All parties resort to advertising and public relations, but the extent to which this dominated what should be the serious work of Prime Minister and ministers is extraordinary – and was surely not the British system of government as we knew it twenty years ago.

It was, moreover, not only party money that was spent on image-making and it was not only party officials that were involved. The government used, and abused, public money (in ministry-financed advertising campaigns that clearly carried a political message) and civil servants (press officers notably) in ways that would almost certainly have been regarded as unconstitutional in earlier times. To give an autumn 1990 example in the press: a £20 million advertising campaign was to boost the government's training and education policy in the run-up to a possible general election the following year; the Prime Minister's favourite advertising agency, Saatchi and Saatchi (responsible for the Conservatives' 1979 election campaign slogan 'Labour isn't working'), were engaged to promote the campaign. The distinction between politician as minister and politician as party advocate, once taken for granted in Whitehall, seemed to have disappeared; indeed, it is doubtful whether it occured to most ministers that such a convention was desirable, at least while their side was in office.

Official information was also manipulated in order to present the government favourably or limit damage to its reputation. Criticism of the deterioration of standards in the publication of official statistics seems to have come to a head recently as the Royal Statistical Society has entered the fray. Of course, there are many ways of calculating unemployment, inflation, health and pollution, different formulae giving different results; and of course there are many ways of presenting such figures, the emphasis given in writing up, for example. What all officials seemed to know as the Thatcher decade

E

went on, however, was that official statistics should show the government in as good a light as possible. There were thirty changes in the way unemployment was counted. Is it a coincidence that only one increased the number of unemployed (and then only a little)? And when the broadcast news announcers told us that unemployment has dropped by a certain number, they rarely added that calculated in the same way as under the last Labour government the total would be far higher – probably because the BBC and ITN were increasingly intimidated by government. We had a government wanting to reduce the inflation rate by changing the way the cost of living index is calculated, excluding mortgage interest rates and the poll tax. That could be a rational proposal, not a politically motivated one. Was it? We were told that other countries put rent levels rather than mortgage interest into the cost of living index and we should too. But wasn't Mrs Thatcher's great aim to replace rented property by a property-owning democracy? We were told that taxes are generally excluded. But wasn't the government's aim in replacing rates to draw the voters' attention to exactly how much their local services were costing – wasn't that why it was called a community charge rather than a tax?

We also have endless examples of reports withheld, rewritten, published too late to catch the news, even on non-political subjects like infected eggs and mad cows, if the government's reputation might suffer. I quote only one example, from a leak to a Sunday paper towards the end of the decade. The government had tried to delay the Metropolitan Police's publication of London crime figures until the Home Office was ready to publish its national figures in order to avoid a double dose of critical headlines. In an internal document Scotland Yard's director of public affairs noted: 'With policing figuring ever more highly on the political agenda, and with the prospect of worsening crime statistics as we approach the general election, it is clear that there are likely to be further calls from the Home Office for co-ordination as they attempt to minimise the polical damage caused by the release of two sets of figures.' Labour's home affairs spokesman rightly described this as a constitutional impropriety of the worst type. The fact that we depend on leaks for much of the information that should not be the government's to edit in any case reminds us that we have the most secretive system of any Western democracy. Governments can employ the Official Secrets Act and civil service regulations to muzzle officials, and the Thatcher government did not hesitate to protect its own reputation by intimidating officials in matters that had nothing to do with national interest and where civil servants elsewhere have a right, in the United States even a duty, to alert the public.

We undoubtedly had a government propaganda system during the Thatcher years. Since we live in a pluralist society with other sources of information, this had limited effect. But one must add that the government tries to muzzle criticism where it could. Thus the continuous pressure on BBC and IBA, partisan appointments, changes in the law, a series of interventions that expressed naked dislike of opposition, indeed any sort of criticism, and a determination to use state power to protect the image of those in power. So intimidated were they that government intervention wasn't even needed. Another example from the press towards the end of the Thatcher period: reports that BBC chiefs axed an interview with convicted former Guinness chairman Ernest Saunders from the *Panorama* programme on Conservative Party finance in which he claimed he was asked to contribute to Tory party funds while lobbying to prevent his 1986 bid for Distillers being referred to the Monopolies Commission; the interview was replaced by one with Norman Tebbit. Why is it that no such pressures were brought to bear on the press which is unashamedly biased and openly partisan; why did the new legislation about broadcasting impartiality not extend to newspapers? It can't be a public/private-sector distinction since the Thatcherite aim was to privatise broadcasting; it can't be a distinction between monopoly and competition since we now have numerous channels separately controlled. Could it be that the press is overwhelmingly pro-Conservative? Power again used for electoral advantage?

We are always told that so long as there are free elections there is democracy. Changes in government can be brought about through the ballot box and with it policies can be changed. There is thus no justification for attempts to force a change in government policy through violence, or even passive resistance (like refusal to pay the poll tax). How does one answer the questioner, though, who asks: do I really have to vote for a government I disagree with in order to get rid of a government I dislike even more because that is the electoral system we have? And, more seriously, if the constitutional system gives such power to the government of the day that it can stack the cards, manipulate the electoral register, fix an election date, adjust policies as it goes to meet that date, use the machinery of government to advertise itself . . . if it can do all the things discussed above and does them, what sort of a democratic game am I being asked to play?

It can be argued that a new breed of politicians colonised the Conservative Party and came to power with Mrs Thatcher, a breed ideally suited to the exploitation of our system of government because it is not constrained by traditional conventions, a breed that either deliberately rejects old rules about the proper conduct of public life for ideological reasons or is simply unfamiliar with them because they are no part of its lifestyle. Much was talked about our conviction politicians, led by Mrs Thatcher, pursuing an ideology and impatient of constraints. They had no time for traditions of consensus, for consultation and negotiation, for bargaining and pluralist power centres. Those who opposed them are the enemies within, indeed, even those who claim to be neutral ranked on the enemy side for there could be no neutrality in Mrs Thatcher's mind. It did not even matter that the public rejected their policies. Like Marxists, Mrs Thatcher believed that this must be false consciousness – people should be forced to be free, individualistic, entrepreneurial – or, less politically, nanny knew best.

But the push behind the Thatcher government was not as ideological as was sometimes made out. Mrs Thatcher had a few simple ideas, the commonplace dinner-table exchanges of her social group, the clichés of that particular chattering class. She was surrounded by people who probably did not even hold such views very strongly, who, indeed, had few serious political views at all. They were careerists who would promote whatever promoted their careers. Those who teach politics like to think that there is a field of activity out there in the real world that is political and can be analysed as such for politics courses. The assumption is that behaviour in political institutions is politically motivated and has a political aim. But that is not necessarily true. Remember Samuel Johnson's view that politics was nothing more than a means of rising in the world? That was true of many in his time and is probably true again. Young Conservatives enter politics as a career option like any other, with good prospects and instant status hard to obtain in other jobs. The House of Commons is increasingly a place of business where members are less likely to pursue professions (law, journalism, even merchant banking) outside the House than to make money as consultants, selling services which they could not sell if they were not in Parliament. The chances of promotion to ministerial office are not bad if one impresses one's superiors. That brings better pay, a car, excellent contacts and lucrative offers after resignation. That is not my theme here, simply that power, and with it the British constitution, have been taken over by raiders whose interest in politics is subservient to their own interests (note: personal not class interests, a different analysis altogether). It is not unlike James Goldsmith's recent bid for one of our largest international concerns. At the time, he justified a takeover bid by talk of unbundling the company, thus promoting managerial efficiency and increased profit for shareholders. It didn't sound unlike Conservative talk about dismantling the state economy and lowering taxes as a result. But the Goldsmith clichés barely disguised the fact that his group hoped to profit itself. One must not exaggerate, of course, so I will restrict myself to the more modest point that such careerists as served the Thatcher leadership saw the conventions of government, the unwritten codes, rather differently from their predecessors, Conservative, Liberal and Labour. The morality of commerce recognises few restrictions apart from those imposed by law (and not always those).

Mrs Thatcher was a different case, but she, too, did not seem to understand democracy as our constitutional system assumes. Here we come to constitutional change. Our system has no superior, entrenched constitutional law. Limitations on government do not depend on a special law enforced by a special court or on a balance of power between branches of government, executive and legislative, between chambers of the legislature or national and provincial authorities. They depend on the unwritten parts of our constitution, the conventions that guide behaviour and constrain power. As the textbooks note, they depend on the willingness of those involved to order their conduct by certain implicit standards. What if those involved have different standards or no standards at all?

It is, of course, hard to know what these conventions are that are supposed to underlie the constitutional order. Because they are not law, there is no clear test that will tell us whether changes in behaviour patterns involve a breach of convention or whether all that has happened is that patterns have changed and there never was a convention at all. The notion of parliamentary government, meaning the responsibility, or answerability, of government to Parliament, is always cited as a fundamental characteristic of the constitution, however. Somehow, it does not seem to fit Mrs Thatcher's conduct. She spent less time in the House of Commons, intervened less in debates, even made fewer set speeches than any of her predecessors according to a survey published in *Public Administration*. Nor did she seem to understand the fundamental British idea that it is the duty of the opposition to oppose and the duty of government to reply: criticism and justification as the discipline of parliamentary democracy. See the Prime Minister's answers to parliamentary questions. The only questions she really answered were, for the most part, planted ones, questions her staff had briefed her supporters to put. At best the opposition got a statement about government policy that praised her record but missed the inconvenient points of the question; follow-up questions were met by a rehearsed repetition, no sign of a mind trying to answer criticism. As often, of course, the answer was an attack on Labour's record in government over a decade before, or on what it might do if returned again – a good propagandist technique (though the strident style into which she sometimes lapsed was counter-productive), perhaps a technique she learnt in her brief training as a barrister: do not answer your opponent but attack his credibility. Whatever the reason for this style, it is a fundamental contradiction of the idea of answerable government which students of British government have long been taught as one of the elements of British democracy.

Much the same can be said of Mrs Thatcher's approach to Cabinet government and collective responsibility, another principle of the British system. Of course, there have been long academic debates about the relationship between Prime Minister and Cabinet, and roles have, of course, changed over time. Domination of the Cabinet, bypassing it through committees, the use of her own advisers to replace ministerial advice, even the announcement of policies on the hoof without consulting her colleagues – all that may just have pushed further along the road several of her predecessors travelled, though it looks more like a qualitative than a quantitative change and certainly led to defeat in her final leadership contest. Her treatment of Cabinet colleagues, her behaviour to them in public for example, the use of her press secretary to undermine them – those clearly went beyond anything that convention, or decent behaviour, would allow.

One could go on about the way in which the style of government changed, asking whether such changes involved a breach of unwritten conventions (the constitution as practice as opposed to law). The way patronage was used might be another example. If there is one virtue in public life, wrote Hugo Young in the *Guardian* recently, that Mrs Thatcher and her circle sought systematically to extinguish, it was impartiality. The result could be seen in every quango from health authority to BBC governors, from university funding body to environmental protection agency, from schools to arts associations. Partiality shrieked from every committee and board. The 'great and the good' were replaced by 'one of us'. The idea of balanced representation also went: the 'us' tended to be small businessmen, at provincial levels at least. So much for the tradition that certain quangos, BBC and IBA, University Grants Council and Arts Council, represented a form of arm's-length government that was an essential part of British democracy. So much for the idea that the representation of interests, unions as well as employers, was another part of that system.

There is another aspect to constitutional change, not changes in the style of those who govern us but changes in the structure of our system of government itself. Here again we have a problem: given our non-documentary constitution, there is no way of knowing what institutions actually form part of the constitutional order. When legislation alters the structure of our system of government, how do we decide whether the constitution has changed or something less important? Fundamental changes in local government, however, must surely be constitutional change: local government, after all, has often been described, certainly to foreigners, as an essential part of democracy. Yet the legislation that altered the system required no special procedures, could be passed by an unrepresentative majority in Parliament with only the sketchiest mandate for such action, much contrary, in any case, to public opinion.

This is not the place to describe the changes. As regards structures, we had the abolition of the Greater London Council (later on the Inner London Education Authority also) and the metropolitan counties, slipped into an election manifesto at the last moment by Mrs Thatcher without sensible planning, leaving conurbations fragmented as in no other West European country and, whatever rationalisation were offered, clearly the result of partisan spite. We have had the dismantling of functions and growing intervention in those that remain. Urban development corporations, appointed by the government, took over in certain areas. There was the forced sale of council houses, followed by housing action trusts, and the forced contracting-out of services. Intervention in education, on teacher's pay, was followed by the national curriculum (shades of Napoleon!), autonomy from local authorities in school management, opting out and business-led (though government financed) city technology colleges. Control over finance was equally dramatic, rate and expenditure capping, followed by the replacement of rates by the community charge. Any or all of these may be sensible reforms (though there hardly seems a majority of opinion for most), but they add up to a fundamental change, not just in structure or functions but in the role local government can play and the independence it enjoys.

Local government changes reflected something else apart from the near-dictatorial imposition of undesired reforms whipped through a disciplined parliamentary party. They showed an amateur style of government that reflected personal rule, ideas picked up by ministers from the clique of ivory-tower ideologists (Adam Smith Institute, Centre for Policy Studies) they talk to, deliberately avoiding Royal Commissions that might give undesirable advice and ensuring that civil servants do not confuse them with such advice either. The result was a record of inefficiency in implementing policies almost unparalled in recent British history. The confusion about services after the abolition of metropolitan councils can only be explained by the fact that ministers were unaware of many of the things the councils actually did. The complications following the introduction of the community charge were unbelievable: ministers had to introduce one alleviating measure after another, reliefs and rebates, safety nets to redistribute income between authorities, then charge capping – which of course destroyed the whole argument that the new tax allowed voters to judge their councillor's stand on expenditure for themselves. The difficulties of collecting the new tax, and the expense this involved, were left for local authorities to shoulder. A businessman who had planned a new production so sloppily would be rightly bankrupted – and perhaps it was only right that market forces should have started the collapse of Thatcher & Co. as market surveys showed the poll-tax offers of a competitor, Heseltine Ltd, were leading voters to switch custom. Inefficiency, caused by the isolation of ideologists and power-holders from real life, was not a special case, however. Many illustrations could be cited. The Department of Employment and the Manpower Services Commission, for example, produced new schemes for job creation and vocational training at what seemed like monthly intervals, each sold as the perfect solution and each replaced shortly after.

Local government reform also shows the use partisan ministers can make of their powers. We noted earlier the way statistics can be manipulated to improve the government's image. They were manipulated to allow the government to help Conservatives and hit Labour. When charge capping was decided, a formula had to be found. Civil servants were doubtless told to run every possible formula through the computer to see which would have the desired effect. How else can we explain the ingenuity of the minister's decision: it allowed twenty authorities, all Labour, to be charge capped, including Brent (expenditure up by 1.4 per cent on the previous year) and Calderdale (proposed charge £297), while excluding Conservative Berkshire (expenditure up 20.6 per cent) and Windsor (charge £449). And when, later, Lambeth appealed against the minister's decision to reduce the charge it had set (taking account of revenues it was unable to collect), and won in the High Court and the Court of Appeal, the government indicated that new legislation would prevent such judicial review in future. Can one really talk of constitutional government when those with a will to do so can exercise such discretionary power in so political a fashion?

Mrs Thatcher said often enough that she was committed to rolling back government, not just in the economy but in the fields of health, welfare and education, where private provision and individual choice were to replace the deadening hand of the nanny state. Much has therefore been made of the paradox of growing central-government power. Some have contrasted the areas in which freedom is to be given, economy and welfare state, with those in which stronger discipline is needed than before, law and order and public morality. That doesn't explain the shift in power to central government as regards local government, however. The explanation there may be that Mrs Thatcher was also committed to the elimination of socialism from British life, and Labour-controlled authorities are socialism to this reversed Marxist doctrine that a dictatorship of Conservatives is needed until the influence of Labour is eradicated, when the state can wither away. Or, a commoner answer to the paradox, that power is needed to destroy power. Or do such ideological explanations miss the point? Is it simply that Mrs

Thatcher was something of a nanny who knew what was right in every case (football matches included) and could not bear others not doing it. It is simply that her ministers (with the notable exception of laid-back Nicholas Ridley who did want his Department of Industry to wither away) could not resist the temptations of power and found that there was little in our system of government to stop them once they had broken traditional self-restraints?

Other fields of change clearly include the core of government, Prime Minister, Cabinet and ministers, though here we are largely back in the unwritten constitution, style rather than law, as suggested earlier. The same is perhaps true as regards the changing character of the civil service. Prime-ministerial intervention in top appointments is an example. Changes in civil service conditions of employment are more formal, though they require no legislation either. Since our politically neutral civil service is supposed to serve successive governments of different political complexion with equal loyalty, perhaps major changes should be agreed between government and the opposition, described in older textbooks as the government in waiting after all. Perhaps one should remember that loyal though the civil service has been to successive masters, it has in the past seen itself, and been seen by many others, as an element of continuity and balance in our system. If Mrs Thatcher turned it into more of a tool of the government in power, its top ranks of can-do yes-men zealously pushing through whatever politicians of the day wanted, is there not a danger that they may serve more dictatorial government with equal vigour – even, though Mrs Thatcher seems not to have thought of it, a socialist one? The dismanting of ministries is another obvious example. The *Next Steps* programme foresees the hiving off of many functions to executive agencies, eventually covering some two-thirds of the civil service. This may seem an administrative rather than political question, and certainly it has not aroused much party conflict. It is a constitutional question nevertheless. The case for taking large chunks of administration out of ministries was that they were not concerned with policy-making, thus politics, but with the implementation of policies, thus management. The phrase used, however, was that they were responsible for delivering services to the public, and if they are at the interface between administration and the public that does raise some issues. The traditional British doctrine of ministerial responsibility is that ministers are responsible for all the actions of their civil servants (even low-level decisions affecting individuals) and must answer for them to Parliament. That doctrine has long been something of a facade, less effective than the system of administrative courts developed in other countries to protect the citizen against administrative decisions. If agencies enjoy managerial autonomy and are run in a businesslike way, will grievances be handled in the same way as customer complaints in your bank or department store? This is not the place to discuss the implications of the Next Steps reform, simply to note once more how easy constitutional change seems to be.

Is privatisation a constitutional issue? Perhaps in so far as the selling off of the family silver is concerned. Shouldn't that have been done with some attempt at agreement of all the family? The assets sold were not the property of the Conservative government but of the nation. And, to return to an earlier theme, though the goal was to expand the market economy and gain the benefits of private enterprise, a by-product, clearly planned for, was that the money received could be used to lower taxes (or at least avoid raising them), thus persuading the electorate to vote for the government. A little more sharp practice, perhaps?

There is no space to run through the many other fundamental changes that occurred, as in the National Health Service. Let us simply emphasise two points in concluding. First, our so-called constitution allows a resolute politician who doesn't want to play according to the unwritten rules, who isn't an officer and a gentleman, almost unlimited power. All the traditional textbook talk about democracy safeguarded by conventions turns out to be nonsense. There is no other way of explaining a government that had 60 per cent of the voters against it when elected imposing policies that even larger numbers rejected. I doubt if there is another democracy where this could happen. Second, because we do not have a documentary constitution, or a body of constitutional law defined as such, we seem hardly aware of the constitutional (as distinct from political) significance of what is happening when what we think of as our system of government is altered – not 'growing like Topsy', the flexible adaptation of which textbooks were so proud, but with radical shifts in power structure. Written constitutions can not stop revolutions or *coups d'etat*, but they help prevent the erosion of democracy by salami-slicing tactics through judicial review and legislative procedures for amendment. They do make it clear that

certain changes in the system of government are fundamental,
flagging them up, demanding that they are handled with greater care,
not whipped through Parliament in the same way as everyday legislation.

The real legacy of the last decade will not, I think, be some
transformation of our society and culture, Mrs Thatcher's apparent
great plan. Indeed, many of her policies may go with her and we may
find ourselves back with something closer to the mixed-economy
welfare state that most West European democracies have hardly
tried to dismantle on her scale. Much of her style of government is
also likely to go and we may find ourselves back at the consensual,
corporate, pluralist system of earlier times. What her decade will
have shown is that we had lived in something of a fool's paradise
before she came to power, thinking that we had a fine constitution,
only to discover that we had no real constitution at all. The lesson, in
other words, is that power needs to be distributed if it is to be tamed.
The project of the next decade, will be to bring Britain back into the
fold of Western democracies by giving it a democratic constitution.

# Voting behaviour and the party system

Voting behaviour is a subject which did not exist when I started my academic career forty-five years ago, so I am something of a museum piece, one who was in at the beginning. It is now a central feature of every textbook and every course on the political system. Talking about it and its evolution enables me to illustrate some fundamental considerations about the study of politics, considerations that every teacher should keep at the forefront of his thinking. What I say will be familiar. Yet I hope it will also be mildly disturbing.

I am proud to have been President of the Politics Association and I am glad that it is the Politics Association and not the Political Science Association. In a long Anglo-American career I have always been unhappy about the phrase 'political science' and about the distractions that the scientific ideal has created in so many approaches to the problems that I regard as a centre of our study, the ways in which man relates to the state and the ways in which power is actually exercised in the modern state. I do not believe that there is anything worthwhile that we can say about politics which is an eternal truth. Every interesting proposition about the ways in which Britain is governed seems to me to be just a probability statement, an assertion about norms, a guess at the rules of the game prevailing at a particular period of time in this particular part of the world. It is not and can never be an eternal verity.

What I want to do today is to illustrate this theme with five propositions about voting behaviour and the working of the party system. Most of the truths on these subjects that I and all other mainstream teachers of politics were trying to inculcate forty years ago are no longer the right thing to say to our students. One of the comforts of aging is that it gives one a longer perspective; first-hand experience of how life was ordered at different moments in history, makes one conscious of Heraclitus' dictum – 'Everything moves', or of the Chinese wisdom – 'No man can jump in the same river twice; both the man and the river change.'

I use British examples to illustrate how the rules of the game change with the passage of time, but I could equally be writing this chapter in a comparative mode to show how the rules of the game work differently in different environments. For twenty years the USA was my second country; then in middle life I encountered and fell in love with Australia; and now in the last decade I have developed a great interest in India and Indian politics. In all these milieux I have tried to use my British experience to understand another country. With the USA this seldom worked, but with Australia and India it worked surprisingly often. In each of these countries there was the same transience about the rules of the game. Each differed from their own institutions a few years back. Each too differed in its own way from the British model which had once shaped their institutions. Each illustrated the relativity of political truths both in space and time.

Let me now turn to my five examples. The first deals with the practical working of the electoral system. To certain temperaments one of the attractions of the study of elections is that, unlike most political phenomena, elections involve well-advertised quantities. Individual votes can be tabulated in many different ways and then analysed. This process involves the certainties of mathematics as opposed to the uncertainties of our ordinary political generalisations – generalisations about, say, prime-ministerial behaviour or back-bench influence. I have spent my life studying elections but I have always been unhappy about too quantitative an approach. Let me cite two reasons. One lies in the vote itself. Many of my friends, when they vote, are making an unqualified ringing assertion: 'By God, yes, I am Conservative and I support my side – or I am Labour and I support my side.' But when I vote I am making an extremely hesitant statement: 'By and large, by a narrow margin, this party is, probably, for the moment, slightly the lesser evil.' Yet my uncertain vote, which could have easily gone the other way, is counted as exactly the equivalent to my friends' resounding statement of faith. Should that be so? Let me offer a second reason for misgivings about building too much on the quantitative analysis of voting. A general election result is a collective assertion of partisan choice at one moment of time.

Rain on polling day, or an extraneous event the day before, may easily affect 1 or 2 per cent of votes – enough to produce a very different version of the nation's verdict, the mandate which the winning party will use as its justification for the next five years. Ultra-sophisticated conclusions about the will of the people based on voting figures always leave me sceptical.

But, leaving those hesitations on one side, electoral systems are seen as arrangements for converting popular votes into parliamentary seats with predictable regularity. As we all know, in Britain, with our majoritarian, first-past-the-post, arrangements, small majorities of votes can be exaggerated into much larger majorities in seats. The greatest moment of intellectual excitement in my life came forty years ago when I was writing my thesis. I stumbled upon the dusty and unread minutes of evidence of the Royal Commission on Electoral Systems of 1910. In them, one John Parker Smith put forward the hypothesis that under the British electoral system, if votes were divided between two parties in the ratio A to B, seats would be divided in the ratio $A^3$ to $B^3$. Applying this long forgotten 'Cube Law' to the results of the latest three elections I found, wonder of wonders, that it fitted almost perfectly. I wrote it up in an article (alas! anonymous) in the *Economist* in January 1950 and the Cube Law suddenly became famous. And it went on working remarkably accurately so that it seemed to offer an 'Iron Law' of British politics. In the elections of the 1950s and the 1960s, it offered a simple description of the way in which a 1 per cent movement in votes produced a switch of seats in Parliament of roughly 3 per cent. Eighteen seats changed hands for each 1 per cent swing. But in the 1970s this law, which had operated with extraordinary accuracy from 1931 to 1970, suddenly went sour. It degenerated from a Cube Law into a Square Law and then into a law of about the power 1.6.

Let us put that into practical terms. Instead of 18 seats changing hands for each one per cent of votes swinging between Conservative and Labour, only 12 seats in 1974, and then only 9 seats in 1983 changed hands for each 1 per cent swing. What had happened was that the number of marginal seats (defined as seats where the majority was under 10 per cent) had fallen from around 180 from the first twenty-five years after the war down to a mere 80 in the elections of 1979, 1983 and 1987. Fewer seats were now vulnerable. If the Cube Law had worked in 1987 as it did in 1959, Mrs Thatcher would have won 450 seats not 376. This arithmetic transformation was not due to any basic change in the way that politics at the centre were conducted. It was explicable in terms of the demographic changes which turned the inner cities to safe Labour and the suburbs and rural areas to solidly Conservative. The contrast in the political map of England between 1950 and 1987 is extraordinary. Liverpool and Glasgow in 1945 gave a majority both of votes and of seats to the Conservatives; now neither city has a single Conservative Member of Parliament. From 1945 to 1966 the Labour Party won seats scattered all over the south of England; now outside London it has only three MPs below a line from the Wash to the Severn. That is my first illustration. In the 1950s and 1960s one could put forward the Cube Law as one of the more certain regularities of British politics. Now it has ceased to be so.

My second illustration is less technical and deals with the style of electioneering. The law governing elections has hardly changed since the 1930s, yet a comparison of what happened in the elections of 1950 and 1951 with what happened in 1983 and 1987 reveals an extraordinary change. At the local level, public meetings went down. In 1950, 30 per cent said that they went to a public meeting; 3 per cent said so in 1987. In 1951, 44 per cent said they were canvassed by the Conservatives; only 19 per cent said so in 1987. The size of the canvassing armies has been much more than halved. The number of constituencies in which the perfect Victorian model, where a complete canvass, a full manning of the polling stations, and an efficient machinery for knocking up was even attempted must have fallen from a few hundred to a few score. At the centre, the contrast is even more extreme. Think of 1950 with Mr Attlee driven around by his wife from great city to great city with only a single detective in the back seat, addressing a big rally each night and a few marketplace and street-corner meetings during the day. Think of Churchill going out about ten times during the campaign by train to a mass rally. Each leader made his appeal through big evening speeches aimed at the morning papers. There were no press conferences to make the headlines; television did not cover the election at all; the radio only put on slightly stilted fifteen or twenty minute talks by party leaders; the new bulletins eschewed all reference to campaign speeches.

Compare that with 1987. Think of Mrs Thatcher and Mr Kinnock sent out by their media advisers for early morning photo-opportunities designed for the lunchtime bulletins; then on to press conferences; then launched into the country by battle-bus or car cavalcade for an afternoon appearance in time for the television bulletins; and then, on several evenings during the campaign, a massive interview with Robin Day, David Dimbleby or Alistair Burnet. The use of time, the language employed, the conscious strategic development of the election massage has been transformed. This transformation has been due more than anything to the way in which the morning newspaper had been supplanted by television as the main means of mass communication. But there have also been technical advances in opinion polling, in market research, and in advertising expertise. The description of electioneering which I set out in *The British General Election of 1951* offers a very obsolete picture of how British democracy elections work in the 1990s.

Let me turn to a third, more technical, matter. Since 1950 one phrase more than any other has been central to the study of voting behaviour. The concept of 'party identification', as developed at the University of Michigan, underlines all modern voting studies. When Donald Stokes came from Michigan in 1963 to help me launch Britain's first nationwide academic study of voting behaviour, he insisted that we should include in our schedule of questions not only the obvious, 'How will you (or how did you) vote?' but that other regular from the Michigan stable, 'As of today, would you describe yourself as Conservative, Labour, Liberal or what?' I argued with him that the latter was an unnecessary question because in Britain people would give the same answer to it as to the voting question. In the surveys that we did in 1963, 1964 and 1966 I was, more or less, justified by our findings – there was a negligible difference between party identification and voting intention. However, in 1969 we conducted a survey at time when the Labour government was at an exceptionally low point in the opinion polls, and we found that, although Labour was 13 per cent behind the Conservatives, a majority of voters still said that they regarded themselves as Labour. Party identification had justified itself.

It has justified itself even more in recent times as the electorate has become more volatile. The strength of party identification has declined spectacularly, although almost 90 per cent of the population are still willing to accept a party label. In the 1960s, 42 per cent said they felt very strongly attached to their party, in 1987 only 19 per cent said the same. When opinion polls, like by-elections, show incredibly sharp short-term swings, it is well to go back to the concept of party identification. Yet the decline in intensity of party loyalty causes the concept of identification to mean something very different from what it did in the 1950s. It is worth exploring briefly why electoral volatility has shot up so much. Let me offer four summary explanations.

The first lies in Britain having become a more educated society. In 1945 more than 90 per cent of the population left school at fifteen. Now no one leaves school before sixteen and the number going on to tertiary education has increased at least fivefold. Education sometimes opens the mind. Even more it encourages the educated to believe that they have an open mind.

Second, the structure of British society has changed. Let two statistics suffice to illustrate a comprehensive transformation. In 1945, 32 per cent of us lived in owner-occupier houses; now 68 per cent do. In 1945 68 per cent of us earned our living in manual occupations; now only 49 per cent do. The politics of a country that is over half white collar are very different from those of the country where two-thirds were blue collar. The politics of a country where two-thirds are house-owners are very different from those of a country where less than one-third were house-owners. But it is not just the change in individual circumstances that explains the change in politics and voting behaviour. This demographic alteration has occurred all over the country and affected almost every family. People no longer live in solidary groups, as the miners in their tied cottages used to among neighbours and friends all linked to the mines. Now some of their family will have gone on to higher education, and even more to white-collar occupations. The 70 per cent plus Labour vote manifest in thirty mining constituencies in 1950 no longer exists. Only in four seats in South Wales did the Labour vote top 70 per cent in 1987.

A third reason for the increase in volatility surely lies in the recognition of Britain's decline in world status and in the failure of any party to check that decline. The end of Empire and the country's slippage in the international economic league table came home to people in the 1960s. At first they could blame the decline on the wicked Tories, with their 'thirteen wasted years'. But then Labour took over and they could blame the silly socialist nostrums of Mr Wilson's government. Then the Conservatives came back with Mr Heath in 1970 and there was the U-turn. Labour got back in 1974 but once again things failed to improve. It became harder and harder in this period to remain a true believer, to stay convinced that any one political party has within it the seeds of truth, the answer to the nation's ills.

However the fourth factor which has surely been the most important in the transformation of electoral behaviour has been the transformation of political communication with the coming of television. Between 1955 and 1965 Britain moved from a nation which had few television viewers and no television coverage of politics to one in which almost everyone had access to a television set and television covered politics comprehensively. In those ten short years, according to the polls, television totally usurped the place of newspapers as the prime source of political information for the great mass of our fellow citizens.

Television coverage of politics is perhaps more balanced in Britain than anywhere else in the world. The BBC (by Charter) and the ITV (by Statute) are required to maintain equity between the parties. They give equal time, if not within programmes, at least between programmes. Very often that has just meant putting one Conservative and one Labour politician in front of the cameras to argue the parties' positions. Wanting to have an articulate discussion, broadcasters usually choose Oxbridge smoothies, who first-name each other and, while they disagree, disagree in a fashion which, both in language and in substance, makes plain how much more they each have in common with their opponent than with members of their own party who are not in Parliament. Moreover, the performers know that, being uninvited guests in people's homes, they must not argue stridently as they do in the hustings or in Parliament; to use that sort of aggressive language would be as disagreeably bad manners as it would be to have a flaming row with your spouse while dining with friends. This muted television dialogue has implicitly taught the public a basic truth about democracy: it only works if 80 per cent of people agree on 80 per cent of the political agenda – if, in Balfour's words, the politicians are so fundamentally united that they can safely afford to bicker. A public that has learnt its politics from the full coverage offered by British television over the last thirty years is unlikely to be as deeply partisan as the previous generation which, living in more socially uniform areas and getting its news from a single partisan newspaper, was less cross-pressured. Volatility has come to stay. When we talk about voting behaviour today we are talking about something decidedly different from voting behaviour in the 1950s.

Let me turn to a fourth issue – a very different one. Do we have a two-party system? It is easy to make the case that we do. Leaving out the Northern Irish, over 90 per cent of MPs elected between 1885 and 1918 were Conservative or Liberal; since 1945 over 95 per cent of MPs have been Conservative or Labour. The only moment when we seemed to have a full-blown three-party system was in 1922 and 1923, when each of three parties got over 100 seats. On the other hand, it is easy to make the case that we do not and never have had a two-party system. Other groups have always existed and always have had the possibility of winning parliamentary seats. From 1910 to 1945 there were only five years when we had single-party majority government. From 1910 to now, there have only been two elections when one party has secured over 50 per cent of the vote.

Obviously in the last twenty years our ideas have gone through considerable change. In 1955 Liberal MPs were elected in only six seats (three of them due to Conservative abstention) and the party secured only 2.4 per cent of the vote. It was then possible to talk unequivocally of a two-party system. In the 1980s it has been much harder to take that attitude. We now have Northern Irish parties which have severed all connections with the British parties. We also have Scottish and Welsh Nationalists with a moderately secure, though small, foothold. And there are the centre parties which have moved up to over 20 per cent of the vote and over twenty seats.

Of course the drama of drastic realignment, which seemed plausible in the first flush of Social Democratic Party success, has evaporated, but are we to tell our students that the apparent return to two-party dominance evidenced in the opinion polls since 1987 is a permanent thing? that parties and voters have once again adapted to the necessary realities of parliamentary government in a reasonably homogeneous country using a first-past-the-post electoral system?

We all teach about the logic that fosters two parties: the rectangular chamber which divides parliamentarians into government and opposition and makes it hard for the lesser opposition party to distinguish itself; and the pressure on the major parties always to try to hold onto the floating central vote that gives the main parties such an enormous incentive to hew towards the middle, leaving no space for a centre party. It was possible to argue that the upsurge of the centre in the early 1980s was almost entirely due to the seeming extremism of both Conservative and Labour and to predict that before long the major parties would move back closer to each other, squeezing the centre. However, although history is very often cyclical, it is not circular: we do not return to exactly the same patterns as before. The new volatility, which made possible those extraordinary triumphs for the SDP and the Liberals early in the 1980s, makes it possible for them or for other parties to do the same again. The Green upsurge in the Euro-elections of 1989 may not be repeated but the possibility of a breakthrough by them or by some other new grouping through the fortunate incidence of a by-election is there. I do not think we should assume that the renewed form of two-party system, to which we now seem to have returned, is there for all time.

My last point concerns party structure. The most influential book on British politics since the war was, I would contend, Bob McKenzie's *British Political Parties*. It was published in 1954. It caused an immense stir because it argued, against all conventional wisdom, that the Conservative Party was in practical terms as democratic as the Labour Party and that, in both parties, power rested in the parliamentary party. It assaulted the traditional idea that in the Labour Party power flowed upwards and that in the Conservative it flowed downwards. Bob McKenzie pointed out that more Conservative leaders have been ousted, or in danger of ousting, than Labour leaders. Bob McKenzie touched up that book once or twice but he died in 1982 just when he was going to attempt a drastic revision. He was a close friend of mine; I saw a lot of him when he was writing the original version and I discussed the rewriting with him. But I never believed that the rewrite was a good idea because the world had moved on. Yet perhaps the original text stands the test of time better than it seemed to do twenty years ago. Bob spent a lot of his time on television and in his lectures defending his original thesis, even when the Labour Party seemed to have changed from the model he saw in 1945–55. In the 1960s the praetorian guard of union leaders ceased to provide a united phalanx around the parliamentary leadership, defending them from the impractical idealism of their rank and file. The Labour Party of Clement Attlee was very far from the Labour Party that Harold Wilson and Jim Callaghan had to contend with in the 1970s. Ten years ago Tony Benn and all that he stood for seemed to have turned McKenzie's thesis on its head. Yet perhaps we have now come full circle and the Labour Party has come to heel. Neil Kinnock has as little trouble with the unions as Clement Attlee, and the parliamentary party today seems at least as solid as

Clement Attlee's was. For a while Bob McKenzie's thesis appeared more threatened by the Conservative Party's switching to direct election of the leader for that, paradoxically, seemed to entrench the leader. But the fall of Thatcher, like the fall of Heath may be regarded as a vindication of McKenzie. However, what I am concerned to show here is simply the variation, over the last thirty-five years, in the validity of his analysis of power in British parties.

These are my five examples – I could have cited others (electoral reform, hung parliaments, nationalisation, devolution) where the wisdom we dispensed in 1960 or 1975 would seem very obsolete today. But my five examples are enough to illustrate how in the last forty years the rules of politics have changed or fluctuated. I hope these examples will serve as a warning that whatever we teach our students now about the working of the political system is likely to be wrong forty years hence. Its not our fault that we get it wrong; the world changes in unpredictable ways. But it will be our fault if we suggest to our students that we are teaching eternal verities, or that the study of politics is more than the study of ephemeral norms which seem to explain current political behaviour.

However, the fact that what we are saying is uncertain does not mean that it is unimportant. It is because the behaviour of our political masters, whether they be our MPs or our fellow-voters does continually affect our own well-being that it is worth studying. For, as Aristotle said, 'The purpose of politics is not knowledge but action.'

# The House of Commons: from overlooked to overworked

One of the most remarkable features of the House of Commons has been the enormous growth in the demands made of it over the past twenty years. Those demands have come from different sources. As a result, Members of Parliament have had to respond in different ways. A consequence has been a massive increase in the workload of the House and its Members. The resources available have increased over the same period but have failed to keep pace. There is the danger of parliamentary overload, of MPs not being able to keep up with the work expected of them. Some are already staggering under the pressure. The most significant challenge faced now by the House is that of coping in the 1990s with the threat of being overloaded.

## A multi-functional House

To understand the demands made of it, one has to look at the nature of the House of Commons. It has never been simply a law-'making' body. As Robert Packenham has observed, legislatures have a number of consequences for their respective political systems.[1] Allocating values through law-making is the one most often associated with them, but often is not the most significant. Law-making is an important function of the United States Congress, but Congress is very much the exception. Packenham identifies eleven consequences under three headings: legitimation; recruitment, socialisation and training; and political decision-making or influence. As he concedes, these will vary in importance from country to country.

In the United Kingdom, political scientists have tended to concentrate on the decision-making function. A consequence has been a general neglect of Parliament. In the 1960s and 1970s, the

burgeoning discipline of political science was concerned with identi-
fying those who did make the decisions. It was not Members of
Parliament. Study of the House of Commons was consequently not
at the forefront of the discipline. What literature there was on the
subject was disparate and criticised by Samuel Patterson for being
unduly atheoretical and anecdotal.[2]

Thus, twenty years ago, the House of Commons was relatively
neglected. There was little recognition of the other consequences that
the House had for the political system. Concentration on relations
between Parliament and government obscured the nature and extent
of the relations between Parliament and the citizen. Yet organised
interests, pressure groups and constituents have variously made
demands of Members of Parliament. How MPs have responded to
those demands has consequences for the political system. And those
demands have increased in recent years.

## The demands made of the House

The increased demands made of the House emanate from at least five
separate sources.

### From government

Legitimation is the oldest function of the House of Commons.
Knights and burgesses were first summoned to the King's Council in
order to give assent to the King's request for additional aids. Not
only does it remain a core function of the House, it has become more
important since the enlargement of the franchise in the nineteenth
century. As Ralph Miliband has noted, election has rendered illegitimate any radical alternative to seeking change.[3] The House is at the
heart of a process accepted by citizens as the sole authoritative
process for rendering legitimate measures of public policy which are
to be binding. Consequently, government is dependent on the House
for giving its approval to requests for money and legislation.

Relatively early in its history, the House of Commons also
acquired for itself the power to discuss the measures brought before
it. It became a deliberative body. The writing of statutes was taken
from the King's scribes and undertaken instead by the Commons.
From that emerged the process which we now have, of a Bill having
to undergo three readings in the House with committee and report
stages between Second and Third Reading.

The increase in government responsibilities in the late nineteenth century and more especially in the twentieth century has resulted in more public general legislation being enacted. The House of Commons has become much busier in having to find the time to discuss and give assent to such measures. This increase has become especially marked in the period since 1970. There has been a remarkable growth not in the number of Bills introduced each year but in their length. Before 1950, no more than 1,000 pages of public general acts were passed each year. From 1950 onwards, the number surpassed 1,000 and by 1970 had reached 1,500 pages. In the majority of sessions since 1980, the number of pages has considerably exceeded 2,000 pages: in 1985 it exceeded 3,000.[4] There has been a similar increase in the number of pages of Statutory Instruments passed by Parliament.

Some of the increase in the volume of legislation is accounted for by consolidation measures, drawing together in one measure existing law on a particular subject. The rest, though, is the consequence of extensive government Bills. Among the more substantial measures of recent years have been the 1986 Financial Services Act, the 1988 Education Reform Act and the 1989 Water Act. The Education Reform Bill needed more parliamentary time (200 hours) than any previous post-war measure. The bill was almost 300 (A4) pages in length. The Water Bill was almost 350 pages. To get such measures through, government has resorted increasingly to the use of timetabling (guillotine) motions. In the 1988/89 session, a record number of guillotines – ten – was used.

Just over half the time of the House is taken up with discussing government Bills. However, the real burden of the increased volume of legislation falls on committees. Since the 1960s, it has been quite common for an average session to witness more than 300 standing committee sittings; before that time, fewer than 200 sittings was the norm. When meetings of standing committees on statutory instruments are added, the figures are starker still. Twenty years ago, such committees did not exist: now there will be between 45 and 95 sittings in a session.

The House is creaking under the strain. There is a limited number of MPs available to serve. Sharp sessional variations in the number of committee sittings are not matched by similar variations in the number of Members serving on committees. The greater the volume of legislation, the greater the demands made on the finite number of members of Parliament.

*From pressure groups*
The House of Commons fulfils other functions identified by
Packenham. These include interest articulation – representing the
needs and demands of the community and of particular groups to
government – and tension release, acting as a channel through which
the views of groups and individuals may be authoritatively
expressed. These are not functions that have been recently acquired.
In the fourteenth century, the House began to make the granting of
aid conditional on a redress of grievances: the first clear instance of
this was in 1309.[5] The House developed as an important conduit for
those in the realm seeking redress from the King.

What is of contemporary relevance is the extensive use made by
pressure groups of the House to articulate their demands and
opinions. Lobbying of Parliament by organised interests is not new –
indeed, as already inferred, it has extensive historical antecedents –
but the volume of it now has served to change qualitatively the
relationship between the House and outside interests. From being a
relatively neglected institution, the preserve especially of hopeless
causes (lobbying MPs when all else has failed), the House of Commons has become a magnet for groups of all descriptions. Since
1980, the House has in effect been discovered by sectional interest
groups.

Lobbyists are now familiar figures at Westminster.[6] Before 1980,
hardly any firms of lobbyists existed. Today, there are more than
thirty such firms and probably several hundred lobbyists of one
description or another. Some firms and pressure groups hire professional lobbyists (political consultants); others, such as BP, have
in-house lobbyists. A 1985 survey of 180 sizable companies found
that more than 40 per cent hired professional help. Another survey
the following year, of 250 organised groups, found that a minority
hired lobbyists but that the vast majority maintained contact with
one or more Members of Parliament (Table 9.1).
A consequence is that MPs are showered with material from outside
groups. Groups employing effective political consultants tend to
target appropriate MPs. Groups relying on their own resources tend
to use more often a blunderbuss approach, sending material to most
or all MPs. Members serving on standing committees will receive
extensive briefing material and requests to table amendments from

Table 9.1   *Organised groups: contact with Parliament*

| Type of contact | % | No. |
|---|---|---|
| Regular or frequent contact with MPs | 74.4 | 189 |
| Presented written evidence to a select committee | 65.6 | 166 |
| Regular or frequent contact with peers | 58.7 | 148* |
| Presented oral evidence to a select committee | 49.0 | 124 |
| Contacts with all-party groups | 47.6 | 120* |
| Contacts with party subject groups or committees | 40.9 | 103* |

Based on questionnaire to 253 organised groups.
*1 respondent did not answer.

*Source:*   M. Rush, *Parliament and Pressure Politics* (Oxford University Press, 1990) 14.

groups affected by the Bills under consideration.[7] A number of groups will request meetings with Members. Extensive contact will take place between lobbyists and sympathetic Members, often in the committee corridor. During the committee stage of the 1986 Financial Services Bill, for example, about eighty references were made by members to the representations they had received from outside groups.

The reasons for this increase in lobbying appear to be several. The House of Commons is relatively more independent in its behaviour. Since 1970, government backbenchers have proved willing on occasion to vote against their own side, on occasion forcing concessions from government.[8] There has thus been a greater potential for lobbying to bear fruit. The most visible and dramatic recent example of such lobbying proving successful was in April 1986, when the Shops Bill went down to defeat on Second Reading: 72 Conservative MPs voted against it.[9] Most lobbying is less visible and less dramatic, focusing instead on achieving amendments at committee stage.

Structural changes have also been important. The departmental select committees introduced in 1979 constitute magnets for organised groups (see Table 9.1). They represent a means of specialisation which previously the House lacked and they offer a channel through which groups can make their case. And whereas the government essentially controls the timetable on the floor of the House, select committees are responsible for determining their own agenda. As government since 1979 has given the impression of wanting to divorce itself from the grip of corporatist negotiation, so groups have perceived a need to find an alternative source of access to government through Parliament. They have thus turned to an institution that appears more relevant and specialised than before, and they have been enabled to do so by the growth in the number of lobbying firms.[10] Televising the proceedings of the House has acted as a further spur, MPs now having a wider audience through which they may raise issues on behalf of particular groups.

The causes are thus several, the combined effect the same: a significant increase in MPs' workloads. Material floods in to select committees and to Members individually. More and more time is taken up having to deal with such demands: even saying 'no' is time-consuming. At least one MP uses a plastic bin-liner to accommodate the unwanted material. However, not all material is discarded. Much is useful to Members: it makes them better informed and they can use it to effect. The real problem is only partially qualitative; the principal problem is a quantitative one.

### From constituents

Members of Parliament are returned as Members for particular constituencies. In the 1940s and 1950s, contact between constituents and their MPs was not extensive. Many Members considered they were returned to serve at Westminster, not to spend time opening fetes in their constituencies. A good constituency Member was often seen as a failed minister.[11] It was a view often shared by constituency activists. One Conservative MP in the 1945–50 Parliament was actually denied readoption by his local party on the grounds he was not going to make it to any future Conservative Cabinet. Some Members, Labour as well as Conservative, were rarely seen in their constituencies. Visits were sometimes annual. Constituency correspondence for some was so small in quantity that they had time to reply in longhand.

This changed in the 1960s and, more especially, the 1970s and 1980s. Constituency surgeries became more common: by the end of the 1960s, more than 90 per cent of Members held them.[12] Letters from constituents became more numerous. In the 1960s, in an average week the typical MP would receive between 25 and 75 letters. Newly elected MPs became more likely to live in or near their constituencies.

These trends have been marked over the past twenty years. The average Member now receives in one day the amount of correspond-ence he or she used to receive in one week in the 1960s. The number of letters Members write to ministers in pursuit of constituency casework has consequently expanded enormously. In the early 1980s, about 10,000 letters a month were written by MPs to ministers; by the end of the 1980s, the figure had reached 15,000, more than 150,000 letters a year reaching the desks of ministers from fellow MPs. A 1984 survey of MPs by the Commons Reform Group found that, of Members who responded, approximately one in five spent thirteen or more days each month in the constituency. A more recent analysis, by this writer, of the addresses given by MPs in *Dod's Parliamentary Companion* reveals that, of MPs first returned to Parliament in 1987, more than half give addresses in or near their constituencies; only a minority of those MPs first returned in or before 1983 do so.

The explanation for this increase is again not mono-causal. It appears to be both demand and supply led. Demand-led in that constituents expect more of their MPs. With the emergence of the welfare state, government departments have impinged more and more on the lives of individual citizens. With economic downturn in the 1960s and since, government has variously had to pursue redistributive rather than distributive policies. Citizens have increas-ingly used their Members of Parliament to try to achieve a redress of grievance or, more often, to achieve an authoritative explanation of why some action was or was not taken. MPs have thus an important tension release as well as grievance redress function.[13] As consti-tuents have found that their MPs can do something for them, the more they appear to have used them. And, on the supply side, MPs themselves have more often than before sought out grievances to pursue. Such casework can form part of a Member's attempt to achieve a higher public profile, useful for promotion prospects as well as, in marginal seats, helping keep the seat. Cain, Ferejohn and Fiorina estimated that 27% of Members adopted a proactive approach.[14] That proportion is likely to have increased in the wake of the new parliamentary intake of 1987; it may also be further encouraged by the recognition that there may be somewhat more electoral reward for such service than was previously realised.[15]

Again, the effect is the same. Members have to devote more time than ever before to constituency work. Several hours a day will now be taken up dealing with constituency casework (writing letters, meeting constituents, meeting ministers); most weekends will be given over to constituency work. Such time has to be carved out of existing commitments.

## From membership of the European Community

Membership of the European Community has added to the burdens of the House. The traditional function of scrutinising legislation and the administration of government has been extended to encompass draft legislation and policy of the EC.

Most work in the Commons has fallen on the shoulders of the Select Committee on European Legislation. It has responsibility for considering draft proposals and other documents, reporting on whether or not they raise political and legal questions, and recommending whether or not such documents should be debated by the House. It reports each week to the House. The amount of material it has had to digest has been such that it has had considerable difficulty in coping. Some documents have been referred for discussion in standing committees, though the number has not been extensive (usually less than twenty each session). Of documents recommended for debate, only a minority are actually debated: the number will vary considerably from twenty to one hundred, though with less than 3 per cent of the time of the House taken up with such debate. Pressures on the timetable are such that it is difficult to find more time.

However, the time of a fraction of Members will now be drawn upon extensively as a result of recent changes. Given the increased importance of EC policy-making as a consequence of the Single European Act, the Procedure Committee in 1989 recommended the appointment of special (to be known as European) standing committees to consider EC policy in particular policy sectors. In October 1990, the House voted to approve the recommendation of the Leader of the House that three such committees be appointed: early in 1991, after problems in getting a sufficient number of members to serve on them, the number was reduced to two. EC documents recommended for debate are now referred (unless the House votes otherwise) to these committees. Any MP, not just those appointed to the committees, can attend meetings and seek to attract the chairman's eye to participate in debate. Though designed to save a little time on the floor of the House, the net effect of the change is likely to result in a number of MPs having to devote more of their time to committee work. Again, this is time that has to be found at the expense of other commitments.

## From Members themselves

Not only have the demands made of Members changed, so too have the Members themselves. Members are not only more active in the House as a result of pressure from organised groups and constituents but also of their own volition. The House serves as a training ground for potential ministers. By convention, ministers are drawn from, and remain within, Parliament. Political advancement thus entails entering the House and making one's mark there. The past twenty years have seen greater competition to gain attention.

What Anthony King described as 'spectator' politicians have given way increasingly to career politicians. MPs are more middle class than before[16] and in the 1970s many began to adopt a different attitude to government: their old deferential attitude was displaced by what Samuel Beer described as a more participant attitude.[17] MPs wanted to be more involved in parliamentary work. The more active MPs became, the more they vied with one another to attract attention. This has encompassed greater activity in the Palace of Westminster and, as we have seen, greater constituency activity.

There are various Member-driven activities that reflect this greater intensity on the part of Members. One is the growth in the number of parliamentary questions. Before the 1970s, a little over 10,000 questions for oral answer were tabled in an average session. Restricting the number that each Member could table produced a decrease in the sessions after 1972–73. However, the number tabled for written answer (on which there are no restrictions on number) increased by about 50 per cent; and, from the mid-1980s, the number tabled for oral answer also shot up again. In the latter half of the 1980s, the number of parliamentary questions receiving oral or written answers in a typical session exceeded 40,000. So numerous were they that in October 1990 the House introduced new rules to try to reduce the number.

Another increasingly used device is that of Early Day Motions (EDMs). These are motions tabled for debate 'on an early day'. In practice, the chances of time for debate being found are virtually nil. However, the motions are published on the order paper and other Members who agree with them may add their signatures. They thus serve as a form of parliamentary noticeboard. An EDM attracting a considerable number of signatures can catch the attention of ministers and help raise the profile of a particular issue. It was through the medium of an EDM, for example, that Conservative MPs Michael Heseltine and Norman Tebbit persuaded the then Education Secretary, Kenneth Baker, to include abolition of the Inner London Education Authority in the 1988 Education Reform Bill. Before the 1960s, no more than 200 EDMs were ever tabled in a single session. In the 1960s, the number occasionally exceeded 400 and in one session exceeded 600. The number increased in the 1970s and 1980s: in 1983/4 the number for the first time exceeded 1,000. In the long session of 1987/88 it exceeded 1,600. In the following, average-length, session it exceeded 1,400.

The more participant attitude has not only driven Members individually to greater action but has also facilitated the creation of the departmental select committees. To subject government to sustained scrutiny was difficult on the floor of the House. One department might escape parliamentary debate for a considerable period. MPs could influence government policy through the division lobbies, but that was an essentially blunt and negative weapon. The departmental select committees were essentially the creation of the House and provided the opportunity for regular and more focused scrutiny of government departments than was ever possible before. The committees have proved popular with MPs: they are keen to serve on them and their output has been considerable. In the first Parliament of their existence, the committees issued 193 reports and in the second they issued 306. In an average session, they will interview more than 1,000 witnesses.

Each of the fourteen extant committees has eleven members and meets each week. The departmental committees thus absorb at any one time the energies of 154 MPs. They exist over and above the other select committees of the House, of which there are twelve. These include the Public Accounts, Procedure, and Services Committees.

Members thus compete for attention in the House. They do so through seeking to fulfil the expectations held of them by government, by organised groups of one sort or another, and by constituents. The professional, as opposed to those remaining spectator, Members now have bulging diaries. They have constituency correspondence to deal with, a variety of meetings to attend (with ministers, with representatives of different groups, with consti-

tuents, with reporters), committees to go to (party, and – if members
– standing and select), meetings to address (in London, in the constituency, or elsewhere), and business on the Floor to attend (Question Time, debates, divisions). At weekends, there are various
demands of the constituency (surgeries, meetings, telephone calls
and just being seen around). The demands show no sign of abating.

Given that many Members still maintain outside interests, a particularly heavy burden falls on those who devote their energies wholly
or almost wholly to parliamentary duties. How well has the House
adapted to increased expectations to allow Members to cope?

### Parliamentary facilities

In the 1940s and 1950s, Members of Parliament were badly paid and
bady resourced. They worked in cramped conditions in the Palace of
Westminster, being allocated lockers rather than offices, with no
secretarial or research support: if they wanted secretarial help, they
had to pay for it out of their own salaries. The 1960s witnessed some
improvement. Pay was increased, various offices were made available for occupancy by some backbenchers, and in 1969 a secretarial
allowance (of £500) was introduced.

In the 1970s and 1980s, pay and facilities expanded to meet the
demands of a more professional and, especially after 1979, more
specialised House. Members' pay was variously increased, Members
themselves forcing a higher level of pay than the government had
recommended. In 1987 the House approved pay being linked to civil
service salaries (at senior principal level). The previous year, it
increased – against government advice – the secretarial and research
allowance by 50 per cent. By the beginning of 1990, an MP had a
salary of £26,701 and a secretarial and research (known as office
cost) allowance of roughly the same amount. It was possible for a
Member to hire a full-time secretary and a part-time research assistant. Office capacity also increased. The acquisition in the 1970s of
the old Scotland Yard building on Victoria Embankment added
considerably to office space. Further space was also created in the
Palace of Westminster and by the end of the 1980s, every MP who
wanted a desk was able to have one. (The one publicised exception
was Labour MP Ken Livingstone.) A new office building in Bridge
Street was also begun.

Facilities available to Members collectively and to committees of the House also improved. The Library expanded both quantitatively and qualitatively. Staff size more than doubled in the period between 1970 and 1990 and a computerised classification index (POLIS, the parliamentary on-line information service) was introduced. The departmental select committees appointed in 1979 were not only given the traditional allocation of at least one clerk but were also permitted to appoint specialist advisers for the lifetime of a Parliament and not, as previously, just for specific enquiries. Most committees have made considerable use of such advisers: in the 1987/88 session, the 13 committees employed 76 such advisers, the Defence Committee leading the field with 13. Provision also exists for the appointment of Specialist Assistants, people with some background in the subject and employed on fixed-term contracts: a number of committees make use of one and sometimes two such Assistants. Some committees have the support of a second clerk and the Defence Committee is now assisted also by two specialists seconded from the National Audit Office.

The House itself has achieved a greater independence over its own resources through the creation of the House of Commons Commission, responsible for staffing and for various expenses incurred by the House.[18] Opposition parties have been able to utilise more resources in carrying out their parliamentary duties through the provision of 'Short money' (named after the Leader of the House, Edward Short, responsible for its introduction, and not after the actual amount of money made available.) This usually facilitates the provision of more office staff. The sum involved now exceeds £1 million a year.

The total identifiable costs of running the House of Commons in the 1989/90 session was put at £95.65 million. (This excludes the maintenance of the Palace of Westminster, put at £26.5 million.)[19] The amount is considerable. But is it sufficient to enable the House of Commons to fulfil the demands now made of it?

The answer is no. Parliamentary facilities have improved but they have not kept pace with the changing nature of the institution. Expectations, as we have seen, have increased. Consequently, in terms of resources, Parliament has to run in order to stand still. Select committees are under threat as members find it increasingly difficult to force the time necessary to prepare for meetings. The committees rely on a small staff. In evidence to the Procedure Committee in the 1989/90 session, the Clerk of the House described the overall staffing level as 'deliberately lean'.[20] With members having limited secretarial support, mail mounts up. Even during summer recesses, there is no escape: there is what one Member describes as the 'kitchen tap' effect, a constant 'drip, drip' of mail. With limited research support, Members have difficulty pursuing issues raised by pressure groups and constituents. With more of their time taken up by parliamentary business, constituents and lobbyists, Members have little time to give sustained thought to major issues; strategic thinking is a luxury that few can now afford. They have little time to do the research necessary to harry government when it needs to be harried.

There is a human as well as a political cost. Some Members suffer from increasing stress. (One Member admitted to me that he had to take tablets to keep going at the end of a particularly demanding session.) The stress may not usually be life-threatening but it does threaten the efficiency of Members of Parliament. The increasing demands also mean that some existing aspects of parliamentary life have to be discarded or given less attention than before. One victim on the Conservative side appears to be the backbench committees. Over the past decade, attendance has declined significantly and a number no longer meet on a weekly basis; one Conservative back-bencher, exaggerating somewhat, has gone so far as to describe them as 'dead in the water'. The most significant victim, though, is the House itself. Without adequate resources, collectively and individually, Members are unable to fulfil the tasks expected of them. The long-term consequence is a fall in public support for the institution. If that is to be avoided, and the House is not to collapse under the strain, corrective action has to be taken.

**What is to be done?**

If Members are to meet the increased demands made of them, they need to be provided with greater resources. This encompasses a more efficient working environment and greater secretarial and research resources. There is now evidence to suggest that Members themselves are generally aware of this. A MORI poll of MPs in 1990 revealed that 58 per cent of those who responded considered the House to be a 'fairly poor' or 'very poor' place to work.[11] A survey of select committee members by the BBC TV *Scrutiny* programme (broadcast 11 November 1990) found that almost half of those who

responded considered the committees were not scrutinising departments effectively and more than half (53 per cent) favoured having
more staff and resources.

The goal of every MP having an individual office by 1995 will not
now be met. The failure to acquire County Hall (former
headquarters of the Greater London Council) for parliamentary
purposes was a grievious one. MPs will have to continue to work in
relatively cramped conditions. There is thus an urgent need to speed
up the Bridge Street development and to engage in more strategic
planning. More immediately, Members need to be better resourced.
Pay and office cost allowances need to be increased in order that each
Member can cope with the growing demands of groups, government
and constituents. Committees need to be better resourced: the
acquisition of a small research unit for each committee would be a
step in the right direction, as would the creation of dedicated offices
(committees at present have to book rooms and most compete for
space on Wednesdays). However, how well resourced a committee is
will be irrelevant if members cannot find time to devote to its work.
Committee members need to be enabled to spend time on committee
work: to this end, the provision of a research allowance – as well as
remuneration – to members has been advocated by myself (in evidence to the Procedure Committee 1990). Some MPs have outside
jobs for which they receive remuneration. Those who dedicate their
time to the work of the House deserve to be remunerated for that
work. A research allowance would permit them to hive off more
mundane tasks, allowing them to concentrate on committee work.
This list is selective, not exhaustive. Such changes are not cost free,
but not to make them would constitute a false economy.

However, the realisation of such changes is hampered by the fact
that responsibility for recommending action is dispersed among the
committees of the House. Both the Services Committee of the House
and the House of Commons Commission have recognised the problems of working conditions and resources faced by Members. The
Procedure Committee, in contrast, has taken a more conservative
view. Reflecting the absence of a consensus among its members, the
once radical committee has resorted to issuing what one Member
termed 'steady as she goes' reports. In 1990, it issued a short report
on oral questions that was narrow and specific and another on the
working of the select committee system: the latter had to be defended
by the chairman against accusations of being a 'damp squib'. The

committee took the view that the select committees had performed well and that only occasional adjustments were necessary. Increases in pay and research resources were rejected. The select committees were thus expected to face the growing demands of the 1990s with the limited resources of the 1980s.

What is needed is a thorough, comprehensive review of the problem. That cannot be achieved through the Procedure Committee as presently constituted. When faced with a similar problem, the Canadian House of Commons set up a Special Committee on Reform of the House. Its scope was wide-ranging. If the House of Commons is to cope with the growing threat of parliamentary overload, it would be well advised to follow suit.[22]

At the heart of what is happening is a paradox. Because there is an increasing perception that the House of Commons can achieve the demands of citizens, greater demands are made of it. Because of greater demands, the House becomes less able to satisfy those demands. It has to run in order to stand still. That is the message to be drawn from the experience of the past twenty years.

### Notes

1  R. Packenham, 'Legislatures and political development', in A. Kornberg and L. D. Musolf (eds.), *Legislatures in Developmental Perspective* (Durham, NC: Duke University Press, 1970) 521–82.

2  S. C. Patterson, 'Review article: the British House of Commons as a focus for political research', *British Journal of Political Science*, vol. 3, no. 3 (1973) 363–81.

3  R. Miliband, *Capitalist Democracy in Britain* (Oxford University Press, 1984) 20.

4  J. A. G. Griffith and M. Ryle, *Parliament: Functions, Practice and Procedures* (London: Sweet & Maxwell, 1989) 288.

5  A. B. White, *The Making of the English Constitution 449–1485* (London: G. P. Putnam's Sons, 1908) 369.

6  C. Grantham, 'Parliament and political consultants', *Parliamentary Affairs*, vol. 42, no. 4 (1989) 503–18.

7  P. Norton, 'Public legislation', in M. Rush (ed.), *Parliament and Pressure Politics* (Oxford University Press, 1990) 178–210.

8  See P. Norton, *Dissension in the House of Commons 1945–74* (London: Macmillan, 1975); P. Norton (ed.), *Parliament in the 1980s* (Oxford: Blackwell, 1985).

9  P. Regan, 'The 1986 Shops Bill', *Parliamentary Affairs*, vol. 41, no. 2 (1988) 218–35; F. Bown, 'The defeat of the Shops Bill, 1986', in M. Rush (ed.), *Parliament and Pressure Politics* (Oxford University Press, 1990) 213–33.

**10** P. Norton, 'The changing face of the House of Commons', in P. Norton (ed.), *New Directions in British Politics?* (Aldershot: Edward Elgar, 1991).

**11** J. Marsh, 'The House of Commons: representational changes', in P. Norton (ed.), *Parliament in the 1980s* (Oxford: Blackwell, 1985) 69–93.

**12** A. Barker and M. Rush, *The Member of Parliament and His Information* (London: Allen & Unwin, 1970).

**13** P. Norton, ' "Dear Minister . . " The Importance of MP-to-Minister Correspondence', *Parliamentary Affairs*, vol. 35, no. 1 (1982) 59–72.

**14** B. Cain, J. Ferejohn and M. Fiorina, *The Personal Vote* (Cambridge, MA: Harvard University Press, 1987).

**15** P. Norton and D. Wood, 'Constituency service by Members of Parliament: does it contribute to a personal vote?', *Parliamentary Affairs*, vol. 43, no. 2 (1990) 196–208.

**16** See C. Mellors, *The British MP* (Farnborough: Sexon House, 1978); and M. Rush, 'The Member of Parliament', in M. Ryle and P. G. Richards (eds.), *The Commons Under Scrutiny* (London: Routledge, 1988).

**17** S. H. Beer, *Britain Against Itself* (London: Faber & Faber, 1982).

**18** P. Norton, 'Independence, scrutiny and rationalisation: a decade of changes in the House of Commons', *Teaching Politics*, vol. 15, no. 1 (1986) 71.

**19** C. Boulton and Sir J. Sainty, 'Note on the UK parliamentary system', *Constitutional and Parliamentary Information*, 159 (1990) 9–20.

**20** Select Committee on Procedure, *The Working of the Select Committee System*, Second Report, Session 1989/90, HC 19 (London: HMSO, 1990), xxiv.

**21** House of Commons Commission, *House of Commons Services* (London: HMSO, 1990).

**22** Just before the 1991 summer recess, the House of Commons went some way in this direction, appointing a Select Committee on the Sittings of the House. However, responsibility for reform remains fragmented among the committees of the House.

# The House of Lords: the best second chamber we have got?

It seems strange that Britain still has a House of Lords in the 1990s. The preamble to the 1911 Parliament Act had declared the intention to replace the House, and way back throughout the nineteenth century many schemes for its reform or replacement had been advanced. But no fundamental reform took place. After the pre-First World War constitutional crisis the House settled for a quiet life, as a dignified comfortable chamber where aristocrats and notables mingled, and where thoughts of wielding power gave way to hopes of exerting influence. Seldom did anyone take much notice of the House. It was useful as a place to pension off former politicians, and helpful as a forum in which legislation could be revised, almost invariably in accordance with the wishes of government. Decay and eventual collapse seemed a more likely outcome for the House than stormy abolition. By the 1950s it was 'dying in its sleep'.[1]

But resuscitation followed in the wake of the 1958 Life Peerages Act. Recruitment to the House broadened. More peerages were created than ever before. 'Working' peers could henceforth be appointed – folk given their peerages not so much as a high public honour, but rather in expectation of the work they might do in the House. Attendance and activity began to increase and has done so steadily ever since. So too did the volume of work to which Parliament was expected to attend. Every government, whatever its initial protestations about reducing the burden of legislation, has always increased that burden. The task of scrutinising this legislation, and holding government to account for all its non-legislative actions, demanded more than the House of Commons seemed able to deliver. Procedural reform, the establishment of more select committees, the introduction of the National Audit Office, all these and other reforms were evidence of the collective effort being made by MPs to keep pace with government activities. But there was continuing evidence that the Commons alone was unequal to this task. A second chamber could demonstrate at least a modest usefulness as a kind of parliamentary long-stop.

Richard Crossman recognised this when he suggested that without the House of Lords the Commons would need at least another two stages for the consideration of legislation. He made this remark when introducing proposals for the reform of the Lords embodied in the Parliament (No. 2) Bill, 1968, a measure designed to modernise the House by removing its hereditary members and providing for a chamber of appointees, among whom the right to vote would be limited to those who committed themselves to regular attendance. The story of how Harold Wilson's Labour government directed its zeal for institutional reform to the House of Lords has been told by Janet Morgan.[2] The proposed reforms had been agreed almost in their entirety by the Conservative Party leadership under Edward Heath. The House of Lords voted with apparent enthusiasm for the change. But in the Commons Labour left and Conservative right combined to defeat the plan. In 1969 the House of Lords narrowly escaped a reform which would certainly have brought into being a very different kind of chamber.

Looking back, what is remarkable is the extent of inter-party agreement on this scheme. The following decade was to see a sharp polarisation between the major parties. Ten years later Labour was committed to outright abolition of the House and to the reform of Parliament into an efficient unicameral body. The Conservatives were to toy with the idea of a reform which would have actually increased the powers of the Upper House, and certainly bolstered its legitimacy in a democratic sense. But in the event nothing was to be done by way of reforming the membership or altering the powers of the House. In 1990 it remained an obvious and glaring anachronism. Its membership in formal terms was still dominated by hereditary peers, and even among the active members peers by succession continued to play a major role. Yet curiously the House of Lords was probably a more significant chamber, in terms of the influence it exerted and the attention it received, than it had been at any time since the crisis years preceding the First World War. Why is this, and what has been going on to cause such a change?

## Membership and activity

The curious character of the House can be illustrated in many ways, several of which have to do with the way the House is composed. Table 10.1 shows how membership of the House has altered since 1970. Despite the introduction of life peers, the hereditary element has remained important within the House. When the Life Peerages Act was passed there had been no explicit intention to reduce the number of hereditary honours. But after 1964 and up to 1983 no new hereditary peers were created. However, after her second election victory Mrs Thatcher recommended her deputy, William Whitelaw, and the former Speaker of the Commons, George Thomas, for viscountcies. In the following year the former Conservative Prime Minister, Harold Macmillan, was granted an earldom. No other hereditary peerages were created prior to her departure from office in 1990, but the modest resumption of hereditary honours after a near twenty-year interval showed how deep seated the reluctance to break with such honours was in some sections of society.

Table 10.1   *Composition of the House of Lords*

|  | 1970 | (Women) | 1990 | (Women) |
|---|---|---|---|---|
| Peers by succession | 757 | (19) | 760 | (20) |
| Hereditary peers of first creation | 101 | | 17 | |
| Life peers created under Apellate Jurisdiction Acts | 20 | | 19 | |
| Life peers created under 1958 Act | 158 | (19) | 358 | (53) |
| Bishops | 26 | | 26 | |
| Total | 1,062 | (38) | 1,186 | (73) |

New life peerages have been created in substantial numbers (on this and other matters see Shell[3]). The most direct result of the 1958 Life Peerages Act was the strengthening of Labour benches in the Lords so that by the late 1960s Labour constituted almost one-third of the active peers, a position retained during the 1970s, though numerically the Conservatives always remained dominant within the House. By the late 1980s however Labour's numbers had dropped while the number of Conservatives had risen. (see Table 10.2). Part of the reason for Labour's fall was the migration of Labour peers to the Social Democratic Party in the early 1980s, but it had as much to

**Table 10.2**   *Party strength in the House of Lords*

|  | 1967/68 | | 1989/90 | |
|  | *Attenders* | *Regulars* | *Attenders* | *Regulars* |
|---|---|---|---|---|
| Conservative | 314 | 125 | 396 | 186 |
| % of total | 46.2 | 43.0 | 48.1 | 48.2 |
| Labour | 113 | 95 | 105 | 87 |
| % of total | 16.6 | 32.6 | 12.6 | 22.5 |
| Liberal/SDP | 37 | 19 | 65 | 45 |
| % of total | 5.4 | 6.5 | 7.9 | 11.7 |
| Independent | | | | |
|   Cross-bench | 215 | 52 | 260 | 68 |
| % of total | 31.7 | 17.9 | 31.5 | 17.6 |
| Total | 679 | 291 | 826 | 386 |

'Regulars': Those who attended one-third or more of the sittings during the session.
'Attenders': Those who attended one or more sittings during the session.

do with the way the Prime Minister starved the Labour benches of new recruits. All told, Mrs Thatcher recommended 203 new peerages, just over half of which went to Conservatives, with only 45 going to Labour Party supporters. Thus the inbuilt superiority for the Conservatives in the House of Lords was intensified during the 1980s. This failure to reinforce the Labour benches was criticised by the Labour leaders in the House. The Party relied on a gerontocracy to sustain its role as Her Majesty's loyal opposition in the Upper House. That the opposition should be so dependent on the Prime Minister of the day to keep itself adequately supplied with recruits to the second chamber is but another aspect of the anomalous character of the House.

A further anomaly concerns the government frontbench in the Lords. While there have always been some senior ministers in the House, including the Lord Chancellor and the Leader of the House, the number of other ministers has varied. In 1974 the Labour government for a time had only fourteen peers on its frontbench (including Whips). This was an exceptionally low number, but never in recent times has there been one minister for every department. Hence Whips are used to act as departmental spokesmen in the Upper House. In the late 1980s, despite the plentiful number of Conservative peers, and the much vaunted collective experience of which the House boasts, it became clear that the government was having difficulty in filling posts on the frontbench. Though in a personal sense those recruited might perform well at the Despatch Box, they lacked the experience of politics now generally regarded as essential for ministers; some were virtually unknown even in the House of Lords itself.

Table 10.3 indicates something of the increased activity of the House. By 1970 the House was already much busier than it had been a decade earlier, with the average daily attendance, for example, almost double what it had been at the time of the passage of the Life Peerage Act. By 1990 attendance had risen further, and the House was sitting considerably more hours than it had been two decades earlier. Despite this the House has not introduced any significant procedural restrictions. In 1971 and again in 1987 the Leader of the House initiated an enquiry among peers, part of the purpose of which was to sound out opinion about the need for procedural adaptation. On both occasions the views of peers generally were against making changes.[4] Thus there is still no procedure for introducing a guillotine or for selecting amendments. There is no set hour for the House to rise, and of course there is no 'Speaker' in the Commons sense of the term. All this may be taken as indicative of the preferred method by which the House regulates its activities, namely one of collective self-discipline and informal sanctions. Such methods appear comparatively successful in a chamber which is one remove from the pressures engendered by the intensely competitive party politics which dominates the Commons.

**Table 10.3**   *Growth in activity of the House of Lords*

|  | 1971–72 | 1989–90 |
|---|---|---|
| Peers on roll | 1,073 | 1,186 |
| Peers who attended at least once | 698 | 826 |
| Peers who spoke at least once | 419 | 528 |
| Average daily attendance | 250 | 318 |
| Total hours House sat | 813 | 1,072 |
| Average length of sitting | 5h. 45m. | 7h. 18m. |
| Sittings after 10.00 p.m. | 28 | 74 |
| Number of starred questions | 494 | 551 |
| Number of questions for written answer | 315 | 1,204 |
| Number of amendments made to government bills | 924 | 2,540 |

Before evaluating the legislative and deliberative work of the House, a general account of how it has related to successive governments throughout this period is given.

## The House and the government

The failure of the 1968–69 attempt at reform had the somewhat curious effect of emboldening their lordships. Clearly they were not to blame for the débâcle. If the Commons couldn't bring themselves to reform the Lords then why should peers restrain themselves to avoid clashing with MPs? Such arguments were soon heard when the House of Lords was faced with the Labour government's attempt to delay the revision of parliamentary constituency boundaries in an effort to confer electoral advantage on itself. The Lords wrecked the Bill and peers made clear that only by using Parliament Act procedures would it ever reach the statute book. But if it were enacted by this method it would be too late, for by then the next election would have taken place on constituency boundaries revised to Labour's disadvantage. The fact that the Labour government found a way to achieve its goal without the need for legislation at all obviated the need for further debate on this Bill. But equally that did not disguise the fact that the House of Lords had gently but firmly bared its teeth.

The Conservatives in office after 1970 were faced by an opposition in the Lords utterly different from the handful of peers that had confronted them in the 1950s. The Labour peers for their part were eager to prove to their party colleagues elsewhere that they could advantageously carry the party struggle into the Upper House. The Heath government's enormous and controversial legislative programme gave abundant scope to the opposition peers to prove their worth. The result was a different kind of House of Lords, with the party battle being fought out in the Upper House with an intensity hitherto unknown. The sum total of changes to legislation, such as the Industrial Relations Act and the Housing Finance Act, resulting from debate in the Lords was small. The government suffered relatively few defeats on legislation (twenty-five all told from 1970 to 1974), but when defeat occurred ministers generally gave way to the House following defeat. And the sort of issues on which the House was now pressing the government were no longer those beloved by right-wing Tory backwoodsmen (as had been allegedly the case in the 1950s, on capital punishment for example) but rather matters favoured by the new lobbies concerned with such areas as the environment, conservation, the disabled and sex discrimination.

The period 1974–79 was very different again. Labour was for much of the time a minority government, and when this was not so its Commons majority was minute. But its very low majority did not inhibit the government from attempting to carry highly controversial and partisan legislation. In this respect it differed from its predecessors in 1950–51 or 1964–66. For the Lords this meant that exercising its function of revising legislation was fraught with difficulty. If Conservative peers sent Bills back to the lower House with hostile amendments, the reversal of these could only be achieved on wafer-thin majorities – if at all. The abstention of only two Labour backbencher MPs in 1976 was enough to prevent the government reversing Lords' amendments which wrecked the Dockwork Regulation Bill. Numerous other changes were made to government Bills by the Upper House, many against ministerial wishes. But where these were reversed in the Commons, peers almost invariably gave way.

The House resisted only on two government Bills. On both these the government resorted to Parliament Act procedures to overcome resistance from the Lords, but in neither case did these procedures run their full course because before they did so compromise was reached. The first of these concerned the issue of trade-union membership and in particular how provisions for a closed shop could apply in the media without threatening journalistic freedom. For most of the time it was Lord Goodman, the prominent cross-bench peer, who led the opposition to the government's proposals in the Lords. But eventually when the Trade Union and Labour Relations (Amendment) Bill was re-introduced in the 1975–76 session, peers let it pass.

In the second case peers insisted on removing ship-repairing from the Bill nationalising the aerospace and shipbuilding industries. It was because ship-repairing had been included that the Bill was found to be hybrid, and this added to the complexities of the matter. Eventually, having re-introduced the Bill in the 1976–77 session, the government decided to cut its losses and simply drop ship-repairing altogether. The Lords then let it through. The Conservative opposition in the House also threw out a private Bill, one which in effect would have nationalised Felixstowe Dock. Though promoted by the Docks and Harbour Board, this Bill certainly had strong government support, and ministers were angry at the action of the House.

The fact that the House of Lords had dared to use its remaining powers at all was sufficient cause for the Labour Party in 1977 to pledge itself to the outright abolition of the second chamber. But it could be argued that the House had actually used its powers with great restraint. The Labour government's hold on power was after all very tenuous, exemplified by its winning some Commons divisions during this period only on the casting vote of the Speaker. After the 1976–77 session the government no longer had a majority in the Commons. Hence the flow of legislation which was controversial in a party-political sense abated.

## The House and the Thatcher governments

With the Conservatives back in office there seemed less likelihood of serious conflict between the two Houses. But the House of Lords was by no means as compliant as ministers might have wished. On a number of occasions it amended Bills against the wishes of the government. One of the first disputes concerned the proposal made in the Education (School Transport) Bill to allow local authorities to charge for transport to schools in rural areas. This stirred opposition in the Commons, where 13 Tory backbenchers voted against the government, and at least as many more abstained. In the Lords 40 Conservative peers cross-voted and the government went down to a notable defeat by 216 votes to 112. The government had the choice of either giving way, or facing further rebellion and possibly defeat in the Commons, with accompanying political opprobrium on this highly publicised issue. Ministers decided to give way. And they did so again on legislation concerning the 'right to buy' council houses; here the Lords voted heavily for restrictions on the sale of accommodation for the elderly and the disabled.

The government's programme was not seriously affected by what the Lords did, but on several Bills significant compromises were made. It could be argued that this exemplified the role a revising chamber ought to have. But there was no hiding the fact that at times ministers were intensely displeased at their Lordship's actions. After the 1983 election two further related factors encouraged peers to exercise their revising role with increasing vigour. The first was the very large majority – of 152 – the government now had in the Commons; this made it relatively more difficult for MPs to oblige ministerial re-thinks about particular provisions, and caused peers to talk of the extra responsibilities thereby placed on their House. The second was the very weak character of the opposition. The Labour Party, having seen a chunk of its support syphoned off to the Social

Democrats, had been led to its worst ever electoral performance by Michael Foot. Many Labour MPs openly doubted the value of spending time in the Commons trying to 'improve' government Bills when they were so heavily outnumbered. The appointment of so senior a figure as the Deputy Prime Minister, William Whitelaw, as Leader in the House of Lords was in part intended to smooth out problems with the House. But his role seemed quickly to become more one of arguing his ministerial colleagues into making concessions and throwing his weight around in Whitehall on behalf of the House, than one of subduing querulous backbench peers.

The 1983–87 Parliament saw the Lords enjoying a degree of attention and effectiveness unmatched under previous governments. Even when the Commons reversed some of their amendments to Bills, peers decided to insist rather than give way – for example on the details concerning the sale of public housing. In 1984 peers obliged the government to alter its strategy for the abolition of the Greater London Council (GLC). Ministers had decided to cancel elections due to take place in 1984, and replace the Labour-controlled GLC with an interim body nominated by the London boroughs, most of which were Conservative controlled. This seemed convenient to the government but it was seen by others as a grossly insensitive way to handle constitutional delicacies. Having prevented the government from following its strategy, peers then compromised and rather than insist that new elections took place, agreed to the proposal that the existing council, still led by Ken Livingstone, continue in office for one extra year until the abolition legislation had been implemented. Encouraged by this snub to the government on the so-called 'paving' Bill, some people apparently thought the Lords would wreak havoc with the substantive abolition legislation the following year. But to do so would have been to oppose a measure which had been clearly included in the previous election manifesto, and this the House has never done since the First World War.

As the Thatcher government embarked on its third term, still with a very secure Commons majority and with a controversial and radical programme of legislation, Lord Whitelaw publicly stated that he expected serious defeats in the Upper House, and went on to emphasise that ministers would have to be prepared to accept some of these and to compromise. But there was to be less compromise with the Lords in the 1987 Parliament than there had been previously. Perhaps Lord Whitelaw's own sudden departure from office (on the grounds of ill-health) in January 1988 had something to do with the change. But it seemed as if Mrs Thatcher was more determined than ever to resist opposition to her measures from the Upper House.

Perhaps she had a point. Giving way to peers seemed to enlarge their appetite to make changes rather than appease it. A different attitude to the House was displayed in the determined efforts that were made to avoid defeat there, especially where the reversal of such defeats would only give further opportunity for Conservative rebellion in the Commons. Thus after facing down her backbench opponents in the Commons on the introduction of the poll tax, the last thing the Prime Minister wanted was defeat in the Lords necessitating further acrimony in the Commons. A heavy Conservative three-line Whip brought unprecedented numbers of rarely attending hereditary peers to the House to vote down an amendment moved by a former chairman of the 1922 Committee in the Commons, Sir Tufton Beamish (who had metamorphosed into Lord Chelwood). The whole episode reflected badly on the House and badly on the government too.

Where the government did suffer defeat in the Lords it showed a new determination to reverse such changes in the Commons, even at the risk of further defeat. This was demonstrated in 1988 when peers voted against the introduction of charges for eye tests and against increases in dental charges. Many Conservative MPs were deeply unhappy with these proposals and had already rebelled in the Commons. After the votes in the Lords no fewer than sixty-one Conservative backbenchers had signed an Early Day Motion in the Commons calling on the government to accept the changes made in the Lords. But ministers determined otherwise. A timely announcement of an extra £3 billion for the NHS just before the Commons debated the Lords amendments helped reduce the number of Conservative dissidents. But the government majority in the Commons fell to single figures on eye-test charges. What was significant was that the government was prepared to risk defeat in the Commons rather than give way to the Lords, even though the issue had assumed considerable public prominence.

Ministerial unwillingness to listen to the Lords was exemplified by the government's introduction of the War Crimes Bill in 1990. Earlier debates in both Houses had given ample evidence of widespread hostility in the Lords to the proposal to alter the law to allow trials of Second World War criminals to be resumed. The Judicial members of the House were outspoken in resisting the proposal. But the government ploughed ahead with the Bill. After it had completed its Commons' stages the Lords threw it out at Second Reading. The Thatcher government announced it intention to re-introduce the Bill and force it through using Parliament Act procedures if necessary. In the event this is what happened, with the Bill attaining Royal Assent in May 1991 despite its rejection for a second time by the House of Lords. It seemed strange indeed for a Conservative government on an issue such as this, which was not a party matter still less a manifesto Bill, to insist on overriding the Lords. This exemplified a hardening attitude to the House. For the first time for over forty years (and the first time ever under a Conservative government) the Parliament Act had been used to carry a Bill to the statute book. While talk of an immediate constitutional crisis was misplaced, the whole episode raised doubts in many minds about the longer-term future of the House of Lords. But before taking up that point a summary discussion of the work of the House is appropriate.

## Legislative work

The revision of government Bills is frequently described as the most important function of the House. This has become an increasingly burdensome task. The most direct reason for this is that governments have been submitting ever more legislation to Parliament. In the late 1960s around 1,500 pages of new primary legislation were enacted every year. By the mid-1980s half as much again was passing through the legislative machine. Not only had such an increase occurred, but experienced parliamentarians complained about the decline in the quality of legislation as first presented to Parliament. This decline was variously attributed to the failure of the government to consult more carefully, or a failure on the part of ministers to really make their minds up about what they wanted done, or simply to inadequacies in the staffing of the parliamentary counsel's office responsible for drafting legislation.[5]

Whatever the cause for the increased quantity and the allegedly decreased quality of legislation, one consequence (so it was argued) was the number of amendments the government was asking the House to make to Bills. In the first three sessions of the 1970

Parliament (1970–73) the House of Lords made 2,854 amendments to government Bills – an average of around 6 per sitting day. In the first three sessions of the 1987 Parliament (1987–90) the comparable figure was 7,868 amendments, or an average of over 16 per sitting day. Government and Commons depended heavily on the House of Lords to get its legislation into reasonable shape before it received the Royal imprimatur and was unleashed on the public. Much of this tidying up of legislation had to be done in a rush at the end of the session. It has been a frequent source of complaint that the effectiveness of the Lords revision of Bills has been handicapped by the fact that it does two-thirds of its legislative work in the final third of the parliamentary session, that is after major Bills have been delivered to it from the Commons. For this reason one peer recently described the House as 'a gilded dustpan and brush'.[6]

But there is also evidence to suggest that outside organisations do make considerable use of the House in their efforts to get Bills amended. A recent survey showed that organised groups found the House of Lords almost as important to them as the Commons for this purpose.[7] Certainly during the 1980s the House of Lords has more and more become a target for lobbyists. From their point of view the whole legislative process would be impoverished if it were not for the opportunities afforded by the House of Lords to amend Bills.

## The deliberative work of the House

The House does not simply revise government Bills. It also debates policy and seeks to scrutinise government activity. The House spends a lower proportion of its time on non-legislative debate than it did twenty years ago, but because the House sits longer, no general decrease in the number of hours spent on non-legislative debate has occurred. There has always been considerable dispute over the value such debates have. Perhaps the fairest conclusion is simply to say that this is very varied. Sometimes a debate has identifiable consequences, at least to those who took part. 'The House of Lords is a devastating place for any failure of argument' was the title given to a newspaper article by Lord Rees-Mogg as he reflected on the debate in which he made his own maiden speech (*Independent*, 11 April 1989). At other times all that appears to result is that a few more columns of *Hansard* are filled up.

The use by the House of select committees has considerably increased. The 1968 White Paper on Lords reform (Cmnd 3799) had suggested that a reformed House might have greater use for select committees. In the early 1970s the House began the habit of establishing such committees on an *ad hoc* basis, either to examine Bills introduced by private members, or simply to look at topics. In 1979 when the Commons abolished its Select Committee on Science and Technology, the Lords decided to establish one for this area. And throughout the Thatcher-dominated 1980s, that committee along with other *ad hoc* committees has done something to keep alive the tradition of experts and politicians mingling to produce reports on the lines of Royal Commissions, the influence of which was often hard to define.

But the major expansion in select committee work followed Britain's entry to the European Community in 1973. There was much more of a consensus about the European Community in the Lords than in the Commons, and it was not surprising that the Lords found it easier than the Commons to supply the manpower for the new task of scrutinising legislative instruments emanating from the European Community. Quite quickly a structure was devised whereby some 100 peers became involved in the scrutiny process operating through a range of subject-orientated sub-committees.[8] The Commons set up its own select committee but with more restricted terms of reference and a smaller membership. The work of the Lords committee has won frequent praise, though as with select committee activity generally it is difficult to analyse precisely its impact. What may be significant is that the committee seems to be taken at least as much notice of in Brussels as in London. Britain's response to the European Community has been criticised as slow, half-hearted, even downright obstinate; without the Lords' select committee such criticism would have even greater validity.

## Reform of the House?

When the Labour Party decided at its Conference in 1977 to abolish the House, the Conservative leader Mrs Thatcher responded by establishing a party committee under Lord Home (the former Conservative Prime Minister) to advise about the future of the House. This recommended phasing out all hereditary peers, by simply withdrawing the right to a seat in the House to those who succeeded

to peerages in the future, and introducing into the House, alongside
the remaining appointed peers, others who would owe their seats to
election. Eventually the House would have become one-third
appointed and two-thirds elected. Those elected would be members
for fixed terms, with a proportion coming up for re-election every
three years. Thus reformed the Home Committee proposed that the
power of the House to delay Bills should be restored to two years.[9]
The Alliance parties in the 1980s also argued for reform along
similar lines. The objection most commonly made to any scheme for
the election of the House is that it would thereby become a rival to
the House of Commons. But the elections to the Upper House could
be on a completely different basis to those for the Commons. And the
powers of the Upper House could be firmly limited.

The Thatcher government showed little interest in reform. During
the early Thatcher years the subject was apparently discussed from
time to time, both at party conferences and by a specially established
Cabinet sub-committee.[10] But the Prime Minister herself was mani-
festly agnostic. And as the decade went by the need to reform the
House lest it fall victim to Labour's abolitionist ambitions
diminished. The Conservatives simply ceased to have any policy at
all in respect of the House.

But towards the end of the decade Labour did bring forward new
proposals at least in outline form.[11] These involved the replacement
of the House with an appointed senate. The primary task of this new
second chamber would be to revise Bills, but no legislation could be
introduced there, and it would contain no ministers, nor would it
have any power to delay Bills. This second chamber would however
have significant powers as a constitutional watch-dog, or at least so it
was suggested by Labour, because it would have the power to delay
for a full parliament any measures which infringed fundamental
rights.

It would be quite unreasonable to expect a future Labour government to do nothing about a second chamber which, because it
remained primarily composed of hereditary peers, retained a Conservative preponderance. On the other hand, reforming the House in
a comprehensive way, or replacing it altogether, could in legislative
terms be an extremely time-consuming business, especially in the
absence of any consensus between the parties on what ought to be
done. Whether Labour in office would really feel that such a course
of action was something which merited a high priority in their

legislative programme seems doubtful. A more worthwhile but perhaps less likely scenario would be the kind of simple straight-forward measure that the Conservatives introduced (without cross-party agreement) in 1958, namely the Life Peerages Act. Perhaps Labour will introduce a Bill which simply excludes all peers by succession. It is the continuation of a very substantial hereditary element which is most glaringly anomalous in the late twentieth century. It is this which undermines the legitimacy of the House in a society which aspires to be democratic. If the removal of hereditary peers were linked with the all-party acceptance of a formula for the allocation of new peerages between the parties (some of which might initially be former peers by succession), the House could continue that process of gradual evolution which has characterised its entire existence. On the other hand, if even a Conservative government demonstrates the sort of indifference to and even contempt for the House which senior ministers encouraged over the War Crimes Bill, then its value and legitimacy is likely to be called increasingly into question. The House of Lords may have been the best second chamber we have got, and a surprisingly useful one given the oddity of its composition, but it is difficult to see it surviving – at least in its present form – into the twenty-first century.

### Notes

1  P. Hennessy, 'Mediaeval relic or mighty oak?', *The Listener*, 5 November 1987, 11–12. An article based on a Radio 4 *Analysis* programme broadcast on 5 November, 'The other opposition'.

2  J. Morgan, *The House of Lords and the Labour Government 1964–70* (Oxford University Press, 1975).

3  D. Shell, *The House of Lords* (Oxford: Philip Allan, 1988).

4  House of Lords, *10th Report from Select Committee on Procedure, 1970–1*, House of Lords Paper 227 (1970–71); and House of Lords, *Report by the Group on the Working of the House*, House of Lords Paper 9 (1987–88).

5  See House of Lords Debates, 31 January 1990, cols. 382–407, 'The quantity and quality of legislation', debate initiated by Lord Simon of Glaisdale, a former government minister and Lord of Appeal in Ordinary.

6  House of Lords Debates, 25 April 1990, col. 614.

7  M. Rush (ed.), *Parliament and Pressure Politics* (Oxford: Clarendon Press, 1990) 160–7, 183.

8  T. St John Bates, 'Select committees in the House of Lords', in G. Drewry (ed.), *The New Select Committes* (Oxford University Press, 1985).

9  Lord Home of the Hirsel, *Report of the Review Committee on the Second Chamber* (London: Conservative Political Centre, 1978).

10  Hennessy, 'Mediaeval relic or mighty oak?'
11  Labour Party, *Meet the Challenge: Make the Change. Final Report of Labour's Policy Review for the 1990s* (London: Labour Party, 1989).

# Part III
# The executive process

# The civil service:
# twenty years of reform

In a four-page advertiser's announcement in Norwich's evening newspaper in November 1990, Her Majesty's Stationery Office proudly announced to the public of the city where it was located that it was 'coming out of its shell'. It was 'moving into the cut and thrust of a competitive market place' and was 'presenting to the world a new face of enterprise, a buzz of excitement, the sharp edge of competition. And you ain't seen nothing yet . . . The last traces of bureaucracy are being cast aside.' Both the substance and the tone of these assertions tell volumes about how the civil service has changed over the past twenty years. In the 1950s and 1960s HMSO was an unremarkable backwater of the civil service responsible for the production of official government publications. In the late 1960s it was moved to the provinces as part of a government dispersal programme. In 1980 its commercial reins were loosened and in 1988 it was chosen as one of the first half-dozen executive agencies to be hived off from the civil service, into semi-autonomous status with its own organisational procedures, recruitment, pay scales and the like. HMSO is meant to bid for commercial work and in return has no monopoly on government publishing, since other government agencies are free to tender their publishing to any commercial company. HMSO is typical of agencies which undertake work of a quasi-commercial nature yet have a sufficient public interest component to render them unsuitable for privatisation. Other typical examples are the Royal Mint and the Vehicle Inspectorate. Some 200,000 civil servants have been transferred into such agencies, and the expectation is that by the end of the century three-quarters of the civil service will be organised as agencies, although not all as commercially orientated as HMSO.

The creation of these agencies, together with allied changes, suggests that the 1980s may possibly rank alongside the Northcote/ Trevelyan period as a period of critical change for the British civil service. Indeed, in some respects the present trends mark a shift away from the ideal of a unified and uniform civil service, imbued with a public-service ethic, which was inherited from the Victorian period. Quite apart from the significance of the dismemberment of the civil service, the eleven and a half years of Mrs Thatcher's premiership have been by any standard eventful, indeed dramatic. These years have witnessed a bitter civil service strike; major debates about the ethics of civil service behaviour sparked off by the Ponting, Westland and Wright affairs; reforms of recruitment and training; the abolition of the Civil Service Department; the much-publicised efficiency drives of Lord Rayner and his successors; and attempts to change the dominant civil service 'culture'.

It would, however, be wrong to see 1979 as marking any absolute turning point. For one thing, the incoming Conservative administration had no blueprint for radical change or grand strategy worked out in opposition. The Thatcher governments' initiatives and reforms as often as not came in response to events or as incremental adjustments in an evolving experiment. Secondly, many of the changes of the 1980s have their roots in developments or initiatives taken in the 1970s or beyond. A striking feature of recent years has been a change in the terms of reference of debates about the civil service. For most of the twentieth century civil service issues were seen as a self-contained area with debate ranging on fairly technical issues. There was a general consensus about the role of the civil service in the state and about its general organisation. The 1970s and 1980s saw a tendency to relate civil service issues much more to general political and ideological concerns. This was particularly marked with the rise to influence of New Right ideas. Under Mrs Thatcher not only were civil service questions accorded sustained, and unprecedented, interest from the very top, they were also related to the sharp end of government policy, to specific policy concerns, such as the desire to cut down drastically government expenditure. Civil service issues, moreover, came to be seen as a part of more general *administrative* reform. It should not be forgotten that the full title of the *Next Steps* reform manifesto of 1988 was *Improving Management in Government: The Next Steps*.[1] Parliament too has been much more concerned with the civil service, in contrast to the immediate post-war period.

## The aftermath of the Fulton Report

Our period begins in 1970 in the wake of the Fulton Report of 1968.[2] The Fulton Report was a major and much-publicised enquiry into the civil service; some of the members of the departmental committee which drafted it explicitly saw themselves as 'doing a Northcote/Trevelyan for the twentieth century'. Commonsense might suggest, therefore, that the history of the civil service over the next twenty years might be written in terms of the implementation of the Fulton Report. Such an interpretation would be far too simplistic.

Fulton was one of the offspring of the reforming zeal of the then Labour government which saw the 'outmoded' institutions of Britain as in need of modernisation. The Report attacked the domination of the generalist elite mandarins, called for the appointment of more specialists and professionals to senior administrative positions and for the abolition of the existing classes within the civil service. It suggested the 'hiving off' of clearly defined sections of accountable work. It also recommended improvements in training and the establishment of a Civil Service College. A new Civil Service Department, independent of the Treasury, should be established to control and organise the service.

There were three basic problems with the Fulton Report. In the first place, the Report was perceived very differently by those concerned with it. On the one hand, the radicals saw it as a manifesto for change. Foremost here was the energetic Norman Hunt (later Lord Crowther Hunt) who had devoted a whole year to working full-time on the committee. The provocative first chapter of the report with its attack on the 'cult of the amateur' represented this viewpoint. Later Hunt was deeply critical of what he saw as the mandarin elite's subversion of the Fulton reforms.[3] On the other hand, many leading administrators, including some members of the committee itself, saw Fulton as an episode in an evolving pattern of administrative change. William Armstrong, who became head of the new Civil Service Department saw the Report as 'an icebreaker', 'a catalyst' which enabled all sorts of ideas to come through which had already been evolving within Whitehall during the preceding years.[4] In this context the substance of many of the Fulton proposals were a good deal more conservative than appeared at first glance.

Another more serious problem with Fulton was certain contradictions inherent in the Report's approach. Its condemnation of generalism and preference for specialism logically pointed towards the break up of the home civil service and greatly increased departmental autonomy, whereas the Report itself urged increased uniformity, particular of grades and salary scales.

Finally, the Report's concern to increase the efficiency of the government machine was hampered by its terms of reference which prevented it from considering issues of ministerial responsibility or the role of the civil service in the state. The Fulton radicals underplayed the political and constitutional constraints imposed upon the civil service. Moreover, Fulton was somewhat imprecise in its definitions of 'efficiency' and managerial qualities. In contrast to the Thatcher years, there was a lack of political interest or 'clout' from the government. In this it shared many of the weaknesses of the 'New Britain' ethos of the reformers of the Wilson era, where time and again rhetoric proved to be stronger than substance.

In later years it became fashionable for senior officials to be dismissive of Fulton, along the lines of 'we made a lot of changes: we renamed everything'. However, if Fulton is viewed less as a blueprint for reform and more as a catalyst, its significance, from the perspective of a generation later, appears greater. It helped to instil certain attitudes into Whitehall which bore fruit in later years: the importance of interchange of personnel with the outside world; the use of planning units; the necessity for more systematic training; the better use of specialists; more flexible career patterns; and, above all, a recognition of the importance of managerial techniques and skills in the work of government in the last decades of the twentieth century. After 1979, however, these ideas were imbued with a sharper edge as they came to reflect in general terms New Right thinking on bureaucracy and in particular the political concerns of the Thatcher government.

Fulton had been especially concerned with three areas of the civil service: its structure and grading, recruitment procedures and in-service training. In all three areas changes were already taking place, largely as a response to changes in British society. Given the meritocratic ethos of the Wilson/Heath years the very term 'class' had unfortunate connotations. One of the key recommendations of the Fulton Report was that there should be a single, unified, grading structure covering all civil servants from top to bottom in the civil service. Linked to this was a desire to abolish the dividing lines between the generalist administrators and the specialist classes. Under William Armstrong, head of the civil service in the post-Fulton period, more was achieved under the first of these headings than the second. The task of reforming structure and grading within the service was initially given to a committee of the National Whitely Council, comprised of senior civil servants and union representatives, which sat from 1968 to 1973 and was presided over by Armstrong. In 1971 the old administrative, executive and clerical classes were merged and the scientific civil service was unified. The logic of these moves had its basis not only in Fulton but in the difficulties which had begun to be experienced in the 1960s in recruiting persons of sufficient calibre to the old administrative elite; increasingly recourse had to be made to promotion from the executive class. Under the new system a series of occupational groups or categories was created, for example, the administration group (comprising nearly half the home civil service), the social-security category, the secretarial category, the professional and technology category, the science category, the legal category and so on.

In one important respect the reforms made little impact: that is regarding the top echelon of administrators. Some recruits to the Administration Trainee (AT) scheme which was created in 1971 were to be 'starred' and thus became high fliers destined for the top. After January 1982 external recruitment to administrative trainee was confined to a fast stream of graduates aged under 28, with internal candidates coming from executive officers within the civil service and a limited number of non-graduates nominated by their own departments.[5]

As far as recruitment was concerned, attention and controversy after 1970 continued to be focused on the continued pre-eminence of Oxford and Cambridge graduates in the examinations for the direct entry into the AT scheme. Between 1968 and 1982 no less than three official committees investigated the charge of bias in selection procedures, accusations which were revealed to be unfounded. What this attention tended to obscure was the fact that after 1970 the civil service was facing more intense competition for graduates and other well-qualified school leavers at all levels. This was especially marked among specialists, but shortfalls in the recruitment of the high-flying AT category became a regular cause for complaint in the 1980s. This was a key consideration which encouraged the development both of in-service training and promotion from the ranks of executive

officer, where in any case graduates were becoming more numerous
following the expansion of higher education after 1960. Another
feature of the period after 1970 was the continuation of the tendency
for departments themselves to be responsible for the recruitment of
the vast mass of civil servant employees below executive officer rank.

One of the chief concerns of Fulton was to attack the philosophy
of the generalist which denigrated specialist training and instead
placed a high premium upon 'learning on the job'. As a result of its
recommendations a Civil Service College was created. The radicals
on Fulton seemed to have envisaged this as a dynamic force capable
of transforming the working practices of the civil service and
pioneering new administrative devices. The vision of something
which approximated to the prestigious French Ecole Nationale
D'Administration ill-fitted the traditions of the higher civil service
and ran up against opposition from the unions, concerned at the
elitist implications. The Civil Service College, in the words of a
critical report of 1974, was expected to 'combine the role of All Souls
and an adult education centre, with some elements of technical
education thrown in for good measure'. The first decade of its
existence was not a happy one. Most training in any case continued
to be undertaken by individual departments. However, by the late
1970s the college was adapting to a more humdrum role of providing
training in applied skills.[6]

During the 1980s the emphasis, as far as both recruitment and
training was concerned, shifted to reflect the new thinking which saw
work in the civil service in more managerial terms; however, in the
Thatcher years 'managerial' was given a more entrepreneurial interpretation. This was a feature which was equally noticeable in other
areas of public administration, such as the health service. Lord
Gowrie, when minister in charge of the civil service spoke in terms of
young civil servants going out into the 'jungle of bureaucracy' to
achieve booty in the form of savings and improved methods of
performance. Although the vocabulary of official sources was more
restrained, the message was essentially the same. A report by Sir Alex
Atkinson in April 1983 called for the recruitment of a 'new profile'
civil servant, more at home in the cut and thrust of the competitive
market-place. Dennis Trevelyan, when First Civil Service Commis-
sioner, stressed how the new breed of civil servants would have to
'develop a bias for action. We need more risk takers, innovators and
doers.' He lectured career seminars at universities with the message

that 'cerebral recluses' were unsuited for a career in the civil service: 'naked intellect' was not enough; what was required was 'action orientated thinkers'.[7] Efforts were also made in the 1980s to promote the interchange between Whitehall and the world of commerce by encouraging civil service secondment to private firms, and, in a more limited manner, recruitment from the private sector into the civil service. The problem has been that the blurring of distinction between the public and private sectors has been something of a double-edged weapon. Throughout the 1980s there has been a haemorrhage of expensively trained, Whitehall talent into the high-salaried and attractive commercial sectors.

New ideas about the kind of civil servant required had more marked effect upon changes in training than in recruitment. By the mid-1980s the Civil Service College was placing more emphasis upon training in financial and management techniques. Departments were obliged to pay the college for their training, but in return were allowed to buy in from elsewhere or to develop their own programmes. In 1984 a report of the Management and Personnel Office argued the case for gradually introducing a Senior Management Development Programme whereby staff set themselves, in conjunction with their superiors, goals of attainment with a view to improving their skills and qualifications. A version of this scheme, which began to be implemented in 1985, was extended to lower grades. At the elite level a Top Management Programme was instituted. Here senior civil servants attended intensive six-week courses with top executives from industry and commerce and from other areas of the public sector. The idea here was to turn out a 'new breed of Whitehall operatives who can hold their own with the best private sector managers'.[8]

Of all the proposed Fulton reforms none proved to be a greater disappointment to its authors than the Civil Service Department (CSD). This was established in November 1968. From the start there were ambiguities concerning its *raison d'être*. For Hunt and the radical reformers the new department was to be 'a sort of battering ram of change'. It was to preside over the implementation of the Fulton 'programme' and to spearhead the reforms which were to modernise the civil service; it was to pioneer the most modern techniques of management and stimulate reform of the organisation of government as and when they were necessary. Within Whitehall, however, the creation of the CSD was regarded as less a radical, novel departure than the continuation of tendencies already in place: the giving of more weight to management issues and the moves to reduce the overloading of the Treasury. A decade later Hunt concluded that the CSD had been an 'enormous disappointment' from the start. It was not, he believed, so much a question of it running out of steam as that 'it never had any steam in it in the first place instance'. There had been no attempt, for example, to staff the new department with people at senior level who had had experience of large organisations outside the civil service.[9]

Certainly, after about 1972 the fortunes of the CSD took a turn for the worse. In the first place, there was a loss of political direction. The CSD was remote from the Prime Minister; junior ministers who headed the department tended to carry little weight, or, if they were figures of substance, to be preoccupied with other duties. On the official side William Armstrong, the first official head of the CSD, enjoyed a close relationship with Mr Heath, but was preoccupied with advising the Prime Minister on economic strategy and the miners' strike. His successors, Sir Douglas Allen and Sir Ian Bancroft, did not enjoy any very close relationship with the Prime Minister of the day: indeed relations between Bancroft and Thatcher verged on the glacial.

Secondly, as the 1970s wore on, less credence began to be placed in reforms in the machinery of government or in structures of administration as a means of effecting change. Subsequently the definition of 'efficiency' within Whitehall began to alter. Whereas in the late 1960s and early 1970s it had been defined in terms of outputs, i.e. the quality of service which government provided, by the late 1970s more attention was being paid to inputs, i.e. to the costs of government. The new emphasis was upon economy in government and in particular manpower reductions. This became very much more marked after the Conservative victory of 1979, but the tendency was already there in the preceding years.

A third factor came to be of critical importance after 1979. This was the tendency for the CSD increasingly to be regarded as the custodian of the interests of the civil service. It was, after all, the bureaucratic department responsible for the civil service and thus in some way was bound to 'fight the corner' of the civil servants. After 1979 the civil service faced ministers, and in particular a Prime Minister, who was temperamentally hostile to officials as a breed, in a way that had not been seen before in the post-war period. It was significant that Mrs Thatcher placed the machinery for promoting efficiency within government not in the CSD, where one would have logically expected to find it, but in her own staff under the auspices of the Cabinet Office. She treated Sir Derek Rayner, her efficiency adviser, seconded from Marks and Spencer, as a kind of unofficial head of the civil service, rather than Sir Ian Bancroft, who seemed to embody all the characteristics of the mandarin class which she most despised.

After 1979 the CSD was clearly 'on probation' as far as the new government was concerned. Arguments were finely balanced as far as a possible merger of the CSD and the Treasury were concerned. The issue was investigated by the Treasury and Civil Service Select Committee of the Commons and debated within Whitehall. The balance of argument favoured the status quo. Within a year there was a striking turn about. The CSD was peremptorily abolished in November 1981 in the aftermath of the civil service strike, and its functions were dismembered. Control over pay, conditions of service and manpower numbers were vested in the Treasury; whereas management systems, recruitment, training and personnel management along with responsibility for the efficiency drives were placed in a Management and Personnel Office (MPO) which was attached to the Cabinet Office. This division of responsibilities in its turn proved to be unsatisfactory. The MPO was abolished in 1987 and its managerial responsibility for civil service pay and conditions of service were absorbed once again into the Treasury. Responsibility for the efficiency unit, however, remained with the Cabinet Office, where prime ministerial superintendence could be close.

## Mrs Thatcher and the civil service

The abolition of the CSD was especially significant in so far as it represented the determination of the Thatcher government to tackle frontally what it saw to be the privileges and the vested interests of a bureaucratic caste. Such sentiments reflected New Right political ideas which held that all public bureaucracies tend to 'over supply' government. Officials are seen as concerned with maximising their budgets and in extending their empires to the detriment of the interests of the consumers of public administration. As far as the mandarin elite was concerned such general ideas were reinforced by Mrs Thatcher's temperamental hostility to the values of the civil service elite and the suspicion that here were the true 'guilty men', the permanent politicians, who had presided over thirty years of economic decline since the late 1940s. Ironically the CSD, envisaged by the radical reformers of Fulton as a dynamo of reform, had come to be seen to embody the worst characteristics of Whitehall conservatism and vested interest.[10]

Although some of Mrs Thatcher's political advisers, notably Sir John Hoskyns and Norman Strauss from the No. 10 Policy Unit, mounted a barrage of criticism in the early 1980s against the mandarin elite, calling for radical changes in the whole constitutional position of the civil service, the Thatcher government seemed reluctant to initiate frontal assaults at this level. It preferred to reform Whitehall from within, the idea being to change the 'culture' of British central administration.

At the rank-and-file level events took a very different turn. It was, indeed, trade-union militancy in the face of government determination to curb civil service numbers and to inject market mechanisms which was in the last resort responsible for the demise of the CSD. Trade-union militancy within the civil service had been growing through the 1970s. The years 1971 and 1979 saw strike action in pursuit of pay claims and the decade was marked by a series of trade-union mergers and an altogether more militant conception of the relations between the 'staff' and official sides. In October 1980 the Thatcher government unilaterally ended the Priestley system of pay research designed to allow negotiations to assist a measure of pay comparability with jobs outside; a Cabinet committee drew up contingency plans to meet the anticipated strike. This duly commenced on 9 March 1981. After a total one-day stoppage, it took the form of a series of selected strikes in places designed to hit the government machine hard, notably the Inland Revenue and the defence establishments. The strategy was to avoid hitting the public wherever possible. The industrial action lasted for twenty-one weeks, only to end in ignominious failure: the financial resources of the unions and the less than wholehearted support from rank-and-file members proved no match for the determination of the government. Although the CSD was prepared for some negotiation, the Prime Minister and many of her colleagues saw a firm approach as a key element in the pursuit of their broader policy objectives: the undermining of union power and triumph in the battle against inflation.

The effects of the action upon defence establishments promoted the first *cause célèbre* of the Thatcher administration: the banning of unions at the intelligence-gathering centre at Goverment Communications Headquarters (GCHQ) Cheltenham. Considering that the civil service unions had openly boasted that Britain's four Polaris submarines were 'trapped' as a result of the selective strikes – W. L. Kendall of the union side had reassured the public that he would 'be on the end of the phone line if anybody wants to ring me up about some great invasion' – some government initiative was inevitable. What was less inevitable was the government's persistent refusal to compromise or negotiate. The refusal of an intrepid handful to accede to the government's terms kept the issue alive as one which could be portrayed in terms of human rights. It further soured relations with the trade-union movement, but equally illustrated just how weak the latter had become.[11]

Morale is a concept which is by its very nature intangible and tends to be avoided by writers on public administration. There is no doubt that in the early 1980s the Thatcher government's increased flexibility in handling civil service matters was purchased at a heavy cost in terms of morale. Ministers sometimes used the hideous word 'deprivilegise' to describe their intentions towards the civil service. However, as Ian Bancroft, in his retirement once remarked on television to describe a hardpressed, nineteen-year-old, female, DHSS counter-clerk in Liverpool as 'privileged' was to risk serious abuse of the English language. Even the elite felt shaken by the uncomfortable experience of serving a government of the right which was unimpressed by the values of the public sector. Pay restraints and staff cuts may not have affected the elite but, in the words of an anonymous official interviewed in September 1984 for *The Times* 'to be told by politicians that they don't want whingeing, analysis or integrity – that we must try and do as we are told and that they have several friends in the private sector who could do the job in a morning with one hand tied behind their back is a bit much'.[12]

What became known as the Efficiency Strategy represented the more positive aspects of the Thatcherite impact upon the civil service. Put simply, the philosophy was to devolve the maximum of responsibility downwards and to encourage civil servants to take initiatives. Alongside this went the view that the civil service was teeming with talent suppressed by the dead weight of petty bureaucracy. By the late 1980s the buzzword was the 'culture' of Whitehall.

The ambition of the reformers of the 1980s was to bring about a fundamental shift in not only the practices but also the attitudes inherent in government. The method of the reformers, in contrast to Fulton, was to avoid any grand enquiry and to work incrementally, developing new procedures as they went along. The Rayner Scrutinies gave way to the Financial Management Initiative (FMI), which in turn led to the *Next Steps* plans for the hiving off of agencies.

In 1979 Sir Derek Rayner was given a small unit within the Cabinet Office. The initial objective was the elimination of unnecessary waste in government. The Rayner Unit developed the technique of the in-depth scrutiny of specific aspects of work within a department in co-operation with officials within the department itself. Scrutineers were encouraged to ask fundamental questions about the way the particular task was carried out, including whether it was necessary at all. As early as April 1980 Rayner presented a Cabinet Paper, 'The conventions of government', in which he made a series of recommendations, including more precise costings of central government, more emphasis upon managerial skills and incentives for individuals who displayed initiative in the elimination of waste. Various reforms followed.[13]

One of the devices which was designed to ensure that Rayner's work continued to bear fruit was the FMI, set up in 1982. The aim here was to promote in each department and organisation a system by which managers at every level were given (1) a clear view of their objectives and a means to measure performances against those objectives; (2) the responsibility for making best use of their resources; and (3) the information and facilities necessary for the effective exercise of these responsibilities. The period from 1983 saw a conscious effort to domesticate the new thinking and practices within Whitehall.[14]

By 1986 Sir Robin Ibbs, then head of the Efficiency Unit, was becoming somewhat disillusioned with the pace and the depth of reform in Whitehall. He commissioned a thorough investigation by members of his unit and the report, *Improving Management in Government. The Next Steps* was published in 1988. The Report was a lucid and short analysis of the problems of Whitehall and was signed by Kate Jenkins, civil service head of the Efficiency Unit and two of her colleagues. In brevity and clarity it was reminiscent of the Northcote/Trevelyan Report of 1853. The *Next Steps* claimed that ministers were overloaded; that too little attention at senior levels was being paid to the delivery of services and the performance of government; and that there were unnecessary controls and restrictions which hampered the performance of managers at the middle levels. The prescription was radical. The civil service was too large and centralised; the time had come to devolve the maximum freedom of management to its components whilst preserving the essentials of ministerial responsibility. Above all, further progress in reform depended upon 'changing the cultural attitudes and behaviour of government'. Specifically, the Report recommended the setting up of executive agencies, in effect the hiving off of vast areas of civil service work. In due course this would leave only a relatively small policy-orientated 'core' at the centre of Whitehall. It suggested the creation of a high-level team, led by a project manager to plan and superintend the process of change.[15]

The Report was not received without controversy. The first draft, on the eve of the 1987 general election, was apparently suppressed on account of its sensitivity – the implication after all was that the last eight years had seen only moderate success in civil service reform – and the Treasury in 1988 baulked at the prospect of the loss of financial control. However, over the next two years rapid progress was made down the road signposted by the *Next Steps* Report. A senior civil servant, Peter Kemp, was appointed project manager and his team, like Rayner before him, received high-level backing. Within a year eight agencies had been established. Some Whitehall departments were more enthusiastic than others at the new developments; indeed a few, like the Department of Social Security, had been thinking along the same lines for years. The Treasury, after initial caution, played a key role in the process, negotiating the terms of reference of the new agencies. Each agency was given a 'framework document' spelling out its responsibilities and targets, with a review to be undertaken after three years. A further significant feature was the interest of the House of Commons' Treasury and Civil Service Committee which over the next two years closely scrutinised the developments and produced reports basically favourable to them, describing the programme as 'the most ambitious attempt at civil service reform this century'.[16] Such broad approval denoted a degree of bi-partisan support for the initiatives, which Whitehall proponents of the reforms were especially keen to foster. By July 1990, 33 agencies with a combined staff of 80,000 had been established:

the target was 50 by the following summer with a staff of some 200,000. At first it had been the small agencies of government, like HMSO, which had witnessed the changes: next in line were the giant employers such as the Inland Revenue and the Customs and Excise.[17]

The development of these quasi-autonomous agencies has, however, raised some controversy. Some have regarded them as perpetuating the old division between policy advice and managerial expertise. Others see the major problem as one of accountability. Certain areas of government scheduled for the agency treatment, for example the social-security side, are ones of great potential political sensitivity. Where does the responsibility of the executive head of the agency end and that of the minister in the sponsoring ministry begin? What are to be the rights and responsibilities of Parliament, given this further weakening of the already frail conventions of ministerial responsibility? The rapid development of moves towards European integration has highlighted a general weakness of administrative control in Britain owing to the entire absence of a tradition of administrative law or codifications over and above the world of politics and administration. This weakness, moreover, is compounded both by the secretive style of decision-making and the adversarial character of party politics.[18]

All this reflects a more general problem in relation to the changes in the civil service over the past twenty years, culminating in the rapid shifts of the Thatcher years. The aim has broadly been to encourage a more entrepreneurial, dynamic and innovative style of administrative leadership with new emphasis placed upon specialist expertise. Top civil servants are expected to be more publicly in evidence than before; at the same time the once rigid barriers between Whitehall and the outside world have been crumbling away, partly of their own volition and partly on account of shoves from politicians. Yet Parliament remains imbued with the old generalist values of the inter-war years and operates according to conventions, such as ministerial responsibility, which may be suited to a bygone age. The entrepreneurial orientation also raises questions about the ethics appropriate for a public servant. The old administrative elite, for all its shortcomings, was cemented by a clear code of conduct enforced by conventions of behaviour. At least politicians and senior officials knew what was expected of each other. The Ponting, Wright and Westland affairs are significant in so far as they illustrated how the conventional pattern had broken down. Detailed consideration is not possible here but no account of the civil service in the Thatcher years would be complete without reference to them.[19]

All of these affairs had implications for the issue of civil service ethics. Clive Ponting was a senior official at the Ministry of Defence at the time of the Falklands War. Subsequently he became uncomfortable at the ministerial responses to later parliamentary enquiries concerning the circumstances of the sinking of the Argentine cruiser, the *General Belgrano*. He sent documents to a Labour MP, Tam Dalyell, a member of the House of Commons Foreign Affairs Select Committee. In a trial which attracted maximum media exposure, Ponting was then prosecuted for providing confidential information to an unauthorised person. His defence was that he was being required to take part in an improper ministerial evasion and deception in order to avoid legitimate parliamentary scrutiny. Ponting was acquitted by the jury, but following this Sir Robert Armstrong, official head of the civil service, issued a memorandum which asserted that the civil servant had 'no constitutional personality or responsibility separate from the duly elected Government of the day'. Civil servants owed their loyalty to ministers; and ministers alone were answerable to Parliament. Civil servants who experienced an ethical problem could and should 'transfer their conscience' by consulting their superiors and, if necessary, appealing to the head of the civil service. This memorandum gave rise to a lively debate among political scientists, lawyers and, not least, MPs. A sub-committee of the Commons Treasury and Civil Service Committee was in the very process of investigating the general question further when the Westland affair broke.

The Westland affair also revolved around the question of leaks, but this time ministerially inspired leaks. The substance of a confidential letter from the Solicitor-General to the Defence Secretary, written at the instigation of the Prime Minister, had been leaked by Department of Trade and Industry officials under the direction of the ministerial head of that department, Leon Brittan, who subsequently resigned. Senior officials at No. 10 had also been implicated. The Defence Committee of the House of Commons were subsequently extremely frustrated on account of the government's refusal to allow them to question the officials involved and at the evident stonewalling of Sir Robert Armstrong who did appear before them.

The government responded to criticisms of both the Defence and the Treasury and Civil Service committees by resolutely maintaining that the confidentiality of ministerial/official relations had to be preserved. Civil servants should not answer questions posed by . parliamentary select committees which concerned their own or their colleagues' conduct. The cross-examination of Sir Robert Armstrong in a Sydney court later in 1986 in connection with the publication of Peter Wright's memoirs added further controversy to the role of civil servants. Sir Robert was forced at one point to admit that he had been 'economical with the truth'. Sir Robert appeared to be acting almost in a political capacity for the government of the day and important questions were raised concerning the propriety of civil servants 'covering up' for their political masters and the degree of secrecy in British government.

The general issue of civil service ethics was brought into focus in January 1990 with the repeal of the old Official Secrets Act with its 'catch all' provisions. A civil service code formed part of the provisions. Information was classified into six categories and disclosure in most instances was no longer subject to the criminal law but subject to the provisions of the code of conduct. The Armstrong Memorandum of 1985 was to all intents and purposes incorporated into the new code. The First Division Association was most unhappy with the new provision. It argued strongly, but in vain, for the establishment of an independent complaints body to which civil servants could appeal when they believed they had been asked to do improper things.[20]

## Conclusion

The period since 1970 has been one of very considerable change at all levels in the British civil service. Much of this change was a response to social and economic developments. It should also be remembered that moves to accentuate the managerial aspects of public administration and the erosion of barriers between the public and the private sector have been part of a European pattern. In some respects the Thatcher decade has seen a hotting up of the pace of change. However, her premiership was marked by a remarkable degree of interest in civil service matters at the highest political level, accompanied by some very striking shifts in both emphasis and structure. ·Civil service issues have also been the subject of considerable controversy in the period since 1979. The successive developments of the Rayner scrutinies, the FMI and the *Next Steps* strategy have undoubtedly changed the face of Whitehall. It would seem likely that under Mr Major a period of less spectacular consolidation will take place. A feature of the Rayner, FMI and *Next Steps* reforms, moreover, has been the extent to which they have won more general approval both within official Whitehall circles and among MPs who have monitored developments in the Treasury and Civil Service Committee. The consensus is that such developments could be shorn of their Thatcherite gloss and adapted to serve other political interests. The Labour Party in opposition, however, has shown scant interest in civil service issues, so that it seems unlikely that an incoming Labour government would either embark on any very radical adaptation or wholly reverse the changes since 1979. In the meantime the issues of civil service ethics and the accountability of the new agencies are likely to surface before the end of the century.

## Notes

1  Efficiency Unit, *Improving Management in Government: The Next Steps* (London: HMSO, 1988).

2  Report of the Committee, *The Civil Service*, 2 vols., Cmnd. 3638 (London: HMSO, 1968).

3  Peter Kellner and Lord Crowther Hunt, *The Civil Servants: An Inquiry into Britain's Governing Class* (London: Macdonald & Jayne's, 1980) 59–99.

4  House of Commons, Expenditure Committee, Session 1976–77, (535), Eleventh Report, *The Civil Service* (London: HMSO, 1977), vol. 2, *Minutes of Evidence*, q. 1499, 656.

5  A full account is given in Geoffrey K. Fry, *The Changing Civil Service* (London: Allen & Unwin, 1985) 36–63.

6  *Ibid.*, 63–9.

7  Lord Gowrie, Radio 4, 13 February 1985; Atkinson, Management and Personal Office, *Selection of Fast Stream Graduates to the Home Civil Service, the Diplomatic Service and the Tax Inspectorate, and of Candidates from within the Service* (London: HMSO 1983); Trevelyan, *The Times*, 23 January 1986.

8  P. R. Coster, 'Training for senior management study', Management and Personnel Office Paper (Cabinet Office, May 1984); *The Times*, 4 March 1985.

9  House of Commons, Treasury and Civil Service Committee, First Report Session 1980–81, *The Future of the Civil Service Department*, Minutes of Evidence, q. 950 37.

10  For a full account of the rise and fall of the CSD see John Greenaway, Steve Smith and John Street, *Deciding Factors in British Politics: A Case-*

Studies Approach (London: Routledge, 1991) Chapter 7.

11   Fry, *Changing Civil Service* 137–43; Peter Hennessy, *Whitehall* (London: Secker & Warburg, 1989) 678–80.

12   *The Times*, 22 September 1984.

13   Hennessy, *Whitehall*, 589–605.

14   *Ibid.*, 605–19.

15   Efficiency Unit, *Next Steps*.

16   House of Commons, Treasury and Civil Service Committee, Eighth Report, Session 1989–90 (London: HMSO, 1990).

17   *Independent*, 31 October 1990.

18   R. A. Chapman, 'The next steps', *Public Policy and Administration*, vol. 3 (1988) 3–10.

19   Useful summaries of all three affairs are to be found in Gavin Drewry and Tony Butcher: *The Civil Service Today* (Oxford: Blackwell, 1988) 1–8.

20   *Guardian*, 27 January 1990.

# The judiciary: justice with accountability?

It is unlikely that men and women will ever cease to wound, cheat and damage each other. There will always be a need for judges to resolve their disputes in an orderly manner. As people grow ever less willing to accept unreservedly the demands of authority, the judiciary, like other public institutions, will be subjected to a growing amount of critical analysis.[1]

## Introduction

By its very function, the judiciary stands exposed to criticism, some of it hostile, from some or other section of the community. Its role is to decide on matters on which there is invariably competing interpretation, if not competing interest. Such decisions are rarely welcomed by both parties, and critical comment on the equity, fairness or standards of justice applied in particular cases has always surrounded judicial processes. What has been a feature of the past two decades, however, is criticism of a rather different order. A case has been assembled which, based on an analysis of a multitude of judicial decisions and statements, points toward fundamental flaws in the role, profile and workings of the British judiciary. The publication in 1977 of John Griffith's *The Politics of the Judiciary* was in many respects a watershed in this development. Moving beyond commentary on the appropriateness of particular legal decisions, Griffith advanced the controversial thesis of systematic partiality in judicial decisions. In what has become a famous passage, Griffith stated that:

on every major social issue which has come before the courts during the last 30 years – concerning industrial relations, political protest, race relations, government secrecy, police powers, moral behaviour – the judges have supported the conventional, established and settled interests. And they have reacted strongly against challenges to those interests.[2]

While not necessarily agreeing with the full weight, and implications, of Griffith's analysis, subsequent critics have nevertheless added to the growing body of concerned commentary which claims root and branch deficiencies in the judicial system. All of which leads one to question why such fundamental criticism has emerged during the 1970s and 1980s. It may well reflect, to return to Pannick's statement above, a greater reluctance on behalf of commentators and the public at large to respect as a matter of course the traditional hierarchy of authority, and therefore that most traditional authority of all, the judiciary, in particular. It may also relate to a shift, or at least perceived shift, in the profile of the judiciary itself. There is a strong case for the claim that, while the judiciary has always had to make decisions of a 'political' nature, the scope for that level of intervention has been enhanced in the relatively recent past. In a number of areas Parliament has determined that the law will play a more significant role than was previously the case – in industrial relations, race discrimination and sex discrimination, for example. Often as a result of indeterminate legal statute, where judicial discretion is unavoidable, this has led to controversial interpretations of the law by top members of the judiciary, some of whom appear to have relished the opportunity to play a more active role in defining the law.

For these reasons, the judiciary has been forced into, or has put itself into, the political limelight in a way not typical of earlier times. However, a central issue for political science, and one which has become more acute with the passage of time, is the extent to which this higher profile adopted by the judiciary can be supported by a judicial structure which has changed little over the centuries. It is essentially a question of accountability. As the judiciary accrues more power to influence if not determine social and political processes, it is increasingly confronted with the accusation of being an 'unaccountable elite'.[3] The social structure of the judiciary, its provisions for the selection and training of judges, its resilience if not hostility to criticism, its mystique and secrecy, are all the subject of growing attention. And there are signs of some attempt at reform. The appointment of Lord Mackay as Lord Chancellor in 1987 appears to have injected a more progressive and open approach into the judicial system. The lifting of the ban imposed on judges on speaking to the media and taking part in radio and television programmes is a modest, but welcome, move in this direction.[4] This, however, will not satisfy those who identify more fundamental problems in the system. For these commentators, the judiciary is still very much 'on trial'.

## The judiciary on trial

Much of the criticism levelled at the social composition, training and selection processes within the British judiciary stems from concern over the way judges actually go about their role, in what they do or say. There is little doubt that such concern has grown over the past two decades. The catalogue of contentious actions and statements has expanded to cover areas as wide apart as industrial relations and rape trials. To some commentators there is a discernible pattern to such cases, a systematic bias, a point to which I shall return later. Whichever way, the record of controversy is extensive.

The activities of the judiciary in the field of industrial relations have of course long been the focus of critical attention. Griffith's study documents a series of judicial decisions prior to 1970, in areas such as the right to picket and the right to strike, which lend weight to his thesis of anti-unionism within the judiciary. However, events subsequent to that were, of course, to plunge judges more explicitly into the fray. The Heath government's 1971 Industrial Relations Act was an attempt to establish legal penalties in certain areas of trade-union activity, including the internal affairs of unions. It established the National Industrial Relations Court (NIRC), which included members drawn from the judiciary, which was granted powers to review complaints arising under the Act and, if it wished, to impose penalties on transgressors. It attained quick notoriety in 1972 when it ordered three dockers to be imprisoned for contempt of court, although the Appeal Court subsequently released them after a request by the official solicitor.[5] Just over a month later the NIRC again made an order of imprisonment, in this case for five dockers, which, amid massive labour protest, it subsequently withdrew. Nevertheless, such events were acute reflections of the tense relationship between the courts and the labour movement which the Conservative legislation had provoked, some would say to its cost. And if the latter half of the decade was to be one of relative tranquility between the trade unions and the (now Labour) government, and therefore between the unions and the courts (the NIRC was abolished in 1974), the 1980s were to see the reverse.

The Thatcher governments, through legislation in the Employment Acts of 1980, 1982 and 1984, and the Trade Union Act of
1984, have unashamedly extended the role of the courts in the
regulation of industrial relations, and thus opened up new chapters
in relationships between the trade unions and the judges. On issues
such as the closed shop, balloting of members and unofficial industrial action, the judiciary has been given responsibilities to determine
the propriety of internal and external matters of industrial relations,
and of imposing penalties where it was deemed appropriate.[6] Two
other developments stand out in the record of judicial approaches to
industrial relations during the 1980s. In 1983, the Prime Minister,
acting on the royal prerogative as head of the civil service, decided to
ban the union at the Government Communications Headquarters
(GCHQ), following several work stoppages. The High Court held
that the ban violated natural justice in that it breached the right of
association. The government appealed, and the Court of Appeal held
in its favour, on the basis that it had acted on grounds of national
security.

By 1989, the last remaining trade unionist had been dismissed at
GCHQ. The other area of controversy surrounded the responses of
the courts to the National Union of Mineworkers' (NUM) strike of
1984–85. The courts were embroiled in two senses, one concerning
civil process, the other criminal. In October 1984, the High Court
fined the NUM £200,000, and Arthur Scargill £1,000 for contempt
of court. This followed a court ruling in favour of two Yorkshire
miners that the national strike was unofficial and unlawful, which
Scargill chose to ignore. Although his fine was paid anonymously,
the High Court set out to sequester NUM funds. When it transpired
that all NUM funds had been transferred abroad, the courts put all
assets in the hands of the official receiver. From a different direction
the courts were to play an important role in the policing of the picket
lines.[7] By sanctioning new, but arbitrary powers of the police to
prevent secondary picketing, by supporting the police case on the
propriety of actions to set up road blocks many miles from the
coalfields, and by accepting police interpretations of offences under
public order law, the courts, according to some critics, were oriented
to reduce the effectiveness of the mass picket.[8]

Accusations that the judiciary has tended to act partially against
the trade unions have been coupled with claims that they have been
less than sympathetic with the political left. Such views were cer-

tainly fuelled by the Greater London Council (GLC) case. A central platform of the Labour Party's campaign for the 1981 GLC elections was a pledge to dramatically cut fares on buses and tubes run by London Transport, one that was honoured within six months to the tune of 25 per cent. One consequence was an increase in the rates levied on all London boroughs. Bromley Borough, under Conservative rule, brought an action to the High Court to challenge the propriety of the move, which was then rejected by the court. However, after an appeal, the Court of Appeal upheld the Bromley case, condemning what it called a 'crude abuse of power' by the GLC. The Law Lords supported unanimously the Court of Appeal decision after the GLC in turn appealed, on the grounds that the GLC was bound by statute to 'promote the provision of integrated, efficient and economic transport facilities and services'. Much rested on their Lordships' ruling on the term 'economic', which they took to mean 'cost-effectiveness', and which they argued entailed an obligation to rate-payers and not just to the transport users. Labour councillors were furious at what they saw as blatant political use of judicial power, to effectively overturn a policy which had been put openly to the local electorate and won support accordingly, and a similar case was raised in the House of Commons, although it was rejected by Mrs Thatcher. Much was made of the apparent consistency between the Law Lords' ruling and the government's own stance on the GLC and its policies.

Claims that the judiciary has tended to side with the government have also surrounded a number of cases on the field of official secrets. The 'exemplary' sentence of six months' imprisonment imposed on Sarah Tisdall in 1984 is one such case. Ms Tisdall was charged under Section 2 of the Official Secrets Act for releasing to the *Guardian* a memorandum issued by the then Secretary of Defence, Michael Heseltine, on the subject of the arrival of Cruise missiles at RAF Greenham Common. Despite pleading guilty, and despite evidence that she acted out of conscience and was of excellent character, Mr Justice Cantley passed down a sentence which was seen by many as excessive,[9] and was explicitly intended as a deterrent to others who might contemplate leaking confidential government documents. At around the same, time, ironically, another case was brewing which led to a series of events which have been described as 'Profumo without the sex', the Clive Ponting affair. There were, of course, a host of controversies linked to the issue at the centre of this case, the sinking of the Argentian heavy cruiser, the *General Belgrano* in May 1982 during the Falklands War, with the loss of 368 lives. Ponting was charged under section 2 of the Official Secrets Act for passing papers relating to *Belgrano* to the Labour MP Tam Dalyell. One of the high points in the subsequent prosecution was the judge's summing-up to the jury on 11 February 1985. In it the judge made a statement which was seen as a mortal blow to Ponting's defence. He rejected the view that someone in Ponting's position could justifiably interpret for himself what is, and is not 'in the interests of the state', as stated in Section 2. Rather, the judge argued, 'in the interests of the state' referred to the policies of the government of the day. Effectively, this directed the jury to ignore the central thrust of Ponting's defence, and all of the odds pointed to conviction. To the surprise of many, not least to Ponting himself, who had apparently consumed a hearty breakfast at the Savoy in expectation that his next would be in prison, the jury unanimously acquitted after no more than three hours. This did not, however, detract from the significance of the judicial interpretation in question, which entered into the catalogue of contentious judicial decisions of the 1980s.

That catalogue, however, goes beyond questions of party politics and the judiciary's attitudes to established organisations like the trade unions. The 1970s and 1980s have also been characterised by a growing concern over judicial attitudes to women. Again, this is no new phenomenon, as controversy over the decisions by the courts on issues affecting women, on questions such as their right to member-ship of professional organisations, has a long history.[10] Neverthe-less, a range of decisions and statements made by judges over the past twenty years has attracted the wrath of commentators from a variety of backgrounds, most importantly the women's movement, whose critique of the courts and the judiciary has done most to highlight the unacceptable face of judges' attitudes to women.[11] Nowhere has this been more apparent than in the area of rape trials, where certain judges have attained notoriety for statements which have been noth-ing less than bizarre. At the Old Bailey in 1976, Judge Sutcliffe directed the jury to be sceptical of the evidence of a rape victim, with the statement that 'it is known that women in particular and small boys are liable to be untruthful and invent stories', and in 1982, Judge Wild summed up at a rape trial arguing that, 'Women who say no do not always mean no. It is not just a question of how she says it, how she makes it clear. If she doesn't want it, she only has to keep her legs shut.' The list of such outrageous statements is extensive, but it goes beyond words. In perhaps the most controversial decision of its kind, Judge Richards in 1982 fined a convicted rapist £2,000 rather than imprison him, on the grounds that the victim was guilty of 'contributory negligence' because she had been hitch-hiking late at night, when the offence took place. This undoubtedly did serious damage to the image of the judiciary, and was probably an important event in subsequent changes to the criminal law in 1988, when the right of appeal by the prosecutuion for 'over lenient' sentences was created. Most certainly, by their statements and decisions in relation to women, judges have attracted criticism, adding to that already within debate on the judiciary, over their social background, selection and training.

In relation to the above, then, the judiciary stands itself very much on trial. The case for the prosecutuion has been further strengthened by decisions surrounding the convictions of alleged terrorists in the cases of the Guildford Four and the Birmingham Six. The decision in 1989 and 1990 to quash convictions in the first case, and similarly a year later in the second, has inevitably fuelled controversy. While all of these cases raise fundamental questions about police powers and methods, and also about current laws of evidence which have allowed convictions on uncorroborated confessions (which differ from Scottish law), they also act as a comment on the propriety of earlier decisions to refuse appeals against wrongful conviction. In the case of the Guildford Four, particular attention has focused on the 1977 Court of Appeal decision, under Lord Roskill, not to order a re-trial in front of a jury after fresh evidence, in the form of admissions from the Balcombe Street gang, had been made available, but rather to hear it themselves in the Appeal Court. The criticism made over the decision at the time, not least by other powerful members of the judiciary such as Lord Scarman and Lord Devlin, looks ever more warranted in the light of those subsequent rulings to quash the convictions. The apparent reluctance to remedy the weaknesses in previous decisions is an issue on which the judiciary stands accused. Indeed, one of the most startling features of the case of the Birmingham Six was Lord Denning's statement in 1980 to the effect that one reason why an action alleging police brutality had to be dismissed was that, if successful, it would mean that the police were guilty of perjury, and that the courts had acted improperly in admitting evidence. In other words, that the convictions were erroneous!

The accusations of injustice levelled at judges, furthermore, have been formed against a backcloth dating back to the 1970s, which has placed the judiciary in a unique position within the processes of justice in Northern Irleand. As a result of the recommendations of the Commission chaired by Lord Diplock, Parliament introduced major changes to the structure of the criminal trial process in the Province with the Northern Ireland (Emergency Provisions) Act 1973. On the grounds that one of the main obstacles to the efficient execution of justice in trials involving terrorist offences was possible intimidation of jurors, and the likelihood of sectarian verdicts in such cases, the Act abolished trial by jury in certain 'scheduled offences', and replaced it with trial by judge alone. Not only would judges enjoy their already powerful position in relation to ruling on the admissibility of evidence and passing sentence, they would also have responsibility for deciding on verdict. The 'Diplock Courts', as they were to become known, with the questions they raise about civil liberties, 'case hardening' (the claim that over time judges have become increasingly inclined to ignore the defence case), and the incompatibility of the roles of adjudicator of both admissible evidence and guilt, have placed the judiciary in a volatile relationship with the politics of Northern Ireland. It is one in which cases like that of the Guildford Four appear to fit all too easily.

Looking over the range of judicial decisions which constitute the case against the judiciary, a question which needs to be asked is whether they together point to a process of 'systematic' bias in the way argued by the Griffith's thesis. Is there a coherent pattern of judicial partiality at work here, running through from decisions in the field of industrial relations to injustices in case of alleged terrorism? The very posing of the question indicates the difficulty of assuming some logical connection between the areas of judicial decision-making involved. It is difficult to draw lines of continuity between them, other than that they act as separate chapters in a growing chorus of criticism which has developed in the recent past.

Furthermore, to talk of a systematic bias in the way of some commentators overlooks two very important features of the current debate over the judiciary. First, it is essential not to ignore or underplay inconsistencies in judicial decisions. We should not forget that, whatever the final ruling in the GLC case, for example, the High Court initially ruled in favour of the cheap fares policy. A similar discrepancy existed between the decisions in the GCHQ case. Due acknowledgment should also be given to the fact that many Court of Appeal and Law Lords rulings are not unanimous, and that there are 'liberal' as well as 'conservative' judges (Lord Scarman being perhaps the most notable of the former category). Judges have often used their discretion in progressive as well as reactionary ways. For example, very recently a judge at Leicester Crown Court made legal history by refusing to accept a husband's immunity from rape charges, stating that, 'I find it hard to believe it was ever the common law that a husband could beat his wife into submission to sexual intercourse'. This could well help establish a new law of marital rape campaigned for by feminist organisations for two decades. And judges do not always side with Conservative governments. One example was the Court of Appeal ruling in September 1990 to uphold the community charge set by Lambeth Council, and refuse the Environment Secretary, then Chris Patten, permission to take his objections to the House of Lords. These cases do not, of course, constitute a full counterweight to the catalogue of criticisms of judicial decisions in other directions. They do, however, require us to be cautious about presuming one-directional and systematic bias.

A second reservation about such presumptions is that they tend to leave little scope for a serious search for reforms to the present judicial system. One pessimistic consequence of the Griffiths' thesis, as Lord Devlin has pointed out, is that, in claiming an inevitable partiality and conservatism in the judicial role, it appears to preclude significant reform to the existing structure of the judiciary.[12]

### The case for reform: towards a more accountable judiciary

Professional discretion and professional autonomy are concepts that have taken something of a battering in recent years. Under the banner of 'accountability', even if behind it lay perhaps the more important slogan of 'economy', established professional groups have experienced government-initiated attempts to reduce their discretion to decide on behalf of themselves and their clients. Doctors' freedoms to prioritise forms of treatment, prescribe drugs and to allow or disallow patients to move to other practices, have been curtailed by GP contracts and fixed budgets. Teachers' freedoms to set the school curriculum and to set and maintain their own professional standards have been subjected to the strictures of a National Curriculum and staff-appraisal systems. Equivalent processes have been under way in the probation, social work and lecturing professions. Above all, performance measurement and assessment have become the symbols of governments' attempts to make such occupational groups accountable and provide 'value for money'. Yet there is little evidence to show that such winds of change have yet begun to bite into the profession of the judge, despite the enormous discretion, autonomy and power which that profession possesses. Indeed, the judiciary is still largely wedded to a system and structure set out in essence in previous centuries. And as its influence appears to grow in ever more areas of political, social and personal life, the degree to which the organisation is equipped to respond to the challenges of public scrutiny and processes of accountability is now the central question for students of the judiciary to address.

The pressures for reform of the judiciary stem from concerns over virtually every feature of the judicial structure, from its recruitment base to its system of review and judicial performance. Even the way judges dress has been the subject of critical comment, perhaps not surprising in an organisation in which the wearing of wigs is still obligatory three hundred years after they went out of fashion. At a time when many public bodies are being required to ask of themselves whether the way they have done things in the past is necessarily the way things should be done in the future, it is only right that the judiciary should face up to the weaknesses of relying upon tradition as the rationale for its organisational structure.

A starting point for reform is with the system of recruitment, selection and promotion which underpins the profession. The unrepresentative nature of the judiciary is well known. In terms of social composition it is almost exclusively male and white, with no one at present under the age of forty, and most over the age of fifty. It is still the case that in terms of educational background, private schooling and Oxbridge constitute the typical profile of the judge. The more one progresses up the judicial hierarchy, the more its unrepresentativeness is exposed. One factor responsible for this is the restricted base for recruitment to the judiciary. Its 'raw material' stems largely from members of the Bar, who have exclusive right to judicial appointment to the High Court and above. Lawyers from the solicitors' branch of the legal profession are only eligible to sit as circuit judges and recorders, and even here they constitute only 10 per cent of membership, despite the fact that nationwide there are ten times as many solicitors as barristers. The organisation of the Bar is such that within itself a socially narrow profile, both in terms of background and attitude, prevails.[13] One possible reform in this context, although one concerned more with the quality and cost of legal services as a whole, is the fusion of the two branches into one legal profession.[14] An inevitable consequence of such a move would be the destruction of existing demarcation between the rights of eligibility to the bench, and thus a widening of the social base for recruitment. Despite the strength of the case against the present division, such a move seems unlikely. However, there have been signs of a shift towards a more reform-oriented approach to the profession, both from within and without, over the past ten years. While many were disappointed with the conclusions of the 1979 Report of the Royal Commission on Legal Services, which essentially recommended maintenance of the status quo, by the end of the 1980s attitudes seemed to have mellowed. In 1986 the Law Society (representing solicitors) and the Bar, set up the Marre Committee to look into the organisation of the legal profession in a similar way to that of the Royal Commission. It recommended, amongst other things, the extension of eligibility to the High Court to solicitors. In 1989, Lord Mackay published a Green Paper on the legal profession which mirrored many such preferences. The scene is very much set for reforms which will widen the base for recruitment to the judiciary in this way. Liberal commentators may welcome such developments, but would like to see eligibility to become a judge widened even further. One proposal is to allow academic lawyers to become judges, and operate at all levels in the judicial hierarchy. Such a move, which would bring Britain into line with many European countries, could well help broaden not just the social base but also the intellectual profile of the judiciary, and introduce other forms of expertise into its decision-making processes.

This relates closely to the question of training. The traditional view has been that the essence of preparation for the position of judge is experience gained practising as an advocate. The need for substantial training above and beyond that has not been recognised within the judiciary. Indeed, Lord Devlin once argued that such training may prohibit the judge from reflecting 'the attitude of the ordinary man applying an intelligent mind to technical questions'.[15] This statement itself will to some provide evidence that experience at the Bar is not itself adequate as preparation for the responsibilities of a judge, and the brief 'training' now provided shows little recognition that the job of judge and that of advocate are very different. If the knowledge gained from disciplines such as psychology, criminology, penology and academic law are not to be brought into judicial decision-making through widening the base of those eligible to sit as a judge, then at the very least they should enter through a full and formal training of potential recruits to the judiciary. As Pannick puts it, 'The amateur approach which the English legal system adopts in this context hinders the effective performance of the judicial function.'[16]

Widening the social base of the judiciary and enhancing its decision-making capacities by judicial training are only a part of an overall package of reforms currently on the table. Others relate more specifically to the question of accountability. Critics have identified three areas in which a need for new structures of accountability exists. First, the processes of appointment of judges to senior positions within the judiciary. This has been described as more on par with a Papal Conclave rather than a rigorous selection of senior law-makers in a democratic society. The Lord Chancellor will recommend candidates to the Queen after a wholly secretive and insular process of consultation with other senior judges. There is no public participation or scrutiny of the process, no open competition on the grounds of professed merit. Nothwithstanding the possibility of allowing candidates from outside the Bar onto the bench, one proposal is to subject all judicial appointments at senior level to a Paliamentary Select Committee on Legal Affairs. Prospective candidates would have their cases reviewed by the committee and its deliberations would be placed on public record.

Also concerned with the issue of openness is the attitude of the judiciary to publicity. Lord Hailsham, as Lord Chancellor throughout much of the 1980s, was notably hostile to members of the judiciary appearing on radio and television, invoking the 'Kilmuir rules' prohibiting such activities in support of his case that they may make themselves vulnerable in so doing. The justification for this restriction is less than convincing, particularly in the light of the high profile of senior judges in out of court committees, such as Lord Scarman on the inquiry into the Brixton disorders, and Butler-Sloss on the inquiry into the child-abuse cases in Cleveland. As long as they do not comment inappropriately on cases in which they are personally involved, there seems little purpose in not allowing the public to have access to the views and values of our judges. Lord

Mackay, as Hailsham's successor, has fortunately relaxed the restrictions enforced previously, and in so doing has helped further the process of creating a more open and public judiciary. This modest reform may help in a small way to begin to disrupt the mysticism with which the judiciary seems intent to surround itself.

The third area in which reforms in the direction of greater accountability have been proposed is in relation to review of judicial performance. Here the contrast with other professional groups, who have had to face up to the processes of external scrutiny, whether by management or public authority, is apparent. Indeed, on a number of occasions during the 1980s Lord Hailsham reacted bitterly to attempts to criticise members of his profession, such as when, in a letter to *The Times* in 1975, he compared denunciation of individual judges to 'mob rule'. It is surely stretching the logic of judicial independence too far when any critical consideration of individual decisions of judges, no matter how questionable such decisions may be, is rebutted in this fashion. In contrast, liberal legal commentators such as Pannick have advocated the creation of a Judicial Performance Commission, an independent body to consider complaints of injudicious conduct. Such proposals have recently been embraced by the Labour Party in its policy document *A Safer Britain*, and would create an equivalent machinery for the judiciary, for example, to that now established for the police service in the form of the Police Complaints Authority. If allied to a Parliamentary Select Committee on Legal Affairs, referred to earlier, a system would be in place to make the judiciary accountable to outside authority. No diminution of judicial independence need transpire as a consequence.

## Conclusion

There are indications from the present Conservative government that reform of the judiciary is in the air. A Green Paper on the issue has recently been proposed, and no doubt many of the reforms discussed above will be under consideration. The government has already made some move to reduce the discretion of judges in one respect with the Criminal Justice Act 1991, which seeks to restrict the scope for sentencers to pass custodial sentences on non-violent offenders. Extra-national limitations to judicial discretion, furthermore, imposed by the European Court of Justice and Community Law, have also been features of the recent history of the British legal system which contemporary analyses of the judiciary must acknowledge.[17] However, no one should underestimate the resilience of the profession to withstand change and to maintain its position and organisation within the structure of British decision-making. While much activity has surrounded the judiciary over the past twenty years, including some modest concessions to the reform campaign, the odds are very much in favour of the view that in twenty years time little radical reform will have been achieved. And the chances are that wigs will still be very much the order of the day.

## Notes

1    D. Pannick, *Judges* (Oxford University Press, 1988).
2    J. Griffith, *The Politics of the Judiciary* (Manchester University Press, 1977).
3    J. Waldron, *The Law* (London: Routledge, 1990).
4    M. Berlins and C. Dyer, *The Law Machine* (Harmondsworth: Penguin, 1989).
5    P. Hain, *Political Trials in Britain* (London: Allen Lane, 1984).
6    D. Farnham and J. Pimlott, *Understanding Industrial Relations* (London: Cassell, 1990).
7    P. Green, *The Enemy Without* (Milton Keynes: Open University Press, 1990).
8    B. Fine and R. Millar (eds.), *Policing The Miners' Strike* (London: Lawrence & Wishart, 1985).
9    D. Hooper, *Official Secrets: the Use and Abuse of The Act* (London: Coronet, 1987).
10   A. Sachs and J. Wilson, *Sexism and The Law* (Oxford: Martin Robertson, 1978).
11   S. Atkins and B. Hoggett, *Women and the Law* (Oxford: Blackwell, 1984).
12   Lord Devlin, *The Judge* (Oxford University Press, 1979).
13   T. Gifford, *Where's the Justice?* (Harmondsworth: Penguin, 1986).
14   M. Zander, *Cases and Materials on the English Legal System* (London: Weidenfeld & Nicolson, 1984).
15   Devlin, *The Judge.*
16   Pannick, *Judges.*
17   N. Nugent, *The Government and Politics of The European Community* (London: Macmillan, 1989).

**13**  *R. A. W. Rhodes*

# Local government

## Introduction

In spite of rumours to the contrary, Britain was not created afresh, and local government did not die, in 1979. British politics has long been distinctive for its traditions and continuity. The story of local government is no exception. This chapter looks at the developments in local government over the past two decades. It focuses upon the changing relationship between centre and locality because this relationship has been the single most important problem. The controversy over local rates and the allegedly high level of local expenditure has fuelled controversy, dominated political debate and created an avalanche of legislation. I argue that, irrespective of party, central government policies towards local government have failed to recognise that the two levels of government are interdependent; that the British administrative structure is fragmented or differentiated; and that private interests, such as the professions and quasi-professions, are institutionalised in government and act as an important source of inertia. As a result, a policy mess has been created in which neither level of government can achieve its policy objectives.

Between 1970 and 1990, it is possible to identify five distinct phases in central–local relations:

| | |
|---|---|
| 1970–74 | partnership |
| 1974–79 | corporatism |
| 1979–83 | direction |
| 1983–87 | abolition |
| 1987–90 | revolution |

This chapter provides a brief description of each phase before providing a brief explanation of trends in central–local relations throughout the 1970s and 1980s. (This chapter draws upon, and at some points paraphrases, my earlier work on this topic.[1])

## Partnership, 1970–1974

Consultation was the 'normal' style of central–local relations throughout the post-war period until the mid-1970s. For most of this time, local service spending was buoyant, and the numbers of local-authority employees grew fairly regularly. A whole series of expectations about reasonably consensual dealings between Whitehall and local government were embodied in the concept of 'partnership'. Ministers often went out of their way to choose modes of implementing policy that maximised voluntary local authority co-operation. For example, in 1965, the Labour Minister of Education, Anthony Crosland, decided on civil service advice to implement comprehensive reorganisation of secondary schools by means of a strong letter of advice (backed up with Department of Education and Science (DES) controls over new school-building), rather than by new legislation to compel councils to change their ways. Over the next ten years nearly nine out of every ten local educational authorities went comprehensive. Although this change was seen at the time as an example of central government's power over local authorities, the truth is that there were never any effective means by which the DES could compel councils to reorganise their schools.

The partnership phase lasted throughout the Heath government's period of office. There were some selective attempts by the Conservatives to develop more stringent controls over council policies. For example, the government forced through changes in council-housing finances against strong resistance. But elsewhere the government was cautious. Sales of council housing were successfully obstructed by all Labour councils. A full-scale reorganisation of local authorities was enacted against much opposition from councils destined to lose many of their powers. However, the government adopted a two-tier system which was more popular with existing councillors and officers than previous Labour proposals for unitary authorities. Staffing and financing arrangements for the reorganisation were tailored to minimise opposition. In fact, the Heath government presided over a bigger four-year growth in local service spending than any 1960s administration.

## Corporatism, 1974–1979

Central-local relations changed fairly gradually in the 1970s towards a more corporatist framework in response to the stringent

economic measures imposed after the oil crisis and at the insistence
of the International Monetary Fund (IMF). Corporatism means that
a few powerful organisations are extensively co-opted into closed
relations with central government, taking on a dual role of representing their members to government and of controlling their members
on behalf of the government. The Labour government made a sustained effort to introduce this kind of top-level, formalised
bargaining into its dealings with local government. Its key innovation was to try to incorporate the powerful local-authority associations (and their joint bodies) into a sort of 'social contract' about
local government spending. For the first time, Whitehall set up a
forum in which to discuss the long-run future of local spending with
the local authority associations. This body, called the Consultative
Council on Local Government Finance, was remarkable because it
brought the Treasury and local-authority representatives into face-
to-face contact for the first time, and explicitly integrated the planning of local spending into the Whitehall system for projecting public
expenditure five years ahead (known as the Public Expenditure
Survey system). The Council's brief was:

regular consultation and co-operation between central and local government on major financial and economic issues of common concern, with
special emphasis on the deployment of resources both in the long term and
the short term. In this way local government can be associated with the
process of settling priorities for the whole of the [next] five year public
expenditure period and local government would be consulted at an early
stage when individual proposals for new policies directly involving local
government were being shaped.

In practice, the government hoped to involve the local authority
associations in policy-making affecting local government, to persuade them of the 'realities' of the economic situation, and thus enlist
them as allies in the battle to keep down the growth of local spending. In the Treasury's view:

Through consultation and persuasion effectively done I hoped we could get
effective control. If we do not get effective control we could not remain in the
position where there was not effective control, and therefore other measures
would have to be considered.[2]

The Consultative Council on Local Government Finance was
successful in getting the local authority associations to persuade their
members to behave with restraint. But there were other pressures in
the same direction. The Council was set up at the same time as a

system of strict cash limits on central grants to local authorities. Under a Labour government, many of the naturally high-spending councils could be persuaded to stay close to government guidelines out of a feeling of party loyalty and concern not to rock the boat. In addition, the swing against Labour in the mid-term local elections meant that the government's policy of restraint dovetailed neatly with the natural inclinations of the new Conservative-controlled authorities. The Council undoubtedly increased the volume of knowledge in local government of Whitehall's problems, and promoted the local authority associations into greater prominence than before. The associations' new role revolved centrally around financial, staffing and economic issues, and the main bodies that found their influence decreased by this change were the many different policy networks promoting increased spending in one issue area or another. Whatever else it accomplished, the Council helped to shift influence with local government away from service-orientated councillors and officers (for example, the school education policy network) and towards local politicians and finance directors more concerned with increased efficiency and financial soundness. In effect, the Council was a Whitehall attempt to build up the influence of the local authority associations and local government finance managers, so that they would be better able to control the rest of the local government system in return for consultation and a direct voice in future planning.

### Direction, 1979–1983

There are marked continuities after 1979: for example, the use of cash limits and cuts in local expenditure. By contrast, the Thatcher government had little faith in corporatist devices. It was committed not only to reducing public expenditure but it also had to ride out a world economic recession. Local authorities were expected to bear the brunt of the cuts. The means for attaining the 'cuts' were provided by the Local Government, Planning and Land Act 1980 which introduced grant penalties. In effect, any local authority spending more than the government's estimate of what it needed to spend would lose central government grant at an increasing rate. The government also reduced the total amount of grant to local authorities from 61 to 53 per cent of their expenditure and imposed tight ceilings on capital expenditure. The response of local authorities was to increase the rates or local property tax to compensate for this loss of grant. Local authority current expenditure – for example, expenditure on salaries, lighting, heating – continued to rise in real terms, i.e. disregarding wage increases and inflation. By 1983 it was 9 per cent higher than in 1979. On the other hand, capital expenditure – for example, expenditure on fixed assets such as buildings – fell by 12 per cent over the same period and the total number of local government employees fell by some 4 per cent. At best, the Conservatives' record of success can be described as mixed.

A government committed to pushing back the frontiers of the state intervened massively in local affairs. Distinctively, it sought direct control of the total expenditure (not just central grant) of each individual local authority; especially high-spending Labour councils. The policy may not have been successful but the search for control was on and the search was not restricted to local finance: for example, the sale of council houses was imposed upon local authorities.

The government's style paralleled its policies. Consultation was abandoned. Michael Heseltine used the Consultative Council to announce what he was going to do, usually after he had briefed the press. This shift epitomised the government's style: it knew best and consequently saw no need to consult and negotiate. Direction was the order of the day.

The response of local authorities to government direction took a number of forms. First, they looked for ways of getting around the legislation. The legal profession was an unexpected beneficiary of government policy as litigious behaviour and the search for judge-proof legislation came to mark relationships. Second, local authorities adopted risk-avoidance strategies. Between 1979 and 1983 there were seven major changes to the grant system. The immediate consequence of so many changes was instability. Local authorities were given various, incompatible spending targets. Even local authorities which supported the government sought ways of avoiding the worst effects of constant changes. Creative accountancy flourished. Expenditures were reclassified. Statistics were massaged. Rates were increased, not to cover committed expenditure, but to build up reserves as a precaution against future changes.

Third, local authorities abandoned co-operation for confrontation. Thus, Labour-controlled local authorities increased their expenditure and exceeded their spending targets. The Greater London Council (GLC) and Inner London Education Authority (ILEA) both exceeded their spending targets to such an extent that they received no central grant. Full-blooded confrontation took place over subsidies for public transport, the most notable being the GLC's 'Fares Fair' policy.

Finally, the policy had a number of unintended consequences. 'Cuts' in local expenditure proved elusive. The record for individual programmes was mixed. Housing expenditure fell by some 49 per cent but law and order expenditure rose by 19 per cent whilst expenditure on education remained constant in real terms. Whatever else the Conservative government may have intended, a continuing increase in real terms in public expenditure in general and local current expenditure in particular was *not* an objective.

The Conservatives' first Parliament ended, therefore, with policy towards local government in a state of some disrepair. Repeated changes to the grant system produced the same outcome, growth in local current expenditure. Direction, was a poor substitute for a system based on voluntary co-operation. It is tempting to conclude that the harder successive Secretaries of State tried, the more they got, of what they didn't want! The government drew a different conclusion; if thwarted, then retaliate.

## Abolition, 1983–1987

As a general rule, the Conservative government of the 1980s avoided structural reform. The policy towards local government after 1983 was one exception. The government abolished the GLC and the Metropolitican County Councils (MCCs). It also created a range of *ad hoc* bodies to replace these councils and to by-pass local authorities. In effect, if local government would not do as it was told, it would be replaced or ignored.

The stated objective of abolition was to:

streamline local government in the metropolitan areas. It will remove a source of conflict and tension. It will save money, after some transitional costs. It will also provide a system which is simpler for the public to understand, in that responsibility for virtually all services will rest with a single authority.[3]

Norman Tebbitt offered a blunter assessment. The GLC was abolished because it was Labour dominated, high spending and at odds with the government's view of the world.

The question of what replaced the GLC and the MCCs admits of no easy answer because the new system is complex. To be brief, functions were re-allocated to private companies, central departments, non-departmental public bodies, district/borough councils, indirectly elected county/London-wide bodies and indirectly elected bodies which cover only part of the county/London. The most visible features are the new joint bodies (some voluntary and some statutory) for waste disposal, consumer protection/trading standards, planning and highways and traffic.[4] More important than the number of agencies is the fact that a significant proportion of them are not directly or even indirectly elected. For example, only 33 per cent of the expenditure on local services in London is by the directly-elected boroughs.

The major consequence of these changes is an ambiguous and complex distribution of functions and institutions. Fragmentation and the erosion of local political control characterise the government of British conurbations. There is also the problem of the muddle of the middle tier. The indirectly elected bodies are under mixed political control and lack political leadership. The re-allocation of functions has fuelled inter-borough and inter-district conflict and yet there is no mechanism for resolving it. Joint committees lack consensus and are slow to respond to new problems. The constituent boroughs of joint boards and joint committees tend to be parochial, complacent and to manifest a narrowness of purpose.[5]

Returning to the government's stated objectives, conflict has intensified, the system has not been simplified, and responsibility does not rest with a single authority. Moreover, although there has been no official analysis of the savings, Skelcher and Leach estimate that expenditure *rose* by 4 per cent between 1984–85 and 1987–88 on the services transferred from the MCCs to the districts.[6] There is one other consequence of abolition: the reformed structure is unstable. Since the Local Government Act (1985) the government has abolished ILEA and the Labour Party proposes to introduce regional government. The future remains unstable. Only one thing is clear:

The future design of London government will be neither the product of administration rationality or academic reflection, nor the by-product of allegedly inexorable economic or social processes. Rather it will be shaped largely as a product of party political interests, political ideologies, party conflicts and coalitions.[7]

By abolishing the GLC and the MCCs, the government removed seven 'over-spending' councils. The policy was one of two prongs designed to cut local expenditure. The second prong was rate-capping. The Rates Act 1984 gave the Secretary of State for the Environment power to determine an 'over-spending' council's maximum rate. The total number of local authorities capped has been small and the policy made only a marginal contribution to slowing down the rate of increase in local current expenditure. Between 1983–84 and 1987–8, local current expenditure rose by 11 per cent in real terms whilst capital expenditure, after rising by some 19 per cent at the time of the 1983 general election, continued its downward trend. The total number of local government employees rose. The government itself conceded that local current expenditure had risen by 1.5 per cent per annum in real terms in the 1980s.

Local authorities remained willing to challenge the government in the courts but their main response to the waves of legislation was political. The GLC and the MCCs mounted a professional public-relations campaign against abolition. Liverpool council drew the Secretary of State for the Environment into negotiations over the city's budget and, by appearing to gain concessions, seemed to win the political battle. The rate-capped councils mounted a united campaign up to the deadline for making a rate when they capitulated. Normally, the Conservatives control the overwhelming majority of county councils. Their control was eroded by the rise of the SDP–Liberal Alliance: after the 1985 elections, 25 of the 46 English and Welsh county councils had no party in overall control. The new urban left flourished in metropolitan areas. It was not content merely to oppose government policy. It also wanted to demonstrate that socialism could work and introduced local enterprise boards to counter unemployment, the effects of recession and regional decline. Even the government was forced to concede that there has been 'a worsening of the relationship between central Government and even the moderate and responsible local authorities.'[8]

Finally, local government's position as the pre-eminent governmental institution beyond Whitehall was challenged by the Conservative government which bypassed local authorities in favour of non-departmental public bodies. The Manpower Services Commission was preferred to local education authorities as the vehicle for improving vocational educational in schools. In the inner cities, the government preferred enterprise zones, free ports, urban development corporations and the Financial Institutions Group to local authorities as the means of economic regeneration. And, of course, the abolition of the GLC and the MCCs produced a whole crop of new agencies. The importance of such framentation should not be under-estimated. Few policy areas are the domain of a single agency. Organisational interdependence is ubiquitous. Effective policy implementation requires inter-organisational co-operation. By proliferating agencies, bypassing local government and restructuring its relationship with non-departmental public bodies, the government fostered obstacles to co-operation and increased policy slippage. The range of agencies involved in the delivery of services increased substantially. The warrior style of the Prime Minister and the predilection for commands over consultation were linked to structural differentiation which dissipated authority between agencies. The response of the government was *Paying for Local Government* (1986) which heralded the community charge, better known as the poll tax. The immediate impact of the Green Paper was muted. The government was waiting for a third term of office before resuming its attack on the 'problem' of local government. There was a stand-off. Grant settlements were more favourable to local government. Volume targets were abolished. The increase in local expenditure continued. The brakes were off. This local government stand-off is one instance of drift in government policy. Such drift epitomises the government's second term of office. It was the lull before the storm.

## Revolution, 1987–1990

After the 1987 election, the narrow fixation on local expenditure gave way to a broader set of themes designed to restructure local government. The government abandoned the search for direct control and pursued a market-oriented strategy designed to return control to citizens, now redesignated consumers. The emphasis fell on accountability to the local electorate, responsiveness to clients, competition and contracting-out to the private sector, greater efficiency and better management.[9]

The centrepiece of the revolution was the poll tax. Accountability was the order of the day. To quote the Green Paper, the poll tax aimed 'to make local authorities more accountable to their electors' by ensuring 'that the local electors know what the costs of their local services are, so that armed with this knowledge they can influence the spending decisions of their council through the ballot box' (1988, pp. vii and 9). The Local Government Finance Act 1988 abolished domestic rates and replaced them with a flat rate charge paid by all adults. The non-domestic or business rate was replaced by the uniform business rate set by the centre. The grant system was (ostensibly) simplified and renamed the Revenue Support Grant.

The immediate consequences of the poll tax were there for all to see: demonstrations, backbench disquiet, poor government performance in the opinion polls and (with rare exceptions) defeat in local elections. The unpopularity of the tax was obvious. The extent of the government's problem was less widely appreciated.

First, the full impact of the new system was never felt because it was phased in. The effects of the poll tax were ameliorated by a set of transitional arrangements, or safety nets, which served, for example, to reduce bills in London. The uniform business rate, also known as the national non-domestic rate, was based on a rating revaluation which led to substantial increases in several areas of the country. However, the government placed a ceiling in the total yield of the tax so that it did not exceed the amount raised in 1989/90.

Second, the administrative effectiveness and costs of the new system were substantial. Each county or metropolitan district and London borough set up a community charge register. Some 38 million individuals were liable to the tax. The size of the registers and the total number of transactions was enormous, far greater than for the rates. The costs in terms of additional staff and administration were high. The cost of enforcing registration and payment further escalated poll tax bills.

Third, the government pursued conflicting objectives. Under the system up to 75 per cent of the total income of local authorities could be decided by the centre. Between 25 and 37 per cent of total local authority income came from the poll tax. As a result, and in theory, the government was in a position to exercise considerable downward pressure on local expenditure. Just to make sure, local authorities with 'excessive' poll taxes were capped. In theory, poll tax clarified the link between services and paying for them, encouraging electors to remove profiligate Labour councils from office. However, in case electors either failed to spot the link between services and poll tax bills, or, in an aberrant moment, voted for high levels of expenditure, the paternalistic govenment stepped in and remedied the oversight by setting the poll tax at the 'correct' level. Accountability was the objective of the poll tax, provided electors did not vote for increased expenditure.

Finally, the new system was unstable. Grant was manipulated to minimise poll tax levels and the 'services-payment' link was further obscured. Financial stability remained a chimera. The government scored a political own goal by introducing the poll tax. It helped to erode their popularity in the opinion polls, cost them by-elections and contributed to the downfall of a Prime Minister. With Michael Heseltine back as Secretary of State for the Environment, the problem was to persuade a reluctant Cabinet that the community charge should be abolished. There were fears that its abolition would exacerbate splits in the party and a sceptical Treasury had to be convinced about the viability of any replacement tax. For example, the income-tax implications of transferring all or part of education to the centre were deemed unacceptable. With a general election looming, however, the fate of the community charge was sealed. It was abolished and policy turned full circle when the government unveiled its new tax – the council tax, known colloquially to us all as the rates. Whether or not this tax gets the government off the hook remains to be seen and will depend crucially on the number of winners and losers. Local government will continue to face an uncertain future. If its finance has been settled, then local authority boundaries and the allocation of functions between councils are on the agenda once more. To date there has been no revolution, only a catastrophe and the story still unfolds.

## Conclusions: explaining the trends

In order to understand the likely outcome of the local government reforms of the 1980s, it is necessary to explore the interaction between national economic problems, party ideology, party politics, bureaucratic tradition and bureaucratic politics.

Interventions in local government affairs do not reflect the government's concern with the state of local government but with the perceived imperatives of national economic management. In the case of the Conservative government, concern with inflation, the public-sector borrowing requirement and the level of public expenditure shaped policy on local government. The Labour Party had a similar definition of the economic problem between 1975 and 1979, and also sought to control local expenditure. However, the Conservative Party's response to Britain's relative economic decline was distinctively shaped by ideology. The control of local expenditure may have been a long-standing concern of the Treasury, but the policies on privatisation and the poll tax and the scale of contracting-out are distinctively Conservative. They also reflect the thinking of the New Right and its various think tanks. Economic problems provided the stimulus to intervene. Party ideology shaped the form and extent of that intervention. Political parties give expression to ideology and are a major source of policy initiation, a counterweight to the inertia of Whitehall and established interests. They are also the focal point of conflict. Conservative policies have politicised and polarised central–local relations. The Labour Party has a majority on a substantial and increasing proportion of local councils. Local government has been simultaneously an area in which the electoral fortunes of the Labour Party have been revived, the test bed for socialist policies, and the main source of opposition to the government. Local government has been a pawn in this increasingly polarised national party-political arena.

The Conservative Party may have initiated a range of policies but intent and result diverged markedly in the process of implementation. The government either did not anticipate, or ignored, the constraints imposed by the extant administrative structure and by policy networks. British government is non-executant; that is, it does not directly deliver services. It has to rely on other agencies. This dependence, allied to policies which have fragmented the service delivery systems, has undermined the government's policy objectives. In its efforts to control individual local authorities, the government adopted a command or directive style. It chose to ignore the simple fact that British government is differentiated: the unitary state is a multi-form maze of interdependencies. As a result, it lacked the hands-on means to impose its policies: the organisational infrastructure of field agents to supervise implementation. It also politicised relationships with local government thereby eroding the latter's 'responsibility ethic' or predisposition to conform to government expenditure guidelines. Failure was built into the original policy design.

To compound the problem, the professional-bureaucratic complexes at the heart of British government – the policy networks – were a break on the government's ambitions. Policy-making in British government is dominated by function-specific networks comprising central departments, professions and other key interests. Outside interests are institutionalised in government, relationships are routinised, the policy agenda is stable and conservative with a small 'c', and policy change is incremental. These networks, especially the professions, were 'handbagged' by the Thatcher government. Unfortunately, their co-operation was integral to the effective implementation of policy. A pattern of authoritative announcement by the centre followed by policy slippage in implementation became all too common. The dynamic conservatism of the policy networks illustrates the recurrent tension in British government between authoritative decision-making and interdependence.

If the government has failed to achieve its major objectives, if the overall result is a policy mess, none the less the record is not one of unrelieved gloom. Elements of the government's several policies have been successful. For example, its ideological message about the virtues of consumer choice and of competition has had some impact. The government has also derived marked political benefits from policies such as the sale of council houses. However, the 'revolutionary' programme has already suffered one major setback with the abolition of poll tax. The outcome from other policies has yet to emerge but the record does not inspire confidence. The prognosis has to be cautious, reflecting not only the fact that the government has had some success but also its persistence. If there is one lesson to be learned, it is that the history of local government is compounded of multiple contradictions – economic, political and organisational. Mono-causal explanations are inadequate. Policy-making for local government has generated a policy mess because of the failure to appreciate that differentiation, interdependence and policy networks are central characteristics of the British polity.

**Notes**

1   See R. A. W. Rhodes, 'Continuity and change in British central–local relations: the Conservative threat, 1979–83', *British Journal of Political Science*, vol. 14 (1984) 311–33; R. A. W. Rhodes, *The National World of Local Government* (London: Allen & Unwin, 1986); R. A. W. Rhodes,

*Beyond Westminster and Whitehall* (London: Unwin-Hyman, 1988); and
R. A. W. Rhodes, 'Now nobody understands the system; the changing face
of local government', in P. Norton (ed.), *New Directions in British Politics*
(Aldershot: Edward Elgar, 1991).

2   Layfield Committee, *Report of the Committee of Inquiry into Local
Government Finance* (Cmnd 6453, London: HMSO, 1976) 327.

3   HMSO, *Streamlining the Cities* (Cmnd 9063, London, 1983) 5.

4   For a detailed summary see S. Leach and H. Davis, 'Introduction',
*Local Government Studies*, vol. 16, no. 3 (1990) 1–11.

5   M. Herbert and T. Travers (eds.), *The London Government Handbook* (London: Cassell, 1988) 91.

6   C. Skelcher and S. Leach, 'Resource choice and the abolition process',
*Local Government Studies*, vol. 16, no. 3 (1990) 41.

7   Herbert and Travers, *Local Government Handbook*, 187.

8   HMSO, *Paying for Local Government* (Cmnd 9714, London, 1986),
5.

9   For further details see Rhodes, 'Now nobody understands the system';
and J. Stewart and G. Stoker (eds.), *The Future of Local Government*
(London: Macmillan, 1989).

# Part IV
# Policy areas

# Government and the economy

It is ten years since, in ... 1968, my predecessor, William Armstrong, described the problems of steering a complex modern economy. These ten years have seen many changes in the economic environment and many changes in public attitudes and in economic thought ... Today the scene is very different ... what was a consensus among those who wrote and thought about macro-economic matters has given way to discord and disagreement (Sir Douglas Wass[1]).

More generally, the power of governments to influence the economy is limited. Even in the confident days of the 1960s it was more limited than was believed at the time, as the difficulties of the 1970s revealed. The key to good government is to recognise the limits of the government's ability to do something about problems which the government cannot solve, and to make sure that those things for which the government *is* directly responsible ... are done as efficiently as possible (Sir Peter Middleton[2]).

## Introduction

A review of UK economic policy over the two decades since 1970 is a rare opportunity to look for patterns over time, for continuity as well as change. Political scientists should not be surprised to find, despite the rhetoric of political actors, a great deal of continuity in policy-making and a large number of obstacles limiting the actions of government.[3] In economic policy-making especially, what looks like comprehensive change is often, in reality, 'policy succession'.[4]

This chapter has three interlocking themes, encapsulated in the two quotes from Sir Douglas Wass and Sir Peter Middleton, the Permanent Secretaries to the Treasury during the 1970s and 1980s. First, that the period since 1970 is one of growing uncertainty in economic theory, and increasing ideological debate and disagreement about the role of economic ideas in policy-making. Second, that as a result of this uncertainty, compounded by policy failure, the confidence of the policy-making elite to influence the economy has waned. Third, and paradoxically, governments since the mid-1970s have been searching for rules and frameworks upon which to anchor economic policy as a means to guide them back to some of the certainties of the 1950s and 1960s.

What follows is divided into two sections. In the first we survey governments' changing macro-economic policy objectives and tools and the politico-economic ideology underpinning them. We then assess UK economic performance against the background of long-term relative economic decline.

## Politico-economic ideology, objectives and policy tools

By the early 1980s, the 'Keynesian Social Democratic' system which had dominated economic policy-making since the end of the Second World War had been overturned. In general terms it is possible to identify a dynamic 'moving consensus'[5] that had formed the basis of economic policy from 1944 to the mid-1970s. This involved the acceptance that governments had a role in ensuring sufficient demand in the economy to maintain full employment.[6] This was buttressed by the economic ideas of Keynes that governments *could* achieve the objective principally by managing demand through the use of public spending and changes in taxation. Internationally, UK governments were active in setting up the 'Bretton Woods' institutions such as the International Monetary Fund (IMF) which were to ensure that domestic Keynesian policies were not overturned by recession in the world economy. A crucial part of the system was the fixing of exchange rates. This was to act as a constraining framework for UK economic policy, since higher inflation would have to be accommodated through squeezing the domestic economy rather than by devaluation. A third element in the consensus was that key 'social actors' such as Trades Union Congress the (TUC) and Confederation of British Industry (CBI) had a role with government in managing the economy. The consensus moved in the late 1950s and early 1960s to embrace a more active interventionist role for government in the supply-side of the economy, rather than just managing demand, spurred on by concern that economic growth was lagging behind France and West Germany. In an effort to emulate the success of French economic policy[7] both the Conservative government and Labour governments of the 1960s introduced experiments in indicative economic planning.[8]

One by one the pillars of this consensus crumbled. The decline of the Keynesian system was gradual, presaged in the 1960s by problems with inflation. A combination of changes in the international economy, the long-term relative weakness of the UK economy, policy failure by UK governments, and concern about the role of the trade unions led to the peculiar crises of the 1970s.[9] At first there was an attempt to shore up the consensus and adopt innovatory policy tools, but finally a 'monetarist' system briefly supplanted the Keynesian system through the radicalism of the early Thatcher years. By 1985 policy had shifted back again towards the eclectic approach of Chancellor Healey in the late-1970s, yet still with rhetorical bias firmly rooted in New Right thinking.[11]

Table 14.1 outlines some of the major characteristics of what can rather crudely be labelled the 'Keynesian' and 'monetarist' systems. It should be stressed that economic ideas become modified when they are utilised by those involved in the political process. What results is often an amalgam of political ideology, pragmatic response to social and political pressures and shades of various schools of economic thought.

### Healey: the first monetarist?

Even allowing for the unprecedented shock administered to the world economy by the 1973 oil price rise, Keynesian economic policy tools had become progressively less successful. In each successive boom inflation was higher and unemployment higher than in the previous one.[12] The advent of 'stagflation' – simultaneously high inflation with low growth and high unemployment – was something which traditional Keynesian theory could not cope with. Policymakers through the Organization for Economic Co-operation and Development (OECD) therefore began a search for techniques which would better deal with the phenomena; the control of inflation was to dominate the agenda.[13]

In the UK, Dennis Healey as Chancellor presided over a major shift in the emphasis of macro-economic policy but one which fell short of an outright repudiation of the post-war consensus. His approach was to use whatever means were at hand to shore up that consensus while responding to the crises of the time.[14]

**Table 14.1** *Differences between the Keynesian and monetarist systems*[10]

| Characteristic | Keynesian | Monetarist |
|---|---|---|
| Policy target | Employment, plus later concern about the balance payments and growth | Inflation (and creating conditions for growth) |
| Time-scale | Short term (one or two years) | Medium term (four to five years) |
| Price bases | Real terms (emphasis on planning in real or volume terms) | Nominal terms (emphasis on current cash terms and nominal GDP) |
| Precedence of fiscal and monetary policy | Fiscal policy dominant, supporting role to monetary policy | Monetary policy dominant with (in UK) a broad money target set, PSBR* set to support this |
| Policy instruments | Emphasis on tax and public spending charges, interest rates and credit controls. Exchange rate used to influence output | Emphasis (in UK) on broad money target achieved by PSBR reduction, funding policy and interest rates. Exchange rate eschewed as tool |
| Foreign economic policy | System initially underpinned by fixed exchange system, followed by attempts to 'manage' exchange rate, desire for international co-ordination of policy, support for exchange controls | Emphasis on allowing exchange rate to follow market, support for free-floating rates and non-intervention, abolition of exchange controls and support for free movement of capital |
| 'Supply-side' policies | Emphasis on direct intervention: regional policy, active industrial policies, public-sector agencies and industries used as policy tools | Emphasis on allowing private sector more freedom, reduction of public-sector intervention, privatisation, de-regulation of markets and labour-market reforms |

**Table 14.1**  *continued*

| Characteristic | Keynesian | Monetarist |
|---|---|---|
| Role of 'social actors' | Tri-partite approach to many economic decisions including involvement in pay and prices policy, and industrial strategy | Only residual contacts between government and TUC and CBI leadership on major economic decisions; de-politicisation of pressure groups |

*Public Sector Borrowing Requirement

The Treasury under Healey began by attempting to deal with the inflationary and deflationary consequences of the oil crisis by using traditional Keynesian techniques. Wage inflation was to be moderated by the 'Social Contract' with the trade unions. This involved government commitments on a whole range of social policies and reform of industrial relations legislation in return for 'restraint' on wage demands. The Public Sector Borrowing Requirement (PSBR) was used as a counter-cyclical instrument, that is allowing it to rise as a proportion of GDP as output fell as a result of the recession. Internationally, these policies were to be supplemented by three approaches. First, Healey attempted to get a co-ordinated response by the major industrial nations to avoid deflationary action in response to the oil crisis exacerbating the world recession. Second, the Treasury tried to obtain an international agreement to support with loans those countries (including the UK) with major balance-of-payments problems. And, in concert with the pro-Western members of Organization of Petroleum Exporting Countries (OPEC), to introduce an active policy to 'recycle' the surpluses being generated by the oil-exporting countries.[15]

Most of these policies were to be untenable. The raft of international agreements Healey hoped for did not materialise. Unfortunately, in the attempt to follow a traditional Keynesian approach domestically and internationally, whilst Britain's competitors reduced their budget deficits, the Chancellor pursued policies out of step with other major economies; this was to make later policy adjustments more painful. The increasingly interdependent nature of the world economy was a restraint on domestic policies. In 1975 the Treasury engineered a 'controlled depreciation' of sterling in an attempt to revitalise domestic production and ease the deficit on the balance of trade. Lack of confidence in UK policy by the financial markets led to the depreciation becoming a free-fall, as the exchange rate fell dramatically. The use of the exchange rate as a policy tool had been discredited and led to a crisis of morale in the Treasury.[16] Market confidence in domestic policies had been affected by the size of the budget deficit and the failure of the Social Contract to cope with the surge of inflation in 1974–75.

In 1976 everything seemed to go wrong with economic policy. The sterling crisis led to a request to the IMF for a loan. Following the subsequent negotiations, the Treasury agreed in December 1976 to adjustments in both the techniques and objectives of policy. Targets for the money supply were publicly announced, the PSBR was to be reduced and public expenditure cut back. Earlier, in July 1976, the Treasury had introduced cash limits on public expenditure in response to the 'crisis of control'.[17] Policy was in disarray. All the features of a classic British economic policy crisis were in abundant evidence – crisis Cabinet discussions, spending cuts, concern about the foreign exchange markets – together with a politically damaging and demoralising submission to the IMF.[18]

These changes in macro-economic policy, introduced under the exigencies of crisis, have been used as evidence for the proposition that the real change of direction in policy occurred under Chancellor Healey rather than under the Conservatives after 1979.[19] This assertion deserves further scrutiny because it lies at the heart of the debate about economic policy since 1970.

In reality it is not possible to evaluate policy change in a dogmatic way, for 'a seemingly dramatic new initiative by government may partially overlap with previous provisions'.[20] By accepting that the Healey chancellorship was marked by a radical shift in policy goals does not rule out the conclusion that *on balance* the period 1979–90 was much more significant. There are plenty of pieces of evidence to support the view that the period 1976–79 saw macro-economic policy move towards the monetarist system as outlined above. The full-employment objective was suspended. In his 1975 budget speech. Healey noted that the budget judgment would not be based on an 'estimation of the amount of demand which the government should put into the economy'. Later in 1977 the Treasury dropped the Medium-Term Assessment (MTA) from the Public Expenditure Survey. Previously the MTA had been one of the cornerstones of spending plans and assumed that policies would ensure that full employment was maintained.[21] There was an element here of the government responding to the inevitable, since employment was rising against difficult circumstances of higher inflation and a poor balance of payments. But nevertheless the UK government had joined other industrialised nations in giving priority to the control and reduction of inflation.

Policy actions during the mid-1970s show how the full employment objective was less sacrosanct. In the period from 1945 to 1973 governments of both major parties had reacted to rising unemployment with an active fiscal policy (increasing public expenditure or reducing taxation) and relaxing monetary policy. From 1975 an increase in unemployment produced a virtually neutral policy response. In no year after 1977 was the PSBR as a proportion of GDP as large as it was in 1974–75, despite the fact that unemployment rose to and remained at post-war historically high levels.[22] In addition, during the Healey chancellorship the PSBR was given a pivotal role in linking fiscal and monetary policy. In 1978 Healey took action to reduce the PSBR when the financial markets became concerned that fiscal policy was out of step with monetary policy as the large PSBR was adding to monetary growth.[23]

The Bank of England began setting internal, unpublished monetary targets in 1973. This was followed during the rest of the 1970s by increasing emphasis being placed on monetary policy in general and broad money aggregates in particular by the Bank and Treasury. This was a trend throughout the OECD as interest rates, the previous guide to monetary policy, were less reliable as an indicator because of rising inflation and fluctuating exchange rates.[24] In the UK from about 1976 such targets were used to influence inflationary expectations and as a means of ensuring that budgetary policy was compatible with the anti-inflation objective.

The degree to which monetary targets were taken seriously in the hierarchy of macro-economic policy tools was evidenced by the action of the Bank and Treasury in 1977. The authorities were faced at that time by an unusual set of circumstances for the period: foreign exchange markets had so regained confidence in UK policy in the afterglow of the IMF loan that, despite falling interest rates, sterling was appreciating. In its attempt to stem this rise through intervention on the exchange markets to sell sterling and buy other currencies, the Bank was endangering the money supply targets. The choice was therefore between stemming the rise in sterling to maintain the competitive position of UK exporting industries or maintaining the money-supply targets. The monetary targets were given priority and the Chancellor took the decision to 'unplug' sterling and allow it to float upwards.[25] The tension between monetary policy and exchange-rate policy was to be a feature of the implementation of the Medium-Term Financial Strategy (MTFS) after 1980. In fact Chancellor Lawson was to face precisely the same dilemma as Healey in the different circumstances of 1988.

Almost as significant was the less tangible change in the rhetoric of senior Labour government ministers and Treasury officials during the mid- and late 1970s pointing to less confidence in the ability of governments to influence the economy. The most famous example was Prime Minister Callaghan's speech to the Labour Party Conference on 28 September 1976 when he stated that:

> We used to think that you could spend your way out of a recession and increase employment by cutting taxes and boosting Government spending. I tell you in all candour that that option no longer exists, and that insofar as it ever did exist, it only worked on each occasion since the war by injecting a bigger dose of inflation into the economy, followed by a higher level of unemployment as the next step.[26]

This was to be quoted approvingly by Conservative leaders and monetarist academics to support the view that the real change in policy occurred in 1976 and the Conservative government merely carried this forward.

All the evidence presented above might seem overwhelmingly to support the view that under Chancellor Healey UK macro-economic policy moved three-quarters of the way to a monetarist system. There are five reasons why this assertion is overstated.

First, while the Labour government explicitly abandoned the full-employment objective, macro-economic policy was not deliberately deflationary during the recession. The neutral policy stance after 1975 was against the background of some growth in output. There was an element of the policy objective of full employment being placed 'on ice' until the economic crisis passed and the task of the government made easier. After the IMF loan was repaid, and in the run-up to the 1979 general election, Labour's Public Expenditure White Papers in 1978 and 1979 showed a renewed commitment to real spending growth. In addition, the Labour government kept faith with the consensual element of the 1944 Employment White Paper by relying on an incomes policy as a means of cutting inflation without excessive reliance on deflationary monetary or fiscal policies.

Second, it was clear that Chancellor Healey downgraded the role of fiscal policy. Public-expenditure decisions were no longer taken with an ultimate macro-economic goal in mind. Control of spending was elevated as a policy goal in its own right. But there is no evidence that policy was guided solely by the need to achieve money-supply targets. Monetary policy was always presented by Labour Treasury ministers and their officials as supporting an anti-inflationary policy which included incomes policy and control of the PSBR. The Conservative leadership when in government was to repudiate the use of incomes policy and the 'corporatist' approach which underlied it and, more significantly, was to reject the notion that Government *could* actually influence employment and output through macro-economic policies.[27]

Third, monetary policy was pursued in a way which supported the view that Labour ministers were 'reluctant' or 'unbelieving' monetarists. In reality policy was 'monetarily constrained Keynesianism' rather than monetarist.[28] The money-supply targets were announced on an annual basis rather than set in a medium-term context. There was concern that 'to pursue a determined and pre-determined de-escalation of the rate of monetary expansion would be to risk imposing serious costs on the economy'.[29] Having set money supply targets for Sterling M3 (£M3) Chancellor Healey ensured that monetary policy still took 'account of the fact that no one indicator can adequately describe all the monetary conditions in the economy'.[30]

Fourth, the medium-term nominal framework[31] regarded as a crucial part of the monetarist system was lacking under Healey. The Labour Chancellor talked of a 'medium-term framework' in his Letter of Intent to the IMF, but this was no more than a grafting on of some longer-term considerations to what were still short-term, *ad hoc* reactions of the Treasury to political and economic developments. No medium-term financial plan was agreed whilst Healey was Chancellor, although this was raised as a possible option. Whilst nominal aggregates such as the PSBR and money supply were brought into policy discussions, public expenditure was still planned in volume or real resource terms with annual cash limits tacked on.

And fifth, rhetoric can be misleading. The statements of senior Labour ministers have to be judged against the particular political and economic background of the time. Callaghan's famous 'monetarist' speech to the Labour Party Conference was a tactical political attempt to achieve multiple objectives: to appease the financial markets, to frighten the Labour Party into accepting the need for tough economic measures, and to make the right impression on the US Treasury Secretary whose support would be vital for the UK to obtain IMF support.[32] It was not a general statement supporting the view that governments should never use fiscal policy as an effective tool of economic management. Rather, in Callaghan's words, it was a speech arguing 'that in the circumstances of 1976 these measures were not appropriate'. Most of Chancellor Healey's statements at the time reflected the approach of an eclectic, flexible political fixer who was responding to the demise of the post-war consensus and its economic certainties.

### 'Believing monetarism', the MTFS and Thatcherism

In contrast, the approach of Margaret Thatcher and her economic team was motivated by a more wholehearted commitment to the monetarist system. The MTFS was to be a far more 'rational' co-ordinated response, when limits to government action were incorporated into economic policy-making as a first principle, than the short-term approach under Healey. Changes and adjustments in policy there certainly were in the 1976–79 period, but we must look to the 1979–82 era for the real decisive break with the Keynesian system.

Throughout the OECD in the late 1970s and 1980s policy-makers developed economic strategies based on medium-term financial and economic frameworks.[33] Most plans were the result of pragmatic responses to the breakdown of Keynesian economic relationships, the tendency to inflation and low growth and the difficulties of funding public-spending programmes. In the UK from 1979, the framework adopted was the result of *ideological* commitment and sprang from a combination of political, economic and intellectual factors.

The late 1960s saw the resurgence of interest in classical economics. A combination of perceived failures in Keynesianism in its practical application in policy, with rising inflation and the stop-go cycle, and revived academic interest in the role of money stimulated by the research of Milton Friedman and the Chicago School began to influence policy-makers in the USA. This followed later in

Britain through the academic activities of Harry Johnson at the LSE who set up the Money Study Group in 1969, Alan Walters, also at the LSE, and David Laidler and Michael Parkin at Manchester University.[34] Later Alan Budd and Terry Burns of the London Business School were to be influential in policy discussions. This revival gained momentum through the acceptance of many of the monetarist ideas put forward by academics, journalists and city analysts by Sir Keith Joseph, Margaret Thatcher and other leading Conservatives in the mid-1970s. Sir Keith Joseph's contribution to the change in the dominant ideology of the Conservative Party in the 1970s cannot be underestimated. His Preston speech on 4 September 1974 is widely regarded as setting the agenda for early 'Thatcherism'.[35]

In the years of opposition Thatcher and her network of policy advisers moved the party towards a policy position which was an amalgam of various schools of monetarism and right-wing populism. But it was this in combination with the failures of the Labour government's attempt at consensus politics which was to provide Thatcher and her supporters with the opportunity to win the policy debate. The creation of what has been called 'Mrs Thatcher's domestic statecraft'[36] was thus the product of a mixture of consequences of events, slowing changing assumptive worlds fed by the contributions of intellectuals, accident and opportunity.[37]

A set of advisers and policy think tanks were influential in shaping the policy positions of Thatcher, Joseph and their closest supporters. The network was drawn from the academic world, the City, Journalism and business. The key institutions included the Institute of Economic Affairs (IEA) which since its formation in the 1950s had published neo-classical and specifically monetarist writings. Notable monetarists such as Friedman had used the IEA as an outlet for their views since the early-1970s. The Centre for Policy Studies, set up in 1974 under Heath's leadership by Sir Keith Joseph and Margaret Thatcher, became a prime source of monetarist advice for the new leader under its director, Alfred Sherman.[38]

A shifting group of academics were drawn upon during the opposition years. The most significant were Alan Walters, David Laidler, Brian Griffiths (Professor of Economics at the City University and later Head of the Prime Minister's Policy Unit), Patrick Minford (Professor of Applied Economics at the Liverpool University) and Douglas Hague (Manchester Business School and part-time adviser

to Thatcher when in opposition). City economists played a
significant part in policy formation. The two most important were
Gordon Pepper and Tim Congdon, both of whom were brought in
later when the Conservatives were in government to occasional
Treasury seminars on the development of policy. There was a small
but influential group of journalists who shared the monetarist line of
the Conservative leader. Sir John Hoskyns (later the first head of
Thatcher's Policy Unit in Downing Street) and Norman Strauss (of
Unilever) were the most influential businessmen to advise Thatcher.

The new Treasury team in 1979 therefore had a mixture of policy
advice and intellectual support for a change of direction in economic
policy. Within the Treasury there was also a receptive climate, at
least from the middle ranks of officials including the future Permanent Secretary, Peter Middleton. Even those senior officials who
were sceptical of the full-blooded monetarist views of Nigel Lawson,
the Financial Secretary, accepted the need for tighter control of
public spending and borrowing and had become demoralised by the
failure of the wages policy and industrial strategy of the departing
Labour government.

The MTFS unveiled in 1980 was the clearest signal that the
economic policy regime had changed.[39] It represented an attempt to
impose discipline on government policy-making by deliberately
limiting the range of options open to the Treasury on monetary and
fiscal policy. Money-supply targets were paramount and were supported by projections for the PSBR and an unprecedented set of plans
to cut public spending in real and volume terms. The MTFS was
explicitly counter-inflationary: governments, it was stated, could
only influence output by supply-side (or micro-economic) reforms.[40]
Initially these reforms were limited, but nevertheless included the
significant act of abolishing exchange controls in November 1979,
some reduction in personal taxation, and a series of Acts reducing
the power of trade unions. Later the supply-side element of the
strategy became more prominent after 1983 with large-scale privatisation, the deregulation of financial markets and tax-reforming
measures.

The strategy was intended to influence the expectations of a whole
set of institutions and markets. For the first time the Treasury was
deliberately reducing the scope for discretionary macro-economic
policy. Financial markets were given a clear, public statement of the
Treasury's policies over the medium term. Whitehall departments

and agencies in the public sector were presented with a framework deliberately set to restrain resources available for public policies. Business leaders and trade-union wage bargainers were, in theory at least, reminded that the post-war settlement had ended: the Treasury would not act to reduce unemployment; inflationary wage demands would not be covered by money-supply increases.

## The evolution and demise of the MTFS

In the course of the ten years from 1980 the MTFS evolved and changed, becoming less and less a rigorous medium-term framework providing clear guidelines to financial markets and other economic actors as it increasingly became no more than an annually updated set of financial figures.[41] It was a return to the same slightly constrained discretionary policies pursued under Chancellor Healey in the 1976–78 period. The MTFS survived partly because of the political embarrassment its shelving would have created, partly because it proved to be a useful vehicle for shifting the substance of policy actions whilst maintaining the aura of consistency, and partly because the annual exercise in setting out PSBR, public expenditure and revenue figures provided the Treasury with a useful weapon in containing public spending pressures. It is on the fiscal side of the MTFS that the Treasury can claim the most success. PSBR targets were more often met and the generation of a nominal budget surplus in the four financial years from 1987–88 to 1990–91 had last been achieved by Roy Jenkins in 1969–70. Although public spending was not reduced in line with 1980 objectives, it did fall as a proportion of GDP from 1982–83 to 1989–90. There is evidence that the Treasury succeeded in reducing the trend rate of growth compared to that prevailing in the 1960s and 1970s, and if measured against the record of other OECD Finance Ministries, the Treasury has been more successful in keeping a lid on the inexorable pressures for higher levels of public spending.[42]

The MTFS failed as a monetary framework if measured against the original intentions in 1980 for four main reasons. First, economic relationships were not as clear and stable as outlined by the Treasury in 1980. The key indicator – sterling M3 – was prone to the distortions created by changes in the financial markets and changes in the way in which individuals used financial instruments. The public sector's deficit was not the most significant cause of inflationary increases in the money supply. In the 1980–82 and

1987–89 period increases in borrowing by the private sector were the most significant factors. Indeed by the end of the 1980s, the public sector was actually in surplus. The interest-rate weapon proved to be a blunt instrument for controlling credit[43] as companies and individuals often acted perversely and increased borrowing despite high interest rates.

Second, an intellectual problem was highlighted here. What was the most appropriate measure of monetary activity? What was the significance of the signals given by monitoring broad or narrow money? How did this relate to economic activity? The debate within the Treasury and No. 10 in 1980–81 created by the simultaneous appreciation of sterling, excess growth of the sterling M3, rising inflation *and* recession and bankruptcy in the private sector was a case study in the sheer intellectual difficulty of trying to run policy using a narrow framework. In the end the Prime Minister's Policy Unit and her economic adviser, Alan Walters, prevailed and monetary policy was eased.[44]

Third, conflicting policy objectives were not eliminated by the simple act of publicly announcing a clear economic policy agenda. Monetary policy was complicated by the abolition of exchange controls as sterling was prone to rapid inflows (and outflows) of capital. The deregulation of financial markets, and in particular the abolition of credit controls in 1982 and the lifting of restrictions on building societies and banks allowing customers to use 'equity withdrawal' as a means of adding to purchasing power, opened the way for a massive explosion of credit in the late 1980s.[45]

Fourth, the original 1980 MTFS almost totally ignored the impact of foreign economic policy on domestic macro-economic policy. The exchange rate was said in 1980 to be determined by market forces. It was only in 1982 implicitly when the exchange was accepted as an indicator, and in 1985 explicitly when it became *the* leading monetary indicator that the Treasury acknowledged the importance of the value of sterling in economic decision-making. It was Chancellor Lawson's conversion to the view that the exchange rate was the most appropriate guide to monetary policy in 1985 that the debate about joining the Exchange Rate Mechanism (ERM) of the European Monetary System (EMS) was joined in earnest in Whitehall.[46] Lawson became convinced of the need to supplement (and effectively replace) the MTFS with a clearer and more easily understood exchange-rate rule through linking sterling to the German Mark.[47]

Indeed the success of John Major as his successor in obtaining Prime Minister's Thatcher's agreement to ERM membership may prove to be the most significant macro-economic policy decision of the last two decades. If the MTFS represented the high noon of a UK brand of monetarism, ERM membership represented the fuller integration of the UK into the European Community and with it a commitment to long-term non-inflationary growth.

### Economic performance: continued economic decline?

This section focuses on whether the economic policies pursued by governments since 1970 have led to a reversal of Britain's economic decline, surely one of the most important litmus tests of 'success' in economic policy.

The concern of policy-makers with the UK's post-war economic decline can be traced back to at least the late 1950s, although decline had been a hundred-year phenomenon.[48] Decline is a relative concept.[49] The story from 1950 to 1970 was that the average Briton had become richer in material terms as measured by per capita income or the so-called 'social wage' (the amount of money spent on welfare services such as education, health and social security). But the average German, Frenchman or Italian had grown even richer using these same measures. Between 1962 and 1972, GDP in the UK grew by 2.2 per cent on average each year, compared to 4.7 per cent in France, 3.6 per cent in West Germany and 3.9 per cent in Italy. The UK's manufacturing industries had sold more goods, but they took a smaller proportion of world markets. In 1950, UK exports of manufactured goods accounted for 25 per cent of the world total, this had declined to 10.8 per cent by 1970.[50] The UK's share of total world exports fell from 10.7 per cent in 1950 to 6.7 per cent in 1970.[51]

### *Reversing decline as a priority of government*

The 1970s and 1980s saw the issue of tackling decline rise on the political agenda. The early approach in 1970–72 of the Heath government involved an experiment with what Harold Wilson dubbed 'Selsdon Man' policies, a 'quiet revolution', in which the dynamism of the economy would be unleashed through tax cuts, less state intervention and reform of industrial relations. Heath was not an advocate of social-market economics, rather he was an advocate of the selective use of free-market solutions if these promised to improve economic growth.[52] The Labour government's attempt to reverse decline, against a mounting economic crisis, involved a much diluted and modified version of the left's Alternative Economic Strategy, with nationalisation, the creation of an Enterprise Board and 'planning agreements', and a more traditional tri-partite 'industrial strategy' bringing together the TUC and CBI in an effort to remove barriers to economic growth.[53] By far the most concerted and deliberate attempt to give priority to reversing decline was that of the early years of the Thatcher government. The responsibility for decline was firmly placed with the governments of the post-war consensus. Chancellor Howe's first budget speech in June 1979 set the tone when he argued that the UK's poor economic performance was due to intervention by governments which had stifled enterprise. He committed the government to a strategy aimed at strengthening individual incentives through tax cuts, reducing the role of the state and liberating the private sector, and reducing public spending and borrowing. Chancellor Lawson's policies from 1985 to 1988 were in effect an attempt to accelerate economic growth in what looked like a period of sluggish output growth.[54] Throughout the 1980s and early 1990s the Conservative governments of Thatcher and Major have emphasised the way policies have created an 'enterprise culture' and 'popular capitalism', the fruits of which will create a more competitive economy. There may be some tentative support for this claim.[55]

*The evidence, 1970–1990*
On balance, the evidence available suggests that the late 1980s may have been a time when relative decline if not exactly reversed was halted, although it should be stressed that much depends on the variables chosen for analysis and the time period.

Table 14.2 for example shows that the 1969–73 period was one of historically high, but nevertheless low relative economic growth, lower than all other major industrial nations except for the USA. During the recessions of the mid-1970s and early 1980s the accumulated weaknesses of the UK economy resulted in very poor comparative GDP growth. From 1984 the UK economy has grown faster than Italy, France and West Germany, and at a historically high rate by UK standards. Taking the 1979–88 period as a whole, 'while exceeding rates recorded in France and Germany, GDP growth remained below the G7 [group of seven major economies], but much less so than in the past'.[56]

Other economic variables also suggest some reasons for concluding that the UK economy emerged from the deep recession of 1980–82 in a relatively better position than at other periods since the 1960s. When analysts have debated whether there has been a 'Thatcher miracle' or a 'Thatcher effect' on economic performance one of the factors highlighted has been productivity. The productivity of the labour-force in the economy as a whole in 1979–88 was 'for the first time in three decades . . . ahead of the G7 average, if only slightly', and manufacturing productivity 'has been impressive, outstripping by a wide margin both the previous United Kingdom trend and the G7 average'.[57] One interpretation has been that, although marked, productivity gains were made against the background of rising unemployment in the early 1980s and a 'huge reduction in international competitiveness which gave workers and managers little alternative but to raise productivity or go under'.[58] Others have stressed that if output growth, productivity growth and the rising rate of profits by industrial companies since 1981 are taken together, a case can be made for saying there has been a marked improvement in the supply-side of the economy and that the industrial and commercial sectors are now more resilient.[59]

**Table 14.2** *Rates of growth of Gross Domestic Product, 1969–88 (average annual percentage rates)*[62]

| Country | 1969–73 | 1974–78 | 1979–83 | 1984–88 | Total 1969–88 |
|---|---|---|---|---|---|
| Japan | 8.8 | 3.3 | 3.9 | 4.5 | 5.2 |
| Italy | 4.6 | 3.3 | 2.5 | 3.0 | 3.3 |
| France | 5.5 | 2.7 | 1.8 | 2.2 | 3.0 |
| W. Germany | 4.9 | 2.1 | 1.3 | 2.6 | 2.8 |
| USA | 3.0 | 2.6 | 1.1 | 4.2 | 2.7 |
| UK | 3.3 | 1.2 | 0.9 | 3.6 | 2.4 |

Using measures on the UK's position in international trade, a less sanguine conclusion must be drawn. Table 14.3 shows that the UK's share of total world exports (primary products and services as well as manufactured goods) continued to decline from 1970 to 1980, down from 6.7 per cent to 5.3 per cent. However, the 1980s may have witnessed a levelling off in the decline in manufactured goods at least.[60] Treasury figures suggest that the UK's share of manufactured trade has stabilised at just over 6 per cent (in value and volume) from 1983 to 1990, after having declined from 9.5 per cent in 1970 to 7 per cent by 1980.[61] In comparison, Japan and Italy have increased their shares of total world exports, and France and West Germany have maintained their 1970 position against a rapidly rising volume of trade. The USA lost its pre-eminent position as the leading exporter rather as the UK did in the late 1950s.

**Table 14.3** *Shares in total world exports by value,* *1970–89 (percentage)*[63]

| Country | 1970 | 1975 | 1980 | 1985 | 1989 |
|---------|------|------|------|------|------|
| USA | 14.9 | 13.1 | 11.8 | 12.1 | 12.5 |
| W. Germany | 11.8 | 10.9 | 10.1 | 10.1 | 11.7 |
| UK | 6.7 | 5.2 | 5.8 | 5.6 | 5.3 |
| Japan | 6.7 | 6.7 | 6.8 | 9.8 | 9.5 |
| France | 6.2 | 6.4 | 6.1 | 5.6 | 6.2 |
| Italy | 4.6 | 4.2 | 4.1 | 4.2 | 4.9 |

*As measured in billions of US dollars.

Specific industry-based studies paint a depressing picture of UK competitiveness. Betwen 1978 and 1985, in all sectors of trade from primary goods to speciality goods (such as entertainment and leisure) UK industries which had lost their share of trade outnumbered those which had gained by 380 to 122. And in only the petro-chemical sector did the UK increase its share of world imports between 1978 and 1985.[65] Just as significant has been the increased import penetration of overseas industries into UK domestic markets. In 1970 imported goods accounted for just under 12 per cent of total UK domestic demand (by volume), by 1988 this had risen to 22 per cent.[66]

Inflation as we have seen came to dominate the policy agenda of all OECD countries since the mid-1970s and Table 14.4 gives clear evidence of a rising trend of inflation as measured by the rise in consumer prices. However, UK inflation rates have been consistently higher on average than the other members of the G7 leading industrial nations. This was particularly pronounced in the 1974–78 and 1979–83 periods, when UK consumer prices rose by 16.2 and 11.3 per cent per year compared to 10.1 and 9.4 per cent respectively in the other G7 economies. The mid-1980s saw a deceleration of UK

**Table 14.4** *Rates of growth in consumer prices, 1969–88 (average annual percentage rates[64])*

| Country | 1969–73 | 1974–78 | 1979–83 | 1984–88 | Total 1969–88 |
|---|---|---|---|---|---|
| Japan | 7.1 | 11.4 | 4.2 | 1.1 | 6.0 |
| Italy | 5.8 | 16.4 | 17.0 | 7.1 | 11.6 |
| France | 4.7 | 10.7 | 11.8 | 4.3 | 7.9 |
| W. Germany | 3.2 | 4.8 | 4.9 | 0.8 | 3.4 |
| USA | 5.0 | 8.0 | 8.9 | 3.5 | 6.4 |
| UK | 5.7 | 16.2 | 11.3 | 4.7 | 9.5 |
| Canada | 4.6 | 9.2 | 9.7 | 4.0 | 6.9 |
| OECD G6 (excluding UK) | 5.1 | 10.1 | 9.4 | 3.5 | 7.0 |

inflation but still some 1.2 per cent a year higher on average than our major comptitors.

Thus the jury must remain out on whether the 1980s presage an economic revival for the UK. The only safe conclusion to draw is that the gap has not widened between the UK and its main competitors in terms of the aggregates of GDP and trade. It has almost become accepted wisdom that there are strong links between the level and quality of education and training and economic performance,[67] and the gap between the UK and Germany here is at its starkest. It remains to be seen whether membership of the ERM leads over the medium to long term to UK inflation rates closer to that of our main competitors.

### Notes

1   From Sir D. Wass, 'The changing problems of economic management', lecture to the Johnian Society in Cambridge, 15 February 1978, reprinted in CSO, *Economic Trends*, 293 (March 1978) 97.

2   From Sir P. Middleton, 'Economic policy formulation in the Treasury in the post-war period', the NIESR Jubilee Lecture, 28 November 1988, reprinted in *National Institute Economic Review*, 127 (February 1989) 51.

3   See R. Rose, *Do Parties Make a Difference?*, 2nd edn (London: Macmillan 1984); and 'Inheritance before choice in public policy', *Journal of Theoretical Politics*, vol. 2, no. 3 (1990) 263–91.

4   B. W. Hogwood and B. G. Peters, 'The dynamics of policy change: policy succession', *Policy Sciences*, 14 (1982) 225–45.

5   Rose, *Do Parties Make a Difference?*

6   Discussed in K. O. Morgan, *The People's Peace: British History 1945–79* (Oxford University Press, 1990) Chapters 1 and 2.

7   See P. Hall, *Governing the Economy: The Politics of State Intervention in Britain and France* (Cambridge: Polity, 1986), especially Chapter 6.

8   G. K. Fry, 'Economic policy-making and planning 1945–70: a survey', *Public Administration Bulletin*, 19 (December 1975) 10–22.

9   See Morgan, *The People's Peace*, Chapters 9—11; and P. Whitehead, *The Writing on the Wall: Britain in the Seventies* (London: Michael Joseph, 1985).

10   Sources: Based on P. Mosley, *The Making of Economic Policy: Theory and Practice from Britain and the US since 1945* (Brighton: Wheatsheaf, 1984), 127; Sir T. Burns, 'The UK government's financial strategy', in W. Eltis and P. Sinclair (eds.), *Keynes and Economic Policy: The Relevance of The General Theory After Fifty Years* (London: Macmillan, 1988) 429; and T. Congdon, *Monetarism Lost and Why it Must be Regained* (London: Policy Study 106, Centre for Policy Studies, 1989).

11   See N. Bosanquet, *After the New Right* (London: Heinemann, 1983).

12   Mosley, *Making of Economic Policy*, Chapter 5.

13   OECD, *Monetary Targets and Inflation Control* (Paris: OECD Monetary Studies Series, 1979).

14   This view comes through clearly in D. Healey, *Time of My Life* (London: Michael Joseph, 1989).

15   See D. Coates, *Labour in Power? A Study of the Labour Government 1974–79* (London: Longman, 1980) for the most authoritative account of this period.

16   Noted by A. Ham, *Treasury Rules: Recurrent Themes in British Economic Policy* (London: Quartet Books 1981); and W. Keegan, *Mrs Thatcher's Economic Experiment* (London: Macmillan, 1984) 88–9.

17   Discussed by M. Wright, 'Public Expenditure in Britain: the crisis of control', *Public Administration*, vol. 57, no. 2 (Summer 1977) 145–69.

18   For a good account of this see S. Fay and H. Young, *The Day the £ Nearly Died* (London: Sunday Times Publications, 1978).

19   See for example S. Brittan, *The Role and Limits of Government: Essays in Political Economy* (London: Temple Smith, 1983), 239–49; and T. Congdon, *Monetary Control in Britain* (London: Macmillan, 1982) 5–7.

20   Hogwood and Peters, 'Dynamics of policy change', 231–2.

21   Discussed by M. Wright, 'Big government in hard times: the restraint of public expenditure', in C. Hood and M. Wright (eds.), *Big Government in Hard Times* (Oxford: Martin Robertson, 1981) 10.

22   See R. C. O. Mathews and J. R. Sargent, 'Introduction: economic policies in a time of troubles, 1977–82', in R. C. O. Mathews and J. R. Sargent (eds.), *Contemporary Problems of Economic Policy: Essays from the CLARE Group* (London: Methuen, 1983).

23   See J. S. Fforde, 'Setting monetary objectives', *Bank of England Quarterly Bulletin*, vol. 23, no. 2 (June 1983) 200–8.

24   OECD, *Monetary Targets*.

25   Congdon, *Monetarism Lost*, 6.

26   J. Callaghan, *Time and Chance* (London: Collins, 1987) 426.

27   See H. M. Treasury, 'Memorandum', in Treasury and Civil Service

Committee, *Monetary Policy* (vol. 2), HC 163–II (London, HMSO, 1981); and 'Background to the government's economic policy', in Treasury and Civil Service Committee, *Monetary Policy* (vol. 3), HC 163–III (London: HMSO, 1981).

28  Discussed in Fforde, 'Setting monetary objectives', 203–4; and D. Smith, *The Rise and Fall of Monetarism: The Theory and Practice of an Economic Experiment* (Harmondsworth: Penguin, 1987), Chapter 5.

29  Noted by Wass, 'Changing problems', 100.

30  *Ibid.*

31  Noted by Burns, 'UK government's financial strategy', 430–2.

32  See Keegan, *Mrs Thatcher's Economic Experiment*, 89–91.

33  See J. C. Chouraqui and R. W. R. Price, 'Medium-term financial strategy: the co-ordination of fiscal and monetary policy', *OECD Economic Studies*, 2 (Spring 1984) 7–50; and OECD, *The Medium-Term Macroeconomic Strategy Revisited* (Paris: Department of Economics and Statistics Working Paper No. 48, OECD, 1987).

34  The key actors are mentioned in Smith, *Rise and Fall of Monetarism*, Chapter 6.

35  Keegan, *Mrs Thatcher's Economic Experiment*, 49–52.

36  J. Bulpitt, 'The discipline of the new democracy: Mrs Thatcher's domestic statecraft', *Political Studies*, 34 (1986) 19–39.

37  For an account of the background to 'Thatcherism' see D. Kavanagh, *Thatcherism and British Politics: The End of Consensus?* (Oxford University Press, 1987).

38  This list is taken from: Keegan, *Mrs Thatcher's Economic Experiment*, Chapter 2; Smith, *Rise and Fall of Monetarism*, Chapter 6; and H. Young, *One of Us: A Biography of Margaret Thatcher* (London: Macmillan, 1989), Chapter 8.

39  Noted by W. H. Buiter and M. H. Miller, *Macroeconomic Consequences of a Change in Regime: The UK under Mrs Thatcher* (London: Centre for Labour Economics, London School on Economics, Discussion Paper No. 179, 1983).

40  This was the theme of Chancellor Lawson's seminal Mais Lecture in 1984; *The Chancellor's Lecture: The British Experiment – The Fifth Mais Lecture* (London: HM Treasury press release, 1984).

41  For more detail see C. Thain, *The Education of the Treasury: The Medium-Term Financial Strategy, 1980–90* (Oxford University Press, 1992).

42  OECD, *The Public Sector: Issues for the 1990s* (Paris: Department of Economics and Statistics Working Paper No. 90, OECD, 1990).

43  A theme in C. A. E. Goodhart, *Money, Information and Uncertainty*, 2nd edn (London: Macmillan, 1989) Chapter 15.

44  For the background to the 1981 Budget see A. Walters, *Britain's Economic Renaissance: Margaret Thatcher's Reforms 1979–1984* (New York: Oxford University Press, 1986) especially Chapter 7; Burns, 'UK government's financial strategy' 435–6; and Keegan, *Mrs Thatcher's Economic Experiment*, 157–170.

45  Discussed by W. Keegan, *Mr Lawson's Gamble* (London: Hodder &

Stoughton, 1989); and Congdon, *Monetarism Lost*.

46   For a discussion of the ERM see: A. Walters, *Sterling in Danger: The Economic Consequences of Pegged Exchange Rates* (London: Fontana, 1990); and 'The Exchange rate mechanism of the European monetary system: a review of the literature', *Bank of England Quarterly Bulletin*, vol. 31, no. 1 (February 1991) 71–82.

47   See N. Lawson, *Stamp Memorial Lecture: Rules Versus Discretion in the Conduct of Economic Policy* (lecture given 26 November 1990 at the London School of Economics, press release).

48   A. Gamble, *Britain in Decline*, 2nd edn (London: Macmillan, 1985).

49   See S. Pollard, *The Wasting of the British Economy* (London: Croom Helm, 1982); and C. Thain, 'The Treasury and Britain's decline', *Political Studies*, 32 (December 1984) 581–95.

50   Gamble, *Britain in Decline*, 17.

51   IMF, *International Financial Statistics Yearbook, 1989* (Washington DC: IMF, 1989).

52   Discussed by A. Gamble, 'Economic policy', in Z. Layton-Henry (ed.), *Conservative Party Politics* (London: Macmillan, 1980): and M. Holmes, *Political Pressure and Economic Policy: British Government 1970–74* (London: Butterworths, 1982).

53   See Coates, *Labour in Power?*

54   Keegan, *Mrs Thatcher's Economic Experiment*.

55   For example, M. E. Porter, *The Competitive Advantage of Nations* (London: Macmillan, 1990) 506–7.

56   OECD, *Economic Surveys: The United Kingdom 1988–89* (Paris: OECD, 1989) 57.

57   *Ibid.*, 58–9.

58   R. Layard and S. Nickell, 'The Thatcher miracle?', *American Economic Review*, vol. 79, no. 2 (May 1989) 218.

59   A view expressed by S. Brittain, 'The Thatcher government's economic policy', in D. Kavanagh and A. Seldon (eds.), *The Thatcher Effect: A Decade of Change* (Oxford: Clarendon Press, 1989) 13.

60   *Ibid.*, 16–17.

61   HM Treasury, *Autumn Statement 1990*, Cm 1311 (London: HMSO, November 1990) 55.

62   *Source:* based on OECD, *Economic Outlook*, 46 (Paris: OECD, December 1989) 166.

63   *Source:* based on IMF, *International Financial Statistics Yearbook, 1989*, 120–1; and IMF, *International Financial Statistics*, XLIII, No. 10 (Washington DC: IMF, October 1990) 76.

64   *Source:* based on OECD, *Economic Outlook*, 46.

65   Porter, *Competitive Advantage of Nations*, 536–9.

66   Brittan, 'The Thatcher government's economic policy', 18.

67   Porter, *Competitive Advantage of Nations*, 720–1.

# Britain and the European Community: twenty years of not knowing

Britain's relationship with the European Community can be summed up as follows. The government lacks any sense of purpose about Britain's role in Europe, and consequently its policies are riddled with contradiction and ambiguity. Any initiative that might result in Britain becoming more deeply involved in European institutions brings these inconsistencies to the surface, with the government then moving into a state of disarray accompanied by bitter party conflict and occasional resignations. There are those who put their Europeanism above party loyalty whilst others, including the Prime Minister, seem prepared to sacrifice Europe for any short-term party political advantage. The Prime Minister's position on the EC issue has invited challenges from political rivals for the key to No. 10. For many, fundamental hostility towards the EC masquerades as arguments about the sovereignty of Parliament, about alien ideologies being thrust upon Britain by the unelected bureaucrats of Brussels or about the undesirable national characteristics of our partners, particularly the French and Germans. In comparison with the government the opposition, which suffered its own divisions in the past, now appears united and positive towards Europe.

This state of affairs refers, of course, to the last days of the Wilson government twenty years ago. But it is remarkable how striking similarities could be found two decades on to the position of Margaret Thatcher's government in relation to Europe. Periodic reassurances from members of that government that it was committed fully to the EC and that what might appear as obduracy on Britain's part was simply how the parternship worked out in practice have to be treated with caution. What is a better indicator of government attitudes than rhetoric is its actual behaviour, and here recently has been seen a government which lurched into crisis whenever crucial decisions had to be made involving a significant European dimension. For example, in addition to the agonising which accompanied the decision on whether or not Britain should enter the Exchange Rate Mechanism (ERM) of the European Monetary System (EMS), the political dramas which will be remembered from the Thatcher years have had European plots and sub-plots. The 'Lawson affair' which ended with the resignation of the Chancellor, resulted from his policy of sterling shadowing the Deutschmark as a prelude to EMS entry; the 'Westland affair' involved rival European and Atlanticist rescue bids for the beleaguered helicopter company from two Cabinet ministers, Michael Heseltine and Leon Brittan, both of whom resigned; and, the 'Ridley affair', which resulted in the resignation of the Trade and Industry Secretary over an assessment of the German character worthy of Walmington-on-Sea's Captain Mainwaring. Finally, of course, the 'Thatcher affair' in which the EC was the key issue which prompted the resignation of her Deputy Prime Minister, Sir Geoffrey Howe and the events which followed, resulting in her own resignation. How can it be that Margaret Thatcher's conviction-led Conservative government inside the EC still suffered from strains in relations with Europe similar to Harold Wilson's consensus-seeking Labour government outside the EC? Can it be possible that twenty years of thinking about Europe has resulted in so little change in British politics?

This chapter considers the political debate on Europe over the last two decades as Britain searched for a new role after loss of empire. It will be argued that successive governments reached the painful decision that there seemed no realistic third-force alternative outside the EC. More attractive roles, either heading the Commonwealth as a third force in world politics or leading a liberal-minded Europe group of countries outside but associated with the six of the EC were pursued for brief periods only to be eventually abandoned as unrealistic aspirations. The only viable third-force role appeared to be within the EC itself, yet this was an international role for Britain which generated little enthusiasm and considerable opposition. Final entry into the EC was accomplished only by insulating the decision from the wider reaches of public opinion.

The chapter concludes by arguing that Britain's ungiving and negative attitudes towards the EC have now proved to be historically justified. Although EC membership was the only and therefore right decision at the time, for what are probably all the wrong reasons Britain's record of blocking, opposition and intransigence as a member of the EC has brought unforeseen advantages. The course of history means there is now much more to Europe than the EC. In a perverse way Britain's traditional distaste of the EC, of its institutions and ways of working, opens the door to the creation of a more outward-looking and politically richer Europe than the EC in its current form could ever become.

## Britain approaches Europe

In her early study of British relations with the EC, Miriam Camps noted a similar sequence in the thinking of first the Macmillan government then the Wilson government in their assessments of Britain's future international role:

first, the flirtation with alternatives to 'joining Europe' – the Commonwealth and EFTA – then the disenchantment, then –'bridge building'; then the cautious acceptance of the idea of membership in the Common Market, on conditions, and with the political overtones played down, ignored or rejected.[1]

As we shall see, Wilson's bid for membership was confused to the point of being a 'policy mess', and the attempt to play down the political overtones of the Treaty of Rome was not so much a tactic to avoid grassroots conflict in the party as it was a sympton of the distaste of party leaders themselves towards the politics of the EC.

### *Labour's European mystery*

Twenty years ago Britain was not a member of what then was referred to as the Common Market or the European Economic Community. Prime Minister Harold Wilson and his Foreign Secretary, George Brown, had conducted a tour of European capitals in order to probe continental responses to a second British application for membership. Judging the time to be ripe for success that application was lodged. At the time Labour leaders appeared to need no effort to convince the party, which was deeply divided on other issues, of the wisdom of such a course of action. The party was, of course, sold a policy dummy which was typically Wilsonian in its magic of appearing to go one way whilst possibly going another.

Labour was not short of policies on Europe; it had three. For the pro-Marketeers in the Cabinet and on the backbenches the Labour government's application for membership of the EC meant that policy was one of positive unqualified support for European institutions and Britain's future role within them. To others, who were considerably less committed to the idea of Britain in Europe, the government's application for membership was viewed in an open-minded and pragmatic manner in which the final decision would rest upon the acceptability of the terms negotiated. Finally, for the anti-Marketeers in the party the application for EC entry was worthy of their support because they felt it would reveal, once and for all, that the terms of entry would be unacceptably high, proving that Britain's future lay outside the EC.

Labour's three policies on Europe co-existed with surprisingly little conflict in the party since, from an early stage in the application process, the French President made it clear that for a second time that he would block British membership. Divisions began to appear when de Gaulle retired from politics in April 1969, thus removing the only major hurdle to Britain's entry to the EC. The storm broke in the last days of the Labour government with the publication of a White Paper in February 1970 which reassessed the likely cost of EC entry in terms of wide-ranging estimates of the burden to the balance of payments. The immediate argument was one about what was or was not an acceptable price for Britain to pay for EC membership. Predictably for the pro-Marketeers any cost, no matter how great, was acceptable whilst for their opponents any cost, no matter how small, proved to be shocking and excessive. The election of a Conservative government, led by Edward Heath, proved too strong a test for Labour's fragile European platform. A bewildered public were then to hear not the nuts and bolts arguments about the costs of EC entry or the advantages and disadvantages of membership which they might have anticipated, but rather assorted Labour leaders in fundamental dispute over what their late government's policy had in fact been. It is worth reporting the words of some of the leading protagonists to illustrate the total disintegration of Labour's policy on Europe. Richard Crossman, for example, argued that:

A search through the cabinet papers of this period confirms that no collective decision was made either upon support for the Common Market principle or upon the modifications and assurances required for British entry . . . there is no truth whatsoever in the allegation that the Labour government was ever committed to 'support for the Common Market' . . . the government's collective commitment was limited to approval first for the making of the application and second for the postponement of a decision until the terms were known.[2]

As far as George Brown was concerned the Labour government had made a very different policy. According to his account there was:

A clear Declaration of Intent and a Decision in Principle by the Cabinet to join. We prudently reserved the final decision actually to sign, and thereby consummate, until the negotiations were concluded and we could see the outcome and terms were indeed satisfactory. That left us freedom to withdraw if it turned out that these were not as we expected them to be. But not the freedom to pretend that we never intended to join.[3]

To make things worse, in January 1971 around half of the PLP, drawn mainly from the left and centre, signed an Early Day Motion highly hostile to British membership of the EC, whilst in May the remainder of the Parliamentary Labour Party signed a full-page political statement in the *Guardian* which expressed strong support for membership. Labour, then, entered the 1970s in extremely poor shape on Europe. It was split from top to bottom on the wisdom of EC membership, with its leaders unable to remember what their policy was or agree on what it should be. This ambiguity tempted two of Wilson's Cabinet colleagues to plot against him, unsuccessfully as it turned out, in bids to replace him.

### Edward Heath and the democratic deficit

Britain became a member of the EC on 1 January 1973. The Conservative government, led by Edward Heath, differed from the Macmillan and Wilson governments that had handled previous negotiations in ways which were to prove critical. Edward Heath was an ardent pro-European to an extent that could never be said of either Macmillan or Wilson. Heath's. support for EC entry was outright, positive and unqualified. It did not result from being nudged towards Europe by an American President, as in the case of Macmillan, or by a reluctant recognition that all the more preferable options seemed closed, as in the case of Wilson. For Heath there was no need for any exploratory exercise to evaluate alternative options for Britain, since on Europe he was, and remains, the post-war Prime Minister most guided by his personal convictions.

Edward Heath's zeal for seeing Britain inside the EC and the successfully completed negotiations which were accompanied by contrived national celebration should not obscure the fact that there continued to be a high level of opposition to membership. Inside the ranks of his own party there was a considerable number of Conservatives who had severe doubts about the government's bid for membership. But the most vocal opposition lay within a divided Labour Party. Dramatic conflicts over Europe became commonplace within the opposition party since many other important issues seemed to touch upon the EC. The management of the economy, the future of the welfare state and the passing of trade-union legislation – all contentious issues in their own right – were seen as bearing upon the EC issue. Labour's pro-Marketeers thus found it increasingly difficult to argue against the Heath government on a wide range of domestic issues but give support on Europe. A young Tribune Group MP, destined for higher office, summed up their dilemma:

For 364 days out of the year on every issue – on school milk, the freeze on public employees, the lot – in Parliament and outside we stridently, without reservation, attack, attack, attack. We have called the Conservatives everything we can lay our tongues to. And then we are prepared to go before the British nation and say on the 365th day – not on a marginal issue, not on a major non-contentious issue, but on the biggest issue of our generation – we are going to put our arms round him and say 'After all Ted, although we hate you for the rest of the time, we think you are right on this one.' It is not on.[4]

In the critical Commons vote, Labour policy was to vote against the Government motion which approved in principle the decision to join the EC. In the event the government received a comfortable majority. If, however, every Labour MP had obeyed the party whip the government would have been defeated

Britain's entry into the EC, a monumental step in constitutional, political, economic and social terms, was accomplished in a manner which may be seen now as being politically inappropriate. Previous Prime Ministers had devised tactics to make easier any move into Europe, but neither had ridden so rough-shod over opposing views. Macmillan attempted to 'sidle into Europe' by playing down the significance of the move through presenting the EC as it was then as an organisation concerned only with commerce. Wilson 'decided not to decide' until such time as a firm decision was required. Unlike Heath, both were sensitive to opposing viewpoints and sought to reassure those who held doubts and reservations. Heath's style on Europe remained to the end that of 'Selsdon Man'. He ignored opposition and his commitment to, some would say his obsession with, Europe was viewed by many agnostics as being a political liability. It was feared that his government would be far too willing to make concessions in the negotiations in order to secure Britain's entry. Mr Heath, in other words, would be a push-over for the Europeans. And in the event many concluded that he was.

In the light of the constitutional arrangements to test the opinion of the Scots and Welsh on devolution, it now seems remarkable that there was no democratic test for the decision on entry into the EC. The wider Labour movement supported the idea of a general election being held in which Labour would oppose entry on the terms negotiated by the Heath government, but the wider public appeared to support the idea of a referendum on the issue. An NOP poll of the time recorded 78 per cent of those interviewed as being in favour of a referendum on entry on the Heath terms. In the context of the European debate this was not a particularly radical constitutional preference, since other applicant countries were consulting their electorates over EC entry. Indeed, as if to rub salt into the wound, the French held a referendum on whether or not the EC should accept new members. For such a divided nation as Britain was at the time to have taken such a crucial step in its history without wider consultation was the first experience of the 'democratic deficit' – a term more generally reserved for the EC institutions than those of member countries.

On 5 June 1975, Britain's first national referendum was held on membership of the EC based on the terms 'renegotiated' by the Labour government. In a turn-out of 63.2 per cent, 17,378,581 voted for continued membership and 8,470,073 voted against. Whilst it was better that this referendum was held than not held, as a consultation of public opinion the exercise was flawed in a number of ways. It was essentially a referendum about withdrawing from the EC rather than joining. Also it was too transparently a device to rescue Labour, divided still from government to grassroots, from the ignominy of still being unable to make a decision on EC entry. In James Callaghan's words, the referendum was 'Labour's little rubber life-raft' rather than an authentic attempt to widen participation on the membership decision.

### The search for a third force role

Retreat from empire left Britain's political elite with much thinking to do about a future role in the world. A position of leadership was sought at the head of what, in the then current configuration of world powers, would be some form of third force. From the outset, options which failed to meet this requirement were ruled out. In his memoirs, Harold Wilson recounted how his Cabinet eliminated in a routine manner a role which involved developing the 'special relationship' into some deeper form of union or existing as an independent ex-colonial power living in reduced circumstances; there was 'general agreement that NAFTA [North Atlantic Free Trade Area] was unreal' and GITA [Go it Alone], it was also widely agreed, was not 'a constructive alternative'. What, then, were the alternatives for Britain as seen by political leaders of the day?

*Global third-force ambitions*
The Attlee government did not participate fully in the Schuman Plan of 1950 when it was proposed that the coal and steel resources of France and Germany should be pooled. Other European governments were invited to join the scheme, which ultimately developed into one of the three foundation stones of the EC. In explaining British reluctance to do no more than send observers the Chancellor, Sir Stafford Cripps, argued that participation in a scheme 'limited to Western Europe' was incompatible with 'our Commonwealth ties'.

The Commonwealth was recognised generally as a force for good by both the major politically parties and public alike. The immediate post-war decades were ones in which there was strong attachment and sentiment across society for the Commonwealth. In retrospect it is probably true to say that at the time the Commonwealth was a rather amorphous concept with Conservatives attracted more to the old White Dominions of the English-speaking world whilst Labour was drawn to the multi-racial, non-aligned and non-capitalist potential of the Commonwealth. These perceptions found articulation at the time of Harold Macmillan's first application for EC membership. Eulogies flowed from all parts of the political spectrum; the Commonwealth was 'something unique in international relations' . . . 'a force both economic and political in world affairs' . . . 'a unique, politically priceless multi-national system of ours' and comparisons, particularly pertinent to this generation, were made between the selfless sacrifice made by the Commonwealth in coming to Britain's aid in the darkest days of the war and the jubilant jackbooted fascism of those whom Macmillan wanted to join.

Labour thinking was captured by this imagery and the party entered the 1964 general election with its 'Commonwealth Plan' policy having preference over any European alternative. In many ways it is true to say of Labour that in 1964 it was 'the Commonwealth' party. The responsibilities of government, however, led to a rapid reassessment of the Commonwealth as forming the basis of Britain's role in the world. It was concluded that the third-force Commonwealth alternative was dead. Harold Wilson expressed disappointment at some of the problems encountered in attempting to strengthen Commonwealth trade:

The developing countries were more concerned with aid programmes. The developed – particularly Australia but, to a small extent, Canada, too – were resistant to closer trading relations. For while they welcomed the continuation, and encouragement, of their long established agricultural exports to Britain, they were not disposed to adopt arrangements which put their own domestic manufacturers at risk. There was the fact, too, that long years of neglect of Commonwealth trade had led to the development of strong non-Commonwealth ties . . . There is in fact nothing under the sun more laissez-faire than Commonwealth trade.[5]

Within months of assuming office, Labour's aspirations about the Commonwealth providing Britain with a leading third-force role were abandoned. Indeed, the Commonwealth 'alternative' was quickly to become the Commonwealth 'problem'. The Rhodesian crisis illuminated how fragile the Commonwealth was as an organisation and in doing so, how politically and economically unrealistic Labour's Commonwealth Plan was from the outset.

## A European third force

At various times during the post-war years there has been support across the political spectrum for the idea of Britain's future being part of a large loosely organised European grouping of nations. In 1956 Reginald Maudling, a senior Conservative minister, had responsibility for negotiating a free-trade area that would include the six countries of what was to become the EC, Britain and any other member of the Organisation for European Economic Cooperation which wished to join. There was opposition to the scheme, particularly from the French, and the Maudling plan foundered. Faced with this failure, rather than apply to join the EC the government established the European Free Trade Association (EFTA). If Britain was now to play a largely European role in world affairs, and a growing number of Conservatives accepted this proposition, then it would be played in a non-federal free-trade organisation. They would have preferred the ambitious Maudling plan to have succeeded but could embrace EFTA as a fallback when Maudling failed.

Before the Wilson government applied for membership of the EC, it experimented with its own version of the Maudling plan. There was an attempt to draw EFTA and the EC closer together through the 'bridge-building' agenda of the Vienna Conference in May 1965. Harold Wilson expressed concern about the 'serious and worsening' division of Europe into two trading blocs and proposed the creation of a new free-trade association covering EFTA, the EC and any other countries willing to join. But as with the Maudling proposals, the Vienna Conference was to fail, and Britain's first preference for a united Europe based on free trade without the federal implications of the EC remained unavailable.

There is also a tradition on the left of British politics which supports Britain's role in a socialist Third Force Europe. For example, Fenner Brockway urged the 1948 Labour Party Conference to support 'the establishment of a United States of Europe, based on public ownership, economic planning and individual liberty'. These attitudes were to survive in the Labour Party within what was known as the Wider Europe Group. The group's members supported Britain's entry to the EC and argued that the EC would at some stage unite with EFTA and the countries of Eastern Europe. The Wider Europe Group accepted that the EC was capitalist in nature, but argued that capitalist integration was a preparatory step towards the centralisation that would be needed for the establishment of the United Socialist States of Europe of which Brockway spoke.

Circumstances in Europe of today have changed in ways which make more possible that which was denied to Reginald Maulding in 1957 and Harold Wilson at the Vienna Conference in 1965. The EC is already experiencing demands for change on both its western and eastern fronts. First, important changes are taking place within EFTA and the long-awaited bridge-building between the old rivals now seems imminent. There is much talk of creating a 'European Economic Space' grouping alongside serious speculation that what is far more likely is the eventual break up of EFTA as its members apply to join the EC. Second, and more significantly, the collapse of communist regimes in Eastern Europe and the changes that are taking place within the Soviet Union have already changed the political geography of the EC with promises of greater change to come. Mrs Thatcher saw the possibilities of a new and wider European order which her instincts preferred to the current and more narrow arrangements. Taking her words at face value, she went on the record in the United States proposing 'that the Community should declare unequivocally that it is ready to accept all the countries of Eastern Europe as members if they want to join'. During a tour of East European countries she went on to tell the Czechoslovak Parliament that, 'We must create the sort of Community which you and others in Eastern and Western Europe truly want to join – a European Community which is fair, which is open, which preserves the diversity and nationhood of each of its members'. Even in her swan-song interview with the press days before her fall, she repeated these themes: 'I am a Europe idealist and I want Europe, the larger Europe. Europe is older than the European Community. I want the larger wider Europe in which Moscow is also a European power.'[6]

It is no longer incredible to think of 'Europe 2000' as stretching from the Atlantic to the Urals. Already there is the proposal for a Parliamentary Assembly drawn from thirty-four nations that emerged at the Paris Conference on Security and Cooperation in Europe. Although the scope of such an assembly would necessarily be narrow, at least in the first instance, its framework reflects the rediscovery of pan-Europeanism from which the EC cannot remain untouched. If the EC of the future expanded to include EFTA members, with the possible exception of Switzerland, as well as in addition to East Germany through reunification, Hungary, Poland, Yugoslavia, Czechoslovakia and some republics from the former Soviet Union it could total around twenty-five members. It would not be the socialist Europe of the Wider Europe Group, but neither would the new Europe simply be the current EC writ large. It would necessarily be loosely knit, with federalism postponed. It would be the sort of Europe of which successive British governments have wanted to be part.

## The EC third force

It was not until 1960 that a reappraisal of Britain's external relations conducted by Sir Frank Lee concluded that the best option was membership of the EC. It was a case of recognising that the least-favoured option was the only option available. Sir Frank's assessment was one which few found easy to accept. The political parties, as reported above, sought without success for other roles before approaching the EC with considerable reluctance. The wider public too shared this resignation; poll data, conference reports and letters to newspapers reflected a general anxiety about both the EC decision and why it was taken. Typical feelings were expressed in a factory-based seminar held in 1962 when one participant, Nurse Robbie, lamented that it was being said that Britain *had* to join the community and asked 'If there were no problems with the Commonwealth, would Britain voluntarily join Europe?'[7] These together with other doubts continued to be held throughout the 1970s, both before and after entry, into the 1980s when Labour's official policy became one of withdrawal from the EC. In the 1990s serious questions are being raised by the government, not over membership, but about the fundamental nature of the Community of which Britain is part. Why, after all this time, has the Community idea such a shallow footing in the conventional wisdom of British political life?

Although those on the political left and right have their own distinct objections to the Community idea, there has remained a shared and instinctive dislike of the concept of a trading bloc designed with the intention of ever-rising tariffs against the rest of the world. The implementation of the EC's only truly Community-wide policy, the Common Agricultural Policy, is mocked for its literally madcap consequences destructive to world trade. British perspectives on the EC have been modified over the years but for many the Community has never shed its narrow inward-looking nature. No amount of rhetoric about Lomé has dented the impression that the true concern of the Community is with the rich West End of Europe. This is currently illustrated by the determined rush led by Jacques Delors towards economic and monetary union, moves which many understand as an attempt to fix Community rules to strengthen further the position of current members to the disadvantage of future members.

In the language of British politics over the last two decades 'pro-Common Market' and 'pro-European' were interchangeable terms. Commentators had a choice in, for example, describing Edward Heath in terms of either and there was no political significance in whichever label they settled on. Now, however, semantic differences have emerged between the two terms. Margaret Thatcher assumed the role of an anti-Common Market yet pro-European Prime

Minister. It will no doubt take another decade of struggle to resolve which tendency will influence the political organisation of the continent. Pro-Europeans will push for an expanded outward-looking Europe which will take into account aspirations of new members: pro-Marketeers will fight to preserve and deepen the EC with demands that new members accept existing arrangements.

## Conclusion

Margaret Thatcher was moved by two European prospects; one was a vision, the other a nightmare. She spoke too little of the former, too much of the latter. The Little Englander nightmare came to dominate her approach to the EC rather than her pan-European idealism. Had the reverse been the case, then perhaps the Thatcher years may have had a different ending.

For the last two decades Britain's relations with the EC have been unfortunate, to say the least, first as rejected applicant then as intransigent member. It is too early to comment on John Major's approach to our EC partners. But what can be said is that he assumed responsibility at a time which bears greater promise. For the third time this century Europe is on the brink of a political reconstruction. One of the possible outcomes is the making of a Europe which closely resembles that which Britain has repeatedly sought but never found.

## Notes

1 Miriam Camps, *European Unification in the Sixties: from the Veto to the Crisis* (London: Oxford University Press, 1967) 194.

2 *New Statesman*, 12 February 1971.

3 *The Times*, 16 February 1971.

4 *Special LPCR* (1971) 38.

5 Harold Wilson: *The Labour Government 1964–70* (London: Weidenfeld & Nicolson and Michael Joseph, 1971) 117.

6 *Sunday Times*, 18 November 1990.

7 *The Cable*, vol. 7, no. 2 (1962) 44.

# Northern Ireland:
# a putting together of parts

The Northern Ireland crisis is a continuing source of what might be called Hobbesian fascination. The question addressed by many academic commentators has been: 'How do politicians devise a rational and just compact amongst themselves and their communities in order to get out of a nasty and brutish state of nature and to secure the conditions of peace?' Much of the suggestive value of this work has been often vitiated by the abstract rationalism of its political science which take too little account (as Hobbes did not) of the passionate nature of human commitment. Moreover, the early attempts to provide a comparative perspective, which drew heavily on the work of Arend Lijphart, tended to confuse what was revealing and significant with what was legitimately applicable; the force of theoretical construction with the resistance of historical experience. In both cases one is reminded of Oakeshott's warning that to follow the example of Zeuxis, who tried to compose a figure more beautiful than Helen's by assembling the perfect features of others, is 'one of the surest ways of losing one's political balance'.[1] That loss of balance is revealed in the frequent oscillation between optimism and despair.

That it is more realistic to despair of than to be optimistic about the Northern Ireland crisis seemed to be confirmed in the recent anniversary which had to do with the arrival twenty years ago of British troops on the streets of Belfast to 'aid the civil power' in the quelling of sectarian riots. The presence of the British army in that role is generally understood to announce the real starting point of the modern 'Troubles'. Clearly, a political crisis logically pre-dated the sending of troops. But the character of that crisis was fundamentally transformed within the year. Struggle for and resistance to reform within Northern Ireland was caught up in the campaign by militant republicans (the Provisional Irish Republican Army) to destroy by arms the Union of Northern Ireland and Great Britain and to create a unified Irish state. At a cost of 3,000 lives it is that campaign which has defined the nature of the problem for most people outside Northern Ireland. The stubborn and bloody persistence of the Troubles has all but exhausted the vocabulary of condemnation. Even the image of the 'cycle of violence' intimates the sense of inevitable and meaningless repetition. And that imagery has been transferred to the political realm in which the 'integrity of their quarrel' remains unmoved, a corrupt and hopeless expression of Burkean 'unchanging constancy'. However, history never repeats itself. It only stutters. What may appear to be the dreary sameness of events and conditions is invariably something different. Those who seek 'progress' in Northern Ireland take comfort from that insight and keep faith with the belief that the different will be for the better. The sceptic must also be allowed the qualification that it could just as well be for the worse. In so far as the whole of the crisis may be understood as an arrangement of its parts, the following considerations may be acknowledged.

## Interpreting the Troubles

The onset of the Troubles signalled the final disintegration of that settlement which had maintained relative stability in Ireland for fifty years. The Government of Ireland Act of 1920 and the Anglo-Irish Treaty of 1921 had been reasonably successful in conjuring the Irish question out of existence for British politicians. To employ the jargon of the present day, four major relationships of the question had been recognised (in principle at least) by Lloyd George's diplomacy. The six counties of Northern Ireland had been given a measure of devolved self-government but the unionist majority had won its struggle to remain part of the United Kingdom. The twenty-six counties of the Irish Free State had been granted national self-determination in the manner implied by the contemporary use of the phrase 'Home Rule'. Provision had also been made for a Council of Ireland to discuss the common affairs of the island of Ireland (the North–South dimension). The Irish Free State was to remain a dominion within the British Empire (the East–West dimension). This arrangement of parts, which British politicians expected to hold together by geography and sentiment, was to be transformed by determined political will.

First, their experience of the 'official mind' in London during the negotiations on partition had led unionist leaders to believe that the British government exhibited little enthusiasm for the Union with Northern Ireland. The terms of the Irish settlement implied that it was up to unionists themselves to ensure that Northern Ireland did not succumb to the 'logic' of Irish unity. This they tried to do by refusing to co-operate with the Dublin government in the Council of Ireland (which became a dead letter) and by fashioning Unionist Party hegemony within Northern Ireland on the resources and patronage made available by devolved government. When it was in its power to do so, the Unionist Party rewarded loyalty and excluded from influence those who were, or were thought to be, disloyal. Second, nationalist politics in Northern Ireland simply mirrored this Unionist response. Having lost in 1920, nationalist politicians excluded themselves from constructive engagement in the system because that would have been tantamount to accepting the legitimacy of partition. The grievances which arose from that disposition were actually functional to a view of the world which asserted that catholics could get no justice under British (or surrogate British) rule. Indeed by constantly associating claims to justice within Northern Ireland with the 'true' justice of Irish unity national-ists only encouraged unionist suspicion of their motives. The solid continuity of unionist rule thus overlay a deeply fractured polity. Third, the southern Irish state established a confessional political identity at odds with its claim to embody the true national aspiration of all on the island whether catholic or protestant. The separate development of Irish Home Rule became manifest with the triumph of de Valera and his Fianna Fail party in 1932. The new constitution of 1937 unilaterally amended the conditions of the 1920s settlement and its articles two and three laid jurisdictional claim to the territory of Northern Ireland. When the Irish state became a Republic in 1948 the links to London and the Commonwealth were formally severed. Finally, Westminster proved itself to be a coy sovereign in Northern Ireland. By excluding citizens there as far as possible from the main currents of state it helped to ensure the perpetuation of the worst features of Unionist rule. A policy of 'out of sight, out of mind' (apart from the Second World War) served Westminster well for fifty years.

Fifty years is a long time in politics. The civil disturbance which broke out in the late 1960s, and from which the IRA campaigns of the following two decades developed, came as a bolt from the blue not only for the British government but for the Irish government as well. When the Stormont Parliament was prorogued in 1972, the British government, ruling 'directly', was thereby compelled to set about reconstructing the parts into a manageable whole. In the course of the next two years the first Secretary of State for Northern Ireland, William Whitelaw, put together an ingenious package of delicate compromises to accommodate and adjust the claims of the contending parties. The Northern Ireland Office recognised that the former Stormont system had had the seeds of disequilibrium implanted from its birth. Enlightened policy had first to redress by institutional means the imbalance of unionist majoritarian democracy within Northern Ireland and so achieve a legitimate framework for sound governance. Second, it had to acknowledge some relationship between Northern Ireland and the Irish Republic. Third, it had to reaffirm that the will of Ulster unionists to remain within the United Kingdom would be constitutionally recognised. Finally, if there was no longer a Commonwealth link between London and Dublin, common membership of the European Community was identified as a valuable forum of association. It was a comprehensive strategy. Despite mounting political violence during the period, a power-sharing executive between co-operative unionists and nationalists had been put in place in Belfast. At Sunningdale in December 1973 agreement was reached between that executive and the British and Irish governments on the establishment of a Council of Ireland. Article five of Sunningdale sought to confirm the existing constitutional status of Northern Ireland. But as a result of the Ulster Workers' Council strike in May of 1974 this strategy collapsed just as comprehensively. What were the reasons for this failure? If we ignore the contingent factors – an unfortunately timed Westminster election in February 1974 which allowed the anti-executive unionist groupings to mobilise successfully and a new minority Labour administration unsure how to respond to a (protestant) workers' strike – then the following considerations were central.

First, the Social Democratic and Labour Party (SDLP), which represented the voice of constitutional nationalism in the executive, attempted to exploit its position to push for a full-blooded implementation of the Irish dimension. Balancing the pressures from within its own ranks, from its own electorate and from the IRA, the Council of Ireland had become for the SDLP the index of success. Not only did the pushing of the Irish dimension at Sunningdale undermine the position of those unionists led by Brian Faulkner in the executive and deflect discussion from immediate tasks; it also appeared to confirm protestant suspicion that the SDLP was determined to pursue a traditional nationalist agenda.[2] Second, the constitutional guarantee that the Irish had supposedly given to Northern Ireland was publicly repudiated by the Dublin government when it was challenged on the principle of contradicting articles two and three. Both the government and the Supreme Court confirmed that the Sunningdale agreement in no way qualified the territorial claim as stated in the Republic's constitution. That this was an admission of some enormity for stablility in Northern Ireland has been ignored in some commentaries on the politics of the period.[3] Third, the hostility of unionist opinion to any apparent qualifications of their statehood had been underestimated. The term statehood is used advisedly. What was not at issue *on principle* was co-operation with catholics in the government of Northern Ireland, although whether power-sharing – permanent coalition – itself was the proper form of such co-operation remains debatable. What was at issue for most unionists was detected by David Miller; namely, that 'Westminster in 1972–74 was unwilling to give meaningful assurances of a determination to make the United Kingdom the state in Northern Ireland.'[4] In the conditions of continuing republican violence, unionist opposition translated this sense of political insecurity into an effective boycott of the new constitutional order.

## Aspects of the crisis

The failure of the initiative of 1973–74 reveals the truly significant grounds of the Ulster crisis. One is the clear lack of trust between the constitutional politicians in Northern Ireland. Unionists took the experience to reveal that the SDLP was not prepared to take seriously the task of contributing to the stability and good government of Northern Ireland to the extent of putting off the goal of Irish unity. Similarly, the SDLP came to believe that the risk involved in outraging hardline nationalist sympathies by co-operating in an internal settlement in Northern Ireland was probably not worth taking. Therefore, the Irish dimension increasingly took prominence in nationalist thinking as a pre-condition of devolution rather than as a structural appendage to it. Another important ground is the contradictory political culture of the Irish Republic. On the one hand the Irish Republic is a modern European state committed, as membership of the European Community demands, to the idea of pragmatic interstate co-operation based on the acknowledgement of existing boundaries. On the other, the Republic is a state with a destiny to re-integrate the national territory, a state the public doctrine of which has (hitherto) forbidden it to recognise clearly the validity of Northern Ireland's position in the United Kingdom. The problem of achieving any stable Irish dimension between Belfast and Dublin, never mind between London and Dublin, has been due in large part to that public doctrine. Finally, the impression given by Westminster that it exercises a reluctant sovereignty in Northern Ireland has been perfectly conducive to instability. Unionists are encouraged to be distrustful of government intentions and the IRA is encouraged in its assumption that where the will is weak there is a way for force. These interlocking hostilities, suspicions and bad faith constitute the substantial problems which define the character of the Northern Ireland crisis which it has been the task of British policy to resolve.

The next decade, 1975–85, was sterile of major political development within Northern Ireland. All the local parties, with varying degrees of enthusiasm, had pirouetted around the prospect of devolution according to ingenious proposals choreographed by British governments, both Labour and Conservative. This became a long-running political show which seemed to bore its sponsors and exasperate those taking part in it. The electorate, though long-suffering, expressed only minor interest in what was going on. As opinion polls revealed, while large majorities expressed support for some form of devolved power-sharing government, there was also little expectation that it would be achieved. The reasons for this pessimism (or realism) become clear when we examine the dispositions of unionist and nationalist politics in this period.

The generality of unionist politicians hankered after some reconstruction of the old order. But it was clear that this could never be. Indeed, what had been essential to the meaning of the old order was now denied to unionists. They could not have exclusive control of security and patronage. There was also suspicion that what the British government was prepared to concede to ensure SDLP participation would not strengthen the Union but weaken it. Thus, while the unionist parties remained publicly committed to devolved government within the United Kingdom, what devolved government now meant as practical politics was something they did not want at all. This was a frustrating and ultimately demoralising position and contributed to the absence of open debate about alternatives within unionism. Under the leadership or, rather, *sotto governo* of James Molyneaux, the Official Unionist Party (OUP), particularly its MPs, moved towards a practical policy of integration, i.e. assimilating Northern Ireland into the administrative and political arrangements relevant to any other part of the United Kingdom. However, the intellectual case for this strategy was never consistently argued. The Democratic Unionist Party (DUP) led by Ian Paisley was fully engaged in a search for some formula that would have returned devolved government to Belfast. For instance, it was the DUP which tried to make a success of the Assembly set up by James Prior in 1982. Defiant Paisleyite posturing should not obscure the reality that in this period it was the DUP which was most in tune with the strategic purposes of British policy. What stymied the DUP in its objectives was that the SDLP, under the leadership of John Hume, had abandoned any interest in an 'internal settlement'.

In the latter part of the 1970s Hume had tried to fashion a 'third way' for nationalist politics between the traditions of violence and non-cooperation. He espoused a felicitous notion of an Agreed Ireland based on the reconciliation of the 'two traditions' on the island. This notion, which was developed in the New Ireland Forum Report of 1984, had been the product of intensive deliberation between the SDLP and the parties of the Irish Republic. The Forum and its Report were designed to provide a democratic alternative to the opportunism of Provisional Sinn Fein, the political wing of the IRA, which had profited from the emotion of the Hunger Strikes to take 40 per cent of the nationalist vote in Northern Ireland in 1983. Its central purposes were to put the Irish dimension back into prominence in any future deliberations about Northern Ireland; to redefine the 'problem' of Northern Ireland in terms of Unionist accommodation with the 'aspiration' to Irish unity in the rest of the island; and to mobilise the resources of the Republic's diplomatic community to push the SDLP's case with the British government. As article 5.8 of the Report reads: 'it would be for the British and Irish governments to create the framework and atmosphere within which such negotiations (with unionists) could take place.'[5] In other words, in any

future attempt to address the Ulster crisis both sovereign governments should first: establish an institutional *fait accompli*
compatible with the idea of Irish unity and second: the British
government should use its influence to encourage the unionists to
consent to it. Reconciliation would have to come in *Ireland* not in
*Ulster* alone.

## The Anglo-Irish Agreement

On 15 November 1985 the British Conservative government
attempted another putting together of parts to answer the whole of
the Irish question. The Anglo-Irish Agreement, which was signed at
Hillsborough by Mrs Thatcher for the United Kingdom and Garret
FitzGerald for the Republic of Ireland, was an event of the utmost
significance. It was the product of an engagement entered into by
both London and Dublin to establish a common frame of reference
within which the two sovereign authorities could encourage a political settlement between the parties in Northern Ireland. It was also
designed to establish the following conditions to the satisfaction of
both governments. For the British government the distinctiveness of
Northern Ireland as a region of the United Kingdom was further
underlined. The discussion of its affairs was set apart even further
from the Westminster norm and constrained by the obligations of an
international treaty. To balance unionism and nationalism as political identities the Anglo-Irish Conference and Secretariat were set up
in recognition of the essentially contested nature of public policy in
Northern Ireland. But it still remained the stated aim of British policy
to foster a devolved power-sharing administration within Northern
Ireland to acknowledge and to accommodate the immediate interests
of catholic and protestant. What was significant about the British
commitment was that it recognised devolution to be a function of the
Irish dimension rather than vice-versa. Indeed, the Irish dimension
had been woven in principle into the whole texture of government in
Northern Ireland and London affirmed its willingness to facilitate
any popular move towards Irish unity. These arrangements were
designed to capture the imagination of world (especially American)
opinion as well as to enrol the support of the Irish government in the
battle against IRA terrorism.

For the Republic the aspiration to Irish unity was in no way
circumscribed. Though article one of the Agreement recognises that

no change in the status of Northern Ireland can come about without
the consent of the majority there, no qualification was made
regarding the Republic's territorial claim. Articles two and three of
its constitution were allowed to remain unchanged. Dublin was
granted a direct influence in the decision-making process within
Northern Ireland but without accountability for the execution of
that policy for which the British Secretary of State retains ultimate
responsiblity. The influence was to be that of a sovereign advocate of
the interests of the minority – which is another way of saying that the
Irish government was to press at the highest level the particular
interests of the SDLP. Therefore, while the Anglo-Irish Agreement is
a short document (thirteen articles and a preamble setting out the
broad principles acknowledged by both parties), its brevity belies its
critical and historic import. As a number of academic commentators
have realised, the Agreement concedes a definition of the Ulster crisis
which has been advanced by nationalists in the 1980s.[6] For example,
the text proclaimed the 'need for continuing efforts to reconcile and
to acknowledge the rights of the two major traditions that exist in
*Ireland*' (our emphasis). The language here is the language of the
Forum Report and confirmed to unionists that the Agreement
embodied an open nationalist agenda announcing a unilateral victory for John Hume. It did nothing at all to reassure them that it did
not embrace a hidden nationalist agenda as well. Unionists had not
been consulted throughout the course of discussions on the
Agreement. As late as the summer of 1985 unionist leaders were still
sceptical about reports of what was afoot. When all was eventually
revealed the shock and outrage were profound. As the historian A. T.
Q. Stewart dramatically captured that mood: 'all was changed
utterly on 15 November 1985. A terrible, unwished-for duty was
born.'[7] Unionists were alarmed into almost universal hostility.

However, the Agreement had been designed to be proof against
unionist boycott. No provincial institution had been erected which
could have acted as the focus of unionist pressure. There was to be no
repeat of the UWC strike. The inter-governmental Conference was
beyond the reach of unionist protest. Unionism had been outflanked
already by the Irish dimension. The potency of the 1974 strike had
lain in its novelty: no one had known how far the strikers would have
gone. It was different in 1985. The British government now knew the
limits and confronted the unionists with the constraints of their own
position. In Mrs Thatcher, unionists recognised a stubborn and

purposeful leader. They too recognised that history was not going to repeat itself. What was required was not just protest but intelligent judgment and effective politics. Nevertheless, the immediate response was the 'Ulster Says No' campaign, in effect, a public withdrawal of consent and a self-imposed internal exile.[8]

To adapt a term which Francis Fukuyama popularised in 1989, one might claim – and not entirely with tongue in cheek – that the virtually unanimous support for the Agreement in the House of Commons, in the British and Irish media and throughout academia constituted an intuition that at Hillsborough, Irish history, as a tale of Anglo-Irish misunderstanding, had come to an end. The Agreement, it was thought, would provide the means to de-ideologise anachronistic political antagonisms and to refashion them in the image of modernity. Reason had realised itself in the intergovernmental Conference. The Agreement embodied all that was dispassionate and bureaucratic, a final triumph of enlightened statesmanship and compromise over and above the unruly forces of prejudice and sectarianism. It seemed that all that was left to do was to tidy up the loose ends of Irish history and there was confidence enough in the early years that the job was well in hand. Unionists, it was believed, would eventually come round to accept the new dispensation and, under British tutelage, find a role in institutions which, while falling short of joint sovereignty, would contain a significant and increasing Irish aspect. The IRA would be isolated and ostracised as nationalists could now work peacefully and constructively to bring about an 'agreed' Ireland. However, Irish history has proved a little bit more cunning than that. Quite rapidly attitudes began to change. From something which was self-evidently correct, support for the Agreement became a political act of faith. Two main justifications were adduced. First, that without the Agreement the problems of Northern Ireland would have been even worse. That is irrefutable – but only because it is unprovable. Second, that all imaginable alternatives would be even worse. In other words, the Agreement had become an end in itself. It had become another part of the Irish problem and not the final nail in its coffin.

The experience of the Anglo-Irish Agreement confirms those essentials of the crisis which were revealed at the time of the Executive. They can be restated simply. First, unionists could have little faith in the prospect of sharing power with the SDLP in the government of Northern Ireland *as part of the United Kingdom* if the

SDLP was only willing to consider ways and means of 'sharing this island together' i.e., sharing power as part of some wider all-Ireland arrangement supported by the British and Irish governments. Second, the leader of the SDLP let it be known shortly after the Agreement was signed that his party had 'no ideological commitment to devolution'. In effect, this was a declaration of a new agenda beyond the devolutionary intent of Hillsborough, a sign of increased nationalist expectation. The possibility which the British government held out to unionists – that the insupportable aspects of the Agreement could be 'devolved away' in some new Northern Ireland arrangement – had been 'ideologically' compromised by John Hume. Third, the Irish Republic continued to show its persistent refusal to accept the legitimacy of unionist opposition to Irish unity. In March 1990, in what was almost a replay of 1974, the Irish Supreme Court delivered the judgment that, the Anglo-Irish Agreement notwithstanding, the 're-integration of the national territory is a constitutional imperative'.[9] Rather than a willing partner in the search for an accommodation of different political traditions, such a disposition on the part of the Republic simply cast it in the role of an opportunistic partisan. Finally, the way in which the British government negotiated the Agreement behind the backs of unionists continued to raise doubts about its commitment to the Union. It has officially sanctioned an open-ended state of constitutional uncertainty which, as W. Harvey Cox remarked, is 'highly destabilising, leaving the Ulster unionists in a perpetual position of distrustfulness'.[10] In John Hume's phrase, the British government was now 'neutral' on the Union, a definition which the new Secretary of State Peter Brooke did nothing to repudiate. These problems, which were glossed over in the public presentation of the Agreement, have frustrated the possibility of restoring some form of local democracy to Northern Ireland.

## The Brooke initiative

The latest attempt to complete that comprehensive agenda (publicly) announced in 1985 has been the so-called Brooke initiative. 'Talks about talks' were conducted by the Secretary of State with local party leaders throughout 1990 and the beginning of 1991. Like the famous moving statues of Ballinspittle, whatever movement was detectable seemed to be in the eye of the believer and in the press releases of the

Northern Ireland Office. Yet, despite the seasoned scepticism amongst political commentators, Mr Brooke has attained his objective of securing 'substantive' talks on the future of Northern Ireland. This has been an achievement in itself. It appeared for most of the preliminary talks period that only the British Secretary of State had any will to see them through to a positive conclusion. Neither the SDLP nor the Irish government wanted to compromise the new Anglo-Irish status quo in return for devolved government in Belfast. The Unionist leaders, Molyneaux and Paisley, though not all of their associates, appeared to reckon that any new settlement could only be achieved at further expense to their expressed position. However, the momentum of the process was such that, having got involved, no one wanted the approbrium of appearing to frustrate it. Both in July and December of 1990 the initiative seemed to have run into the sands only to be resurrected by the indefatigably polite (and astute) Mr Brooke. At the time of writing (May 1991), the final stage of the Brooke initiative has got underway. Like the previous fifteen months all consultations are to be held in secret. The goal is a comprehensive putting together of parts which will address what Charles Haughey, the Irish Prime Minister, once termed the 'totality of relationships' within these islands. That, as the experience of Northern Ireland has shown, is easy to say yet so difficult to achieve. Indeed, the publicly stated positions of the parties appear to be so irreconcilable that no negotiation seems possible to resolve them.

For the Unionists, the object is to secure 'an alternative to and a replacement of' the Anglo-Irish Agreement. They also seek the removal of articles two and three of the Republic's constitution; a devolved assembly in which parties would have 'a role commensurate with their support in the community'; an external affairs committee of that assembly to deal with problems of common interest between Northern Ireland and the Irish Republic; and confirmation of British sovereignty in Northern Ireland such that all other matters concerning North–South relations will be dealt with on the basis of *inter-state* relations.[11] What Unionists want, in other words, is a settlement which is substantially *British* and only residually *Irish*. The SDLP's public position is exactly the reverse. What it wants is an agreement which 'transcends' in importance the Anglo-Irish Agreement. It hopes that the talks will reveal to Unionists the hopelessness of their current position. The British government, it believes, should become a 'persuader' encouraging

Unionists to make a new arrangement with Dublin. Devolution is to be part of their agenda only if the focus of sovereignty shifts from London to Dublin. Therefore, what the SDLP wants is a settlement which is substantially *Irish* and only residually *British*. Those are enormous distinctions and illustrate the gap between talks and the possibility of success. Indeed, in Northern Ireland politics, 'success' can bring great danger, for success must mean compromise and compromise has often been defined as betrayal. But failure is a prospect whose name no one dare speak (even if they may contemplate it). The paradoxical conclusion at this juncture of the Northern Ireland crisis is that success may be dangerous but failure has its terrors.

## Conclusion

In terms of the sort of comprehensive settlement of the Ulster crisis which has been the subject of this chapter and which has been the major stated aim of successive Secretaries of State, the last twenty years have not been fruitful ones for British policy in Northern Ireland. Nevertheless, all governments have taken comfort in the fact that they have prevented even greater bloodshed and violence than might otherwise have been the case if direct rule had not been imposed when it was in 1972. That attribution of 'negative' success actually does less than justice to the policy experience of the last two decades. There are significant and positive achievements of direct rule in broad areas of government policy which many commentators (for a mixture of motives) tend to overlook. In terms of housing policy; strategies for equal opportunity in employment; the maintainance of necessary public expenditure in the National Health Service, education and personal social services, Northern Ireland has done well. With a seat in Cabinet and a large portfolio of 'special cases', Secretaries of State for Northern Ireland have been able to make effective representations for those concerns which have been their responsibility. One of the illusions about Northern Ireland has been that there is a large constituency which longs for devolved government. The longing is not necessarily for devolved government but for good government. These two things are not one and the same. The benefits accruing from direct rule are material ones which few catholics or protestants wish to see threatened. Therefore, the 'fourth dimension' of the Northern Ireland question is one which remains important even though the other three might be properly addressed under the Brooke initiative. That dimension is the dimension of proper democratic procedure for the conduct of Northern Ireland affairs at Westminster. To stress this point is merely to stress the political realities of power and prevailing influence.

British policy in Northern Ireland over the next two decades (with the assistance of the Irish government where necessary) must confront unrealistic nationalist ambitions – be they political or military – and address unrealistic unionist fears. This returns us to the beginning of this chapter. History never repeats itself. It merely stutters. Irish nationalism is no longer the imagined virtue of the 1916 Rebellion. In the practice of the Irish state it has become effectively Europeanised. The Union is not what it was in 1912 or even 1920. The British state is not the political heart of a great empire. In both cases, nationalists and unionists in Northern Ireland must reassess their own politics. There are intimations that such a reassessment is indeed under way, though what may issue from it is beyond the competence of this chapter to predict.

### Notes

1 M. Oakeshott, *Rationalism in Politics* (London: Methuen, 1962) 131.

2 P. Bew and H. Patterson, *The British State and the Ulster Crisis* (London: Verso, 1985) 64–8.

3 See, for example, P. Arthur, *The Government and Politics of Northern Ireland* (London: Longman, 1980).

4 D. Miller, *Queen's Rebels* (Dublin: Gill & Macmillan, 1978) 164.

5 New Ireland Forum, *Report* (Dublin, 2 May 1984) 30.

6 See, for instance, M. Connolly and S. Loughlin, 'Reflections on the Anglo-Irish Agreement', *Government and Opposition*, vol. 21 (1986) 148.

7 *Spectator*, 11 January 1986.

8 On this see Arthur Aughey, *Under Seige: Ulster Unionism and the Anglo-Irish Agreement* (Belfast: The Blackstaff Press and London: C. Hurst and Co., 1989).

9 For details see K. Maginnis MP, *McGimpsey and McGimpsey v Ireland* (Dungannon, 1990).

10 W. Harvey Cox, 'Managing Northern Ireland intergovernmentally: an appraisal of the Anglo-Irish Agreement', *Parliamentary Affairs*, vol. 40 (1987) 84.

11 *Irish Times*, 27 February 1990.

# Part V
# Political education

# 17  *Bernard Crick*

# Citizenship and education

My concern is not with the kind of citizenship that is appropriate to an autocracy, nor with how the idea of free citizenship can sustain itself under autocracy – as the events of 1989 in Eastern Europe so dramatically demonstrated, against the expectations of all expert opinion: that in itself a vindication of freedom. I am concerned with true citizenship, the idea of individuals interacting for public purposes in a civic community: the citizenship associated with the existence and exercise of civil liberties by a free people.[1]

Historically there have been two main ideas of civil liberties and of the kind of citizenship appropriate to each of them: the one, sometimes called 'liberal', that civil liberties are a framework of law to protect individuals against the state; and the other, sometimes called republican, that civil liberties are the positive means by which citizens may influence affairs of state. Much educational practice still falls under the first paradigm, despite a remarkable revival of scholarly interest in the republican tradition.[2]

In the last two years of the reign of Margaret Thatcher, the concept of citizenship stepped onto the political agenda of Britain in an unexpected manner. Government ministers suddenly began urging a distinctive idea of active citizenship. Foreign observers might be pardoned any surprise that a debate on the nature of citizenship is, for the majority of people in British public life, such a late, sudden and enigmatic guest at the feast. But then Britain is not the United States nor France neither, two countries whose very national identity is still perceived in the light of different ideas, or myths if you prefer, of active citizenship – originally indeed a *revolutionary* tradition, bourgeois revolutions but, like those of 1989, revolutions nonetheless. To them even the mild word 'active' in 'active citizenship' should be quite unnecessary. What else is a citizen, would say John Doe or Jean Françoise, than someone who is active in public affairs? Indeed, but let us not exaggerate: modern American and French citizens are not a hyper-active ancient Athenian citizen elite; yet they know that there is a kind of official, even constitutional, blessing on being at least spasmodically active; or at least not feeling peculiar if they are.

In Britain, however, the qualifying adjective for citizen has less often been 'active' than 'good'. *Good citizens* have a respect for law and order, pay their taxes (even poll taxes) know their place in society (what the philosopher F. H. Bradley called, in a once-celebrated essay, 'My station and its duties', keep their noses clean and are ever so grateful to be governed so well; although we British do rather pride ourselves (or used to) on knowing our rights. And these rights are held to include civil liberties, but then liberties perceived as part of a legal order, not primarily a political or a citizen order. We should be able to go to court to protect ourselves not merely from nuisances by strangers or neighbours or public bodies, but even against the state. Only recently on environmental issues have neighbours begun to combine for political or 'community' action.

There can be, of course, a good Conservative case for a constitution to protect our rights against radical innovations, just as there is now, and quite a novelty, a radical or republican case to reform the constitution in order to enable a positive and participative citizenship. I refer, of course, to Lord Hailsham's former views on Parliament as an 'elected despotism' and to the Charter 88 movement. The House of Lords has just opined that it would be a good idea to set down our rights in fundamental law just to be sure what they are, and Charter 88 adds that we might as well improve them a bit while we are trying to find them to embalm them.[3] But too many good Brits believe that if our rights are well protected by the courts and not heavily abused by the state, as on the whole they think they are not, we can stay safely in our homes, even in our Welsh or Highland second homes, and sing madrigals, watch the television, make love, even walk the streets safely at night (so long as you are not a woman), or otherwise kill the time pleasantly without public obligations.

Less than a century ago the matter was clearer because editorials would habitually refer, on the one hand, to the restive and excessively democratic American or French *republican* spirit (which everyone knew did not simply mean no monarch; indeed, a republican spirit famously existed in Holland and other lands where there was a monarch); and on the other hand, leader-writers before the First World War would flatter their British readers as 'good subjects' or 'loyal subjects'. I believe it was the slaughter and the conscription crisis in 1916 that turned official rhetoric from 'subjects of the King' to, well, not quite 'fellow citizens' but at least citizens of the realm, 'British citizens'. But nowadays, even when Mrs Thatcher used to talk with admirable realism if gross constitutional impropriety about 'my ministers', she would never say 'my subjects'; indeed, incredibly she spasmodically began to demand that people should exhibit more citizenship. Citizenship was held up as an individual moral virtue. Suddenly the idea of 'the good citizen', which hitherto was simply that of being 'the good subject' who voted occasionally in public elections, has proved insufficient even for a Conservative view of things. Douglas Hurd, Kenneth Baker and Chris Patten stretched their minds to elaborate this primal thought of citizenship as an individual moral virtue in speeches which are at least wonderfully useful as essay assignments by political philosophers to average students.[4]

By citizenship Mrs Thatcher meant that individuals have a duty to help strangers as well as family, especially those less well off. Rights and duties are morally correlative, and so they should be; each implies the other, both John Stuart Mill and Emmanuel Kant said that; so far so good. But they should be done by individuals voluntarily, and when so done they enhance the individual. In Hurd's version, that was the main object; but Chris Patten's variant had a hint or a hope that it actually helps others. All agreed, however, that voluntarism is the mark of moral citizenship. Helping others must not be done, or as little as possible, by public authorities out of all our pockets, nor by churches from moral blackmail based on eccentric and unministerial readings of the scriptures.

Now as often with Margaret Thatcher – her critics still ignore this at their peril – there was a thumping big half-truth here. Let us say a reverential 'Amen' to a half-truth and let those of us who are without sin cast the first civil-disobedient stone. Why has the Labour Party (which, for better or for worse, in sickness and in health, is my own party) not made a virtue of active, republican citizenship; or not until very, very recently, and then in a tentative and intellectually

unimpressive manner?[5] Presumably because it has long been possessed by a crusading spirit to get hold of the centres of power to use
them in the interests of the poor, the dispossessed, the disadvantaged
and the handicapped (or should I now say 'to manage a mixed
economy more efficiently'?). If standards of secondary education
had not fallen (as is now matter of faith to all British statesmen) I
could have put that more briefly in Latin by saying that they too
share the *libido dominandi*. But this crusading spirit, while a
generous impulse in practice, often meant a cock-sure knowingness
about what was best for other people. 'We know what people want
because we have been elected; how else could we have been elected?',
say the old councillors. Or as the poet Auden once put it, 'we are all
here on earth to help each other, but what the others are here for,
God only knows'. The old Labour project also carried with it a
formidable commitment to using, indeed strengthening, central
power – as shown by the divisions of the Scottish Labour Party in
1978 and 1979, and a continued ambivalence about any radical
devolution or Home Rule.

For the Thatcherite half-truth is that people are very open to the
suggestion that they would rather, if empowered, help themselves
than be helped and to choose for themselves when to help others and
whom. The idea of a public-welfare society as a gift of the state did
begin to grate; or could be seen, even by some of its managers and
clients, either to be overdone or to be so full of accumulated historical accidents and anomalies (like the supplementary benefit regulations) as to have lost all coherence, hence comprehensibility, hence
self-confident or self-evident justification.

The half-untruth in Thatcher's rhetoric of citizenship is, however,
the belief that voluntary effort can fill the gap left by the deliberate
under-resourcing of social services, especially those associated with
local authorities as a plurality of centres of power, and those where
the 'clients' are the least able to organise themselves in effective
pressure groups: the very old, the very young, the mentally and
physically handicapped and the long-term unemployed. So suddenly
the ancient idea of positive citizenship becomes confused with
charity, or is seen as part of privatisation; and privatisation not just
of industry but of large parts of the social services, public responsibility for the arts, industrial training and education. The remaining
public-welfare bodies are asked to work with voluntary bodies, as in
the Griffith Report on caring for the elderly. And being so

under-resourced, they have little choice, however spasmodic, insufficient, eccentric or commercially self-interested the voluntary support can prove to be.

Nonetheless, there has always been a good involvement of volunteers in areas of need. It would be hard to envisage any state of affairs where extra volunteers cannot help (even in schools); at the very least, sit with and talk to the lonely, or shop for those infirm foolish enough not to have loving families, tasks well within the capabilities even of untrained people of commonsense and common feeling. It is good to help others and it gives us a feeling for others. Professionalism in teaching, the personal social services and even in some aspects of medicine, can be carried too far. An excessive professionalism in the social services has sometimes discredited itself. The real needs of clients can be confounded by a claim to professionalism that is a mixture of old battles for disciplinary status and relatively new (for the professions) trade-union concerns. This is another question. But undoubtedly the public is sometimes confused as to whether they are being harangued to save the NHS or to save NUPE. This has given the new perverse sense of citizenship its opportunity and its plausibility.

The new sense of citizenship as individual voluntary social or charitable work is perverse for one obvious reason, and one less obvious but more profound that goes to the heart of the dilemmas of our culture. The obvious reason is that in a mainly voluntary system in no way can resources be matched to needs or rational priorities followed – indeed logically it could not be a 'system' at all. Priorities would, figuratively speaking, follow whether the Princess Ann or Glenda Jackson broadcasts 'The Week's Good Cause' rather than how good it is. Certainly each of us have a moral and a civic duty to give (as 'giving' is extolled as a virtue in placards in American buses and subways), whether from the private pocket, the corporate cheque-book or the widow's mite. All that is easy, but to engage ourselves, with hands, feet and head as well as purse and heart, to commit precious time and physical effort to regular voluntary work, this would be, on the scale needed, both highly demanding to ordinary individuals and could be highly threatening to the conventional state.

It could threaten because if people did engage their own time and effort, then they would then surely do so, be they ever so law-abiding good subjects, *critically*. They may come to think about what they are doing, not just do it as in a routinised job. The heart and the head, not just the purse, would want a say both in *what* should be done and in *how* it should be done. And this points to the deeper inadequacy and incoherence of the new view. For if the voluntary involvement of masses of people under the banner of 'citizenship' in the running of social services is crucial or critical, people will become critically minded and will expect to find some effective forum in which to air their criticism; or, still worse, if part of the criticism is that there is no such forum, or only a quite ineffective one, then they may want to make one. And the volunteers themselves, nominated in the twin names of individualism and economy, may themselves become effective lobbyists for more public resources. Deciding how the edict on spelling is going to be implemented will not mend the school roof. In other words, no idea of citizenship can be totally individualised, removed from a public realm, removed from a commonsense sense that some things are better done publicly than privately, and that some things can only be done publicly; and, further, that to have any public effect means (in Hannah Arendt's simple argument) 'acting in concert'.[6] What on earth is he talking about? Come down to earth! Well, she started it: 'there is no such thing as society' said the former Prime Minister.

Citizenship cannot be re-presented as charitable work. Giving by individuals is in itself a good thing and it can make us each feel more virtuous or less guilty, which is no bad thing: but it is only when individuals combine through active citizenship that both public policy and public behaviour can be influenced. Free societies must debate, and a constantly shifting debate it is: what is the proper sphere of the private and the public, the individual and the social; or in economic terms, what is the most efficient and the most acceptable mix of a mixed economy? Public decisions have too important an effect on the lives of individuals to be left entirely to a multiplication of random individual decisions with the government pretending to be the mere umpire of natural market forces.

Public decisions are too important to be left to governments, especially to any government that tries to narrow to the absolute minimum the extent of those benefits, goods and services that can only be provided, or most efficiently provided, publicly; and while mocking 'society' invents a 'community' into whom the long-term mentally ill can be discharged. While the concept of society should not, indeed (the half-truth again), be used as an excuse for avoiding individual responsibility ('I'm not to blame, it was society; it was me upbringing', etc.), surely a sense of *sociability* in individuals is a virtue as well as a psycho-biological human characteristic; or to use an old-fashioned political and military word, 'fraternity'. The radical right will allow one legitimate area of non-individualistic, non-competitive, altruistic behaviour: the family. That is one reason why they make so much of it. But, remarkably, some parents try to bring their children up to care for others; and families by themselves can as easily be hunting-packs of nepotism and special advantage as they can be schools of virtue.

It follows that any education for citizenship must involve both education and the training for effect on public issue through acting together. If we educate for citizenship we may get citizens, individuals who are interactive and publicly active. Citizens' actions, like all free actions, are unpredictable; government in a citizen culture becomes less easy to conduct, but perhaps more effective and more interesting when it has to and can carry people with it. People are more interested in following and working for results, in politics as much as sport, which are not foregone conclusions. I don't think we should sound solemn and say that with more political education democracy will work better. Who knows? Some exercise of civil liberties may destabilise some governments. Tough.

By civil liberties I mean those things we need to be able to do without interference from the state in order to maintain what we ordinarily call a free society, or what J. S. Mill called 'representative government'. Note that civil liberties are more specific and many than human rights. Human rights are few and basic. No modern philosopher doubts that, but in the classroom 'rights' are multiplied, used and abused promiscuously. Yet it obscures clear thinking and takes away any sense of cost from moral choices to call everything we want, everything we think to be a need or think good, a *human right*. What it is to be a human being is not necessarily to be a fully paid up or fully supported, credit-card-carrying member of a consumer society; or even of a democracy. Inhabitants of autocracies have human rights, even supporters of autocracies, even enemies. Wants and basic needs are to be distinguished, just as civil rights and human rights should not be confused. Human rights are few and are universal moral imperatives; civil rights are many and specific and relative to particular societies.[7] Advanced civil rights may set a general goal and a standard, but they are not inherent to human nature. They are historical and cultural achievements. To call everything we want or think good a *right* confuses understanding, and stakes a claim without delineating a means.

Let me draw a practical inference from this abstract point. I see both the advocacy and the teaching of civil liberties and citizenship not as a campaign for everything we think as right, nor (as philosophers would say) for substantive values but for procedural values.[8] A Council for Civil Liberties (now called 'Liberty') was once unwise enough to confuse matters by commenting, for instance, on the truth of Mr Duncan Campbell's allegations about the covert activities of our famous national security forces, rather than on his right to make allegations, whether true or false, and the methods by which the government tried to stop him. Nor was it wise to comment on the justice of the miners' strike, still less to allow no criticism of their tactics and behaviour, but only those of the police. As citizens we can and should all comment loudly on the policies of the state, but to protect civil liberties as *educators* we must make our remarks strictly relevant, but then to make them all the more strong, to *the procedures and methods* of the state and its agents. Civil liberties enable free politics to be pursued, participative citizenship to be practised and, in extreme cases, basic human rights to be defended.

But this calls for the encouragement of and a training for political action, not simply 'respect for the rule of law' as is so often said. Does 'political action' sound too harsh? I don't see why. Aristotle regarded all relevant analysis and criticism as a form of action.[9] No one has ever tried to teach action as an end in itself. No one (except some anarchists and all Dadaists) favours mindless, thoughtless, unpremeditated, instinctive action. But equally, if it is citizenship we are concerned with (and not just routine teaching for 'good results' in an examination syllabus), the teacher cannot be held responsible for the use the young citizen makes of his acquired knowledge and skills, or rather the emphasis should be, skills and knowledge. Again, the actions of free men and women are unpredictable. If we teach to induce the correct substantive attitudes (whether 'respect for the rule of law', 'proper individualism', 'the classless society' or whatever), it is not then politics or citizenship we are teaching: it is something at best paternally approved, our old quasi-autocratic friend, the 'good citizen', say, rather than subject. And at worst it is, indeed, attempted indoctrination. Successive government ministers instinctively dislike the educational value of empathy because it obviously implies a sympathetic understanding of alternatives.[10]

Of course, the word favoured on all sides is not 'action' but is 'participation'. I've no objection, so long as watching is not thought to be, however knowledgeable the spectator, as participative and healthy as having a share in the action. Citizenship is among a rather small group of important human actions in which anyone can have a share in the action, unless of course, as in so many happy lands, restrained by fear of force.

Unhappily, official opinion still leans towards a late Victorian view of citizenship education as being concerned primarily with good behaviour rather than active participation. The Speaker of the House of Commons set up late in 1988 a Commission on Citizenship which reported in 1990. The recommendations of the Report seemed very close to the kind of ministerial thinking discussed at the beginning of this sermon. Its recommendations envisaged education for a world of voluntary service and community service, in which any political decisions are made purely by elective representatives of the people in Parliament (and 'Parliament is sovereign' whatever we've signed, whatever the European Court of Justice says) and any ambiguities in legislation are decided by courts and must, of course, not merely be respected but obeyed. The individual is protected by the laws. He has little need to do anything by way of corporate action: pressure groups and parties are never mentioned!

Quoting a comparative empirical survey, they say with pride:

On responsibilities, the views of the British citizen were clear: 'Far and away the most commonly cited British duty, however, was obedience to the law ... combined with a more general emphasis on civility or obedience to community norms.[11]

Early-nineteenth-century satirists had an alternative version of John Bull called Lickspittle. Happily this empirical reaffirmation of an alleged English national characteristic is at least problematic. The true behavioural test is behaviour, not simply expressed attitudes. At the time the Commission was polishing up its anodyne report ('untouched by human mind') the Scottish poll tax rebellion was spreading to England, eventually bringing down a Prime Minister. But it is probably right; most people, if not 'the British citizen' (as an imaginative corporate entity), obey the law simply because it is the law, as if Socrates and all the political philosophers had never lived to draw a distinction between law and justice, to point out courageously that the state is not always right. But to the extent that that is true, it points to the problem our country faces, not to the fortunate inherited solution. It is the difficult task of a genuine citizen education to shake this bland belief that good citizenship consists simply in some voluntary service and a general respect for the rule of law.

Yes, indeed. If the laws are good laws. I cannot examine all laws and how they are interpreted and enforced, so pragmatically I give them the benefit of the doubt – with that reservation. May I quote from *Political Education and Political Literacy* on this point crucial to the character of our political culture?

Many people say that any civilised behaviour necessarily presupposes a belief in a 'rule of law', that is obedience to rules – so that even if the rules are unjust, we should only try to change them according to accepted rules. (Sometimes this is the *only* concept introduced into political education when taught – so incompletely – as 'British Constitution' or 'The Institutions of British Government'.) But two problems arise: (i) what if the rules are so constituted as to avoid change? (ii) Is it true that all complex activities pre-suppose legal rules? Consider again 'fairness' and the young footballer: he learns to play football by playing football, not by reading the rules . . . and his concept of what is fair (or just) does not in fact depend on knowing all the rules (only on observing behaviour and convention), nor logically need it – for the rules could be unjust, ambiguous or self-contradictory.[12]

The Commission on Citizenship carefully avoids any discussion as to whether the rules are just or can be changed – any incitement to thought: 'As we have said, in the UK there is no comprehensive list of entitlements. Individuals' freedoms exist to the extent that Parliament has not enacted restrictions.'[13] How can any group of so-called citizens say that without even raising the possibility that some legitimately enacted restrictions have gone too far, or even hinting that every other country in the European Community has a litigable Bill of Rights. Was this handpicked group nervous, stupid or excessively conventional? It is actually easier to think freely in most classrooms.

Even an Education Minister could be more imaginative and state the problem better. Mr Alan Howarth addressed the Politics Association on its twenty-first anniversary:

The issue of politics in the classroom seems to me part of a wider one of how to encourage discrimination (in the best sense of the term), good sense, and rational judgment in young people . . . It is never going to be easy. It has to be faced squarely that political education entails consideration of politics and politics is about choices which so affect the lives of citizens that emotions are likely to run high.[14]

'Citizenship' was mentioned as a cross-curricular theme in the National Curriculum – a vague and minimal direction, it must honestly be said, a sad climb down from when a future Conservative Secretary of State for Education, Mr Kenneth Baker, joined with me in presenting the Hansard Society's Report, *Political Education and Political Literacy* (totally ignored by the Speaker's Commission, incidentally) to the last Labour Secretary of State, Shirley Williams, arguing wholeheartedly, or so it seemed, for its official adoption.[15]

Nonetheless, the mere mention of 'citizenship' sensibly stimulated the Politics Association to seize the opportunity to issue a crisp, short leaflet, *Citizenship: The Association's Position.* It asked 'what should citizenship involve?' and gave short notes towards good answers under 'Knowledge' and 'Attitudes'; but on my marking would come down a class on 'Skills'. True 'participation in the democratic life of their community' came under 'Attitudes' to be encouraged, but skills were all internalised towards readily commendable and respectable educational objectives, 'the ability to distinguish between fact and opinion', etc. So that while it spoke of the ability 'to evaluate differing views and arguments', as a skill it did not speak of the ability actually to argue, to make an argument, to present a case; and the opportunity to speak about 'action skills' (an explicit category in the old *Hansard* report's specification of skills) was passed over.

Perhaps I make too much of this. Perhaps just an omission in drafting? But in hard times it is not politic to trim the sails so much that the boat gets blown backwards. 'Politics', 'Citizenship', call it what you will, is a good educational subject; but it is more than a school educational subject. That is what is difficult about it. If it cannot reach outside at least it must point outside the classroom. That is what citizenship is about.

I am the ghost at this feast. Perhaps Banquo owed Lady Macbeth an apology for upsetting the guests and criticising the family silver. I am vastly impressed by all the printed material produced (much like most of the content of this book) to help teachers with the factual side of GCSE examinations, by how well the latest academic knowledge is being mediated into fifth and sixth forms, yet I am depressed to see how little material and thought has been produced for the rest of the school, for the non-examination levels – those whom Lady Plowden once famously and simply called 'all our nation's children'. The journal has recently changed its name from *Teaching Politics* to *Talking Politics*. I see some gain for a particular constituency but a greater public loss.

To my recollection the motives of the founding fathers could be expressed under five heads. (1) To give comfort and companionship in adversity to, back then, some very isolated teachers. This has been well done. (2) To provide practical help with teaching materials. This has been well done too, but mainly for university or polytechnic candidates. And these academic departments will quite often help sixth-form teachers, mainly because they want students; but they give little thought to educational values, the rest of the school or citizenship as the aim rather than Political Science. (3) That materials and methods should engender political thought, not simply learning constitutional rules and institutional facts. This battle sways back and forth: when examination boards try to force thought by the strategy of real questions about real problems, memorisable cribs to thoughtful seeming answers are published (even by yourselves). (4) To provide a bridge between secondary, further and higher education. It is my impression that the bridge to and from further education is in a bad state of repair (admittedly the opportunities are less). (5) To spearhead a crusade for citizenship education throughout the school. That was my primary motivation, and I suspect Derek Heater's, Ian Lister's and Alex Porter's too. This motivation now seems at rather low ebb – despite one shrewd and public-spirited protest.[16] Times are inclement. Some public authorities are positively hostile, unless citizenship can be redefined and debased to mean law-abiding good subjects either doing occasional voluntary service or gratefully receiving a Charter or placatory consumer rights. 'We are all here on earth to help each other', said the poet Auden, 'but what the others are here for, god only knows' – certainly not to be active citizens. But the educational and national need to ferment true participative citizenship has never been greater.

### Notes

1   This is a revised version of an address given to the twenty-first Annual Conference of the Politics Association (of which the author was the first President) at Manchester, 21 September 1990.

2   Historians of political ideas who might once have written about the history of liberalism, now see that as what Germans would call a *Rechtstadt* (a framework of legal rights), which is not necessarily 'republican', indeed sometimes hostile to too much participation and positive citizenship. See J. A. Pocock, *The Machiavellian Moment: Florentine Political Thought and the Atlantic Republican Tradition* (London: Princeton University Press, 1975); Quentin Skinner, *The Foundation of Modern Political Thought*, 2 vols. (Cambridge University Press, 1978). And applying these ideas to a modern context, see Adrian Oldfield, *Citizenship and Community: Civic Republicanism and the Modern World* (London: Routledge, 1990); James Boswell, *Community and the Economy: The Theory of Public Cooperation* (London: Routledge, 1990); Raymond Plant, *Community and Ideology* (London: Routledge, 1974); and his *Equality, Markets and the State* (London: Fabian Tract 494, 1984); and Geoff Andrews (ed.), *Citizenship* (London: Lawrence & Wishart, 1991). Many of these ideas are well-mediated for teachers in Derek Heater, *Citizenship: The Civic Ideal in World History, Politics and Education* (London: Longman, 1990); otherwise they have not reached the sixth-form textbooks which still struggle with the greater ambiguities of 'liberalism' and, of course, 'democracy'.

3   Charter 88 has a useful short leaflet *A Bill of Rights*. A full, reasoned proposal is *A British Bill of Rights* (London: Institute for Public Policy Research, 1990); and a philosophical discussion is Ronald Dworkin's *Taking Rights Seriously* (London: Duckworth, 1977).

4   For detailed references see Derek Heater's excellent 'Citizenship: a remarkable case of sudden interest', *Parliamentary Affairs* (April 1991) 140–56.

5   *Democratic Socialist Aims and Values* (London: Labour Party, 1988). David Blunkett MP and this author tried to do better in *The Labour Party's Aims and Values: An Unofficial Statement* (Nottingham: Spokesman Pamphlet, No. 87, 1988).

6   Hannah Arendt, *On Violence* (London: Allen Lane, 1970) 44.

7   H. L. A. Hart, *The Concept of Law* (Oxford: Clarendon Press, 1961), 181–207, especially pp. 189–95, 'The minimum content of natural law'.

8   Bernard Crick, 'Procedural values in political education', in Bernard Crick and Alex Porter (eds.), *Political Education and Political Literacy* (London: Longman, 1978).

9   Hannah Arendt, *The Human Condition* (University of Chicago Press), 7–17.

10   Bernard Crick, 'Review of the National Curriculum Working Group Final Report', *Political Quarterly* (October 1990) 486–91.

11   *Encouraging Citizenship*, Report of the Commission on Citizenship (London: HMSO, 1990) 6.

12   Crick and Porter, *Political Education*, 58–9.

13   *Encouraging Citizenship*, 7.

14   Speech of Mr Alan Howarth MP, Minister of State for Education, to the Politics Association, 4 July 1990, reprinted in this volume: see pp. 318–26.

15   See this author's letter to the *Independent* of 6 October 1987.

16   See Bernard Jones, 'Political education 14–16: a role for the Politics Association', Discussion Paper, Politics Association, 1988: 'We must put more eggs in the basket of pre-sixteen education in order to legitimise our position, to help provide a teaching role for our members, to help provide future generations of graduates and teachers, and, of course, to fulfil our moral purpose,' p. 5. Of course. And since writing this chapter, there has appeared Frank Conley (ed.), *Political Understanding Across the Curriculum* (London Politics Association, 1991) in which most of the contributors at least state the case for looking at the whole curriculum. Is this a change of emphasis or a gesture? Time will tell.

# Britain, Europe and citizenship

## Two decades ago

Three weeks after the founding conference of the Politics Association, the Prime Minister, Harold Wilson, declared, 'If they, the Six, are ready for negotiations to begin, we are ready. If, in these negotiations, we achieve terms satisfactory for Britain, on the lines we have outlined, then negotiations will succeed.'[1]

De Gaulle's curt brush-off of Wilson's coy advances had taken place two years before. The European mood was now more receptive to courtship: in June 1969 de Gaulle was replaced as President of the Fifth Republic by Georges Pompidou; and three months later in the same month as Wilson's speech at the Labour Party Conference, Willy Brandt became Chancellor of the Federal Republic of Germany. Both new leaders desired British membership of the European Community. It was left, of course, to Edward Heath to take advantage of the new receptive atmosphere. It was he who signed the treaty of accession in Brussels in January 1972 (the same year, by the way, in which the journal *Teaching Politics* was launched).

And so it came about that, some two decades ago, Britain made the moves which finally took her into membership of the Community – an association which occupies so much of our political and economic attention today. Yet the contrasts between 1970 and 1990 are instructive. The coolness of Margaret Thatcher in membership served but to remind one of the ardour of Edward Heath in seeking it. The frustration of the French Commission President Delors in trying to coax Britain along the road of European union is the very antithesis of the French President de Gaulle's deep anxiety to prevent Britain from placing a foot on the approach-path at all.

Furthermore, when we turn our attention to British public opinion, the shift in attitude is quite dramatic. In 1970, whereas

nearly two-thirds of the citizens of the Six favoured Britain's accession, the same proportion of Britons opposed.[2] In 1970 a bare 19 per
cent in Britain supported their country's membership of the
European Community; twenty years later 42 per cent already considered themselves to be 'Europeans', while 72 per cent viewed the
possibility of a United States of Europe as an attractive prospect.[3]

Two assumptions explain much of the hesitation about Britain
enthusiastically throwing in her lot with continental Europe – a
hesitation which existed in the past and still exists residually in the
minds of those who have formed the Bruges Group. These assumptions are that Britain is somehow different from its continental
neighbours and that she cannot be on terms of really comfortable
friendship with France. These beliefs may be illustrated by two
anecdotes from the French Revolution, in the bi-centennial
celebrations of which Mrs Thatcher so awkwardly participated. The
first concerns the organisation of a cricket XI to be sent across the
Channel in the early summer of 1789 to teach these strange con-
tinentals the orderly and gentlemanly game as an antidote to
anarchic revolutionary hysteria. The second illustration concerns the
Grande Peur, which burst forth in the high summer of the same year.
In Aquitaine the defensive panic reaction against the mythical
marauding brigands took the form of rumours of the imminent
arrival of the English, so deeply imprinted was the folk-memory of
the Black Prince's depredations in the Hundred Years War!

## Historical background[4]

Even so, in the long history of schemes for European union – and it *is*
a long history – the participation of England has often been considered as absolutely crucial; and particularly by Frenchmen. Inter-
mittently in the Middle Ages and as a continuous tradition from the
seventeenth century, paper schemes were drafted to urge the creation
of some kind of confederal European structure. Four of the most
famous of these, all composed by Frenchmen, recognised the necessity of England's playing a key role. These plans were as follows: *The
Recovery of the Holy Land* by Dubois; the 'Grand Design' of Sully;
*The Reorganisation of the European Community* by Saint-Simon;
and *The Project for European Union* by Briand.

Every age and every writer viewed the ideal of European union
from the perspective of a particular and characteristic concern. Each

of our four authors had quite different priorities, yet all were at pains to show that England's involvement was absolutely essential.

The fourteenth-century lawyer and pamphleteer, Pierre Dubois, produced a fascinating scheme for a form of European union. Its purpose was to reduce internal Christian quarrels; to facilitate campaigns against the Muslim infidel; and to open up the Middle East to European trade. The plan was dedicated to a number of European rulers, pride of place being accorded to the English monarch, Edward I. The reason for this is probably not far to seek: Edward's zeal for resuming the crusades was well known. It is doubtful whether Edward took the plan seriously, but he died the following year in any case.

Three centuries later the Duc de Sully, the former chief minister of Henry IV, was working on his *Memoirs*. When they eventually saw the light of day at the end of the seventeenth century, they contained a 'Grand Design' for a European 'Christian Commonwealth', falsely attributed to that assassinated French king himself. It became the most famous of all such schemes. When Churchill addressed The Hague Conference which launched the Council of Europe in 1948, he declared:

There are many famous names associated with the revival and presentation of this idea [i.e. United Europe], but we may all, I think, yield our pretensions to Henry of Navarre, King of France, who, with his great Minister Sully . . . laboured to set up a permanent committee representing the fifteen – now we are sixteen – leading Christian States of Europe.[5]

Sully was a complex character: a soldier-turned-administrator; a strait-laced Huguenot who organised bawdy soirées in his home. He also had one obsession: hatred of the Habsburgs, whose empire in central and southern Europe and the Americas was so vast. His plan for European union also involved taking the Habsburgs down a peg or two. And what more natural ally than England, who had supported the revolt of the Netherlanders and faced the threat of the great Armada?

We may scarcely be surprised then to read in his *Memoirs* of missions he had made to Elizabeth I and James I. Reporting an interview with the English Queen in 1601, Sully wrote:

I found her deeply engaged in the means by which this Great Design might be successfully executed; and nothwithstanding the difficulties which she apprehended . . . she did not appear to me at all to doubt of its success . . . A very great number of the articles and conditions, and different dispositions, is due to this queen.[6]

The understanding that Europe's two most respected monarchs – Henry the Great and Gloriana – were the originators of the Grand Design was undoubtedly a cardinal factor in keeping the plan in the forefront of attention for so long. It is a pity, therefore, that what Sully reports about their co-authorship is complete fabrication! For example, he did not even visit England in 1601, let alone have a conversation with the Queen!

The point is, however, that Sully was so convinced of the need for England's enthusiastic association with his scheme that he felt impelled to manufacture for posterity the deep commitment of her government.

Less than a generation after the publication of the final volume of Sully's *Memoirs* there broke out the Nine Years War between the France of Louis XIV and an opposing alliance including England. It was the start of a veritable second hundred years' war between them; the two countries were in a state of intermittent conflict from 1689 to 1815.

At the (Napoleonic) end of this period of Anglo-French warfare, Saint-Simon, with the help of his young associate Thierry, rushed into print their pamphlet on *The Reorganisation of European Society*. The hurry was occasioned by Saint-Simon's unrealistic ambition of influencing the statesmen assembled at Vienna to redraw the map of Europe. Henri, the Comte de Saint-Simon, was an even more colourful personality than Sully; successively soldier, speculator and scholar. My favourite story relates to an Arthur Daley-style deal he concocted with the *ci-devant* bishop Talleyrand. This was to strip off and sell the lead from Notre Dame cathedral! The story goes that he turned up with a cart-load of *assignats*, but the government agent with whom he hoped to clinch the deal judged these notes too depreciated in value to equate with the work of such an expanse of expensive roofing material. Instead, Saint-Simon found himself flung into jail in the clean-up of speculators instigated by Robespierre, 'the Incorruptible.'

By the turn of the century Saint-Simon was concentrating on literary activities. These included the formulation of his political ideas that government should be reduced in function to administration and that scientists and industrialists would be better suited to this task than the 'new priesthood' of lawyers. If only such men could predominate in British-style parliaments in European states and in a supra-national European parliament. Much of the pamphlet is, indeed, a remarkable eulogy of the British constitution:

What people [he asked] is freer and richer internally, greater externally, more skilled in industry, sea-faring and commerce? To what can we attribute this unrivalled power, if not to the English government, which is more liberal, more vigorous, more favourable to happiness and national glory than any other government of Europe?[7]

Saint-Simon envisaged an Anglo-French union as the start of a process of building a European confederation by accretion. As other states adopted British-style constitutions so they would be eligible for membership.

The nineteenth century was the age of great enthusiasm for some form of European union. Federalism was in vogue. Proudhon expounded the principle; the United States of America, tested in the gruesome Civil War, practised it and provided the model for numerous thoughts about a United States of Europe. The concept of a federal United States of Europe threw into sharp relief the issue of sovereignty, which had in large measure been ducked hitherto. In the 1920s and 1930s it had to be addressed in the context of powerful new forces: the horror of war lodged in the memory of the First World War; the belief in national self-determination as a panacea; the existence of the League of Nations; the economic chaos of the Great Crash and Depression; and the rise of aggressive state power, especially in the guise of Nazism.

It was against this complex background that Briand produced his plan. Aristide Briand spent much of his life in ministerial office – he was Prime Minister eleven times, the very personification of the Third Republic's stable instability. He was persuasive alike as conciliator and orator. And, above all, his bushy moustache, from under which dripped a constant fag-end, was a gift to cartoonists.

In 1929 he decided to launch an appeal, through the medium of the League of Nations, for a kind of European regional league, though with greater emphasis on economic co-operation. This 'Project for European Union', as he called it, was canvassed in a speech in Geneva in that year and presented as a Memorandum for European government responses the following May. The sympathetic Stresemann died in 1929 and, in any case, Germany was concentrating now on serious internal problems. Mussolini was dreaming thoughts of empire. The Soviet Union was not even a member of the League. Any hopes for Briand's Project rested with Britain. Ramsay MacDonald was Prime Minister and Arthur Henderson, Foreign Secretary. Both were keen internationalists and Henderson particularly a loyal supporter of the League. Unlike the previous schemes, which were little more than theoretical kite-flying essays, here was a practical plan to which the British government was required to respond.

The response was handled with dishonest cunning.[8] Within a fortnight the Foreign Office had drawn up a memorandum of reservations. But the government did not wish to offend the French by presenting its objections immediately. Instead, it waited for other governments to express their criticisms. The Quai d'Orsay had asked for the British reaction by mid-July at the latest. On 16 July a 'preliminary and tentative' reply was delivered to the French ambassador: Britain's true hostility was cloaked in the excusing fog of the need to consult the Commonwealth. The friendly tone of the reply was a deception.

In fact, despite England's assumed indispensability over the centuries to any form of European union, the idea generated little interest this side of the Channel. True, Sully's *Memoirs* were read, and translated, and the Quakers, William Penn and John Bellers, each produced their own versions of his Grand Design in reaction to the carnage of the wars of Louis XIV. A century later Jeremy Bentham wrote his *Plan for a Universal and Perpetual Peace*. But he was as much concerned about imperial and commercial causes of war as about the aptness of European unity. Not until 1940 did Englishmen produce draft constitutions for a united Europe. These were the books entitled *Federation of Western Europe* by that great constitution-monger, Ivor Jennings, and *Federal Europe* by that enthusiast for federalism and (later) Labour MP, R. W. G. Mackay. These publications were reflections of an enthusiasm for the idea, shared by *inter alia* Attlee, Beveridge, Hayek and Harold Wilson, which can at last be discerned among certain politicians and intellectuals (though not the top civil servants) in the early days of the Second World War.

## The issue of European citizenship

Circumstances are now, of course, totally different. A form of European integration does exist and Britain *is* a member. However, the European Community is not static. Its political structure (let alone its economic arrangements) is still evolving. I have already suggested that different ages have had different political priorities with regard to European integration. For Dubois it was the crusade. For Sully it was the undermining of Habsburg hegemony. For Saint-Simon it was the creation of technocratic parliaments. For Briand it was economic and administrative co-operation for the preservation of peace. In each case England was perceived as an essential participant.

What is the key political need in the European Community today; and could Britain play a significant role in its achievement? Let me suggest that the issue is European citizenship and that Britain is well placed to make a major contribution to its definition and development.

Why is the idea of European citizenship so important? In a basic, negative sense the matter simply cannot be ignored. To cite the eighteenth-century parallel American constitutional debate, in so far as 'the powers of the Confederation operate immediately on the persons and interests of individual citizens',[9] then those citizens must have rights *vis-à-vis* the Confederation. The principle is, in truth, already conceded: European citizenship does exist in embryonic form. For instance, we are now enfranchised to vote in European parliamentary elections. However, the Community is evolving, and rapidly so. The implications of the status of European citizen are bound to evolve too. And so, in a positive sense, it behoves us to try to ensure that this evolution takes place with conscious regard to democratic ideals and principles.

There are three possible scenarios. The first is that the move towards tighter integration grinds to a halt with the achievement of the Single Market. The second is that a federal European Union comes to pass. The third possibility is an adaptation of the second, namely, the development of a variable-association ECocentric continent (if I dare coin the term!). This model projects a central core of tightly federated states (of which Britain may or may not be a member); an inner ring of, for example, European Free Trade Association (EFTA) states closely associated with this Community;

and an outer rim of, for example, Eastern Europe, only loosely linked.

In the event of calling a halt at '1992' the matter of European citizenship must be considered in the light of two pressing questions. One is the so-called 'democratic deficit'. From the Schuman Plan through to the Treaty of Rome the growth of the European Community was largely due to people like Jean Monnet with primarily administrative mentalities. The operation of the Commission – the 'Eurocrats' – has been crucial to the Community style of organisation. Then with the creation of the European Council of heads of state or government in 1974, what is in effect the executive branch of the Community became very powerful. The weight of the European Parliament is too slight to provide a truly effective counter-balance. Already, let alone after 1992, the Council and Commission are insufficiently accountable to the citizens of the Community. Communications between MEPs and their constituents need to be improved and the power of the European Parliament expanded.

The second urgent question concerns the Social Charter, so controversial in this country. If the strength of multinational big business is going to be enhanced by the Single Market, then the rights of social citizenship need to be standardised and guaranteed.

However, if European Union – the federalisation of the Community that has been canvassed by the likes of Altiero Spinelli – if that tighter integration comes into effect, then this minimum enhancement in the character of Europen citizenship will be insufficient. The civic rights and duties of the citizen will then need to be harmonised across all the component states. The Parliament will need to become a fully fledged legislative arm of the Union with all that implies in terms of accountability to the electorate. And thirdly, the sense of European identity must be brought more vigorously to life. Just as in the Federal Republic an individual will think of him or herself simultaneously as a German and, say, a Bavarian, so in our continent (or sub-continent) an individual will need to feel a European as well as a Briton.

There are, it goes without saying, enough federal states to copy or from which we can learn – particularly legal and constitutional practices. Where we would be venturing into exceedingly complicated territory is in the event of the third hypothetical development taking place. Citizenship, as I hope to indicate later, is, even at the simple unitary nation-state level, a complex of feelings, rights and responsibilities. If, however, we shall at some time in the future be living in a Europe where there are several degrees of integration, then a clear specification of what it means to be a European citizen will be extraordinarily difficult to define and could become a legal minefield. Such a prospect renders it all the more imperative to clarify the status and meaning of European citizenship both today and as it would be in a straightforward federal union.

How well placed is Britain to provide guidance in this task? If interest, study and debate are indicators, then Britain has a great deal to contribute. Since 1988 few political concepts have been more widely discussed than citizenship. As Hugo Young wrote in the *Guardian*, 'Something is rotten in the state of Britain, and all the parties know it . . . The buzz-word emerging as the salve for this disease is something called citizenship.'[10] What in fact happened, to mix the journalist's metaphors really thoroughly, was that citizenship became a party political conceptual football.

The Conservatives, with Douglas Hurd, the then Home Secretary, in the vanguard, equated citizenship with 'active citizenship' and self-help. This is a kind of amalgam of the Abbé Sieyes and Samuel Smiles, despite the claims of the Home Office to originality of thought. The Labour Party, through their academic spokesmen, Professors Crick and Plant, emphasised the centrality of fraternity and social citizenship respectively. David Marquand, representing the views of the Social and Liberal Democrats, as they then were, identified citizenship in a proper sense as a status missing from the British polity because of the peculiar nature of the constitution. In fact, a wide centre–left segment of the political spectrum took up the cry for reform with the Charter 88 movement. It is possible to accord to citizens the true dignity of their status, so it has been argued, only if their civil and political rights are clearly set forth in a proper constitutional instrument.

Yet in all this lively debate, the issue of European citizenship was virtually totally ignored. Not even Professor Marquand discussed the problems. Despite his background and interest in the European Community he contented himself with showing how effective democratic monitoring by the European Parliament was being inhibited by 'the absolutist view of power which permeates Britain's political culture'.[11] In other words, the doctrine of the sovereignty of the Westminster Parliament is a barrier to the exercise of a true citizenship in Britain, either national or European.

In the meantime, however, a group organised by the Federal Trust for Education and Research has been tackling the problem. The project calls upon the expertise of the British Institute of International and Comparative Law, the University of London Institute of Advanced Legal Studies and a number of individual specialists from other Community countries. The study has had two central objectives:

– in a Community context, to contribute to reflection and action designed to achieve a genuine European citizenship as a necessary and integral part of European Union; – in a British context (i) to create a group of experts knowledgeable about, and with a continuing interest in, issues relating to European citizenship; and (ii) through the work of this group, its report and subsequent activities, to contribute towards the creation of a better and wider understanding of the issues related to European Citizenship among British decision-makers and opinion formers.[12]

The group has studied six topics, namely: the concepts and the substance of citizenship as general problems; the framework of citizenship in public international and comparative national law; the experience of other developing unions of states; 'European citizenship' today and the potential for further development within the Community framework; a model for European Community citizenship; and targets and strategies for implementing the recommendations. At the time of writing these findings are due to be published as a Draft Charter and a book of background working papers.[13]

It therefore could well be the case that, despite the weakness of the British tradition of citizenship and the frailty of its commitment to European Union, the contribution of this country to clarifying, extending and consolidating the concept and status of European citizenship will be invaluable. Indeed, precisely because we do not have a clearly defined national citizenship status analogous to that developed in France since 1789, for instance, it may be that we can bring more flexibility of thought to the problem. A large proportion of public opinion has been alerted by the news media to the pronouncements of politicians, the appointment of the Speaker's Commission, the activities of Charter 88 and the concern of the Prince of Wales in this matter. It is precisely now, when political, scholarly and popular debate is engaged concerning the nature of British citizenship, that the European dimension should be incorporated in any conclusions that are reached. The experience and lessons could then have wider implication throughout the Community. In such an event, the age-old confidence that England has a vital role to play in any scheme of European political unity would be confirmed.

## A People's Europe

We do not, in fact, start with a *tabula rasa*. Certain facets of citizenship have already been identified and some action taken to render them realistic. After a hesitant prologue, the story effectively starts in June 1984. The European Council, meeting at Fontainebleau, decided that measures were needed for the development of a 'People's Europe'. (We may wonder, incidentally, whether this particular translation of the French 'Europe des Citoyens' is evidence of a deliberate English reluctance to accept the idea of citizenship.)

For this purpose a committee was created under the chairmanship of Pietro Adonnino. Its remit was an extraordinary rag-bag of political, social, cultural, educational, sporting and economic matters. The committee lodged two reports the following year with the European Council, which approved them. For our purposes it is the Second Report which is the more relevant, particularly Section 2: 'The special rights of citizens', and Section 9: 'Strengthening of the Community's image and identity'.

How far does this report take us towards constructing a European citizenship? It is convenient to distinguish five elements in the complex concept of citizenship. It involves the exercise of rights and obligations in three arenas – civil, political and social. It requires citizens to have a sense of political identity and it requires them to be possessed of the quality of civic virtue.[14] It may be helpful to keep these five elements in mind while outlining the work of the Adonnino Committee.

Implicit in its very appointment was the belief that it is unreasonable to expect the inhabitants of the Community to behave as good citizens if the very status of citizenship lacks any practical meaning and content. Placing the committee's work in a broader context, the European Commission has noted that 'In its resolutions Parliament has laid particular stress on devising a policy which involves European citizens in the creation of a living Community and on transforming the technocrats' Europe into a people's Europe.'[15]

Clearly it is not possible to be a good citizen if you do not consider that you are a citizen at all. In the words of the Second Adonnino

Report, they felt it necessary to identify 'longer term objectives which would make the Community more of a reality for its citizens'.[16] As a result, the committee made the following recommendations, some of which have already been implemented. Symbols should be adopted in the form of a European flag, emblem, anthem and postage stamps.

In the area of civil or legal rights we may notice the recommendation that the adoption of European passports, already agreed as early as 1975, should be handled with a greater sense of urgency. The committee also suggested that 'steps be taken to accelerate the systematic codification and simplification of Community law, priority being given to those areas of greatest importance to the citizen in his daily life'.[17]

For the citizen *qua* political participant the committee made a variety of recommendations. These include the harmonisation of electoral procedures for the Parliament; enhancement of the facilities for the citizen's right of petition to the Parliament; and the right to participate in local elections in one's place of residence irrespective of one's nationality status.

In the field of what might be termed 'social citizenship' – the right of the citizen to a certain quality of life – the Adonnino Committee identified a number of areas for development. These included more mobility for workers and students and more general access to health care.

In 1988 Carlo Ripa di Meana, the member of the Commission with particular responsibility for a People's Europe, issued a communication taking stock of progress. This document also listed priorities for future action. These embraced the enhancement of communication and information facilities, particularly Europe-wide television, as essential means of strengthening the sense of European identity. Improving access to information and advice was also considered crucial for the better protection of the European citizen's rights. In addition the document suggested the possibility of a Charter of Citizens' Rights to complement the European Convention on Human Rights (an idea, incidentally, which the Parliament adopted with alacrity). Specific changes which had been advocated by the Adonnino Committee but which had not been implemented were listed. Among these were the matter of voting in local elections, already mentioned, and Community driving licences, both for their symbolic and practical value.

## The issue of multiple citizenship

And yet, for all this interest, concern and activity about European citizenship, little attention has been devoted to the problems of relating the budding status at the Community level with the fully flowered status at the national level. It is really not good enough for the members of the Commission and Parliament in their enthusiasm for a federal Community to try to underpin their ideal with a new supra-national citizenship regardless of the existing component national laws, conventions and sentiments. True, if the Community is to mean anything more than an administrative convenience, then some notion of European citizenship is necessary. But *qua* European citizen I really must understand how that status affects and relates to my status as a British citizen. It certainly cannot totally replace it.

In strictly legal terms the principle that Community law takes precedence over national law already ensures that the individual's rights as European citizens are often synonymous with his or her rights as citizen of a member state. However, even at the simplest level we should be able easily to discover on which issues uniformity has been achieved and on which it has not.

Too often discussions about European citizenship have focused on rights (or 'entitlements', to use the vogue term) and their definition. It must be remembered, on the other hand, that citizenship involves feelings of identity, loyalty and responsibility and a desire to discharge one's duties. It cannot always be assumed that these features of citizenship at the national level will automatically and comfortably blend with those same features at the European level. How do I cope with a Community policy designed to enhance the autonomy of regions at the expense of the cohesion of a unitary state? How do I relate to an MP and an MEP who pursue contrary policies on, for example, trade-union rights? How do I cope with a national government which seeks to protect national interests at the expense of the common interests of the Community?

Conscientious citizens can manage these problems only if there is a clearly articulated concept of multiple citizenship. This must embrace not just legal definitions concerning the relationship between an individual's status at Community and national levels (and state level too where a nation has a federal constitutional structure). Important though such definitions would be, there is the more subtle problem of how the citizen orders the priorities of his or her civic loyalties and activities.

I would like to suggest that the principle of subsidiarity might provide a useful guideline. This is an idea which originated in papal political thinking and has gained considerable currency in recent years in the European Commission and Parliament. In his Encyclical *Quadragesimo Anno* of 1931 Pius XI declared that

it is an injustice, a grave evil and a disturbance of right order, for a larger and higher association to arrogate to itself functions which can be performed efficiently by smaller and lower societies . . . The State therefore should leave to smaller groups the settlement of business of minor importance . . . it will thus carry out with greater freedom, power and success the tasks belonging to it alone . . . Let those in power, therefore, be convinced that the more faithfully this principle of subsidiary function be followed, and a graded hierarchical order exist between various associations, the greater will be both social authority and social efficiency, and the happier and more prosperous the condition of the commonwealth.[18]

A generation later, in *Pacem in Terris*, John XXIII extended the principle by asserting that 'the relationships between the world government and the governments of individual nations must be regulated according to the principle of subsidiarity.[19]

How, one may wonder, did this concept of subsidiarity enter the Community lexicon? It was almost certainly through the channel of the Christian Democratic parties, which so enthusiastically supported the idea of European integration in the post war period. The concept may indeed be found in the principles enunciated by the Italian cleric-politician, Don Luigi Sturzo. He was the founder of the Catholic Popular Party after the First World War, the precursor of the Italian Christian Democratic Party. But by whatever route, it is now firmly established. Thus President Delors, addressing the Parliament in Strasbourg in January 1990, referred explicitly to its crucial importance. Commenting on the need to augment the powers of the European Parliament and its relationship with the national parliaments, he said, 'There will have to be consultations on this question . . . and the concept of subsidiarity will have to be clarified and reflected in the institutional and legal arrangements.' He went on to declare that 'subsidiarity . . . must be the watchword underlying any scheme for allocating responsibilities between the Community, the national authority and the regional authorities . . . the principle of subsidiarity will have to act as a constant counterweight to the natural tendency of the centre to accumulate power.'[20] In fact 'sub-

sidiarity' has come to be so widely but so loosely used that the
European Parliament has deputed Giscard d'Estaing to compile a
report to define its meaning.

It is clear from these quotations that, whether in 1931, 1963 or
1990, the term 'subsidiarity' has referred to the exercise of political
authority and the power of decision-making. What, then, can be its
relevance to citizenship? Simply this: that what is sauce for the state
goose is sauce for the citizen gander. If government should be most
aptly conducted on the basis of acknowledged geographical hierarchy, so citizenship should be thus exercised. If there be potential
conflict in the mind and heart of the citizen regarding his or her sense
of identity, feeling of loyalty, demand of rights or performance of
duties, let subsidiarity be the principle that resolves the conflict. Let
us, as embryonic citizens of Europe, behave as citizens of our locality
in the first instance and so on upwards, leaving our sense of civic
responsibility to the Community to those larger issues which clearly
fall within the decision-making remit of Brussels.

In a sense, we already do. For although I might feel impelled to
approach my MEP about the pollution of the North Sea, problems
relating to the emptying of my dustbins are obviously more appropriately addressed to my local councillor. Even with the less tangible
issue of identity, the same principle can operate. For if, as it is surely
true, that no person has only a finite quantity of loyalty, then
portions can be attached to the objects of social identification as
befits the circumstances. An individual can feel passionately attached
to Bingley, Yorkshire or Great Britain in different contexts; and
perhaps, who knows, in the foreseeable future, Europe. But in the
event of war, to take an extreme example, one would expect the
commitment to Bingley or Yorkshire to be overshadowed by a higher
loyalty.

The idea of multiple citizenship within the context of Europe is
practicable, even though difficult and complex; and, as yet, barely
thought through. I have suggested that historically and for diverse
reasons England has been identified as the provider of essential
leadership or style in plans for European unity. What could Britain's
characteristic contribution be to a definition of multiple citizenship
specifically, in addition to the general academic discussions to which
I have already alluded? They are twofold.

The first service is in a sense negative. Where other members of the
Community have clear-cut definitions, Britain has a tradition of

muddling through. From the British Nationality Act of 1948 through that of 1981 to the embarrassment concerning the citizenship rights of the inhabitants of Hong Kong, Britain has struggled with definitions in complicated circumstances. The complications have arisen from the confused legacy of Empire compounded by the retention in the metropolitan country of the crown–subject rather than the creation of a modern state–citizen relationship.

In the process we have learned how difficult it is to define citizenship in delicate and tricky situations; and, what is more to the point, how easy it is to generate a law of confused injustice. The situation in the European Community raises problems of comparable difficulty. What is to be the relationship between national and Community citizenship? Is there to be developed any realistic form of provincial citizenship? What are to be the rights of the alien guestworkers? What is to be the status of citizens of other European states which might negotiate forms of association with the Community in a broad common European home, to use Gorbachev's phrase? How far should a definition of citizenship extend from the civil and political to the social spheres? What are to be the rights of inhabitants of former overseas empires where there are vestigial rights *vis-à-vis* the metropolitan state? (By way of a parenthesis I could point out that after 1992 the inhabitants of Macao, by virtue of the concession of Portuguese citizenship to the whole population, will have more rights in Britain as Community citizens than those inhabitants of neighbouring Hong Kong who have been denied British citizenship.) It is precisely these kinds of questions which could be clarified by reference to British experience and mistakes over the last four decades.

The other distinctive contribution which Britain could make relates to its own urgent need to put its constitutional house in order, Northern Ireland cries out for a solution, the Scots have deep grievances. The number of Britons who are forced to seek redress on human-rights violations from the Council of Europe is a scandal.

At the same time and paradoxically, the opportunity for change could be facilitated by British flexibility. For the belief that Britain is an inflexible unitary state is a myth. Citizens of the Irish Republic have voting rights, the Isle of Man and the Channel Islands have their own legislatures. Scotland has its own legal system.

Charter 88 has placed constitutional reform on the agenda for active consideration. If it could be persuaded to forge a link with the

Federal Trust, the issues of British and European citizenship could be tackled, as they properly should be, simultaneously. Such a collaborative venture would benefit Britain and the European Community. It would also benefit the status of citizenship, which, although firmly established in the ancient world, requires its ideals and basic principles to be constantly refurbished to meet the conditions of each age. Their refurbishment for the new European home is a worthy call upon the craftsmanship of British lawyers and political scientists – not to mention, of course, the teaching profession.

### Notes

1  H. Wilson, *The Labour Government 1964–70* (Harmondsworth: Penguin, 1974) 887.

2  See V. Kitzinger, *Diplomacy and Persuasion* (London: Thames & Hudson, 1973) 33.

3  Mintel, quoted in the *Guardian*, 7 February 1990.

4  For details, see D. Heater, *The Idea of European Unity* (Leicester University Press, 1992).

5  Quoted in S. de la Mahotière, *Towards One Europe* (Harmondsworth: Penguin, 1970) 7.

6  *The Memoirs of the Duke de Sully, Prime Minister to Henry the Great* (transl. Charlotte Lennox, London: William Miller (1755) 1810 edn), vol. 5, p. 80.

7  H. de Saint-Simon, 'The Reorganization of the European Community' (in *Selected Writings*, ed. F. M. H. Markham, Oxford: Blackwell, 1952) 45.

8  See D. Carlton, *MacDonald versus Henderson* (London: Macmillan, 1970) 83–7.

9  *The Federalist* No. 33, quoted in M. Forsyth, *Unions of States* (Leicester University Press, 1981) 112. It should also be noted that Forsyth classifies the European Community as a confederation and not a system *sui genaris* as is usually the case.

10  H. Young, 'Citizens! The cure-all rallying cry' in the *Guardian*, 1 September 1988.

11  D. Marquand, *The Unprincipled Society* (London: Cape, 1988) 245.

12  Federal Trust for Education and Research, *European Citizenship – Progress so far: Perspectives for the Future* (mimeo), November 1988.

13  Some thirty papers have been compiled. Information about the work of the Study Group may be obtained from Gary Miller, Director, Federal Trust for Education and Research, 1 Whitehall Place, London SW1A 2DA.

14  See D. Heater, *Citizenship: The Civic Ideal in World History, Politics and Education* (London: Longman, 1990) Part Two.

15  Commission of the European Communities, *Bulletin of the European Communities, Supplement 2/88: A People's Europe* (Luxembourg: Office for Official Publications of the European Communities, 1988) 6.

16  Commission of the European Communities, *Bulletin of the European Communities, Supplement 7/85; A People's Europe* (Luxembourg: Office for Official Publications of the European Communities, 1985) para. 1.7.

17  *Ibid.*, para. 2.4.

18  Reprinted in M. Oakeshott (ed.), *Social and Political Doctrines of Contemporary Europe* (London: Basic Books, 1940) 58. One may also note that E. F. Schumacher cited this encyclical in *Small is Beautiful* (see Abacus edn., London, 1974) 203–4.

19  Para. 140.

20  Transcript of speech (mimeo), 17 January 1990.

# New curricula, new directions

For twenty-one years the Politics Association has provided an important forum for promoting and debating key issues and strands in political education. For example the Crick and Porter case for political literacy as part of the educational entitlement for all students co-exists and has often been disputed with Fred Ridley's priority for supplying street-wise political tools for the urban survival of sixteen-year-old school leavers. More consistently and persistently present, and only occasionally challanged, has been the distinguished and practical support given by the Association through its conferences, publications, *Teaching Politics* and *Talking Politics* and PARB (Politics Association Resource Bank), to politics and government taught by specialists to a more restricted group of older students. But now we have a National Curriculum for all pupils aged five to sixteen. Although political education is not identified as a required component, 'Citizenship' is one of several cross-curricular themes which all subjects must take account of, and issues that are currently politically controversial can be identified in the recommendations of, for example, the History and Geography Working Groups and in the statutory instruments for the teaching of science. No longer is learning about politics just to be a specialist study for some pupils over the age of sixteen. It is to be part of the curriculum for all pupils from the age of five. So new directions are suggested in a more diverse agenda with different priorities. It is an exciting prospect for the Politics Association as it enters its majority.

There are of course still many reservations and doubts about the emerging National Curriculum. Soon all formal consultation on its proposals will be over. So must we not accept that no longer do we have *a* curriculum emerging but *the* National Curriculum established? It is a view likely to be held by ministers and their civil servants and doubtless by some members of the National Curriculum Council (NCC). Undoubtedly the Department of Education and Science (DES) and the NCC will urge us to accept statutory instruments as *faits accomplis*, as 'game-set-and-match' statements. It is a view we must resist. It remains *a* national curriculum, not yet *the* National Curriculum. At the end of 1990, the final reports of the History and Geography Working Groups' recommendations, the ministerial responses to them and the statutory instruments have been part of a paper debate. Much of what has been written deserves serious consideration, some to be influential, but they have not yet earned the right to be uncritically accepted as a complete policy or, above all, as practical working documents usable in classrooms. Until the first class is taught, all that has been written and said remains a hypothesis waiting to be tested. Only Chapter 1 of a much longer story has appeared. Not only do we need to test the proposals for the new curriculum in classrooms, we need further discussions to clarify the proposals themselves. There are, at the time of writing (December 1990), too many lurking assumptions, hinted values, absent or ill-defined criteria, generalisations and ambiguities in the statements coming from the DES and NCC which a continuing debate must first clarify.

There is a good democratic case for such a debate on the grounds of accountability. For a long time teachers have been reminded of *their* accountability by, for example, the statutory requirement of examination results to be published, the publishing of HMI reports on the performance of their schools and departments, on proposals for teacher appraisal and testing and of their obligations to defend and explain and increasingly to be influenced by tax payers, who resource them and pay their salaries. But accountability is not a vehicle that travels only in one direction unless, that is, we fail to distinguish being citizens from being subjects. Taxes pay not only the salaries of teachers, but the salaries and expenses of the Secretary of State and their civil servants, of HMI, of the subject working groups and of the National Curriculum Council. We are all thus entitled to ask the centre for a clarification of intentions, for assumptions to be explicit and argued, values to be identified, criteria to be defined and judgments supported by evidence. No doubt we will not get answers to all our questions, but they must not be allowed to disappear from the public agenda.

But we do not want to debate just as a matter of political principle and right. So far, many of the responses to the subject group reports and to the ministerial responses to them have been too narrowly based and sometimes far too deferential. The recommendations of the Working Groups for History and Geography were often, puzzlingly, far more restrictive than their ministerial terms of reference required. Such evidence as exists permits us at least tactfully to speculate that their thinking may, on occasions, have been blocked, diverted or blunted by being too easily persuaded that certain recommendations would not be politically acceptable. The messages from the two groups of course were mixed. The historians, for example, certainly argued persuasively and with considerable effect, against the views held by two Secretaries of State and by the then Prime Minister on the nature and status of knowledge, views more uncritically accepted by their colleagues on the Geography Group. However, both groups accepted without declared doubts or analysis the complex strategy of assessment proposed and accepted by ministers of the Task Group for Assessment and Testing (TGAT). These proposals are central to the strategy of the whole National Curriculum and will have a direct affect on teaching and learning styles. Their complexity and importance deserved a considered discussion by the historians and the geographers in their respective groups. Although their terms of reference only asked them to 'bear in mind' and 'take account of' the TGAT proposals, they were in fact, uncritically and baldly accepted. Too much deference, or were they nobbled? The recommendations of the working groups were made by independent, unpaid professionals. Their role was, within their broad terms of reference which remain unamended and publicly available documents, to make recommendations to the Secretary of State on what kind of history and geography should be taught and why, to relate their recommendations to evidence of how pupils think and on the necessary classroom conditions for their learning and its assessment. The persuasiveness and particularly the authority of their recommendations stemmed from the maintenance of their professional independence. Their task was neither to flatter nor to second-guess ministerial attitudes. Nor was it to seek a confrontation with or to vex them. If they had appeared to do either they would have blurred the important distinction between the giving of independent, professional advice and the taking of political decisions. It is a distinction on which the independent advice and the

public credibility of HMI has long depended, a characteristic recognised and greatly valued by some previous Secretaries of State and
which now, more than ever, needs fiercely to be defended.

Deference may have blunted the edge or diverted some of the
possible recommendations. Too many of the responses from professional associations and unions have also touched an unnecessarily
humble forelock, have readily accepted the assumptions lying behind
curricular proposals and displayed a timid lack of curiosity in their
values. Understandably, many of the responses have concentrated on
those aspects of the recommendations which have a most direct
impact on teaching and learning in classrooms, on the content pupils
will be expected to learn and its assessment. The agenda is too
narrow, if concerns about the amount and nature of content, does
not at the same time seek to ferret out the criteria by which it was
selected. Doubts about procedures for assessment just as much as the
case for their need, depends upon some agreement in advance about
their underlying principles and their function. It is not just enough to
know what procedures of assessment *are*, but what they are *for*.
Where, for example, in the History Report are its assumptions, its
thrust, its heart? A reader of it constantly stumbles against its
vocabulary and seven words in particular on which much of its
thinking depends and is described. They are:
Breadth
Balance
Coherence
Appropriate
Relevant
Sufficient
Objective
Cognoscenti will recognise DES- and HMI-speak. Of course they are
all clichés and the first three are metaphors. Clichés are dull but not
necessarily wrong, but their familiarity may not breed contempt
so much as an uncritical acceptance. Metaphors are familiar
features, together with others, such as 'dimension', 'core', 'foundation', 'spiral', of much talk and writing which drives curricular
discussion, sometimes into dead ends and in wrong directions. There
is nothing wrong with metaphors provided they are recognised as
such and there is at least some *shared* recognition of the concrete
circumstances they are designed to illuminate. What all these words
have in common is that they are arm-twisters. They are concealed

bully words. They demand acceptance. Who could possibly oppose them? Is anyone foolish enough to defend 'imbalance', 'narrowness', 'incoherence', 'subjectivity', 'irrelevence'?

But what kind of learning do they describe? 'Breadth' is a spatial metaphor, which has lost its usual companion, 'depth'. It runs the danger of encouraging rapid journeys over clearly mapped territory, but allowing little time for repose or reflection, or to make rewarding visits to sites which, as Michelin would say, 'are worth the diversion'. If 'breadth' suggests area, 'balance' raises the image of equilibrium between contrasted but equally weighted elements. Too often it has been used to justify a simplistic study of complex issues polarised into two contrasted points of view, sometimes at the expense of understanding either. It can urge the search for a kind of compatability of worth which can inhibit commitment, threaten moral outrage: 'Well, next week boys and girls – the case *for* Auschwitz.' Confusion is compounded when balance seems to be made synonymous with 'impartiality'. 'Coherence' either ignores or underestimates the random, the eccentric, the individual in the learning of young people and the excitement and motivation it can give them. Of course we should welcome coherent thinking, but that is not how the document uses the word. It wants coherent *content*, in which all the constituent parts bear some visible and organic relationship to the other. It is not how adults operate. We do not impose a coherence on ourselves when we decide which book to read, gallery or museum, or historic site to visit, article to write or television programme to watch. Should not such approaches to learning be able to play some part in that of pupils in school? A centrally defined agenda of coherence is likely to tidy up and iron out the unpredictable variety of interests and enthusiasm which can emerge in any class. 'Objective' is a bit different. It is not a metaphor, nor quite a cliché. It seems to support a bluff commonsense Clapham-omnibus point of view, which sees history and indeed, the humanities and social sciences, as pursuing truth and transmitting accurate and publicly acknowledged facts. Things are a touch more complicated than that. HMI, in their publication *History in the Primary and Secondary Years: an HMI view* (HMSO, 1985) made a distinction between objective content and objective procedures. The former, HMI suggested, is a myth. Content is inevitably selected, although by whom and for what purpose is not always made clear. It is a process which confers status on what is selected and diminishes

L

what is not. It cannot either be objective or value-free. *Procedures* on the other hand are objective when they cannot be modified either by the ideas we examine or by the conclusions we hope to reach. They are procedures which insist constantly that statements made about human beings, individuals or groups, must be consistent with available evidence linked to them by what we might broadly call 'rational thinking'. They are not only the procedures of history, they also give political education its pedagogical stature and intellectual cutting-edge. And as for 'relevant', 'approprate' and 'sufficient', unless they are qualified by a preposition followed by a concrete phrase, they are meaningless. They conceal just who defines what is relevant, appropriate and sufficient, for whom and for what purpose. *All* these words are familiarly scattered throughout much of the writing on the National Curriculum. As they are used, they do not encourage debate, but hold it at arm's length. It is thinking through slogans, curricular development through incantation. Language has been used to build barricades rather than lines of communication.

Debate on the National Curriculum needs further to be broadened to encounter two other aspects which have not yet received sufficient prominence. They are both imbalances. The first is an imbalance in favour of teaching rather than learning. It favours the teacher as an agent of the centrally defined curriculum, as a monopolist of knowledge and experience as opposed to the perceptions and diverse experiences and previous knowledge which pupils bring with them when they first enter primary schools. It is an imblance which may stem from the feeling that education is synonymous with schooling and thus ignores the resource of pupils' experience. There are many young people in schools who have experienced violence, racial abuse, drugs, encounters with the police or, more positively, the experience of other cultures, beliefs, of living in other countries, of artistic or sporting success outside the experience, indeed perhaps the comprehension, of some of their teachers. This is not a plea for a child-centred or negotiated curriculum (more misleading metaphors). Nor is it an attempt to undermine the authority of teachers, but merely to suggest that it often lies less in their need to tell, inform and mould, than in their ability to help pupils distinguish between myth and reality and acquire procedures which help them categorise, reflect on and critically evaluate, extend and apply their own knowledge and experiences. If citizenship in the National Curriculum is to concern itself with currently controversial and sometimes politically sensitive issues such considerations are of a crucial importance to its teachers. They have pedagogical as well as content implications.

There is a second imbalance running through much of the educational policy coming from central government. It is between a prescriptive centre at the expense of the professionalism of teachers. There were some early warning lights. The proposals made to the Secretary of State on the teaching of history and geography were made by groups drawn from the world of education. Only two out of ten were teachers in the History Group while in the Geography Group there was only one practising teacher, although we must add to it the presence of a retired head teacher. The National Curriculum Councils' History Task Group did a bit better with three teachers out of eleven members. The Celts did even better. The Welsh had four teachers out of a total of fourteen, while the Northern Irish had eight teachers in a larger group of sixteen. This imbalance, running through much of the Education Reform Act, is helping deprofessionalise teachers. We are still in danger of an easy acceptance of a National Curriculum which seems unwilling to identify, let alone enhance and learn from the professionalism of teachers. The History Report again has its own straws blowing in a more general wind. It paid a just tribute to the contributions of teachers to curricular development and assessment in the past. But it is a contribution which appeared to have mainly an antiquarian interest, as there were no comments or suggestions as to how best these past achievements could be seen as an investment in the future.

But what about citizenship in the National Curriculum? The National Curriculum Council *Curriculum Guidance No. 8: Education for Citizenship* (NCC, 1990) has now appeared, a year after the publication of the final History Report and some six months after that on Geography. The History and Geography Working Groups had identified links with and described the potential contribution of their subjects to citizenship. Neither defined the term or had much in the way of practical guidance on how it might be related to the proposed study units or to levels of attainment. What they wrote was sound but there was not very much of it. There was some impression of hurried, last-minute writing designed more to satisfy the Working Group's terms of reference than as a support to learning. Some coherence with the main body of the reports would have been welcome. The separate membership, quite different timetabling and determined autonomy of the History and Geography Working Groups and the National Curriculum Council Citizenship Group failed to demonstrate in their working the kind of curricular thinking or professional liaison which their recommendations demanded of teachers. So perhaps it is not surprising that *Curriculum Guidance No. 8* is a pallid, feeble affair. It compares badly in appearance, length, practicality and detailed recommendations with its cross-curricular predecessors dealing with Economic and Industrial Understanding and Environmental Education. The lack of co-ordination between the publication of advice on related areas of curriculum is further compounded by the citizenship document's references to social sciences, despite the fact that nothing so far has been published on this important area of the curriculum by the end of 1990. HMI has not yet published its long-planned and discussed suggestions on social sciences in its *Curriculum Matters Series*. At the outset, messages from the centre on citizenship seem to be muddled and to diminish and marginalise it. Statutory instruments for the teaching of History and Geography were published in the summer of 1991. They encapsutated the attitudes of Kenneth Clarke; they severely limit the opportunity of geographers to discuss values in many issues and terminate history in 1970 (originally 1960). Such responses were not only confused and wrong but they emasculated two key subjects where knowledge and procedures have given the study of contemporary issues some depth and rigour. How crass and blinkered it is when rarely in history has the nature of citizenship been so publicly debated, disputed and fought over than in 1989 and 1990!

However, *Curriculum Guidance No. 8* does suggest a framework on eight components which, potentially, provide usable initial agenda for thinking about a syllabus. They are:

Community
A Pluralist Society
Being a Citizen
The Family
Democracy in Action
The Citizen and the Law
Work, Employment and Leisure
Public Services

These components are supported by cross-curricular skills and a set of 'positive attitudes' and 'moral codes and values' they are designed to promote. (What are negative attitudes, by the way? Are they undesirable, or those that are merely uncomfortable?) But what messages do the proposed structures give us? What values underpin this document? How would we recognise a citizen educated in its terms? What kind of society are they likely to live in? The educated citizen would be able to 'argue a case . . . e.g. for or against changes in the local community' and detect 'opinions, bias and omission', and 'make choices in the light of available evidence, e.g. decide upon a particular course of action', exercise 'democratic responsibilities and rights'. They will have 'independence of thought on social and moral issues', and 'active concern for human rights' and an 'appreciation of the paramount importance of democratic decision making'. So far, so reasonably good. The citizen will be able to make decisions between alternative points of view, using skills which are, on the whole, more mind opening than socialising.

In sum, we have a clutch of skills, attitudes and ideas that would sit uncomfortably in a closed or authoritarian society. Implicitly they would not always be entirely comfortable nor necessarily deferential, and yet we read references of a 'respect', a favourite word of this document, for 'different ways of life', 'beliefs', 'opinions and ideas', for rational argument and 'non-violent ways of resolving conflict'. We read of shared values, such as 'concern for others, industry and effort'. There are suggestions about comparing 'values and beliefs held by themselves and others in order to identify common ground' and 'consider solutions to modern dilemmas, personal and social'. A feeling is beginning to set in that perhaps the messages are just a touch cosy, seemly, even smug. To identify common ground in other beliefs and values without understanding the differences is bland and misleading. Do dilemmas always or ever have solutions? Is the educated citizen to be protected from understanding, or forbidden to choose violent means of resolving conflict? Has the NCC been nobbled by the Campaign for Nuclear Disarmament (CND) and the Society of Friends? Are other views to be respected *just* because they are different? And *all* views? Anti-semitism, Sexist, homophobic discrimination? Certainly good citizens should have the means critically to understand and *where possible* to accept and respect other views, but at the same time be obliged to declare why some attitudes do not merit respect. Are there no flaws within democratic societies, or other ways of running things? Does power vested in Parliament always understand and guarantee the rights of minorities? Tolerance and respect are fine, but they are fragile unless they can mobilise intellectual and political weapons to use when faced with disrespect, intolerance and sheer bloody-mindedness. These comments are in no way intended to suggest that the messages that do emerge are in any way threatening or undemocratic, but merely that they are a sight too confident, safe and self-satisfied. May they not too easily assume that certain values *are* shared? If so, by whom? Are a society's values necessarily valuable?

The uneasy cosiness is not dispelled when we look further at the exemplary issues and activities for developing pupils' skills and attitudes. Sensibly, the emphasis, particularly for younger pupils, is on the experience of their immediate environment at home and in the school. Such priorities can remind schools that the first experience young people have of the ability of adults to organise a community, to make rules and impose sanctions, deal with disputes, recognise and value minorities, is their school. The importance of helping old people in their homes, on the very young in their crèches, of carol singing in hospitals, organisations such as the Guides and the Scouts and the St John's Ambulance Brigade, Outward Bound, Operation Raleigh, or of the contribution of the police service is clear and welcome. What about Friends of the Earth, CND, Amnesty International, organisations protesting against the building of motorways or the closing of hospitals, or the opting out of schools? There is an uneasy feeling that there is an imbalance in favour of respectability at the expense of the tough reality of the lives of many young people. There is a similar unease in the single paragraph on the contribution of the police service. No other organisation enjoys such emphasis in the whole document. We read, 'Police forces can help in developing the ethos of a school.' Well, yes, but the prominence given to the contribution of the police suggests perhaps more a reaction against the few and overpublicised dimwits who encouraged anti-police attitudes in schools than a balanced and sensitive recognition of the role of the police in a community, of the varying perceptions of them held by many young people and, in some communities, as an issue of great political sensitivity.

In an outline syllabus contained in the document, suggestions are made how each of the eight components might be tackled. In the four key stages under the heading of 'A pluralist society' the words 'racism', 'racialism', 'discrimination', 'prejudice' do not even appear. It is not so much that the suggestions proclaim values that are unacceptable, just that key values appear to be absent. However, there are some positive suggestions. Pupils aged eleven to fourteen, it is suggested, might gather information to compare employment prospects in their community for different groups, 'manual and professional, male and female, Asian, Afro-Caribbean' Pupils should share their findings, it is proposed. But please, Sir, what now? For pupils aged fourteen to sixteen it is suggested that they 'chart the history of and identify the reasons for migration to and from this country'. Miss, what happened then? The experience of many pupils and their families will supply some of the answers. The document does not suggest this follow-up. It does suggest at another point that pupils should acquire an understanding of 'the importance to society and the individual of wealth creation'. Fine, but many individuals are less immediately concerned with the effect of wealth creation than its distribution.

Many of these proposals may be implemented in 1992 and so rightly there are references to Europe. Phrases such as 'links with Europe', 'relations with national, European and worldwide communities' suggest an insular separation from the mainland, which is both geographically wrong and politically partial. Surely by the end of 1990 curricular documents issued from the centre should be referring to, for example, 'other European countries' or 'the European mainland'? Where, incidentally, is the NCC's document of guidance to schools with suggestions about using the curriculum to develop a European dimension in it? After all, there is a very clear government commitment to this embodied in the Resolution of the Council of Ministers of May 1985 and signed by Kenneth Baker.

Many of the skills and attitudes and examples imply citizenship should encourage young people to debate and discuss issues that are publicly controversial. But issues that affect pupils are sometimes not only controversial, they are also sometimes politically sensitive: funding and management and resourcing of their own schools, relations with the police, squatting, the rights of the unemployed (just as important as the responsibilities of the employed), the publicity about and the funding of research into Aids, Gay Rights, Clause 28. That these issues are delicate and require sensitive teaching is clear. Equally so that they often affect directly or potentially many young people, but such issues do not appear in the document. Their absence, we suppose, may be a tactful matter of political deference. It is certainly timid. We read, quite rightly, about voting and debating. What about other legal political activity in a democratic society, marches, carrying banners, petitions, sit-ins, pestering people with letters?

Finally, the document is conceptually inadequate. No definition of 'citizenship is given. The distinction between 'citizen' and 'subject' is not made, between 'political' and 'social citizenship', or between what is 'just', 'fair' and 'legal'. The relationship between rights and obligations is not raised. Is the former conditional upon the latter, a kind of reward for being good? Or is Ralf Dahrendorf correct when he writes to the Speaker's Commision on citizenship, 'There are rights of citizenships and there are obligations. Both are absolutely valid if they are valid at all, but we shouldn't turn them into a quid pro quo.' And no indication is given that citizenship is itself a controversial political issue.

Whom is *Curriculum Guidance No. 8* for? What is it for? Clearly it is not a publication for pupils. It may be that it could offer a reassuring and comprehensive description of a part of the curriculum which parents and governors could read with some profit and little alarm. But for most teachers, apart from some specialists in politics, social sciences, some historians and geographers and teachers of religious education, it offers little help. Nevertheless, we have a document that deserves to be taken seriously. Education for citizenship *is* a serious issue and it is a required theme in a national curriculum, and this document endorses it and gives it status. The preliminary agenda it gives us has some merit. Its flaws are seriously distorting, but not yet quite fatal. In the main it suggests, recommends and exemplifies but rarely, if ever, prescribes. What it does not specifically forbid, it implicitly allows. What is ambiguous and ill-defined can be variously interpreted. But it needs to be taken by the scruff of the neck and given some professional bite. Meanwhile, it need not seriously threaten professional autonomy. However, to turn *Education for Citizenship* into a teachable programme that not only recognises the realities of the 1990s but also gives it a pedagogy that seeks to give democratic power to pupils without patronising them, is going to require considerably more public discussion, specialist support, access to a variety of resources and much in-service training. These needs suggest a prominent role for the Politics Association.

We have never had a National Curriculum before. It is wholly novel, not only in its concept but in its vastly complicated network of study programmes, skills, concepts, targets and levels of attainment and assessment procedures. It is neither surprising nor dishonourable if in its early stages it is flawed, contradictory, often unworkable or just plain daft. There remains a powerful argument which has cross-party support for a national curricular framework, but based on declared assumptions, carefully argued and agreed criteria together with a recognition that a common curriculum does not necessarily require uniform syllabuses. Whatever its final form, its implementation ultimately will depend upon the goodwill and professional experience of teachers. Its effective evaluation, modification and evolution must depend upon public debate and on a publicly defined working partnership between the centre (DES, HMI and NCC) and teachers seen as independent professional *partners*, not as carefully chosen and ministerially approved part-time consultants. The debate will not take place automatically, nor necessarily in the kind of educational forum that has been suggested unless the profession, particularly the organised profession, including, for example, the Politics Association, wants it. But without such a debate we are in danger of stumbling and sleepwalking into a national curriculum imposed partly by tradition, influenced by political whim and maintained by inertia. 'What is to become of poor students . . . if their notions of history are to sway this way and that according to majorities in the House of Commons?' asked J. A. Froude in 1855. With a debate we may, just, if we are stubborn and if we are lucky, achieve a national curriculum that enhances the professionalism and status of teachers and the learning of pupils. In an open, democratic society a curriculum can help make a persuasive professionally based case for education concerned with the examination of values rather than their transmission, not primarily as a socialising but as a mind-opening process. In this debate there is a central role for the Politics Association. It should, without much difficulty, carry us from our twenty-first birthday to our golden jubilee.

# Political education:
# a government view*

It gives me great pleasure to be here, through the good offices of Bob Dunn, to address you on the occasion of your twenty-first anniversary. He too, I know, spoke to the Political Association on political education some years ago. My colleague Robert Jackson has also been your guest more recently. You have heard, I gather, from politicians as diverse as Ken Livingstone and Enoch Powell. I recognise the privilege accorded to me in attending your coming-of-age celebrations. I understand that the Association now has nearly 1,000 paid-up members and 300 or more school student members covering the spectrum of politics education, from secondary schools to further and higher education. You are well established and set fair for the future. I know from experience that the Association's growth and development will have been due in no small measure to its officers and supporters. I note that your President Elect is Professor John Slater, lately of HMI and Staff Inspector for History. I am sure that his inside track knowledge of the DES will be of advantage to the Association.

In promoting the study and teaching of politics the Association has much to its credit. Its journals, meetings and courses help to raise the profile of the subject and encourage improvement in the quality of political teaching. I gather that *Talking Politics*, now two years old, is a valuable resource for 'A' level politics and government students

*This chapter is the text of a speech given by Alan Howarth MP, Parliamentary Under-Secretary of State for Education, at a special reception held in the House of Commons to celebrate the Politics Association's twenty-first anniversary on 4 July 1990. Also in attendance were Lord Joseph, Robert Dunn MP, Austin Mitchell MP and other parliamentarians concerned with political education.

and that your sixth-form conferences have proved very popular. One can only speculate how many of these young people will, as a result of the experience, forsake the imminent prospect of jobs in – say – accountancy or teaching for the headier attractions of a career in politics. Not too many I hope! It is an awesome responsibility the Politics Association may have to bear.

I know that the Association will continue to make its views known to government and others on curricular issues, as it has done for example on political education and citizenship in the National Curriculum. It is important to do so, to contribute to the continuing discussion, especially in areas which are not statutorily defined. That brings me to the Education Reform Act (ERA) 1988. Section 1 requires a balanced and broadly based curriculum in maintained schools which promotes the spiritual, moral, cultural, mental and physical development of pupils at the school and of society; and prepares such pupils for the opportunities, responsibilities and experiences of adult life. The National Curriculum is the key curricular innovation. Its introduction offers a new challenge to political education. Inevitably, schools will concentrate on teaching the ten foundation subjects and the five cross-curricular themes identified by the National Curriculum Council (NCC). I accept that none is labelled 'political education' as such, but 'citizenship' is of course a cross-curricular theme and has a strong affinity with political education. I will come on to citizenship a little later. Let me say a few words now about the foundation subjects.

As you know, the ten foundation subjects are those which the government believes need to be included in a broad and balanced curriculum for all pupils of compulsory school age. There will be many opportunities for discussing political ideas and concepts within the core and other foundation subjects, not least in English, history and geography. Political education is thereby anchored in contexts which may increase its attractiveness. For example, the History Working Group's suggested history study units on Life in Britain since 1930, Britain in the twentieth century and East and West Europe: 1948 to the present day would provide potential entrées. Through the foundation subjects, political education will become the experience of the many rather than the privilege of the few. This is achieved without putting yet more pressure on an overcrowded timetable or jeopardising the broad and balanced curriculum. It also becomes part of the pupil's work which is assessed, a possible additional incentive to learning!

Balance and breadth in the curriculum are important. I have heard the fear expressed that the National Curriculum might squeeze out worthwhile options. While the Secretary of State emphasised in his speech to the Society of Education Officers (SEO) on 25 January 1990 that we should not try to overcrowd the curriculum, I should point out that this does not rule out such options. I know that the Politics Association has long advocated the teaching of politics as a single subject by a specialist. I recognise that a foothold has been established for discrete government and politics courses in the fourteen–sixteen curriculum and that there are fears for the future. You may, I imagine, be looking for reassurance. You will forgive me if I do not comment substantively in advance of NCC and Schools Examination and Assessment Council (SEAC) advice on the possibilities for subject combinations leading to a GCSE. However, John Macgregor emphasised that the availability of reduced courses of study for the foundation subjects other than the core subjects, combined or on their own, is intended to help ensure that schools have time to include options such as a second foreign language or classics when they want. This is clearly an indicative not a complete list of options. So the possibility of political education as a discrete subject leading to a part or full GCSE is by no means ruled out by the measures taken so far to implement the National Curriculum.

I recognise also that the Politics Association is concerned about the future of 'A' levels and 'AS' government and politics examinations. I am sure that members will study the development of present 'AS' level courses with interest: I understand that two boards are now offering the qualifications in the area of government and politics and entries are in the high hundreds. I can well appreciate the argument for a route to 'A' level and beyond, into further and higher education, for those who have a serious interest in political studies. I hope that here provision matches the need in the marketplace.

Perhaps I can say a word about the sensitive and difficult question of bias in political education in schools. As a preliminary observation, I think that it must be recognised that some people sincerely believe that bias is inevitable and one way of avoiding the problem is not to teach politics in school at all. For my part, however, I think this should not be ducked and we look to teachers to help young people get to grips with issues, learn how to make a case and set out their personal position rationally. You will remember, perhaps, the sardonic yet penetrating comment attributed to Robert Lowe when contemplating the 1867 extension of the franchise that 'we must educate our masters'. (I understand that he actually said: 'I believe it would be absolutely necessary that you should prevail on our future masters to learn their letters . . . From the moment that you entrust the masses with power their education becomes an absolute necessity.' Which rather lacks the bite of the sub-editor's paraphrase!). If no attempt is made to teach political education – in the professional and measured way we expect of schools – the result is hardly likely to be a vacuum. Many pupils would leave school with untested opinions or prejudices picked up from less than disinterested sources.

The issue of politics in the classroom seems to me part of a wider one of how to encourage discrimination (in the best sense of the term), good sense, and rational judgment in young people. It is so difficult these days for people at school to plot their way through the barrage of advertising, propaganda and slogan mongering. Language is all too often used to blur rather than clarify meaning. Verbal gestures are made calculated to achieve the maximum of impact and the minimum of definition. Efforts are constantly made to persuade the young to conform to the fashion of the day. It must surely be the role of education to equip the individual with the wherewithal to stand up to this constant barrage and to identify and maintain his individuality and independence. As has been well said, style is being yourself, fashion is copying someone else's style. It is never going to be easy. It has to be faced squarely that political education is about politics and politics is about choices which so affect the lives of citizens that emotions are likely to run high. On the other hand, we have the long British tradition of accepting that rational men and women can hold quite contrary political views but that the way of resolving the great political issues of the day is through the decisions of a Parliament given authority by the people through periodic elections. I believe that political education at school which presents fairly the diversity of opinions in our society but is firm on the resolution of differences through our democratic institutions and the courts of law best serves the interests of young people.

The 1986 Act is clear that the school-room is not the place for party-political propaganda. It forbids the promotion of partisan politial views in the teaching of any subject. I see political education in schools as a preparatory activity offering information, criteria against which to judge it and guidance on how to come to a point of view and defend it cogently. After all, only the very oldest pupils in sixth forms are entitled to vote and only a minority of those will actually have the occasion to vote. I agree with the view of your former Chairman, Dr Bill Jones, quoted in the *Times Educational Supplement* article on the Politics Association's new guidelines on political education: 'The purpose of such education in a liberal democratic society is to enlighten children about various available explanations of the world, to interest and challenge them to reach their own decisions. Teachers who merely impart their own prejudices are not serving these ends.' I should add, in parenthesis, that I rather like Sir Keith Joseph's formulation in a speech some six years ago to the National Council of Women of Great Britain that:

If asked by his pupils for his own views the teacher should, as appropriate, declare where he himself stands but explain at the same time that others, in particular the pupil's parents and their teachers, may disagree.

Let me turn now to citizenship. A former High Master of Manchester Grammar School, John Paton, once said: 'Education is the science which deals with the world as it is capable of becoming.' Education for citizenship is that part of it which deals with the potentiality of young people to take responsibility within their communities. Albert Mansbridge, founder of the Workers' Educational Association, wrote in 1917 that the purpose of any school 'must be to bear its part in developing to the utmost the powers of body and mind and spirit for the common good . . . developing citizenship, which is the art of living together on the highest plane of human life'. Mansbridge reminded his readers that in 1895 Arthur Acland, then Minister for Education, had introduced a detailed syllabus for citizenship into the Elementary Code. This had met with general approval at the time although, Mansbridge tells us, 'the elaborate nature of Mr Acland's syllabus tended to defeat its object, and some held it to be psychologically unsound, but there has also been a lack of suitable text books'. 'In general however,' Mansbridge adds firmly, 'the whole subject depends peculiarly upon the personality of the teacher, who feels no lack of text books if he is alive to the interest of his lesson.'

Education for citizenship is not, then, a new concept. How citizenship should be taught today, and what its contents should be, are the questions I want now to address. Section 1 of the Education Reform

Act requires, as I noted earlier, that young people should be prepared for 'the opportunities, responsibilities and experiences of adult life', and that not only their personal development, but also the needs of society, should be taken into account. As the Secretary of State told the National Conference of the Commission on Citizenship in Northampton in February 1990, 'Unless citizenship forms a part of what schools seek to convey to their pupils, these aims, as set out in the Act, will not be achieved.' Education for citizenship is one of five major cross-curricular themes identified by the NCC, and one on which the Council proposes to publish detailed guidance for schools very shortly. I know that this Association has contributed valued evidence to the NCC Task Group on citizenship: indeed, I gather that, wearing different hats, some of its members were also members of the Task Group.

Education for citizenship, like the other themes, lends itself more readily to a cross-curricular than to a subject-based approach, because its elements permeate the whole curriculum and, indeed, the whole life of a school. The cross-curricular themes contribute to personal and social development in a number of ways. As NCC has put it:

they explore the values and beliefs which influence the individual and his or her relationship with others and the wider world;
they help pupils to respond to their present lives and prepare them for adult work and life;
they emphasise practical activities, decision-making, learning through experience, and the development of close links between the school and the wider world;
they provide relevant ways in which skills might be developed.

'Every subject taught in a school should serve the needs of the larger citizenship', wrote Mansbridge, 'but there has been much discussion concerning the relative importance of the development of community spirit in schools, and the introduction of the direct teaching of citizenship.' If Mansbridge could eavesdrop on the current debate, he might find the arguments of the protagonists very familiar, for there continues to be considerable debate about what education for citizenship should consist of, and where it should be located in the curriculum. But within that debate, I think there *is* broad agreement about the areas of knowledge and concepts which should be included in its study. Among them are: the organisations and structures of society; the rule of law; freedom, justice, democracy; the responsibilities and duties, as well as rights, of individuals; and the boundaries between individual freedom, the rights of others, and the needs of society. I think everyone would agree too that citizenship impinges upon all areas of experience: at home, school and work; on our participation in democratic processes; on the state and voluntary services which we provide and use; on our adherence to agreed codes of conduct and the law. I hope that young people will, as well, see their rights, responsibilities and duties in the wider context of the European and the world community. There has never been a more pressing need for us all to think of our world home, and to unite our effort to sustain its precious life-support system and limited resources.

That said, two issues in particular stand out. First, citizenship is not simply a body of knowledge, which can be neatly separated from other subjects and delivered in 35 or 40 minute periods. It is also, crucially, concerned with equipping young people with the appropriate skills and attitudes they will need to cope with the many different aspects of their lives as workers, voters, consumers, and members of a widening and overlapping series of communities. Individually, it is about making confident, independent, well-informed judgements and decisions. Collectively, it concerns the development of co-operation, tolerance and mutual respect at home, at school, in the local community, and in relation to national and international life. Citizenship is also, I believe, about nationalism in the best sense of that difficult word. Perhaps 'nationhood' is a more apt description for the sense of group identity, pride, commitment and continuity – the sense of belonging – which we feel ourselves, and recognise and respect in our world neighbours. Too often 'nationalism' is trivialised by tabloid stereotypes, or made sinister by the actions of extremists. One important task in educating young people for citizenship is to give them all a feeling of sharing, of being active participants in, and of not being excluded from, the national community.

Second, many of these concepts, and the opportunities to develop the skills and attitudes which should accompany them, already have their natural place within foundation subjects of the National Curriculum. History, of course, has a particular role to play in helping young people to understand the complex forces and tensions which have contributed to the creation of our own modern society, and to the political and social systems of other nations. English, my own specialist subject, has I believe an important place in the teaching of citizenship. Reading Chaucer, or Swift, or Dickens or Orwell, for example, makes limited sense without some explanation and understanding of the social and political issues which fired their imaginations, and their indignation. And rigorous training in the analysis and use of language will help young people to resist the barrage of sloganising to which I referred earlier. Of course, the extent to which citizenship is included in National Curriculum foundation subjects will vary from school to school. This is part of the very democracy of our own education system – one of the proper values of a liberal state. That flexibility will enable each school to review the extent to which opportunities and activities related to citizenship already exist, in foundation subjects and in other areas; and to what extent new ones need to be created.

Reviewing existing practice will be an essential step in producing a whole school policy. It will also be a particularly challenging task. Every school is a microcosm on society. The total school experience of each child is, therefore, a significant contribution to his or her preparation for citizenship. To an evaluation of the taught (and received) curriculum must be added consideration of the whole texture on a school's relationships, expectations, values, rules and activities all of which contribute to what is often called the climate, or ethos, of a school. Teaching about democracy will have greater meaning if pupils know that they have themselves some means of representation, such as a school council. Learning about responsibility will be real learning, only if pupils are allowed and encouraged to become actively responsible for and towards each other, both within the school community and through, for example, voluntary service, which extends this sense of responsibility into the wider community. We tend often to underestimate the potential of young people to rise to a whole range of challenges, acquiring as they do so new confidence and self-esteem.

Voluntary service has a special role in education for citizenship. Many young people do, of course, belong to church and other voluntary orgnisations in their local communities, but there is much that schools can do to create opportunities and encourage pupils to take them up. Community Service Volunteers (CSV), has for many years worked closely with schools, and its advisory service receives funding from my Department. One new initiative, with which CSV is connected, is the Prince's Trust Young Volunteers' Scheme and I

M

particularly welcome what it is setting out to do. The scheme, which starts this autumn, will give young people between the ages of 16 and 24 a variety of opportunities to undertake planned programmes of voluntary service, including community and environmental activities. A key aspect of the scheme will be planned teamwork, and the fostering of skills development and self-assessment among the young volunteers. It will therefore contribute directly to their personal and social development, and will enhance the education for citizenship provided by schools. It is a most exciting venture, and I wish it every success.

Education for citizenship is not, however, only the concern of schools and voluntary groups. It begins in the home, and should continue to be, like every other aspect of education, pursued in partnership with parents. Sometimes this is easier said than done; and sometimes teachers feel that they are held wholly responsible for education, and then for all of society's ills, where education fails. It is, I feel, most important for schools to seek ways of working closely with parents; and equally important for young people to understand the value and place of family life in society, as one aspect of citizenship. Other organisations too have legitimate interests in education for citizenship. I have already referred to the Secretary of State's address, earlier this year, to an audience of some 100 students, educationists and representatives from industry and the voluntary sector, at the National Conference of the Speaker's Commission on Citizenship. The Commission has been debating the nature of citizenship, sponsoring research on current school practice, and encouraging discussion of its rationale and teaching. We all await, with great interest, the publication of its report. At that conference, the Secretary of State also paid tribute to the valuable work of the Council for Education in World Citizenship, which celebrated its fiftieth birthday last year.

But tonight it is of course to the Politics Association that I extend my congratulations, on the occasion of your twenty-first birthday celebrations. Through its publications and resources, its local and national activities; and above all, through its continuing, informed, lively debate on all aspects of politics and citizenship, the Association makes an impressive contribution to these very important subjects.

*Peter Hennessy*

# Epilogue:
# Reasons to be cheerful

I'm one of those people who gets cross with his maker for not putting him on these islands at certain other moments of twentieth-century British political history. Who, for example, can read George Dangerfield's *The Strange Death of Liberal England*[1] and not wish they had been around to see Lloyd George grappling with the House of Lords or Asquith applying his exquisite intellect to the Irish Question? The year 1940 must have been quite something, and, as a political journalist, how I would have relished prising a few mono-syllables from Attlee in 1945 about the welfare state he was intent on constructing or, in 1947, prodding Ernie Bevin to tell me what a devious bastard he thought Molotov to be.

Yet I wouldn't have missed the turn of this decade for anything, the moment when Mrs Thatcher passed tearfully into the arms of the political historians, when one Cabinet minister told *The Economist* his colleagues were like the prisoners in Beethoven's *Fidelio* walking blinking into the sunshine[2] and another, with incredulity in his voice, recalled for me, as if it were some great historical enormity, just how 'haphazard' Cabinet government had been under the *ancien régime*: 'You never knew when there was going to be a discussion. It wasn't on the agenda and, suddenly, you'd find yourself discussing some-thing the PM had heard from someone she'd met or someone she'd spoken to the day before and the hapless departmental minister was quite unprepared.'[3]

It was plain from John Major's first Cabinet ('who would have believed it?', he asked as he called the meeting to order[4]) that genuine collective discussion was back, that the chapter entitled 'Conviction Cabinet'[5] was closed and another opened. As if that wasn't enough to set the pulse of British political science racing once more, within seven weeks of assuming the premiership Mr Major was required to set up the fourth 'war cabinet' since 1945.[6]

But, quite apart from the more immediate and dramatic excitements, there were plenty more stimulants to make the writing and teaching of politics a vintage experience. Take the constitution, traditionally *the* great soporific of our trade. Lazarus-like, it came alive in the late 1980s. At last there was a reawakening of interest in the hidden wiring of our political system.[7] The ground rules under which the political contest is conducted became of acute interest once more from the electoral system to the second chamber, from regional government to reducing the 'democratic deficit' with Europe.

The raw material of debate emerged from both the usual mines – Charter 88 and the Constitutional Reform Centre – and some unexpected lodes too, like the free-market Institute of Economic Affairs[8] and the Sheffield No. 2 Branch of the Workers' Educational Association.[9] Perhaps the most impressive input of all came from the Labour-sympathising Institute for Public Policy Resarch with its detailed blueprint for incorporating the best European, American and United Nations thinking into a new 'culture of liberty' in the United Kingdom[10] and its draft written constitution.[11]

One of the two major parties, Labour, went some way to accommodate this reformist surge. In January 1990, the party's Deputy Leader, Roy Hattersley, unveiled a slate of proposed Bills on privacy, freedom of information, oversight of the security and intelligence services and equal opportunities which, he claimed at a Fabian Society weekend in Oxford, amounted to a 'charter of rights', which, when added to Labour's proposals for an elected second chamber and regional government, would, if implemented, 'add up to the greatest constitutional reform this century'.[12]

Neither at Ruskin in 1990 or at the Queen Elizabeth II Centre in January 1991, when he launched a more polished version of *The Charter of Rights*, would Mr Hattersley contemplate a written Bill of Rights or the incorporation of the European Convention on Human Rights into the law of the land, largely for fear that an unreformed judiciary would use it to dilute the reforming tide of a radical government.[13] Nevertheless, the adoption of so much reformist thinking marked a major step forward and promised an intensely interesting period for the thinkers of political thought should Labour form a government at any time in the 1990s.

Parliament (apart from Tony Benn's successive drafts of his Commonwealth of Britain Bill[14], and Graham Allen's Written Constitution[15] and Human Rights Bills[16]) remained depressingly supine about its own powers *vis-à-vis* the executive. The 1990 report from the Procedure Committee on the role of select committees was as self-satisfied a document as I've read from the House of Commons in recent years.[17]

You would not think that a rival pole of parliamentary influence existed in Strasbourg, with another one in prospect in Edinburgh. In fact, the near certainty of devolution to Scotland by the turn of the century and even the meagrest outcome imaginable from the intergovernmental conference on European political union seemed set to push out the frontiers of UK constitutional change, however reluctant the local political class might be to depart from its 'this is England' syndrome which leads so many of us to see our nation as a special case, glorious in its traditionalist inertia.[18]

By contrast, across the road from Westminster, Whitehall was undergoing its most thorough peacetime overhaul since Mr Gladstone's day, as the process of turning large blocks of civil service work, under the *Next Steps* project,[19] into free-standing executive agencies continued apace, and promised to do so throughout the 1990s, even if there was a change of government. The Head of the Home Civil Service, Sir Robin Butler, acknowledged publicly that the programme had been designed with political transferability in mind,[20] the all-party Commons Treasury and Civil Service Committee endorsed this approach[22] and the government purred with pleasure when they did so.[24]

There was, however, no sign that Mr Major would tread where Mrs Thatcher had forsworn to go and initiate a policy-making revolution to accompany the managerial changes in Whitehall. The Central Policy Review staff went unrestored, though it's almost certain that had Douglas Hurd won the Conservative leadership in November 1990, the 'think tank' would have risen from the grave in which Mrs Thatcher had interred it after the 1983 general elction.[23] Neil Kinnock, by contrast, promised to restore a think tank for the Cabinet should the electorate propel him into No. 10, and to make the Whitehall machinery generally more responsive to the needs of our membership of the European Community.[24]

All in all, the prospects for the writers, teachers and consumers of political education in the 1990s are pretty glittering – a fistful of alluring, developing themes set against a still rising trend of the number of students taking Politics 'A' level and sitting for Politics degrees of various kinds with no Secretary of State for Education telling us (unlike the historians) that we have to turn off our thinking processes when we reach the 1960s. If political education does turn out to be dull, stale, flat or unprofitable in the coming decade, it will be *our* fault and nobody else's. There is *every* reason to be cheerful.

### Notes

1   George Dangerfield, *The Strange Death of Liberal England* (London: Paladin, 1983).

2   'Bagehot,' 'Selling a new spirit', *The Economist*, 8 December 1990.

3   Peter Hennessy, 'Whitehall watch: war gives Major a new gravitas', *Independent*, 21 January 1991.

4   Colin Brown, 'Happy days are here again . . .', *Independent*, 17 December 1990.

5   See Peter Hennessy, *Cabinet* (Oxford: Blackwell, 1986), Chapter 3, 94–122, based on Mrs Thatcher's famous declaration of a few months before becoming PM that: 'It must be a conviction government. As Prime Minister I could not waste time having any internal arguments', *Observer*, 25 February 1979.

6   Peter Hennessy, 'Falkland memories will guide Major', *Independent*, 16 January 1991.

7   See Peter Hennessy, *The Hidden Wiring: Power, Politics and the Constitution* (London: Fabian Discussion Paper No. 2, Fabian Society, 1990.

8   Frank Vibert, *Constitutional Reform in the United Kingdom: An Incremental Agenda*, IEA Inquiry, No. 18, September 1990.

9   *The Last Closed Shop?* WEA, Sheffield, No. 2 Branch, September 1990.

10   Anthony Lester *et al.*, *A British Bill of Rights* (London: Constitution Paper No. 1, Institute for Public Policy Research, 1990).

11   *The Constitution of the United Kingdom* (London: Constitution Paper No. 4, Institute for Public Policy Research, 1991).

12   Roy Hattersley, Speech to the Fabian Society Conference, Ruskin Hall, Oxford, 6 January 1990.

13   *The Charter of Rights: Guaranteeing Individual Liberty in a Free Society* (London: Labour Party, 1991); Peter Hennessy, 'Constitutional tinkering that may create a culture of liberty,' *Independent on Sunday*, 13 January 1991. Later in the year, Mr Hattersley softened somewhat on the Bill of Rights.

14   *Commonwealth of Britain, A Bill*, presented by Mr Tony Benn and ordered by the House of Commons to be printed 20 May 1991 (London: HMSO, 1991).

15   *Written Constitution, A Bill*, presented by Mr Graham Allen and

ordered by the House of Commons to be printed 13 December 1990 (London: HMSO, 1990).

16  *Human Rights, A Bill*, presented by Mr Graham Allen and ordered by the House of Commons to be printed 10 December 1990 (London: HMSO, 1990).

17  *House of Commons, session 1989–90, Select Committee on Procedure, Second Report, The Working of the Select Committee System*, House of Commons Paper 19–I (London: HMSO, 1990).

18  See Hennessy, *The Hidden Wiring*.

19  *Improving Management in Government: The Next Steps*, Efficiency Unit, Report to the Prime Minister (London: HMSO, 1988).

20  He was speaking on 'Whitehall unbound', BBC Radio 4, *Analysis*, first broadcast on 31 May 1990.

21  House of Commons, Session 1989–90, Treasury and Civil Service Committee, Eighth Report, *Progress in the Next Steps Initiative*, House of Commons Paper No. 48–1 (London: HMSO, 1990).

22  *Progress in the Next Steps Initiative*, The Government reply to the Eighth Report from the Treasury and Civil Service Committee, Session 1989–90 (London: HMSO, 1990).

23  Peter Hennessy, *Whitehall* (London: Secker & Warburg, London 1989) 312.

24  Peter Hennessy, 'Whitehall watch: Kinnock would restore 'think tank', *Independent*, 25 February 1991.

# Notes on contributors

*Arthur Aughey* is Senior Lecturer in Politics at the University of Ulster at Jordanstown. His recent publications include *Under Seige: Ulster Unionism and Anglo-Irish Agreement* (1989). He has just completed a study of British and American conservatism and is currently researching the politics of cultural identity in Northern Ireland.

*Rob Baggott* is Senior Lecturer in Public Policy at the Leicester Business School. His current research interests include pressure-group politics and health policy. He has published widely in a range of academic journals, including the *Journal of Social Policy, Parliamentary Affairs, Public Administration* and *Talking Politics*, and is the author of *Alcohol, Politics and Social Policy* (1990).

*David Butler* is Fellow of Nuffield College, Oxford. Apart from his regular appearances on television and articles in the press he is best known for *Political Change in Britain* (1969 with Donald Stokes) and his *Nuffield Studies* of successive British general elections since 1950. He has also written widely on the British electoral system, European elections and Indian politics. Dr Butler was President of the Politics Association from 1983 to 1987.

*Bill Coxall* was formerly Senior Lecturer in Humanities at Brighton Polytechnic. His publications include *Parties and Pressure Groups* (1981), and, with Lynton Robins, *Contemporary British Politics* (1989). He has been a member of the Politics Association since its foundation and was the first reviews editor of its journal, *Teaching Politics*.

*Bernard Crick* was Professor of Politics at Sheffield University and later Professor of Politics at Birkbeck College, University of London. His many books include *In Defence of Politics* (1962, 3rd edn 1992), *Reform of Parliament* (1964), *Political Education and Political Literacy* (1978, with Alex Porter), *George Orwell: A Life* (1984) and *Political Thoughts and Polemics* (1990). He is now Emeritus Professor but remains a prolific writer and broadcaster. He was joint founder of the Politics Association and its President from 1969 to 1976.

*David Denver* is Senior Lecturer in Politics at Lancaster University. He is the author of *Elections and Voting Behaviour in Britain* (1989) and of numerous articles on elections. He is a regular commentator on elections for BBC Television in the north-west and with Gordon Hands has undertaken a major study of the political attitudes of sixth-formers.

*John Greenaway* is Lecturer in Politics in the School of Economic and Social Studies at the University of East Anglia. He is co-author (with Richard Chapman) of *The Dynamics of Administrative Reform* and has written widely on the British civil service. He is currently working on a study of the Liquor Question and British Politics since 1830.

*Gordon Hands* is Lecturer in Politics at Lancaster University. He is co-editor of *Issues and Controversies in British Electoral Behaviour* (1982) and has published widely in that field. He is currently directing a research project on local campaigning in the forthcoming general election.

*Derek Heater* held a number of educational appointments including that of Head of the Department of History at Brighton College of Education. He was also the Founder-Chairman of the Politics Association.

*Peter Hennessy* worked as a journalist for ten years on *The Times*, *Financial Times*, and *The Economist* before becoming a political historian, freelance journalist and broadcaster. He is Visiting Professor of Government at Strathclyde University and a Visiting Fellow at several other university politics departments. As a broadcaster he presents Radio 4's *Analysis* and has presented several television documentaries on British politics. His books include *Cabinet* (1986) and *Whitehall* (1989). He is a Vice-President of the Politics Association.

*Alan Howarth* was educated at Rugby and Cambridge University where he read History. He worked as a Research Assistant to Field Marshal Montgomery for a while before taking up a teaching position at Westminster School. In 1975 he became Private Secretary to the Chairman of the Conservative Party and was Director of the Conservative Research Department from 1979 to 1981. In 1983 he became MP for Stratford-upon-Avon thereupon serving in the Whips' Office, the Northern Ireland and Environment Departments, before becoming Parliamentary Under-Secretary of State for Education in 1990.

*Stephen Ingle* took up the new post of Professor of Political Studies at the University of Stirling. He is the author of books on politics and literature, politics and health, and British political parties. He is currently preparing a book on the political thought of George Orwell.

*Bill Jones* worked for two years in Whitehall before joining Manchester University's Extra-Mural Department in 1973 as Staff Tutor in Politics. He has been Director of the Department since 1987. His books on politics include *The Russia Complex* (1978), *British Politics Today* (4th edn 1991 with Dennis Kavanagh), *Political Issues in Britain Today* (editor, 3rd edn 1989) and *Politics UK* (editor 1991). He also writes on political education and continuing education. He was Vice-Chairman of the Politics Association from 1979 to 1983 and Chairman from 1983 to 1985.

*Dennis Kavanagh* studied Politics at Manchester University and returned to lecture there for a number of years before becoming Professor of Politics and Head of Department at Nottingham University. He is author or co-author of fifteen books, including (with David Butler) the series of Nuffield Studies of British General Elections. Among his books are *British Politics: Continuities and Change* (1990), *Thatcherism and British Politics: The End of Consensus* (1990). He is also a regular contributor on British Politics to *The*

*Times* and other newspapers. He was President of the Politics Association from 1987 to 1990.

*Philip Norton* is Professor of Government at Hull University. Among the many books he has authored and edited are *The Constitution in Flux* (1982), *British Polity* (1990), *Conservatives and Conservatism* (1981), *The Commons in Perspective* (1981), *Parliament in the 1980's* (1985) and *Legislatures* (1990). He has served as President of the British Politics Group in the USA and has given evidence to parliamentary committees in the UK and Canada and to a New Zealand Royal Commission. He has been a regular contributor to Politics Association conferences and publications for many years.

*R. A. W. Rhodes* is Professor of Politics and Head of Department at York University. His recent publications include *Beyond Westminster and Whitehall* (1988). He is editor of *Public Administration*, the journal of the Royal Institute of Public Administration.

*Fred Ridley* studied at the London School of Economics and the Universities of Paris and Berlin before becoming a Lecturer in the Department of Political Theory and Institutions, Liverpool University. He was appointed Professor in 1965. He was editor of *Political Studies* from 1969 to 1975 and has edited *Parliamentary Affairs* since 1975. His books include *Public Administration in France* (1964), *Studies in Politics* (1975) and *Policies and Politics in Western Europe* (1984). He was President of the Politics Association from 1976 to 1981.

*Lynton Robins* is Course Leader of the Public Administration and Managerial Studies degree in the Leicester Business School. He is co-author of *Contemporary British Politics* (1989) and co-editor of *Public Policy Under Thatcher* (1990). He is editor of the Politics Association's journal, *Talking Politics*.

*Stephen P. Savage* is Principal Lecturer in Criminology and Police Studies at Portsmouth Polytechnic. He is author of *The Theories of Talcott Parsons* (1981) and co-editor of *Public Policy Under Thatcher* (1990). He has published variously in the areas of social theory, political sociology, police studies and the politics of law and order.

*Donald Shell* was educated at the London School of Economics and Essex Univerity. He is currently Lecturer in Politics at Bristol University; author of *The House of Lords* (1988) and a regular contributor to *Parliamentary Affairs*. He is a member and Academic Secretary (1988–91) of the Study of Parliament Group. He speaks regularly at Politics Association conferences.

*John Slater* was HMI with national responsibility for History and Political Education from 1974 to 1987. From 1980 to 1990 he was Visiting Professor at the University of London Institute of Education where he is now based. He is currently President of the Politics Association.

*Colin Thain* was educated at Manchester University before moving to Exeter University's Department of Politics in 1984. He has written several articles on politics and the economy and his book on *The Education of the Treasury* is due to be published in 1992. He is currently researching into the politics of public expenditure, planning and control.

# Officers of the Politics Association 1969–1990

*Presidents*

| | |
|---|---|
| Professor Bernard Crick | 1969–76 |
| Professor Fred Ridley | 1976–81 |
| Professor Anthony King | 1981–84 |
| Dr David Butler | 1984–87 |
| Professor Dennis Kavanagh | 1987–90 |
| Professor John Slater | 1990– |

*Vice-presidents*

Lord Edward Boyle
Lord H. M. Maybray King
Colonel F. W. E. Benemy
Professor Fred Ridley
Professor Bernard Crick
Brian Lapping
Professor Hugh Berrington
Professor G. Moodie
Professor Peter Hennessy
Professor John Slater
Dr David Butler
Tom Brennan

*Chairmen*

| | |
|---|---|
| Derek Heater (Brighton College of Education) | 1969–73 |
| John Sutton (Southwood School, Corby) | 1973–79 |
| Tom Brennan (Bingley College) | 1979–81 |

| | |
|---|---|
| Gareth Beavan (Crewe and Alsager College) | 1981–83 |
| Dr Bill Jones (Manchester University) | 1983–85 |
| Bernard Jones (Sheffield Polytechnic) | 1985–88 |
| Geoffrey Prout (Dartford Grammar School) | 1988–(91) |

*Vice-chairmen*

| | |
|---|---|
| Diane Brace (Brookland Technical College, Birkbeck College) | 1970–74 |
| Tom Bennan (Bingley College of Education) | 1974–79 |
| Dr Bill Jones (Manchester University) | 1979–83 |
| Geoffrey Prout (Dartford Grammar School) | 1983–88 |
| Steven Brice (Rutland Sixth Form College, Totton Sixth Form College) | 1988–(91) |

*Treasurers*

| | |
|---|---|
| John Sutton (Sir Wilfred Martineau School) | 1970–73 |
| Gary Weaving (Sir Wilfred Martineau School) | 1973–77 |
| Geoffrey Prout (Dartford Grammar School) | 1977–83 |
| Steven Brice (Rutland Sixth Form College) | 1983–88 |
| Graham Thomas (Reading Technical College) | 1988–(91) |

*Secretaries*

| | |
|---|---|
| Colonel F. W. E. Benemy (William Ellis School, Highgate) | 1969–72 |
| Alex Porter (Kings Heath Grammar, Technical School, Birmingham Solihull Sixth Form College) | 1972–76 |
| Gareth Beavan (Crewe and Alsager College) | 1976–80 |
| Sharon Markless (Westminster College) | 1980–85 |

Colleen Dicks
(Havering Technical College)                                    1985–89

Frank Conley
(Harvey Grammar School, Folkestone)                             1989–(91)

*Executive secretaries*
Gareth Beavan
(Crewe and Alsager College)                                     1974–76

Edward Sallis
(Acton Technical College)                                       1976–77

Rhys Evans
(South Trafford College)                                        1977–79

Sharon Markless
(Westminster College)                                           1979–80

Mike Bagley
(Basingstoke Technical College)                                 1980–82

Lorna Fowler
(Notting Hill and Ealing High School)                           1982–84/5

Sylvia Llewellyn
(Helston School)                                                1984/5–87

Stephanie Marshall
(University of York)                                             1987–89

Clive Thomas
(Millfield School                                               1989–(91)

*The Politics Assocation's journal*
Ken Mosley and Derek Heater were early editors of *Teaching Politics*.
Lynton Robins took over in 1979. In 1988 the name of the journal was
changed to *Talking Politics*. Assistant editors of the new journal include
Derek Heater (1988), Bernard Jones (1989) and Robert Pyper (1990–).
Reviews editors include Bernard Jones (1988–89) and Stephen Page
(1989–).

# Index

Acland, Arthur, 322
Adam Smith Institute, 43
Adonnino, Pietro, 297
Allen, Graham, 329
Anglo-Irish Agreement, 263–6
Ashdown, Paddy, 26
Asquith, Herbert, 327
Attlee, Clement, 250, 327

Bagehot, Walter, 24
Baker, Kenneth, 275, 283, 315
Bancroft, Sir Ian, 180–1
Beamish, Sir Tufton, 164
Benn, Tony, 329
Bevin, Ernest, 327
Brandt, Willy, 287
Briand, Aristide, 291
British Commonwealth, 250–1
British Medical Association (BMA),
    40, 43
British Nationality Act (1948),
    301–2
Brittan, Leon, 244
Brooke, Peter, 266–8
Brown, George, 245, 247
Browne, John, MP, 48
Budd, Alan, 231
Burns, Terry, 231
Butler, Sir Robin, 329
Butler-Sloss, Lord, 202
by-elections; Orpington, 24;
    Torrington, 24

Cabinets; and collective
responsibility, 122–3;
Conservative, 6–8; and
educational background, 6–8;
and end of 'Conviction Cabinet',
327; Labour, 6–8; and social
class, 6–8, 82
Callaghan, James, 29, 228, 230, 249
Campaign for Nuclear
    Disarmament (CND), 313
Campbell, Duncan, 280
Camps, Miriam, 245
Centre for Policy Studies, 43, 231
Charter 88, 274, 295–6, 302, 328
Chelwood, Lord, 164
Chicago School, 230
Churchill, Winston, 289
citizenship; background and
definitions, 274–5; and civil
liberties, 273–5, 279–80;
Commission, 323; and Europe,
324; and human rights, 279–80;
and the Labour Party, 275–6; and
the National Curriculum, 283,
311–13, 316; and participation,
281–2; and political education,
322–3; and the position of the
Politics Association, 283–4; and
Thatcher, 273, 275–6; and
voluntary effort, 276–7
Civil Service; and change, 173–4;
College, 178; Department (CSD),
179–81; and Efficiency Strategy,
183–4; and Financial
Management Initiative (FMI),

184, 189; and Fulton Report, 175–81; and Her Majesty's Stationery Office (HMSO), 173; and House of Commons Treasury and Civil Service Committee, 185; and inservice training, 178–9; and local government, 206; and The Next Steps (1988), 184–5, 189; and Ponting affair, 187; and recruitment procedures, 177–8; and reform, 183–6, 329; and repeal of the Official Secrets' Act, 188; structure and grading, 176–7; and Thatcher, 174, 176, 181–8; and trade-union militancy, 182–3; and Westland affair, 187–8

Clarke, Kenneth, 312

coalition government, 34–5

Common Agricultural Policy (CAP), 254

Communist Party, 104

Community Service Volunteers (CSV), 325–6

Confederation of British Industry (CBI), 222

Congdon, Tim, 232

consensus in two-party politics, 33–4

Conservatism, 26–8

Conservative Associations; and class, 8–9; and educational background, 8–9; and women's participation, 13

Conservative party; and citizenship, 295; and European Community, 244, 247–9; and House of Lords, 157–8, 160–1, 162–5, 167–9; and ideology, 26–8; and leadership, 6; and new breed of politicians, 120; and social background, 17–18; and women's membership, 11–12

Constituency Labour Parties (CLPs); and class, 9; and educational background, 9–10; and ethnic minorities, 15; and women's participation, 13

Constitution; and Cabinet government, 126–7; and elections, 114; and electoral roll, 115–16; and electorate, 111–13; and funding of campaigns, 116; and Labour party, 328; and local government, 123–5; and parliamentary government, 121–3, 329

Constitutional Reform Centre, 328

Consultative Council on Local Government Finance, 207–8

Council for Civil Liberties, 280

council housing sales, 206

Crick, Bernard, 295

Cripps, Sir Stafford, 250

Crosland, Anthony, 206

Crossman, Richard, 246

Dangerfield, George, 327

Day, Sir Robin, 54–7

De Gaulle, Charles, 287

Delors, Jacques, 254, 287

Democratic Unionist Party (DUP), 262

Department of Education and Science (DES), 306, 317

de Sully, Duc, 289, 293

Devlin, Lord, 201

Dubois, Pierre, 289, 293

economy; and attempts to reverse decline, 235–6; and European Monetary System (EMS), 234; and evidence of decline (1970–90), 236–9; and Exchange Rate Mechanism (ERM), 234; and full employment objective, 227–8; Healey and monetarism, 223–30; Keynesian and monetarist systems; a comparison, 224–5; and Keynesian Social Democratic system, 222–3; and Medium-Term Financial Strategy (MTFS); evolution and demise, 233–5; Medium-Term Financial Strategy (MTFS) and Thatcherism,

230–3; politico-economic
ideology, objectives and policy
tools, 222–35
Education Act (1986), 321
Education Reform Act (ERA), 28,
311, 319, 322
elections; and funding, 116
electoral system, 50, 130–2
equal opportunities, 11–14
Erroll Committee, 39
ethnic minorities; and population
figures, 15; and representation in
politics, 14–17
European citizenship; and the
Adonnino Committee, 297–8;
and Britain, 287–8; and conflicts
with British citizenship, 299; and
European integration, 293–7;
and European Parliament, 294;
and Federal European Union,
293–5; and Federal Trust for
Education and Research, 296,
302; and historical background,
288–92; and issue of multiple
citizenship, 299–303; and a
people's Europe 297–8; and
principle of subsidiarity, 300–1;
and Single Market, 293; and
Westminster Parliament, 295
European Community (EC); and
approach by Britain, 245–9; and
Common Agricultural Policy,
254; and Commonwealth,
250–1; and Britain's search for a
third force role, 249–55; and
Heath government, 247–9; and
House of Commons, 146–7; and
House of Lords select committee,
167; and judiciary, 203–4; and
Labour Party, 245–7; and
national referendum, 249; and
pressure groups, 46–7, 49–50;
and relationship with Britain,
242–5; and Thatcher, 243,
253–5, 287
European Council, 297
European Free Trade Association
(EFTA), 251–2, 293

European Monetary System (EMS),
234, 244
Exchange Rate Mechanism (ERM),
234, 244

Faulkner, Brian, 260
Federal Trust for Education and
Research, 296
feminism, 11
FitzGerald, Garret, 263
Friedman, Milton, 230, 231
Froude, J. A., 317
Fulton Report, 175–81

General Certificate of Secondary
Education (GCSE), 320
Geography Working Group, 306–7,
311–12
Giscard d'Estaing, Valéry, 301
Go it Alone (GITA), 250
Goodman, Lord, 161
Greater London Council (GLC),
123; and abolition, 163, 210–13;
and cuts in local government
spending, 209–10; and the
judiciary, 195
Green Party, 231
Gross Domestic Product (GDP), 237

Hague, Douglas, 231
Hailsham, Lord, 202–3, 274
Hattersley, Roy, 328
Haughey, Charles, 267
Healey, Dennis; and fiscal policy,
229; and inflation, 225–6; and
monetarism, 225–9; and the
'Social Contract', 225
Heath, Edward, 235, 246, 247–9,
254, 287
Her Majesty's Inspectorate (HMI),
309, 317
Her Majesty's Stationery Office
(HMSO), 174
Heseltine, Michael, 215, 244
Hill, Lord (BBC Chairman), 59–60
History Working Group, 306–7,
311–12, 319
Home, Lord, 167

Hoskyns, Sir John, 232
House of Commons; and
  constituents, 144–6; and Early
  Day Motions (EDMs), 147–8;
  and educational background, 6;
  and ethnic minority
  representation, 9, 14–15; and the
  European Community (EC),
  146–7; and improvement of
  resources, 151–3; and legislative
  process, 141; and Members,
  147–8; a multi-functional House,
  139–40; and Parliamentary
  facilities, 149–51; and pressure
  groups, 142–4; and Select
  Committee on Members'
  Interests, 47–8; and Select
  Committee on the Treasury and
  Civil Service, 49, 185; and social
  class, 6; and standing
  committees, 141–2; and women's
  representation, 11–12, 19
House of Lords; and abolition of the
  Greater London Council (GLC)
  163; and attendance, 159; and
  deliberative work, 166–7; and
  European Community (EC), 167;
  and eye charges, 164; and
  government, 160–2; and
  legislative work, 165–6; and Life
  Peerages Act (1958), 157–8;
  membership and activity, 157–9;
  and outside organisations,
  166–9; and poll tax, 164; and
  reform, 155–7, 167–9; and select
  committees, 167; and Thatcher,
  162–5; and War Crimes Bill,
  164–5; and women's
  representation, 11–12
Howarth, Alan, 282
Howe, Sir Geoffrey, 236, 244
Hume, John, 262, 264, 266
Hunt, Norman (Lord Crowther
  Hunt), 175
Hurd, Douglas, 275, 295, 329
Hussey, Marmaduke, 60

Inner London Education Authority

(ILEA), 209–11
Institute of Economic Affairs (IEA),
  231
Institute for Policy Research, 328
International Monetary Fund
  (IMF), 207, 222
Italian Christian Democratic Party,
  300

Jenkins, Roy, 233
John XXIII, Pope, 300
Johnson, Harry (LSE), 231
Jones, Bill, 322
Joseph, Sir Keith, 231, 322
Judiciary; and anti-union
  legislation, 193–4; and attitudes
  to women, 196; and bias,
  198–99; and Criminal Justice Act
  (1991), 203; and European Court
  Justice and Community Law,
  203–4; and Greater London
  Council (GLC), 195; and
  National Industrial Relations
  Court (NIRC), 193; and National
  Union of Mineworkers (NUM),
  194; and Northern Ireland, 198;
  and official secrets, 195–6; and
  publicity, 202–3; recruitment,
  selection and promotion, 200–1;
  and reform, 199–203; and review
  of performance, 203; and its role,
  191–3; and terrorists, 197; and
  training, 201–2; on trial, 193–9

Kant, Emmanuel, 274
Keynes, Maynard, 222–3
Kinnock, Neil, 29–30, 329

Labour Party; and citizenship,
  275–6, 295; and civil service,
  175–6, 189; and constitution,
  328; and European Community
  (EC), 245–7; and House of
  Lords, 157–8, 160–2, 167–9;
  and ideology, 28–30; and
  leadership, 6–7; and social
  background, 17–18; and
  women's membership, 11–12

Laidler, David, 231
Lawson, Nigel, 232, 234, 236, 244
Lee, Sir Frank, 253
Liberal Democrats, 25
Liberal Party; and alliance with
  SDP, 25–6; and two-party
  system, 24–5
Lijphart, Arend, 256
lobbying of parliament, 142–4
local government; and abolition of
  Greater London Council (GLC)
  and Metropolitan County
  Councils (MCCs), 210–13; and
  accountability, 213–14; and
  Conservative government
  policies, 215–7; and Consultative
  Council on Local Government
  Finance, 207–8; and corporatism
  (1974–79), 206–8; and cuts in
  local expenditure, 208–10; and
  direction (1979–83), 208–10;
  Finance Act (1988), 214; and
  Liverpool City Council, 212; and
  national economic management,
  215–17; and new joint bodies,
  211; and non-departmental
  public bodies, 213; and
  partnership, 206; and phases in
  central–local relations, 205;
  Planning and Land Act (1980),
  208; and poll tax, 214–15; and
  the Rates Act (1984), 212; and
  revolution (1987–90), 213–15
Lloyd-George, David, 257, 327
Lowe, Robert, 321

MacDonald, Ramsay, 292
MacGregor, John, 320
MacKay, Lord, 192
McKenzie, Robert, 24
Macmillan, Harold, 54–6, 250
Major, John, 236, 255, 327–9
Mansbridge, Albert, 322
Marquand, David, 295
Maudling, Reginald, 251–2
Medium-Term Financial Strategy
  (MTFS), 228, 230–5
Members of Parliament (MPs); and

constituents, 144–6; and
  lobbying, 142–4; and
  parliamentary facilities, 149–51;
  and pay, 149; and social
  background, 18–19; and stress,
  151
Metropolitan County Councils
  (MCCs), 210–13
Middleton, Sir Peter, 221, 232
Mill, John Stuart, 275, 279
Minford, Patrick, 231
Molyneaux, James, 262, 267
Money Study Group (1969), 231
Monnet, Jean, 294

National Curriculum, and
  accountability, 306; and
  citizenship, 311–13, 316;
  Council (NCC), 306, 317,
  319–20, 323; and Europe, 315;
  and History and Geography
  Working Groups, 306–7,
  311–12; and imbalances within,
  310–11; and recommendations,
  308–9; skills and attitudes,
  314–15, 324–5; and Task Group
  for Assessment and Testing
  (TGAT), 307
National Farmers' Union (NFU), 40
National Front, 103–4
National Health Service (NHS); and
  doctors' pay dispute (1965), 40;
  and government policy, 33; and
  the NHS Bill (1990), 44; and pay-
  beds in hospitals, 41; and Royal
  Commission, 39
National Industrial Relations Court
  (NIRC), 193
North Atlantic Free Trade Area
  (NAFTA), 250
Northern Ireland; and Anglo-Irish
  Agreement, 263–6; and Anglo-
  Irish Treaty (1921), 257; and
  aspects of crisis, 260–3; and
  Brooke Initiative, 266–8; and
  Council of Ireland, 257, 259–60;
  and Democratic Unionist Party
  (DUP), 262; and Government of

Ireland Act (1920), 257; and interpreting The Troubles, 257–60; and Irish Home Rule, 258; and New Ireland Forum Report (1984), 262, 264; and Official Unionist Party (OUP), 262; and Provisional Sinn Fein, 262; and Social Democratic and Labour Party (SDLP), 259–62, 264–8; and Unionist Party, 258

Official Unionist Party (OUP), 262
Organisation for Economic Co-operation and Development (OECD), 223
Owen, David, 25

Paisley, Ian, 262, 267
Parkin, Michael, 231
Parliament; and accountability, 31–3; and constitution, 328; and ethnic minority representation, 14–15; and Prime Minister's Questions, 32; and women's representation, 11–12
party ideologies, 26–30
party political broadcasts, 54
party system in Britain, 23
Paton, John, 322
Patten, Chris, 275
Pepper, Gordon, 232
Pius XI, Pope, 300
Plaid Cymru, 25
political broadcasts; and exploitation of other media opportunities, 63–4; and finance, 60; and Fourteen Day Rule, 54, 60; and media management, 62–3; and opposition to particular programmes, 60–1; and Peacock Committee, 60; and political campaigns, 61; and power of appointment, 59
political class; and civil servants, 85–7; and MPs' educational background, 80–1; and MPs' social class background, 81–2; and party leadership, 79–80, 91;

and political entrepreneurs, 87–9; and politicians, 79–85
political communication, and voting behaviour, 135–6
political education; and bias in schools, 320–22; and citizenship, 322–5; and Education Reform Act (ERA), 319–22; and National Curriculum, 319–20; in the 1990s, 329–30; and Politics Association, 318–20, 326; and school policy, 325; and voluntary service, 325–6
political interview; and external context, 59–62; and impression management, 65–6; and internal context, 62–70; now and future, 70–6; origins and nature, 54–9; and performance skills, 67–70; and politicians' use of anger, 61; and Robin Day, 54–9; and rules of engagement, 64–5; and the set, 66–7
political participation, 101–2
political parties; and accountability, 31–3; and educational background, 4; and efficiency, 35–6; and ethnic minority representation, 14–17; and leadership, 6; and occupational background, 4–5; and party identification, 133–4; and policy programmes, 30–1; and power sharing, 34–5; and social background, 17–18; social class and party elites, 3–6; and two-party consensus, 33–4; and two-party system, 136–7; and women's representation, 4–5, 12–14
political socialisation; and education system, 98–9; and family, 98; and mass media, 99; and party preference, 102–3; and political extremism, 103–4; and political knowledge, 100–1; and political participation, 101–2; and recent changes in the

agencies, 98–100; and 16–19
Initiative, 97–8; and 'Thatcher's
Children', 104–6; and Young
People in Society Initiative, 97;
and young voters, 94–8
Politics Association, 317
poll tax, 164
Pompidou, George, 287
Ponting, Clive, 187, 195–6
pressure groups; changes and
developments, 45–9; and
consultation, 38–9; and electoral
system, 50; and Erroll
Committee, 39; and Europe,
46–7, 49–50; and future, 49–51;
and House of Commons, 142–4;
and 1970s, 38–41; and political
consultancy, 47; and political
culture, 50–1; and public
participation, 46; and Royal
Commissions, 39; and Thatcher,
41–5
Prince of Wales, 296
Prince's Trust Young Volunteers'
Scheme, 325–6
Prior, James, 262
privatisation, 125–7
proportional representation, and
women, 14
Provisional Irish Republican Army,
257, 259, 265
Provisional Sinn Fein, 262

Quinton, Antony, 26

Rates Act (1984), 212
Rayner, Sir Derek, 181
Rees-Mogg, Lord, 166
Ridley, Nicholas, 244
Ripa di Meano, Carlo, 298

Saint-Simon, comte de, 288, 290–1,
293
Scarman, Lord, 202
Schuman Plan, 294
Schools Examination and
Assessment Council (SEAC), 320
Scottish National Party (SNP), 25–6

secrecy in government, 32
Select Committee; on European
Legislation, 146; on Members'
Interests, 47–8
shadow cabinets; and class, 82; and
educational background, 6–8;
and social class, 6–8
Sherman, Sir Alfred, 231
Shops Bill (1986), 44
Short, Edward, 150
Single European Act, 146
16–19 Initiative, 97–8
Slater, John, 318
social class and party elites, 3–11
social context of British politics,
17–19
Social Democratic and Labour Party
(SDLP), 259–62, 264–8
Social Democratic Party (SDP),
25–6
Socialist Workers' Party, 104
Society of Education Officers (SEO),
320
Society of Friends, 313
Stormont Parliament, 259
Strauss, Norman 232
Sturgo, Don Luigi, 300

*Talking Politics*, 318
Task Group for Assessment and
Testing (TGAT), 307
Tebbitt, Norman, 210
Thatcher govenment; and advisory
bodies, 42; and Confederation of
British Industry (CBI), 42; and
trade unions, 41-2
Thatcher, Margaret, 27; and Anglo-
Irish Agreement (1985), 263–5;
and anti-union legislation, 194;
and citizenship, 273–6; and civil
service, 85–7, 174, 176, 181–8;
and collective responsibility,
122–3; and constitution,
111–14; and the European
Community (EC), 243, 253–5,
287; and House of Lords, 157–8,
162–5; and judiciary, 194; and
local government, 123–5,

208–10, 216–17; and monetarism, 230–3; and No. 10 Policy Unit, 88–90; and official statistics, 117–19; and Ponting affair, 187; and Prime Minister's power, 83–5; and privatisation, 125–7; and public image, 117; and public opinion, 116–17; and Rayner Unit, 184, 189; and resignation, 327; and Westland affair, 187–8

think tanks, 88–9

trade unions; and pressure groups, 41; and Thatcher, 41–2

Trades Union Congress (TUC), 222

Trevelyan, Dennis, 178–9

Unionist Party, 258

voting behaviour; and electoral system, 130–2; and party identification, 133–4; and party structure, 137–8; and political communication, 135–6; and style of electioneering, 132–3; and two-party system, 136–7

Walters, Sir Alan, 231

War Crimes Bill (1990), 164–5

Wass, Sir Douglas, 221

Westland affair, 187–8

Whitelaw, William, 163, 259

White Paper; Lords Reform (1968), 167; Public Expenditure (1978, 1979), 228

Williams, Shirley, 283

Wilson, Harold, 28–9, 53, 56, 235, 244–5, 247–8, 250–2, 287

women; in government, 12; in House of Commons, 19; in House of Lords, 12; in politics, 11–14; and representation in Parliament, 11–12

Workers' Educational Association (WEA), 322

Young, Hugo, 295